Also by Timothy Wilson-Smith

Delacroix (1992)

NAPOLEON AND HIS ARTISTS

Gérard's Napoleon in his coronation robes (1805), commissioned by the Foreign Office, is probably the most accurate portrayal of the Emperor in his finery (château de Fontainebleau).

Napoleon and His Artists

Timothy Wilson-Smith

CONSTABLE · LONDON

First published in Great Britain 1996
by Constable and Company Limited
3 The Lanchesters, 162 Fulham Palace Road
London W6 9ER
Copyright © 1996 Timothy Wilson-Smith
ISBN 0 09 475600 7
The right of Timothy Wilson-Smith to be identified as the author
of this work has been asserted by him in accordance
with the Copyright, Designs & Patents Act 1988
Set in Monophoto Poliphilus 12pt by
Servis Filmsetting Ltd, Manchester
Printed in Great Britain by
St Edmundsbury Press Ltd
Bury St Edmunds, Suffolk

A CIP catalogue record of this book
is available from the British Library

For Pam

Contents

Illustrations

Acknowledgements

The writing of this book, which aims to make accessible to a general public the researches of scholars, has been an agreeable occupation thanks to the help of several institutions and many people. I have had access to the resources of Cambridge and London university libraries, of the Courtauld Institute library and of the libraries of Eton College. I have enjoyed the pleasure of using the first edition of Denon's *Voyage dans la haute et la basse Egypte* and the second edition of the *Description de l'Egypte* (the first edition's plates have been reproduced in facsimile). Modern French publishers have reprinted the journal of Napoleon's architect, Fontaine, and Delécluze's reminiscences of David, Napoleon's painter. The Dover Press has published the engravings of Percier and Fontaine and those of Beunat. Usually I have relied on secondary sources. Among Napoleon's anglophobe biographers Vincent Cronin still remains after twenty five years the most readable. Among professional historians no modern Englishman has rivalled the energy of Jean Tulard, who seems to publish something on a Napoleonic topic annually, or of François Furet, who has revolutionized views not just on the French Revolution but also on the hundred years of French history which followed it.

After the flurry of attention to the art of the Revolution in 1989, it was refreshing to note in 1994 and 1995, as this text was nearing completion, that Napoleon's artists are beginning to receive their due from art historians. A campaign to save a sculpture for the nation brought Canova back to public notice in England; and the refurbishment of Apsley House means that 'Napoleon as Mars' can again draw the eye of the visitor to the staircase of Wellington's London home. Works of art outlive changes in taste. The Wallace Collection with its most beautiful of Napoleonic miniatures remains the most delightful monument to French art in London and thanks to the Windsor fire anyone who lives near that castle has been reminded of the splendid array of Napoleon's enemies in the Waterloo chamber. There is no substitute, however, for knowledge of the art on show in France. Eton College's How Fund enabled me to see the exhibition of Egyptomania at the Louvre and a letter from the Provost of Eton College, Sir Antony Acland, opened to me the doors of the Hôtel Beauharnais, which de Gaulle returned to the Germans to be their residence in Paris, and the Hôtel Charost, which must be the most beautiful British Embassy in the world. I owe much to the courtesy of staff at the châteaux of Compiègne and of Malmaison, where Joséphine's roses always seem past their best, and Bois-Préau, with its poignant reminders of Napoleon's last years in Saint-Helena, but I have a special sense of gratitude to those at Fontainebleau who enabled me to see the *petits appartements* of the Emperor — Fontainebleau has been given the private collection of the head of the Bonaparte family — and to Madame Claire Constans, Conservateur en Chef at the châteaux of Versailles and Trianon, who gave me access to the Napoleonic rooms which are closed to the public. A few years ago the librarian of the Senate showed me one of the special bookcases built in the Egyptian style to house the *Description de l'Egypte*. In Paris, whenever possible I have enjoyed the hospitality of the Sulpician fathers, whose lay students are no fans of Napoleon. All over Paris the spirit of Napoleon presides — in the streets that he laid out, in the *projets de prestige* of François Mitterand, in the office of the President himself.

This book has developed out of conversations with Richard Dodman of Constable's and I owe much to his enthusiasm and to the shrewd support of Ben Glazebrook. I have learnt much from discussions over the years with two colleagues, David Evans and Nigel Goodman. My love of French history and French art dates back to 1950, when I first stayed in postwar Paris, but it has been sustained above all by my wife, who is always on hand to improve my French grammar or my English prose style and who has long wanted me to share her admiration for Napoleon. I dedicate this book to her.

Chronology

DATES	POLITICAL AND MILITARY EVENTS	ARTISTIC EVENTS
1789		
May	Meeting of Estates General (later National Assembly)	
July	Fall of the Bastille	At the Salon David shows
August	Declaration of the Rights of Man	'Brutus receiving the bodies of his
October	Women march to Versailles	sons'
1790		
	Re-organisation of France into departments	David starts to work on 'The tennis-court oath' (abandoned 1792)
July	Civic constitution of the clergy	
July 14	First Feast of the Federation	
1791		
June	Louis XVI's flight to Varennes	Voltaire's ashes are taken to the Panthéon
July	Massacre of Champ de Mars	Guilds are dissolved
October	Legislative Assembly meets	
1792		
April	first use of guillotine France declares war on Austria	
June	Prussia declares war on France	
August	Attack on Tuileries – fall of monarchy Fall of Longwy	

DATES	POLITICAL AND MILITARY EVENTS	ARTISTIC EVENTS
September	Fall of Verdun; massacres	
	Proclamation of the French Republic	
November	Battle of Valmy	
	Battle of Jemappes	

1793

January	Execution of Louis XVI	David in charge of funeral of Lepeletier
February	France declares war on Britain and the Netherlands (war of First Coalition)	
March	Revolt in the Vendée	
June	Fall of the Girondins – the beginnings of federalist revolts	
July	Danton leaves the Committee of Public Safety	David in charge of funeral of Marat
	Robespierre joins the Committee of Public Safety	
August	British are given control of Toulon	David in charge of Fête de la Réunion
September	Drawn battle of Hondschoote	David's Commune des Arts in charge of Salon: Girodet's 'Sleep of Endymion'
October	French victory at Wattignies	
	Execution of Marie-Antoinette	David sketches her en route to her death
	Execution of the Girondins	(during year academies, including French Academy in Rome, close. So too Journal de la Mode et du Goût)
December	Bonaparte responsible for recapture of Toulon	David organises the celebrations

1794

April	Execution of Danton	
June	Festival of the Supreme Being (Robespierre's great day), masterminded by David	
	French victory at Fleurus clears the way for the first French acquisitions of masterpieces of Belgian art	
July	9–10 Thermidor fall of Robespierre – Bonaparte arrested, David put on trial	

DATES	POLITICAL AND MILITARY EVENTS	ARTISTIC EVENTS
1795		
January	Occupation of Amsterdam	during summer David spends time with the Sériziats
October	Annexation of Belgium Establishment of the Directory Riots in Paris during Vendémiaire – Bonaparte helps to crush them	
1796		
March	Bonaparte sent as general of the Army of Italy to fight Austria and Savoy	
May	Conspiracy of the 'Equals'	in Genoa Joséphine 'discovers' Gros
1797		
February		Treaty of Tolentino – Pope 'gives' away art
October	Peace of Campo Formio – of partners in First Coalition against France only Britain left	
1798		
May	Bonaparte leaves for Egypt, together with Denon	Percier & Fontaine bring out book on Roman palaces
1799		
April		Joséphine acquires Malmaison
August	Bonaparte leaves Egypt	
October	Bonaparte arrives back in France to cope with Second Coalition	At Salon David shows 'Sabine Women'
November	Bonaparte's Brumaire coup d'état creates Consulate	
1800		
	Foundation of the Bank of France Law of 28 Pluviôse establishes prefectorial system Pacification of the West	
June	Bonaparte's victory at Marengo	

DATES	POLITICAL AND MILITARY EVENTS	ARTISTIC EVENTS
December	Bomb in the rue Niçaise, Moreau's victory at Hohenlinden	Fontaine made Consular architect
1801		
February	Treaty of Lunéville with Austria	David's 'Bonaparte crossing the Saint-Bernard'
August	French in Egypt surrender to British	Britain acquires the Rosetta stone
1802		
March	Peace of Amiens with Britain	(during year publication of
April	Concordat with the Papacy	Chateaubriand's 'Le Génie du christianisme' and Denon's 'Voyage dans la Basse et la Haute Egypte')
May	Bonaparte Consul for Life	Bonaparte moves to Saint-Cloud, Denon put in charge of museums; Canova's first visit to Paris
1803		
May	Renewal of war with Britain Sale of Louisiana to the U.S.A.	Creation of the Napoleonic Institute
1804		
March	Promulgation of the Civil Code Cadoudal plot Execution of the duc d'Enghien	
May	Proclamation of the Empire Napoleon at Boulogne	Gros exhibits 'Napoleon at Jaffa' Napoleon orders review of army uniform
December	Coronation of Napoleon masterminded by Fontaine, Percier & Isabey	
1805		
April	Napoleon King of Italy, Eugène de Beauharnais Viceroy of Italy	
August	Third coalition formed (Britain, Austria, Russia)	David at work on 'Pius VII' and 'Sacre de Joséphine', Ingres
October	French victory at Ulm, British victory at Trafalgar	paints the Rivières
December	French victory over Austrians and Russians at Austerlitz	

DATES	POLITICAL AND MILITARY EVENTS	ARTISTIC EVENTS
1806		
January	Peace of Pressburg with Austria	during year Percier and Fontaine work on Arc du Carousel
February	Joseph Bonaparte King of Naples	
June	Formation of the Confederation of the Rhine	
	Louis Bonaparte King of Holland	
October	French defeat Prussians at Jena-Auerstädt	At Salon Gros exhibits 'Battle of Aboukir' and Ingres 'Napoleon on the Imperial throne'
November	Berlin decrees declare economic war on Britain. Jérôme Bonaparte King of Westphalia	
1807		
February	Drawn battle of Eylau (against Russia)	
June	French defeat Russians at Friedland	Vignon starts work on the Temple de la Gloire (later the Madeleine)
July	Treaty of Tilsit with Russians	
October	French invade Portugal	
November	Milan decrees tighten economic blockade	
1808		
	Establishment of the University	Canova is commissioned to
May	Joseph King of Spain, Joachim Murat King of Naples	sculpt Napoleon's sister Pauline as 'Venus victrix'
November	Napoleon's brief campaign against British in Spain	At Salon Gros shows 'Napoleon at Eylau', Guérin 'Napoleon pardoning the rebels in Cairo' and Girodet 'The funeral of Atala'
1809		
January	British retreat from Coruña (Corunna)	
March	Invasion of Portugal	
May	Annexation of the Papal States (followed by imprisonment of the Pope)	
July	French defeat Austrians at Wagram	

DATES	POLITICAL AND MILITARY EVENTS	ARTISTIC EVENTS
October	French make peace of Schönbrunn with Austria	
Dec 31	Napoleon tells Joséphine that he will divorce her	during year appearance of the first volumes of the 'Description de l'Egypte', not in its complete form till 1828

1810

April	Marriage of Napoleon and Marie-Louise of Austria, consummated at newly redecorated château de Compiègne, celebrated in the Louvre, where the ceremonies were masterminded by Percier and Fontaine	
		Canova's conversations with Napoleon. Salon: David's 'The Distribution of the Eagles', Girodet's 'The Revolt of Cairo', Gros' 'Battle of the Pyramids'
	Marshal Bernadotte elected King of Sweden	and Gérard's 'Battle of Austerlitz'
	Louis ejected from Holland	Award of decennial prizes to Percier and Fontaine, David and Girodet

1811

	Year of economic crisis, which will affect even the furniture business of Jacob-Desmalter	
	Birth of the King of Rome, for whose future Percier and Fontaine are asked to draw up plans for a palace	

1812

June 24	Napoleon crosses the Niemen to invade Russia	Percier and Fontaine publish decorations in full
September	Battle of Borodino leads to occupation of Moscow	At Salon critical triumph for Géricault's 'Charging chasseur' David paints 'Napoleon in his study' for Lord Douglas
November	Crossing of the Beresina by retreating French	

DATES	POLITICAL AND MILITARY EVENTS	ARTISTIC EVENTS
1813		
May	French win battles of Lützen and Bautzen	Beunat publishes book of decorations
June	British victory at Vitoria leads to flight of Joseph from Spain, so Wellington takes many art treasures	
October	Allies defeat Napoleon at Leipzig Wellington crosses the Pyrenees	
1814		
Jan–March	Campaign of France	
April 6	Abdication of Napoleon Death of Joséphine	Salon patronised by Louis XVIII David shows 'Leonidas at Thermopylae'
1815		
March 1– June 22	Hundred Days	David goes into exile, Denon resigns

The Style Fit for a Hero

IN 1824 Eugène Delacroix, a youthful Bonapartist, confided in his *Journal*: 'The life of Napoleon is our century's epic for all the arts.'

Born just eighteen months before the coup of Brumaire* brought Bonaparte to power, young Delacroix had no childhood memories of a time when Napoleon had not ruled France. He had been educated at the Lycée Impérial, once the Collège Louis-le-Grand, both his father and his brother-in-law had been imperial prefects, his two brothers had fought for the Empire, in one case had died for the Empire and in the other case had been ennobled by the Empire. He knew that with the fall of the Empire the glory of France had passed away too.

Napoleon was not responsible for going to war against most of Europe – that distinction had fallen to the revolutionary leaders of 1792 – but from 1796 he pursued war in a more spectacular fashion than anyone else and except during 1802–03 he was involved in warfare directly or indirectly every year till 1815. In 1792 the French government had gone to war to save the revolution. Under Napoleon war became not a means but an end, a way of life not only for professional soldiers like him, but for all France.

As a commander Napoleon was lucky and inventive. In 1796 and 1797 he beat larger armies than his by rapid manoeuvre; technological superiority lay behind his crushing defeats of Egyptian and Turkish forces in 1798 and 1799; in 1800 at Marengo he was almost too daring and was just saved by the timely arrival of relieving troops. By 1805, as a commander he had matured; and that year's campaign is usually held to be his masterpiece. His armies first fanned out to give the Austrians

---

*Brumaire, the 'foggy' month, the second month of the 'revolutionary' year, which ran from 22 October to 20 November.

the illusion that they faced isolated detachments of Frenchmen and then concen-
trated to envelop them at Ulm; and at Austerlitz he risked vacating high ground to
split the Austrians from their Russian allies before picking off first one army and
then the other. For the next four years he went on adding to his tally of victories.
After Jena he followed the fleeing Prussians with unprecedented speed and forced a
humiliating surrender. He survived a battle for survival in a snowstorm against the
Russians at Eylau and reasserted his mastery by catching them off guard in the
summer at Friedland. He pushed the Austrians aside on his way to Vienna (by way
of diversion, he had temporarily chased the British out of Spain, while securing
Madrid).* He was able to dictate to the continent. But in trying to seal off Europe
from the Atlantic to the Urals he attacked Russia with the largest forces the world
had ever seen. It was too much. He could control neither his army nor the weather,
and the invasion ended in disaster. His enemies had learnt his tricks. At Leipzig he
was beaten by larger coalition armies skilfully co-ordinated. He was still able to win
a series of battles while for the first time defending France, but his opponents, by
never retreating, made him retreat; and at the end he could retreat no further. The
coda to his career, the Waterloo campaign, had an inevitable conclusion.

Though he had defeated each of them singly, it is hard to see how he could have
defeated the four other major powers of Europe acting together. At the last it was
not enough that on the undulating plains of Belgium he could not repeat his
Austerlitz gambit: the British and the Prussians were never decisively divided. They
combined to outmanoeuvre him, the British by adapting the defensive system they
had used on his marshals in Portugal and Spain, the Prussians by copying his own
pursuit of them after Jena.

Napoleon won because his ambition was limitless and he lost for the same reason
– there was always one more battle to win, one more opponent to crush.

Epics are more enjoyable to read than to live. The Napoleonic epic involved
destruction on a massive scale. Haydn had shut out the boom of the French can-
nonade to play softly his hymn to his beloved Austria – it was a sound familiar in
every continental capital apart from Paris. The flames that lit up Moscow in 1812
may burn more brightly in popular memory than other fires, but hundreds of buildings elsewhere had been wrecked before. Monasteries lay in ruins and abandoned
wherever the French had passed, works of art had been rifled except when the
owners had concealed them or fashion explained their neglect, the produce of
innumerable farms had been requisitioned. All over Spain guerrilla warfare had
added a new word to a savage fight for freedom. It is hard to estimate how many
enemy soldiers or neutral civilians the French had killed over twenty years.

---

*The first British attempt to frustrate Napoleon's invasion had led to the famous retreat of Sir John Moore to
Coruña, the English Corunna, in north-west Spain.

Bonaparte fights in Egypt, as seen by the Manufacture Creil et Montereau
(Musée de l'isle de France, Sceaux, *c.* 1840)

Even in the brief period that elapsed between his defeat at Waterloo and his death
on St Helena, Napoleon had begun to make himself into a legend, a subject for the
artists of the future. He reinvented himself as a new kind of person, who had
declaimed the famous cheering words to his soldiers on the eve of the Italian campaign, who was a lover of religious and political freedom and who was a believer in
the national aspirations of the Italian people. This was the material out of which his
nephew, the future Emperor Napoleon III, was able to concoct his book on
Napoleonic ideas. Napoleon had indeed achieved a lot for France, by reconciling
her, more or less, to the Pope, by providing her with a whole system of law and by
trying to open a career to all the talents in the nation which lowly birth and social
prejudice had often stifled in the past. This was not how the artists would remember his legendary deeds. Even during his last years some like Horace Vernet pictured
the wide panoramas of his battles, like that at Montmirail in 1814. Others like
Charlet lingered on more intimate moments: soldiers warming themselves by the
fire, soldiers cooking, soldiers marching in the winter. Then, Frenchmen had experienced some social cohesion which snobbish *émigré* nobles and the right-thinking
bourgeoisie of Restoration France preferred to forget. For over a generation men had
marched all over Europe in their uniforms, which memory recalled as more resplendent than they ever had been; and, though there had been many who never came
back and though in the end there was too much taxation, too much recruiting of
boys and middle-aged men and the enemy on French soil, there was a passion and

a glamour to Napoleon's France which made the new system of government seem endlessly drab. In retrospect, people made mistakes. They forgot the insidious actions of the police – there were more political prisoners, arbitrarily arrested, under the Empire than there had been under Louis XVI – and they chose to forget the parvenu attitudes of the Napoleonic ruling class, of which the Bonaparte family furnished some of the worst representatives.

This selective amnesia was partly the result of Napoleon's careful control of artistic expression during his own reign. While he had ruled, there had been no alternative to the Napoleonic myth. As in revolutionary France, so in Regency Britain there was a strong tradition of caricature which feared no official censor. Gillray the cartoonist dared to be even ruder on the defects of the Prince of Wales, the acting head of state, than he was about 'Boney'. Napoleon had not silenced all his critics – he was not very successful at wooing men and women of letters – but he had control of what was shown, if not of what was written. As a result hundreds and hundreds of paintings had lauded his military genius, his compassion, his wisdom; and there were many triumphal arches and commemorative statues all over France. Perhaps he did not rule long enough for the French to become cynical about him. He was hardly the first French monarch to boost his authority by use of visual propaganda. For over fifty years Louis XIV had presented himself as the Sun King round whom his château of Versailles was orientated and whose mythic qualities were expressed in the statues and fountains of the gardens. Even the rooms of state were named after antique gods, heroes or ideas. To decorate Versailles and the other royal palaces Louis had employed a veritable army of craftsmen to provide the furniture and the tapestries for the rooms and costumes for the courtiers who stood in them waiting to catch a glimpse of the King.

Napoleon was still more enthusiastic in his patronage of the arts. Even if he could not tempt Chateaubriand to write for him, as Racine had once written for Louis XIV, he tried to give work to a small army of workers, to the silk weavers of Lyon and the textile weavers of Jouy, to the cabinet-makers, carpenters and ceramicists of Paris. Though he was anxious that the manufactory of Sèvres should be modern in its technology, this was not just a question of national pride, for he was appalled at the thought of wide unemployment. He was aware how much people had suffered in Paris during the revolution because the patterns of trade had been disrupted. He himself would disrupt trade, because his obsession with defeating the English meant that he did not care for the female fashion for muslin, which came from British India, nor for the fashion among furniture-makers for mahogany, which was imported by Britain from tropical America; and the French Atlantic ports had no great love for what Napoleon did to their local economies. But within his limitations he was enlightened in his concern for artisans.

At the top of the artistic meritocracy ranked the painters, the sculptors, the architects, who hoped to become famous and prosperous. It was they who provided the designs and images on which the myth of Napoleon depended. Once David had decided that Napoleon was a hero like the heroes of antiquity, a whole school of painters followed him in his enthusiasm. One painter-pupil was executed for repub-lican ideals, but he was exceptional. David had been lost when he had lost faith in Robespierre. While he was a convinced revolutionary, he had specialized in martyr-dom scenes, and in the diseased, putrefying body of Marat he had found a source of noble consolation, but now he believed in Bonaparte he shook off morbid thoughts and could exult in everyone's idea of a hero – young, handsome and triumphant. It is difficult to appreciate how Napoleon dazzled his contemporaries. Even those who knew how he could be discourteous to women, moody, cruel or garrulous were cap-tivated by his imagination, his charm, his boundless ambition and boundless self-confidence. He seemed more than just one subject for artists: he was all-engrossing. Architects vied with one another to provide the setting for him, sculptors to make his presence felt all over France and painters to recall every incident in his career. Engravings of their patterns or pictures gave ideas for the artisans to work on.

The Napoleonic industry embraced all crafts from the making of furniture, silverware and carpets to the manufacture of fashionable clothes and military uniform. The intricate marquetry of the eighteenth-century *ébénistes* was abandoned and the Napoleonic court had to make do with silver gilt and without the elaborate court dress of the previous century. Above all Napoleon delighted in providing uni-forms for everyone who worked or fought for him. He knew that baubles like the ribbon of the Légion d'honneur or the sash of civil office or the jacket of a hussar would bind people to him; and while he studiously cultivated sobriety and was nor-mally dressed in the simple clothes of a colonel, he encouraged those round him, like his wife Joséphine, who was an arbiter of fashion, or his brother-in-law, Murat, or his brother, Jérôme, to indulge their love of extravagance until, in the case of Jérôme, it became ridiculously expensive. He stood above all, he liked to think, for sound finance. At the same time, therefore, as fostering a sense of luxury, which was good for French luxury industries, he was determined to be tight with money.

David had once said that artists should paint as men lived in Sparta. Under Napoleon men lived as in Corinth and the manner that suited them had to be opulent and grandiose. The *style empire* was not invented by Napoleon – it was in a way a logical development of the *style Directoire* that had preceded it – but it looked as if it had been invented for Napoleon. Because Neo-Classicism was the dominant style at the time, there were only certain forms that art could take. The *style empire* enlarged the vocabulary of European art, for instance by adding motifs from Egyptian art to the classical repertory, but it came back to familiar sources – above all the sculpture and architecture of the Hellenistic age (the period after Alexander the Great) and of imperial Rome, to which could be added something of the so-called Etruscan style, which partly derived from the linear art of Greek vases and partly from modern fantasy. What Napoleon liked was size and splendour; and the larger the room in which he received people, the more remote his throne, the better he was pleased. Other monarchs from older families lived simpler lives. Napoleon aimed to overwhelm those who came to see him, just as he aimed to overwhelm his enemies on the battlefield. He reintroduced formality to French life.

This gave every action of his a personal importance. He could not rely on inherited position or wealth and affected to despise them, but in the crisis of his career, in the period 1812–13, he admitted that he felt precarious when he compared his destiny to that of the Russian Tsar or the Austrian Kaiser. They could be defeated and yet survive; he must always win. He had seemed invincible for so long that the disasters of the Russian and German campaigns of those years came as a shock not only to himself but to those who conquered him. Everyone had come to believe in Napoleon's propaganda and they forgot that it was an artistic creation which defied mortality and even human weakness. In time the defeats came to seem as heroic as the victories, but that is not how Napoleon viewed them at the time. He did not give up easily – he was as tenacious in 1814 as he had been in 1796 – but the magic had left him, his secrets were known. The vision he had had of the star that led him ever onwards and upwards was a mirage. It was fortunate for the artists that the last Napoleonic Salon took place in 1812, before the bad news of defeat and retreat from Moscow had arrived. They could still devote themselves to his past triumphs and did not have to cope with the facts of present failure.

Looking back to the ancient world, men compared him to Alexander the Great or to Julius Caesar, those two heroes out of Plutarch's *Lives*, or to Augustus. He shared Alexander's restlessness, but he did not die like Alexander, lamenting that there were no more lands to conquer. Like Julius Caesar, he used his prestige to subvert a republic, but he did not die for doing so. Unlike Augustus he did not bring a permanent peace to the lands he ruled, but he had started to match the work Augustus did for Rome, which he had found brick and turned to marble. Napoleon aimed to make Paris what Rome had once been, the cultural centre of Europe. The works of art he brought to Paris, the buildings and streets he constructed in Paris, the painting, sculpting and porcelain-making he encouraged in Paris, gave his capital an importance it had not experienced under the Bourbons, who for a century had ruled from Versailles. While there had been a Louis on the throne for 180 years, Napoleon was monarch of France for only fifteen years and yet he changed more than any king that had reigned before him. He centralised the whole administration, much of the economy and most of the arts in Paris. If Paris is expected to have a special role in forming European taste, that is in part because of Napoleon's legacy; and it is a role that has outlasted his empire and any number of revolutions that have been based on Paris too.

PART ONE

THE ARTISTS AND BONAPARTE

CHAPTER 1

The First French Revolutions

R EVOLUTIONS need their heroes. On 14 July 1789 a crowd of Parisians swarmed to attack the Bastille, fearing that its armaments would be used to subdue the city. Most of them were artisans from the eastern parts of the city. As many as one-sixth were *menuisiers*, *ébénistes*, *graveurs* or *doreurs*, men who made their living by fashioning beautiful inlaid furniture for the rich, by gilding chairs, frames and mounts for all or by reproducing fine pictures for the less well off. They depended for their living on a stable society, where the works of their hands were valued, but poor harvests and bad political management had put everything in jeopardy. Sure of the bad faith of the government, for why else were troops massed outside the city, they reacted in self-defence. With professional help they forced the surrender of the fortress and its tiny group of prisoners, victims more of their own inadequacy than of ill-treatment; and in a moment of mob revenge the governor who had declined to fire on them was lynched. Their exploits became legendary: by taking the Bastille artisans had ended the *ancien régime*. They were the heroes of a new society. Everyman was like a king.

Conversely the King was like everyone. Before 1789 he was a sacred figure, who at his crowning at Reims was anointed with the oil of St Remigius like all kings from Clovis before him. He had healing powers. Though subject to the fundamental laws of France, as an absolute monarch he could issue binding edicts and tax and imprison at will. There were limits to what he could do, partly because no king had any control over much that happened in France and partly because he had to rely on the support of the two privileged orders. Churchmen and nobles – virtually the same class of people, since most abbots and bishops were aristocrats – had private rights that he was unwise to ignore. When Louis XVI tried to reduce their immunity from taxation, they obliged him to call the virtually obsolete Estates General.

From then on events took on an irresistible momentum. The privileged, wanting to keep their privileges, did not want the non-privileged or Third Estate to equal their combined total of votes — popular fury forced through a 'doubling of the Third'. A majority of them, like their king, wished the orders to meet as distinct bodies — the liberal minority joined the Third Estate and on the Versailles tennis court took an oath in favour of a unicameral National Assembly. The King wavered between repression and concession — the 'people' of Paris seized the Bastille. Soldiers were expected to attack villages — the peasants grabbed documents defining seigneurial rights and destroyed them. Back in the Assembly high-minded lords offered to give up those rights — most of the others hurried to join in renouncing them. Finally, in October, women from Paris marched to Versailles. They went to find 'the baker, the baker's wife and the baker's son', for King Louis, Queen Marie-Antoinette and Louis the Dauphin were meant to give them their daily bread. They brought the royal family back to the Tuileries palace in the middle of their city. They did not bring down the price of bread, but the first revolution was over. The King was left with less power than the King of England. He was hardly even a constitutional king.

It had been a bad year for craftsmen. Many were out of work and many works of art, especially in country *manoirs* and châteaux, had been hacked to pieces or burnt. The painters, however, carried on with their trade. Since 1737, every two years at the Salon the most distinguished artists in France showed off their paintings to polite society. In 1789, while the jury made their choice of exhibits, the National Assembly was drafting the Declaration of the Rights of Man and the Citizen. Outside, poor people in the city were more intent on finding food to eat; and art like politics was scarcely on their mind. When the Salon opened its doors in September critics noticed some depictions of recent events, like Hubert Robert's *Demolition of the Bastille*, but they discussed them only in terms of the artist's skill: to their minds the subject did not matter. Robert shows Parisians in the process of destroying a symbol of royal oppression. The Fourteenth of July 1789, like the Declaration of the Rights of Man and the Citizen, has been seen as a great achievement for the ordinary man. Yet the Bastille had fallen because the guns trained on it were manned by professional soldiers and the Declaration was penned partly as a panic reaction to the peasant 'Great Fear'. According to the myth of the French Revolution, Liberty was goddess of the people, but in reality Violence stood at her side from the first. The year 1789 saw the end of the *ancien régime* in France. It also marked the start of a political revolution, whose end no one could imagine.

Among the paintings of that year's Salon only one, planned some time before, captured that autumn's mood. Louis David produced, as he normally did, a masterpiece with its theme from ancient history, this time *Lictors returning to Brutus the bodies of his sons*. He had a liking for stern stories from Livy or Plutarch; and this one was one of the sternest. Brutus was the first Roman consul, the man who led the fight

David's 'Brutus' (Musée du Louvre, Paris), the most important painting of the
1789 Salon, was soon to become a republican icon.

against the tyrannical Tarquins and valued civic loyalty before all other ties. When
he found that his sons had conspired against the new republic, he felt bound both
to sentence them to death and to watch their execution. David invented a moment
when the boys' bodies are brought home. While the household women cry out in
pain, writhe in agony or weep under a sheet, Brutus sits brooding in the shadow,
tragic and alone. Revolutions are made by men.

The *Brutus* was scarcely mentioned in the journals of the year. For once David's
habit of delaying the date on which his works were revealed backfired on him.
Political events mattered most to the journalists; they also made clear that nature need
not follow art. It was the women who clamoured to go to Versailles in search of food.
Whereas men pulled down the King's dungeon in town, women dismantled the
power he exercised from his palace in the country. They made David's glorification
of his own sex look irrelevant. Their problems were immediate; he looked to the
distant past.

In 1789 the painting of *Brutus* had no republican meaning: the conviction it expressed was aesthetic. It was the product of a recent revolution in taste. In 1775 David had gone to Rome as the scholarship student in painting for that year. For him Rome came to mean not the principal see of Christendom, the place where the apos-tles Peter and Paul had died for Christ; rather Rome stood for antique virtue and austere taste. Besides forgetting Peter and Paul, David forgot Nero, who had put the apostles to death. He dreamt of an uncorrupt Rome, not the Rome that after con-quest turned to cruelty and luxury, circuses and bread.

The link between Paris and Rome went back to the previous century. Apart from one short stay in Paris, the most famous French painter, Nicolas Poussin, had spent most of his adult life in Rome, where his pictures had recreated an antique world by deft quotations from the buildings, statues, pillars and sarcophagi around him. He inspired younger artists at home, especially when Classicism was naturalized as French by royal consent. When Louis XIV wanted a new east front for his palace of the Louvre, Perrault designed a colonnade with overtones of a Roman peristyle. The plays of Corneille and Racine at court drew their plots from Greek fiction or Roman fact. Le Brun, Poussin's brightest pupil, took in hand the decoration of the palace of Versailles; if inevitably the movable furniture or *meubles* designed by Boulle, the tapes-tries fashioned at the Gobelins and the carpets at the Savonnerie were modern, many rooms were named after gods and many statues in the gardens were of gods. As for Louis XIV, as Sun King he danced the role of Apollo and he behaved like a Caesar.

It was Louis XIV, not the artists or the craftsmen, who had approved the ways in which the arts and crafts were to be regulated; and it was because of him that the grandeur of the *grand siècle* turned to pomposity at Versailles. Taste in his old age, and still more in the time of Louis XV, his great-grandson, grew weary of the effort. There was a search for lightness, whimsy and frivolity as Baroque was replaced by Rococo. Yet it was precisely in one corner of Le Nôtre's magnificent gardens – a landscape by Poussin brought to life among parterres and walks and fountains – that in the mid-eighteenth century the architect Gabriel turned back to simplicity. Le Petit Trianon is constructed as a cube, its exterior is unadorned, its scale is intimate. The critics' call for classic, classical art was heard at the court which delighted in the pearly nymphs and bronzed fauns of Boucher. Le Petit Trianon was to be a retreat for Louis XV and his *maîtresse en titre*, Madame de Pompadour (the *maîtresse en titre* was the 'official' mistress). She died before she could enjoy it, but she had given the immense prestige of her liking for a new classicism in design. Silversmiths were looking to urns and vases as models for their tureens and ewers, to columns for their candles. The services cast for aristocrats and kings were decorated with laurel and palm leaf swags, with rams' heads, putti and terms. It was smart to seek purity of style. It was dowdy to stand also for purity of morals, until Louis XVI, a young man with bourgeois tastes, succeeded his sensual grandfather.

David's 'Belisarius' (Musée des Beaux-Arts, Lille) was the painting which
made the painter's reputation at the Salon of 1781.

When the new reign began in 1774, in almost all the arts the new taste was established. For the coronation, Robert-Joseph Auguste fashioned a Neo-Classical gold
crown and chalice. For the new Queen Marie-Antoinette Pitoin sculpted candle-
sticks with caryatids to be put in one of the *petits appartements*, the private royal apartments, at Versailles. In her boudoir at Fontainebleau Jean-Henri Riesener, *ébéniste du
roi*, supported her work-table with lyre-shaped legs. On the Mont de Paris, Soufflot
worked on his coldly rational church of Sainte-Geneviève (which revolutionaries
would rename the Panthéon). Only in painting had the new manner produced
nothing of quality. Comte d'Angiviller, appointed Directeur des Bâtiments* at the

---

*The Directeur des Bâtiments: the man whose principal care was the royal palaces, hence he was keeper of the
royal art collection.

very start of the reign, called for 'history' paintings, pictures with their stories from the Bible or the classics (the sophisticated preferred the classics). Next year the count put Vien in charge of the French school in Rome. As Vien, in his insipid way, was Neo-Classical, Poussin's legacy would be secure.

For many years the Prix de Rome had been the prize for which all ambitious art students competed. David tried to win it three times and after one failure even went so far as to think of suicide. When he won it he was quite old for the prize – he had been born in 1748. He set off for Rome with Vien, determined that antiquity would never seduce him. He returned to Paris seduced. Throughout the 1780s he would listen to d'Angiviller's call. Civic virtue would be his theme, classicism his style.

He became instantly famous on his return to France in 1781, when he imitated Poussin with *Belisarius begging for alms*, an incident taken from the old age of a Byzantine general whose dismissal by his master the Emperor was then a story well known to French advanced opinion. It was not till two Salons later that he pushed his art to a new extreme of more primitive intensity. For his showpiece of 1785 David went back to a famous story from the period of the early Roman Republic. One of Corneille's plays, then enjoying a new vogue, took its plot from Livy and Plutarch: the story of the Horatii.

David was drawn to the tough morality of this tale. The three Horatii brothers were chosen to fight for their city's freedom against three Curiatii brothers from Alba Longa. In the battle that followed two of the Horatii were killed and the three Curiatii wounded. The one Horatius left, still unscathed, ran away, so giving himself the chance to kill his enemies one by one (a chance he took). As sole sur-vivor of the fight he came back to Rome in triumph, draping across his shoulders the cloak of one of his dead opponents. By the city gate he met a sister of his, who had been betrothed to the young man whose cloak he carried. She burst into a pas-sionate lament. He reacted swiftly and brutally. Scorning her concern for the fate of their city's foe, he drew his sword and plunged it into her heart. For such behaviour he was bound to be tried. He was saved from death by his father's plea: the girl not he had deserved to die.

At first David thought of painting the meeting of brother and sister. In the end he claimed that he found his picture not in the classics but in Poussin and Corneille. By this he meant that he took details from a series of Poussin paintings on classical stories – *The Testament of Eudamidas*, *The Rape of the Sabines* and *The Death of Germanicus*. As for the debt to Corneille, he had been struck by the last act of a 1782 performance of *Horace* and made a sketch of it. Yet the scene he eventually portrayed – the three young men swearing an oath before their exultant father and their wilting womenfolk – has no precise literary source; and no picture of Poussin's has that sense of suppressed hysteria which gives *The Oath of the Horatii* its power. The manner-

David's 'Oath of the Horatii' (Musée du Louvre, Paris), in the context of the
1785 Salon, was a call to patriotic virtue and artistic rectitude.

isms may be Poussin's: the staged set; the symbolic use of Tuscan Doric as the most
primitive, masculine order of architecture; the near-symmetrical disposition of the
figures; the economical gestures; the unmixed colours. But whereas Corneille and
Poussin worked within a stoical tradition that had ultimate meaning in Christian
revelation, David has opted for a scheme of purely human values. There is a story
that on catching sight of one of Poussin's altarpieces of the *Seven Sacraments* Bernini
fell to his knees. David's art elicits a different sort of devotion: it calls to action, not
to prayer. Nothing in life matters more than being a father's son, a child ready to die
for the fatherland, *la patrie*.

David was conscious of his important task. To make sure that he would achieve
something great, his father-in-law paid for him to return to Rome. After the 1783
Salon he had met and married the daughter of the royal builder, Pécoul. For David
it was a good match, for Pécoul had position and wealth. David was only too aware
that, compared to other painters, he was well educated and well born. He was not
averse to a fine dowry and prosperous relations. It did not make him any more

David's 'Death of Socrates' (Metropolitan Museum, New York), which was
shown in 1787, is the most careful of his classical reconstructions.

gracious in his next narrative picture towards women, whose only role was to be
pathetic. Heroism was an exclusively male virtue. Just as his work had the hardness
of antique stone, so it was grandiose in scale and harsh in lighting and colour. In the
twentieth century it could have been Fascist art. In the eighteenth century it was
merely Revolutionary.

As yet the only political revolution of the 1780s had occurred in America; and
in French liberal circles American patriots like Franklin with his disarming
combination of technical inventiveness and a homely manner, Jefferson with his
quirky learning and Washington, a Cincinnatus who had won victories for his
country and then retired to his estate at Mount Vernon, each in his way exemplified
the republican ethics of ancient Rome. David mixed with liberal reformers. He had
discussed the subject of the Horatii at the hôtel of Monsieur de Trudaine; one of
Trudaine's sons was a friend of Lafayette, Washington's protégé; and the two sons
gave him his next commission, *The Death of Socrates*. Socrates was the ideal hero for
a political reformer with Neo-Classical tastes. Like a modern radical, he had been
accused of subverting the young. In choosing to accept the drink of hemlock
unjustly imposed by the City rather than trying to escape, he behaved like Horatius,
as a patriot.

No other painting by David is so doggedly Neo-Classical, none so marmoreal. There is a somewhat fussy concern with archaeological correctness. The fatal hemlock is offered to Socrates in a cylix, a scroll lies at the foot of the couch, a lamp on its stand shines against the wall, the owl of Athena is cut into the side of a stone seat. Jefferson, then American ambassador in Paris, wrote to the American painter John Trumbull about that year's paintings, stating: 'The best thing is *The Death of Socrates* by David, and a superb one it is.' Sir Joshua Reynolds was even more enthu-siastic: *The Death of Socrates* is 'the greatest effort of art since the Sistine Chapel and the Stanze of Raphael in the Vatican. This work would have done honour to Athens at the time of Pericles.' Count Potocki, a Polish liberal whom David had painted on horseback in Rome, was also full of praise. Nobody looking at *The Death of Socrates* could have guessed that it was painted in a time of political collapse.

During 1781–7 France suffered from the consequences of its most recent foreign policy success. The war on behalf of the Americans had bankrupted the govern-ment; and it was out of weakness that Louis XVI agreed to call a meeting of the Estates General for May 1789. The Estates General had last met in 1614 and 1615 and it had failed; and its failure then had seemed to justify the view that France could be governed well only by an absolute monarch. For ten years from the early winter of 1789 to the early winter of 1799 there was a political consensus that there should be no untrammelled supreme executive power. What mattered was the will of the people, however expressed. While devotion to *la patrie* was his compatriots' ideal, David had found the perfect theme for his art. The values proclaimed by his *Horatii* and his *Socrates* inspired his *Brutus* too.

He soon realized that the status of artists and artisans, so closely bound up with the *ancien régime*, was bound to change once the *ancien régime* no longer existed.

The rules that governed the lives of artists and artisans, like so many French lives before 1789, had been fixed in the reign of Louis XIV. Until his reign there was strictly no difference between artists and artisans. All were tradesmen, all were gov-erned by laws that laid down conditions of apprenticeship, all aspired to become members of a guild – in the case of a painter, the Guild of St Luke, who in his gospel had 'portrayed' the Madonna and child. From Italians, however, painters and sculptors learnt that their crafts were not just the work of their hands. Art, based on the theory and practice of design, was an intellectual activity, like writing. While Louis was still a minor, the Royal Academy of Painting and Sculpture was founded in 1648; and it was revived in 1663, soon after his personal rule began. Architecture, which appealed to trained scientists, like Christopher Wren in England, got its Academy in 1671. The fine arts had become professions; and well-to-do young men, like David, could take to painting without losing social cachet. Those most successful, the academicians, achieved a kind of nobility, like the *noblesse de la robe** which made up France's meritocracy. They were the first order among those who created. The guild system ensured that lesser men, still mere artisans, kept to their inferior place in society.

The hierarchy was maintained when the lesser were controlled by the greater, as when Le Brun, chief painter at Louis XIV's court, was given charge of the Gobelins tapestry factory. Another method was to patronize by the granting of official royal approval. André-Charles Boulle was made *premier ébéniste du roi*, a title that gave him prestige but did not save him from bankruptcy. He had, however, had his workshops in the Louvre. Working for the King was the mainspring of his business. Royal favour was everything to the craftsman; and control of the crafts was a part of royal policy. If Louis XIV wished to know what his subjects made, he had only to consult the *Description des Arts et Métiers* prepared by his Academy of Science. While he worked long hours at his beautiful *secrétaire*, his workmen were at their benches making other beautiful desks for him, for France, for the country's wealth and glory. In 1672 he was the first French king to go to war not so much for dynastic reasons, as for trade.

In the eighteenth century the system was modified. The establishment in 1737 of the biennial Salon to show off pictures placed a new emphasis on the Paris art market. Versailles remained the centre of government but not of taste. Despite the beneficent influence of La Pompadour, who arranged for her brother the Marquis de Marigny to be Director of Royal Buildings and who herself is for ever associated with the soft paste factory at Sèvres, Louis XV showed little aesthetic sensibility beyond a simple love of the dimpled bottoms of Boucher's models. His grandson Louis XVI did not share this taste. He loved clocks. His Queen, Marie-Antoinette, was more adventurous. She liked dressing up *en bergère* and milking cows in her rustic village, *le hameau*.† Her favourite portrait painter was Madame Elizabeth Vigée-Lebrun, the most charming of artists. Madame Vigée-Lebrun had an eye for the textures of chiffon, cotton or silk, for graceful gestures and for sweet smiling faces. She responded sympathetically to the cruelly maligned Queen, who was frivolous and extravagant, but neither hard nor lustful. At a time when the scandal of

---

*The *noblesse de la robe*, literally the nobility of the gown, as distinguished from the *noblesse de l'épée*, the nobility of the sword. Whereas the more ancient *noblesse de l'épée* owed its titles originally to military service, the *noblesse de la robe* had achieved nobility from hereditary office (its training was often legal so its members wore gowns).

†*En bergère*: 'as a shepherdess'. It has been pointed out that Queen Marie-Antoinette's idea of the life and costume of a shepherdess owed more to porcelain figurines than to the experience of looking after sheep. The *hameau* or hamlet contained a rather large, picturesque house (meant to be a cottage), a watermill, two dairies, a barn, which doubled as a ballroom, and a farm.

the diamond necklace* affair spread the lie that Marie-Antoinette was a flirt – a cardinal was duped by a prostitute dressed up as the Queen – Madame Vigée-Lebrun
brought an old-fashioned dignity to her painting of the Queen and her children.
The reward was fitting: thanks to the King, the painter was elected to the Academy.
France was no longer a country where, as under the great Louis, the King wrote an
account conducting his reader round his park. In the time of Louis XVI, as
Madame Vigée-Lebrun wrote many years later, women were the rulers. France had
gone soft.

In other ways art had slipped out of royal hands. The most impressive representation of France's crafts is found in the many volumes of plates from the *Encyclopédie*,
a mammoth dictionary of the arts and sciences brought out largely by the art critic
Diderot against the wishes of the official censors. Under Louis XIV the great
writers, on the whole, supported Church and State. Now they were alienated from
the Church and indifferent to the State. When he looked for enlightenment in a
monarch, Diderot looked to Catherine the Great of Russia, not Louis XV.
Enlightened monarchs, like Louis XVI's brother-in-law, Joseph II, tended to
abolish outdated institutions; and in 1776 there was a chance that Louis XVI
would sanction the abolition of the guilds. But by 1781 they were back in full force;
and now more careful accounts were kept of workers' performance.

A more insidious criticism of the arts came from the writings of Jean-Jacques
Rousseau, whose literary career began with a prize-winning essay on the corrupting
effects of culture and who went on to advocate a sentimental love of simple taste.
France was famous for its excellence in the production of luxuries: Lyon silk, inlaid
marquetry, Sèvres porcelain. Its artisans relied on the rich, its artists flattered the rich.
Chardin, the only painter to achieve simplicity, sold to kings. Unchecked, simplicity would ruin thousands of workmen and hundreds of masters. In the end they
were made desperate by the price of bread.

---

*The scandalous affair of the queen's diamond necklace has been blamed for the coming of the revolution. In
1785 the cardinal de Rohan, worried that he was out of favour at court, became the dupe of an avaricious scheming lady of ambiguous gentility, Jeanne de la Motte, who had insinuated herself into the entourage of the king's
sister, Madame Elisabeth. The cardinal was sure that his fortunes would revive if he could gain the Queen's protection. Jeanne de la Motte was sure that her status would be restored if she could touch his seemingly unlim-
ited wealth. She persuaded the cardinal to give her money, with which she said she was winning over
Marie-Antoinette; and he went to meet the 'Queen' (a milliner dressed up for the role) at night in the gardens of
Versailles. Jeanne's final throw was to pretend to a desperate jeweller that the cardinal would act as go-between
to enable the Queen to buy a famous diamond necklace in four instalments. The jeweller was not paid, the Queen
did not wear the necklace at court and Jeanne's lover and her husband, both acting in collusion, found it hard
to dispose of the necklace and did not have the cash to pay for even the first instalment. When the plot came to
light, the cardinal and Jeanne were put on trial, he was acquitted, but she was branded with the letter 'V' as a
voleuse, a thief, before being imprisoned and escaping to London, from where she poured out her vitriol in vicious
attacks on the real victim of her crimes, the innocent Queen, whose reputation was for ever after ruined.

Since the time of Louis XIV textiles ranked first among French industries. They provided employment in the towns of Picardy – Arras, Abbeville and Amiens – and in the vicinity of the capital, in Rouen, in Jouy, in Beauvais and in Paris itself – as well as in Lyon and Nîmes. Next to food clothes and warm furnishings are the prime necessity of life; and in good years textile manufacturers did well. But if food is short then old clothes will do and sheets, cushions and hangings need not be replaced. On 13 July 1788 a freak hailstorm was so fierce that it killed men and beasts and devastated crops just ready for the harvest. The winter that followed was the coldest in living memory; in the south vines and olive-trees died in the frost, in the north there was ice and snow till April. Everywhere textile workers were thrown out of work; and most poor people, the majority of Frenchmen, had to spend two-thirds to nine-tenths of their money on bread. The price of a loaf mounted steadily and peaked in Paris just one year after the freak hailstorm, on 14 July 1789. The artisans who attacked and sacked the Bastille were hungry.

The *Grande Peur* in the countryside which followed soon after the fall of the Bastille destroyed much more of France's artistic heritage. How many châteaux and *manoirs*, how much fine furniture or furnishings disappeared for ever is unknown. By early August the society of privilege that these goods represented had gone, never to be replaced. The system of the arts, which catered for that closed world of the *ancien régime*, would have to go too. David was coming to hold that the arts would flourish only in a free society. He sat brooding on the ills that academies caused artists like himself, a modern Brutus in the shadows. By the time the Salon opened in September 1789, his painting had a revolutionary meaning, for Brutus was an honourable man, who gave himself to a new style of government.

It was only gradually that radicals came to see that the new regime must be a republic. To some ultra-royalists the tendency of events was clear early on. As early as 17 July 1789 the King's youngest brother, the Comte d'Artois, headed for the north-east frontier and exile; and in subsequent months other *émigrés* left their homes, often for ever.

Madame Vigée-Lebrun, with her remarkable instinct for survival, decided that she too must leave. Her court connections made her vulnerable, her home, the grand Hôtel Le Brun, was dangerous, and she took refuge with the architect Brogniart and his wife, who had an apartment in Louis XIV's military hospital, the Invalides. From the windows she saw vulgar *sans-culottes*, workmen who did not wear breeches, shaking their fists at her. Outside she heard workmen discussing how they would wring money from those they denounced. The mob seemed all-powerful. The governor of the Invalides was sure that he could hide arms from them, but someone betrayed him. What brought forward her flight, however, was the forced move of the royal family to the Tuileries. She was terrified of having to cross the faubourg Saint-Antoine, from which area most of the forcers had come, but by good luck the long march to and from Versailles had left everyone exhausted; and the public coach she rode in passed through dark, silent streets unmolested. She left France for Savoy; and only then could she feel any joy. Behind her lay a career of critical success, which had culminated weeks before at the Salon of 1789, where her study of the painter Hubert Robert showed how well she could capture the spirit of an energetic man. Ahead lay a career of social success among the European nobility. She would not return permanently to France till the King's brother, the Comte de Provence, was restored as Louis XVIII; and she would see the portrait of Marie-Antoinette and her children, which Napoleon had turned to the wall, once more restored to its setting in the salon at Versailles.

Few artists were as single-minded. Regardless of political events, Hubert Robert loved ruins under dramatic lighting. That year he showed the Bastille being demolished by night. Nine years later his subject was young girls dancing by a broken obelisk before a massive pyramid while storm-clouds darken the sky – it was the year Napoleon went to Egypt. Others were aesthetically linked, in style and theme, to the old world. Fragonard's light and delicate scenes of sexual seduction lacked gravity and pandered to degenerate nobles' fantasies of pleasure. In one of Fragonard's most delectable paintings a count gazes longingly up the legs of his mistress, while she is pushed on a swing by a priest. Now he got no commissions and had to rely on David for some work on one of the committees of the Louvre. Greuze, so sentimentally moralistic, almost a Rousseau on canvas, was too much the *bon bourgeois* for rough times. At the revolutionary Salons he was a flop and he died forgotten and poor.

Hard times hit the purveyors of luxury goods even harder. Most eminent of cabinet-makers, Jean-Henri Riesener had been made *ébéniste ordinaire du roi* on the accession of Louis XVI in 1774. By 1784 he was proving too expensive for the King, but into the early years of the revolution he still worked for the Queen. His large bills could not be paid and he had to endure the indignity of buying back his furniture in the hope of selling it again. This proved to be a naïve manoeuvre, for the people who could not pay his bills in the 1780s, even if they were alive and living in France, were even less able to pay them in the 1790s. In 1797 he was asked to remove royal emblems from his own works; and he agreed. His fate was a little better than that of the silversmiths. In October 1789 the National Assembly passed a decree appealing for silver to be handed in to be melted down at the Mint. The great – the King, the Queen, the King's sister-in-law, the King's aunts, the royal Duc d'Orléans, the King's ministers – competed in displays of public virtue by offering the bulk of their collections to the nation; and much of the most beautiful silverware in France was melted down. It was not replaced. There was some point in making furniture of a politically correct kind; and David, who helped Fragonard, also helped the firm of Jacob. But David had no time for extravagant displays of wealth. 'Despise diamonds and gold,' he advised right-thinking women. 'Be adorned in the virtues of your sex.' When he pronounced these words, it was year two in the revolutionary calendar. France was a republic. Brutus had triumphed over Tarquin.

Right up till 1794 David moved with the times. Every turn the revolution took he took too.

In 1790, while the lawyers of the National Assembly had a field-day drafting a new constitution for a rational France, he was fervently committed to the principles of 1789. In spring 1790 he started to work on *The Tennis Court Oath*,* a picture to commemorate the founding of the National Assembly. He would show the spirit of unity among Christians – a Protestant, a monk and a priest embracing – and unity of purpose among deputies, as they raised their hands like his own ecstatic Horatii. He was careful to sketch the setting, he modelled the heads of the political leaders and posed Martin Dauch, the one deputy who would not take the oath, as a cross-limbed Judas, self-tortured and alone. In 1790 David was still friends with the enlightened élite who met in the hôtel of the brothers Trudaine, who had given him advice with the *Horatii* and the *Socrates*. There he met their schoolfriend-poet André Chénier, and the chemist Lavoisier, whose wife had been his pupil. In 1788 he had painted a double portrait of them and in 1791 he painted Madame Trudaine de Montigny. In these three years his style had undergone its own revolution. Lavoisier and his wife are crisply painted, glamorous and sleek, a couple at ease with their fame as eminent chemist and his assistant. Experiments for them were simply matters of good order. By 1791 Madame de Trudaine had no such confidence in her role. She wears her patriotism anxiously. Painted sketchily in the sombre black of the Third Estate, with blue sash and white *fichu* against a red ground, she looks worn-out. She belonged to the party that quickly lost control of the revolution – she would die on the guillotine and David would do nothing to help her.

In the 1780s David had been received by political reformers. As early as September 1789 he was campaigning for the posthumous admission to the Academy of Drouais, a favourite student of his who had died the previous year in Rome. By December he was demanding that the Academy should be more democratic. In the course of 1790 he became still more radical. He became the mouthpiece of the artists who wanted to cut down the privileges of the Academy, as surely as the lawyers cut down the privileges of feudal lords. He argued his case in a speech to the Constituent Assembly (as the National Assembly was now called) and the deputy Lepeletier, a former aristocrat, was so impressed that he ordered the printing of the speech. Temporarily frustrated in his aims, David founded a rival

---

*The real tennis court at Versailles became the site where members of the three estates adjourned and swore to reconstitute themselves into a single national assembly.

organization, the Commune of the Arts. He was asked to become the official recorder of the tennis court oath, the drawing for which had been triumphantly shown at the 1791 Salon.

At that Salon he also showed the great set-pieces of the three most recent Salons, the *Horatii*, the *Socrates* and the *Brutus*. It was a shrewd move, for now those revolutionary works of art could be reinterpreted as politically correct works of art. David's self-transformation into the chief visual witness of the revolution had already begun. In November 1790 Voltaire's play *Brutus* had been shown at the National Theatre. The audience had divided itself into royalists who cheered Tarquin and radicals who cheered Brutus. But David had taken pains to make clear the production's intention, for on one side of the stage he had placed a copy of a bust of Brutus he had brought from Rome and on the other side Houdon's bust of Voltaire. At the end of the play the actors arranged themselves into the poses of his painting. The revolutionary painter had designed a tableau for revolution.

More tableaux were needed: 1790 was also the year when the first great revolutionary festival was held in Paris. On 14 July, one year after the fall of the Bastille, a series of large processions made their way to the Champ de Mars, the open space beside the Ecole Militaire. Before a congregation of 400,000 grouped round the *autel de la patrie* under pouring rain, Mass was sung by the liberal bishop of Autun, Talleyrand, and then Lafayette took the oath of the representatives, the *fédérés*, who had come from all over France to swear their loyalty to the new constitutional monarchy. Louis XVI joined in the holiday mood by using for the first time his new official title as King of the French; and even the Dauphin sported the tricolour uniform of the National Guard. To the participants it was as if the clouds had parted and new light shone on France.

A year later the mood in the capital had darkened. More and more impotent and worried about the safety of his family, Louis XVI had tried to escape to the eastern border, but got no further than Varennes. At the Cordeliers Club, which met in a former convent, politicians recalled that after the rape of Lucretia by Tarquin's sons Brutus had vowed to destroy the family of Tarquin and that the Romans had shut Tarquin out of the city. It was an apt moment to honour the author of *Brutus*, the playwright who had inspired David: Voltaire.

On 11 July 1791 the remains of Voltaire were transported to the Panthéon, the gaunt Neo-Classical shrine originally erected to glorify Sainte Geneviève, Catholic patroness of Paris. But the Church had been nationalized in 1790; and for the rational religion of the new France Soufflot's building had enough the look of an ancient temple to be a suitable resting place for heroes of revolution. It had already received the body of Mirabeau. Now it would be the last resting-place of Voltaire. A small committee, which included David and the architect Quatremère de Quincy – an ally in the fight against the Academies – designed a huge classical chariot to hold the sarcophagus on top of which a statue of Voltaire slept smilingly on an antique bed; a broken lyre lay at his side and at his head Eternity. In this fashion his remains were taken to rest in triumph.

There was a sad sequel. On 17 July a large group of republicans called for a demonstration on the Champ de Mars. Fearful of rioting, Lafayette persuaded the mayor of Paris, Bailly, to proclaim martial law. In the confrontation that followed some of the crowd were killed by members of the National Guard, on the spot where one year before, to national rejoicing, Lafayette had proclaimed national unity. The revolutionary cause was now a cause of division.

Potentially, divisiveness had been present as soon as the Conventional Assembly sold off Church property as national goods (at Talleyrand's suggestion), closed religious houses, turned the secular clergy into servants of the state and demanded of them an oath of loyalty. Despite its Christian roots the 'constitutional' Church thus established was like the civic religion dreamed up by Rousseau or the religion of humanity taught by Voltaire. It was comprehensive, utterly tolerant. Parisian lawmakers could not conceive that anyone in their rational France was attached to the superstitions of the past, to the rituals of the Catholic liturgy and to a pathetic figure like Pope Pius VI, who seemed more intent on keeping hold of Avignon than on standing up for his flock. His flock alas still existed. There were *émigrés*, whom loneliness had attracted to piety, and peasants who had not read their Rousseau and bourgeois who did not mock with Voltaire. By mischance Louis XVI felt like them; and that made him into a counter-revolutionary sympathizer. Though he agreed to the constitution that set up a new Legislative Assembly (David painted a delicate domestic portrait of Madame de Pastoret, wife of its first president, with their child), Louis vetoed the laws against *émigrés* and priests.

The year 1791 thus marked a parting of the ways. While they were increasingly cut off from their ancient sources of patronage – the King, the Church, the nobility – the artists were also freed from privilege. The guilds were abolished, an event that some journeymen artisans celebrated by going on strike, and in place of the painting Academicians David, Quatremère de Quincy and four others were given charge of the Salon. In the same year a law removed the care of royal buildings from the Academy of Architecture to a newly formed Council of Civil Buildings. Conservatives worried that the spirit of democracy would lead to a decay in standards, a view argued by the architect Renou to the Assembly on 30 August 1792. The Academy of Architecture might purr with pleasure, the demagogues had just shown their teeth. On 10 August a mob had burst into the Tuileries, hacked the Swiss guards to pieces and carried off the royal family to the Assembly. The monarchy was overthrown. A few days later a guillotine, the people's humane instrument of execution, was set up in the palace courtyard. Like a church, the new republic would cultivate new martyrs, establish new feasts and demand new sacrifices. In every venture David would cast himself in a leading role. Much like his friend, the actor Talma, however, he was a man whose politics consisted largely of gestures. The chief creators of the republic, the principals in the unfolding action, would be Girondins (Brissot and Roland), Indulgents* (Danton and Desmoulins) and Jacobins (Marat, Lepeletier, Robespierre). David would be little more than an observer, an extra.

It was Brissot, a fiery journalist, and his allies, some of them deputies from the department of the Gironde, who saw in war relief from the political tension in France. Late in 1791 he had called for war. War would show whether Louis XVI stood by his people or not, whether other kings of Europe would intervene to support him, whether France's Rhenish neighbours would continue to protect the *émigrés*. Robespierre stood out against the mood of national folly, but the fools had their way and war was declared on Austria. Brissot's friends became ministers, among them an ageing former inspector of manufacturers, Roland, who took over the Ministry of the Interior. Roland was important politically because he had an able and ambitious wife, a political hostess so imbued with love of Plutarch that she saw in war a school of virtue. To David her husband was a bitter enemy, for Roland had charge of the royal art collection. During the course of 1792 Roland made a political comeback. One of the last exercises of political power by Louis XVI had been the dismissal of the Girondin ministers; so when Louis fell, they reemerged. The very day after the massacre of the Swiss guards, Roland nominated a commission of six to take charge of the royal collection of paintings, which was to be installed in the Grande Galerie of the Louvre. The citizens of Versailles tried to stop the transport of *their* works of art to Paris – and in the case of the *Mona Lisa* for a time they succeeded – but their opposition was as nothing to the fierce attacks of David and JeanBaptistePierre Le Brun, his spokesman.

Like Roland, Le Brun was less famous in his own right than as a husband, in his case as husband of the *émigrée* painter Elisabeth VigéeLebrun, but he was a capable dealer and connoisseur and he expected to be on Roland's commission. David for his part was furious because Roland had favoured Academicians and, most galling of all, had named one of them, Suvée, a rival from student days, as Director of the French Academy in Rome. To Le Brun's jibes Roland replied that Le Brun's interest in dealing could conflict with his work on the commission and, as for David, Roland thought him 'distinguished but too easily led'. The pair settled on a new plan of attack: Roland had faulty ideas about picture restoration. This tactic worked

*The Indulgents were so called because in their policy they were relatively merciful. The Jacobins took their name from their club, which met in the former convent of SaintJacques.

and Roland lost his post in January 1793, the month in which Louis XVI lost his head.

In the course of 1792 more extreme politicians than the Girondins had come to run the politics of Paris. France was in danger from enemies within as well as without, the Prussians had crossed the frontier, Lafayette had given himself up to the Austrians, the fortresses of Longwy and Verdun had fallen. To be safe the Commune of Paris filled prisons with anybody looking suspicious – Catholic priests, royalist editors and royalist printers and royal servants, anyone who had petitioned in favour of Lafayette, even Beaumarchais, once thought subversive for the smiling wit of *The Marriage of Figaro*. Marat, with a pen more virulent than Brissot's, posted placards round the city, urging good citizens to run priests through with a sword. The citizens were good enough to take him at his word. While Roland discreetly avoided intervening, they murdered almost 1500 enemies of the people in the early days of September. The following month Brissot was expelled from the Jacobin club, Marat's club. The Girondins, who had once seemed so intemperate, now fought to delay the execution of the King. They were outvoted, Roland and his friends lost their posts and David was triumphant. Most of all, he was overjoyed that he had helped to kill the King.

CHAPTER 2

The Republic becomes Dictatorial

THE REGICIDES called Louis XVI 'Louis Capet', so recognizing the astonishing unbroken line of royal descent through the male line from the tenth to the eighteenth centuries. But the kingship that they wished to destroy had a more recent origin. For all its medieval and Renaissance trappings, the monarchy Louis XVI had inherited was in its essentials the monarchy of Louis XIV. The Jacobins thought in 1793 that they had brought monarchy to an end. In 1799 Bonaparte brought it back. In 1793 David exercised semi-dictatorial powers over the arts in favour of the new republic. After 1799 he worked for Bonaparte, who was to be a monarch more powerful than Louis XIV had dreamt of being.

For the year and a half from Louis XVI's death to Robespierre's that prospect was unthinkable. In terms of David's art 1793–4 was the period of the three martyrs.

The first martyr was one of the regicides. The day before Louis' execution Michel Lepeletier, once Marquis de Saint-Fargeau, was repeatedly stabbed in the chest by a former member of Louis' bodyguard. From David's sketch of the victim when alive it is clear that Lepeletier had one of the ugliest heads in France: in death David made him take on the beauty of an antique hero, who deserved the splendid pagan funeral he organized in place Vendôme. There, placed high on a pedestal, the corpse, with the bloody shirt at its feet, was approached past smoking urns.

The painting made by David in collaboration with Gérard, one of his most gifted pupils, was damaged irreparably by the martyr's daughter, who became a passionate royalist. From the engraving, the main plate for which she only mutilated, it is possible to make out a sword suspended over his body. During a speech in March to the Convention David explained that the sword pierced a paper on which were inscribed the words 'I vote the death of the tyrant'.

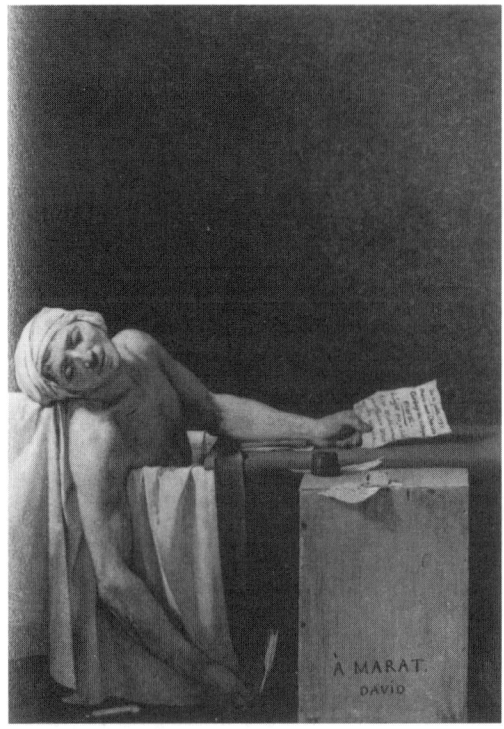

David's 'Death of Marat' (Musées Royaux, Brussels) is the only one of his three martyr paintings of 1793 which was finished. He took it with him into exile.

His second martyr painting was even more concerned with words. Marat had incited the bloodletting of the previous September. Rather belatedly the Girondins set out to have him tried for violent language, not against prisoners, but against the Convention; and this time they won the vote. He eluded them, appealed to the Commune of Paris, was acquitted by a revolutionary tribunal and was treated as a patriotic hero – it is thus that the Lille painter Boilly depicts him, carried on men's shoulders and warmly greeted by men and women of every class. His release from prison meant that the Girondins had been discredited. Though a member of the Convention, his immunity had been ignored – early in June theirs was too, and they were excluded. To their supporters he became a marked man. This time it was a woman who delivered the *coup de grâce*. Armed only with her birth certificate and the thoughts of Plutarch, Charlotte Corday set out from Caen. In Paris she bought a knife from a butcher's shop and made for Marat's house. He was difficult to gain access to because he used to work in a bath to cool his skin, which was inflamed with a form of psoriasis, so she had to send in a message to him: she knew about Girondin plots. He took the bait, she had her meeting and, by plunging the dagger into his heart, she made best use of it. Next day in the Convention Deputy Guirault inveighed against the 'parricidal hand' that 'has snatched away from us the most fear-

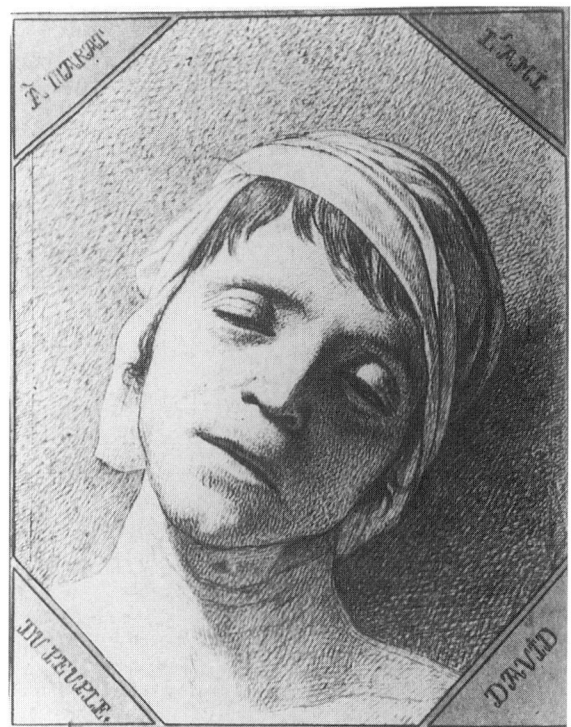

David's head of Marat (Musée du Louvre, Paris) was engraved, so that the martyr could be known throughout France. At the corners are inscribed the words: To Marat Friend of the People David. 'The Friend of the People' was Marat's newspaper.

less defender of the people . . . he is on the bed of death. Where are you, David? You have passed on to posterity the image of Lepeletier dying for the fatherland. There is one more painting yet for you.' 'I shall paint it,' cried out David, greatly moved. It would be painted by him alone.

The Death of Marat is arguably David's greatest painting, a work that transcends both his aesthetic and his political obsessions; and yet it was perfectly adapted to the circumstances of mid-1793. David set out to portray the death of a post-Christian martyr. Marat's body, immaculate but for the slight incision mark in his chest, is tilted lifelessly towards the spectator from his blood-filled bath. On the floor in front lies the fatal knife, the instrument of his passion, but more prominent are the evangel-ical signs of his journalistic vocation: one quill clutched in his limp left hand, another with paper on a wooden box inscribed À MARAT DAVID. The stark wall fits the frugal room of the people's friend – *L'ami du peuple* was the name of Marat's paper – and his charity is stressed by the letter he still clutches in his right hand. David did not mention Girondin plots but wrote 'it is enough that I am unhappy to have the right to your consideration' – his own version of a letter Charlotte Corday had carried close to her breast, Judas-like in her hypocrisy. Once again David juxtaposed art and life. He exhibited the picture beside the sanguinary bathtub; and Marat's

Looking like a hermaphrodite, Barra lies dying, by David (Musée Calvet, Avignon).

body would have been shown too, had not putrefaction and the sores made it too repulsive to smell or look at. In the event the body was hidden by a damp cloth. For those who could not be present, David designed an engraving of Marat's head in an octagonal border with eyes half closed in the sleep of death. In the four triangular corners were the words: À MARAT L'AMI DU PEUPLE DAVID. David and the cult hero were at one.

The third martyr had all the charm of innocence and youth and all the mystery of the unknown (David had never met him). In the summer of 1793 anti-Jacobins were becoming bolder. The provincial distrust of Paris which motivated Charlotte Corday to murder drove whole areas of France to rebel: the Midi, the Lyonnais, the Gironde, above all the Vendée, Brittany and Normandy, where pious peasants who knew no Plutarch could crusade. Terror became the order of the day. Some Girondins fled, but that autumn twenty-one of them who had been captured were dispatched in one day, including Brissot; and Madame Roland was guillotined a week later. Others, one of them her husband, played to the last the role of noble Romans and died by their own hands. Was antique virtue becoming the mark of the enemies of the one and indivisible republic? In these circumstances, at the end of the year, news reached Paris of the death of a thirteen-year-old boy, Joseph Barra, who had been hacked to pieces for refusing to surrender two horses. This was valour of a beautiful kind; and for months David struggled to find an adequate icon. In the end he created a fragment, a youthful hermaphrodite dying on undifferentiated ground who clutches to his heart the national cockade. The event had ceased to matter: it was the thought that counted.

To Robespierre, Barra's story was useful because it could be incorporated into a revolutionary mythology. With higher ideals than the somewhat sordid politicians who surrounded him, impeccable in his private life, Maximilien Robespierre needed to project his fantasies of a republic of virtue. In David he found the perfect master of ceremonies, an artist who could turn a political demonstration into a rite.

The republic was not just a kind of government: it was also a way of life. In 1793 France acquired its own form of calendar, backdated to the moment when the republic officially came into being (so it operated for the first time in year two). The months began with vintage-time,* went through fog, cold, snow, rain and wind, to springtime and times of flowering, haymaking, harvesting, roasting in the heat and ripening. Each month consisted of three *décades*. Most of the year, then, was given over to glorying in the bucolic enjoyments of an existence close to nature. The spare five days slightly redressed the balance by being *sansculottids*, to celebrate the urban working class. In the leap year there would be one extra day for everybody, the Day of the Revolution.

Along with the Gregorian calendar had disappeared Easter, Christmas and Whitsun. Revolutionary piety demanded that revolutionary feasts replace the Christian ones. As long ago as 1790 the Fête de la Fédération had reinforced the memory of the fall of the Bastille; and by 1890, under the Third Republic, the Fourteenth of July was fixed as the French national holiday. In the days of the First Republic this was not yet so; and David became involved in the search for new dates to commemorate. The year 1793–4 was the great period of David's political pageantry as well as of his political paintings. In 1793 he organized the funerals of Lepeletier and Marat in January and July, on 10 August he organized the Fête de la Réunion – it was a year since the crowds had invaded the Tuileries – and on 30 December the feast for the recapture of Toulon from the English (and so for the first time David was involved with a young Corsican artillery officer named Buonaparte). In 1794 there was only one feast, the Fête de l'Etre Suprême on 8 June, but he was planning a second one, for Barra and for another young boy, Viala, when

---

*The months so translated were Vendémiaire, Brumaire, Frimaire, Nivôse, Pluviôse, Ventôse, Germinal, Floréal, Prairial, Messidor, Thermidor and Fructidor.

Robespierre and he fell from power.

Though all these feasts were ephemeral, they were planned as carefully as monumental paintings. The feast of 10 August moved from place de la Bastille via boulevard des Italiens and place de la Révolution to the Champ de Mars. Each site was
marked by a gigantic edifice: an Egyptian woman (Nature) from whose breasts
poured water, a triumphal arch, a figure of Liberty enthroned and finally Hercules,
representing the French people, crushing a monster standing for federalism. At the
first station the President of the Convention indulged in ceremonies mimicking
baptism and communion. At the second station pretty actresses crowned with
laurels deputized for the tough women who had marched to Versailles. At the third
flames burnt royalist emblems and doves were released – flames and doves were pen-
tecostal.

It was at the fourth station that the most interesting transformation of ancient
symbolism occurred, for Herculean qualities had been familiar attributes of
Renaissance princes and Rubens had painted Henri IV, the first Bourbon king, as
the Gallic Hercules. Now David proposed that a gigantic bronze statue of the hero
should be placed on the Pont Neuf, cast from the cannon of France's defeated
enemies. Hercules meant virility: the milky breasts of Liberty were too soft for savage
times. It was as though David reinforced the contrast he had once made between the
male Horatii and their womenfolk. The festival Hercules alluded to this ideal of
masculine severity, for in his left hand he held a model of the Roman fasces, symbol
of the fatherland bound together as one by force.

Hercules reappears on David's projected curtain for a production at the Opéra
entitled *The Meeting of the Tenth of August* or *The Inauguration of the French Republic*.
The second version is the grandest of his revolutionary designs. Drawn by powerful oxen, the massive demigod sits on top of a huge antique triumphal carriage,
holding his enormous club, with tiny figures of Liberty and Justice beside him. In
front of the oxen two citizens race forward with swords to kill two counter-revolutionaries, one of them the King; the car crushes royalist accoutrements littering the
ground; and the processional float is followed by virtuous republicans. Cornelia and
the infant Gracchi lead Marat, who waves Charlotte Corday's letter, and William
Tell and his son, who holds the apple, Lepeletier, a child martyr and, to be up to
date, two good Jacobins whom the British had hung in Toulon.

David's finest hour as revolutionary impresario was his last, when he created the
machinery for the festival which brought him closer than ever to Robespierre.

Late in 1793 Fouché, representative of the central government *en mission* in the
central department of the Nièvre, began the process of dechristianization. Having
seen the Vendée, the ex-priest well understood the force of Catholic fanaticism – he
would develop a countervailing, wholly modern fanaticism that would be politically correct. For 22 September he devised a Feast of Brutus, at which he denounced

religious sophistry. As simple truth was evident to all, there was no need to express publicly the bizarre beliefs of any particular cult. Fouché strongly disapproved of celibacy, which he thought was socially harmful – he had not consulted the celibate Robespierre – and he wished to bring clerics into line with admirable people like himself. Example was contagious; and soon many others could take their pleasure in smashing windows and images, pulling down crosses, ripping out altars and gravestones. It was for the people's good, after all, that they acted thus. On 12 November a philosophic festival was held in the Temple of Reason (once Notre-Dame-de-Paris); and gradually any church within reach acquired an abstract name. Towns and streets were stripped of their Christian significance. Robespierre did not approve.

With lofty confidence in his own convictions, he preached to his fellow deists in the Convention the value of toleration. Frenchmen could be united only by affirm-ing a common creed. Gradually he felt his way towards drafting the fifteen articles of a national religion which he recommended on 7 May. After he had been elected president of the Convention on 4 June, he was free to put the faith into practice. For 8 June, which would be Whit Sunday for old believers, he commissioned David to devise a festival of dedication to the Supreme Being. Under a brightly shining sun, between banks of roses, girls in white carried baskets of fruit, while a vast choir (some 2,400 strong) sang a commissioned hymn to the Supreme Being and then one verse of a better-known new song, the Marseillaise. Robespierre, resplendent in blue, white and red, advanced to speak up for Justice, Liberty and Virtue before setting light to Atheism, easily combustible for the occasion. Later in the day a huge chariot, drawn, as in David's operatic design, by oxen, and containing a plough and a printing press – tools of socially acceptable work – moved solemnly towards the Champ de Mars, where David had constructed a high plaster mountain, topped by Hercules clasping a Lilliputian Liberty in his hand and standing by a large Tree of Liberty. The deputies went up to the sound of music, but Robespierre descended in a silence, a new Elijah, a new Moses. It was, he felt, a day like the day of creation itself. Before two months were out, he would go to meet the Supreme Being in person. Robespierre fell, and David with him, because Robespierre's rivals were ter-rified of the Terror.

No more than in the case of Robespierre is it possible to disassociate David's work (in his case largely connected with the arts) from the policy of repression that began in July 1793, the month in which Danton left the Committee of Public Safety and Robespierre joined it. During the period that ran from midsummer 1793 to mid-summer 1794 this Committee, the number of whose members varied between nine and twelve, became virtually the executive branch of the government of France. Its rival, whose functions were confined largely to police work, was the Committee of General Security; and of this body David was a permanent member. As David was in addition one-time president of the Convention and one-time president of the Jacobin Club, he was heavily implicated in the hysterical politics of the time. He authorized the arrest of hundreds of political suspects. He was determined to show no mercy to the enemies of the republic. He signed the death warrants of the King, the Queen and Alexandre de Beauharnais (whose widow Joséphine would marry Napoleon), he refused the request of the painter Carle Vernet to intervene for his sister, Madame Chalgrin, he had the painter Hubert Robert and the architect Quatremère de Quincy (a friend who went back to student days in Rome) put in prison, he witnessed the deaths of Danton (who had been kind to him and whose massive, coarse head he had sketched) and Camille Desmoulins (whom he had painted with his family), he made no comment as the tumbrils took away former friends – Madame Trudaine, her husband and her brother-in-law and the poet André Chénier (whom he had met at the Trudaines' hôtel) – and sympathetic former clients – like Lavoisier – and many heroes of the tennis court oath. He had made his own the severe morality of the Horatii and Brutus. For enemies of the republic he had no mercy. He treated them with the same coldness as he showed towards Marie-Antoinette. He sketched the woman he most hated on her way to death, toothless, poorly dressed in a loose morning gown, with her hair, cut short for the axe, just protruding under a simple bonnet. All glamour is gone: only her human dignity remains. A revolution in values had been accomplished.

While he virulently pursued all anti-Jacobins, he found it comparatively easy to achieve his policy for the administration of the arts. The Academies of Painting and Sculpture and of Architecture closed their doors in 1793; the Rome prizes were not awarded; and the detested Suvée was unable to take charge of the French Academy in Rome, because Roman fear of revolutionary attitudes among French students had effectively closed the school down. In 1793 there was a Salon exhibition, but one patronized by David's Commune des Arts. It was from the moment when the Academies closed that, according to his biographer Etienne Delécluze, 'David had the dictatorship of the arts in France.'

Delécluze's comment is an exaggeration. It was not David who had ruined the luxury trades in silver, porcelain and silk-weaving (one reason why Lyonnais had no great love of the republic), it was not David who insisted that the kind of furniture he put in the *Brutus* should become the style *à la mode* (it did), it was not David who was in charge of the Louvre (he was merely contemptuous of the commission that was and worked to have its members replaced). Above all he was neither an architect nor a sculptor. It would be foolish to see his relationship to Robespierre as something like that of Albert Speer to Adolf Hitler. Intoxicated by the wine of political upheaval, he was yet no more a Fascist than Robespierre was a Führer.

As painted by Mme. Vigée-Lebrun c. 1783, 'Queen Marie-Antoinette' (National Gallery, Washington) wears the figure-hugging *chemise à la reine.*

Besides, whereas the Third Reich left nothing worthwhile on canvas or in stone, David in his republican fury created one supremely moving painting: *The Death of Marat*. The painter may have been deluded about the nature of his subject, but the delusion is given a timeless beauty. David was not at ease with everyday life, he was more comfortable with ideals than with fashions.

Nothing became the *ancien régime* like its rules on dress. When he became King in fact as well as in name, Louis XIV had deliberately forced his courtiers to spend a fortune on clothes, as if the principle of *noblesse oblige* obliged the nobility to look as well as to be aristocratic; and even though Louis XVI and his wife affected a simpler style of life, the simplicity, at least so far as the Queen was concerned, was contrived. The muslin *chemise à la reine*, which became the rage among the Petit Trianon set in the 1780s, was expensive – it was imported from British India – and the large pat-terned silks demanded by court or formal dress helped to keep 15,000 looms at work in Lyon. High fashion was big business. At Versailles it was meant only for those whom birth placed high. When in 1789 the Estates General was to meet there, the Marquis de Brèze, Grand-Master of Ceremonies, sent out instructions which made clear that, whereas the First and Second Estates, the clergy and nobility, would be adorned in the splendour of their status, the Third Estate must wear only black. The Comte de Mirabeau, who had been elected as a member of the Third Estate,

Boilly's portrait of Robespierre c. 1791 appears to be a provincial lawyer of the *ancien régime*. It is now in the provinces, in the Musée des Beaux-Arts, Lille.

protested against this discrimination; and after October everyone dressed as he chose. One obscure lawyer from Arras, a certain Maximilien de Robespierre, continued to dress with old-fashioned elegance and chose not to drop his '*de*' till all Frenchmen became equally citizens. In the portrait of him by the Lille artist Boilly, he wears a coat of shot silk, breeches with diamond buckles, buckles on his shoes and a powdered wig on his head. He stood out from politicians like the raffish Mirabeau, whose reactions were more in tune with those of ordinary people, but then Virtue, to which Robespierre's life was dedicated, never tries to seek popularity and never alters.

Speedily, conventions of the *ancien régime* became remote. Till recently there had been minute differences in the *robes* appropriate for women's court dress, varying with the formality of the occasion, yet always insisting on the tyranny of tiny waists. Then rich women could rely on fashion to bring excitement into their lives. Now, after a revolution, fashions could be exciting also for men.

During that summer of 1789 Lafayette designed the emblem of political correctness, the tricolour. White was the Bourbon colour, red and blue the colours of Paris, and all three colours, King and capital, made up France. When it was rumoured that royalist regiments had stamped on the tricolour, a Paris crowd went to Versailles

David's elderly 'Sieyès' (1817, now in the Fogg Art Museum, Harvard) still wears the Titus hair-cut that had been revolutionary in the 1790s.

to escort the royal family to the Tuileries, so that white was at one with blue and red. Thereafter on suitable occasions Louis would tactfully don the tricolour, in the form of the national cockade, on his hat. Soon political leanings were reflected in other details of dress. In 1790, according to the *Journal de la Mode et du Goût,* while unre-pentant aristocrats wore full mourning for the monarchy's decline, patriotic former nobles mixed red with black as symbols of their 'half-converted' beliefs. Boots were radical, buckled shoes, except in the case of Robespierre, were reactionary.

As royalists took flight or were taken to prison, Louis XVI was compelled to demonstrate his loyalty by covering his wig with the red Phrygian cap of Liberty. His cousin, formerly Duc d'Orléans, now Philippe-Egalité, took to a short jacket, long trousers and a sailor's scarf. Both men were levelled by the guillotine, in 1793 and 1794, for during the Terror any hint of social privilege was dangerous. Men who supported the revolution no longer even powdered their hair, let alone wore wigs. They followed the short cropped style* that the actor Talma had adopted for the part of Titus in Voltaire's *Brutus.* At all moments they wished to be seen to be true believ-

*Those who adopted the hair style used by Titus, one of the sons of Brutus in productions of Voltaire's play were said to wear their hair *à la Titus*

ers. While awaiting trial and death for following Danton, the journalist Camille Desmoulins was painted by his fellow prisoner Hubert Robert in light breeches, a slender greatcoat, a striped waistcoat and an 'Armenian' hat, an accessory once worn by Rousseau. Coarser-fibred souls threatened to take control. In street politics cleanliness smelt counter-revolutionary. For a while real power lay in the fists of Parisian *sans-culottes*, workmen who spurned knee-breeches and gloried in their baggy woollen trousers, their short jackets, their wooden shoes and their pipes.

As *chic* became more political, women were not to be left behind. In 1790 the *Journal de la Mode et du Goût* had a fashion plate for women *vêtue à la constitution* and in 1792 one for those who wished to adopt a 'Catholic costume' to show their loyalty to priests who would not take the oath to the Church which the constitution had prescribed. But such even-handedness looked trivial. In 1793 the *Journal de la Mode et du Goût* ceased to appear. Its fashion plates of expensive materials were irrelevant, when the manufacture of luxury textiles, of silk, lace and embroidery, had declined. Besides, fashion was an affront to *sans-culotte* womenfolk. They were distinguished by woollen skirts, jackets, aprons, thick stockings and the ever-present wooden shoes, standard and unchanging features of peasant costume in the eighteenth century. If many of them had lost jobs in the fashion industry, that was because the notion of fashion was itself outmoded.

Political influence gave *sans-culottes* confidence to demand that their standard of living should be protected; and for a time it was. They needed wool, linen and wooden shoes; and these were included in the list of essential goods to which in 1793 the National Convention assigned a maximum price. Unluckily the proto-socialist plan did not work. In 1794 controls were relaxed and the *sans-culottes* felt let down. They showed less enthusiasm for the cause of their middle-class allies; and there was no mob adequate to save the Jacobins. In 1794 pre-revolutionary *muscadins* had returned. In defiance of working-class taste young fops sported tight breeches, short waistcoats and bizarre frock coats. The drive for equality had ended: in future liberty would lead fashion.

Not all revolutionaries had stooped to cultural levelling. David consistently sought to ennoble rather than to degrade the cause. As early as 1792 he had designed a republican costume for men, based partly on a Spanish style: a white coat with slashed sleeves under a red cape draped over one shoulder. In addition the republican emphasized his bellicose bravado with pistols at his belt and a sabre at his side and a round hat with ample feathers on top; and his blue trousers added a democratic element. Two years later David had opted for a kind of theatrical costume more in keeping with his artistic credo. He envisaged a citizen in tunic and 'classical' tights – a compromise between the bare legs of the ancient world and the close-fitting breeches of the modern – and a deputy with the addition of a cloak fastened on the shoulder in the antique manner. These styles were approved by the Committee of

Boilly's 'Chenard as sans-culotte' (1792, Musée Carnavalet, Paris) shows a famous actor playing the role of a man of the working class.

Public Safety; and David was instructed to have his designs engraved, so that thousands of copies could be distributed nationwide. But despite Talma's faithful adherence to the master's ideas – they were so eccentric that the actor was taken for a spy for putting them into practice – David's ideas never caught on. Talma himself had had much more success with his *Titus* haircut. In this one case nature followed art. Otherwise it was only on the stage, where there was a tradition dating back to the theatre of Corneille, Molière and Racine, that French men managed to look convincing as updated Romans or Greeks. French women were more at ease: for almost a decade they could adapt *haute couture* to a Davidian aesthetic. They were Neo-Classical with exquisite grace.

One of David's costumes was military. In 1789 the French armed forces had been royal. Early in 1792, when Louis XVI declared war on his brother-in-law, the Holy Roman Emperor, there was a fanatically royalist army, made up of *émigrés*, and a lukewarm army of the King of the French. The French army that was to win the great victories of the French people would be republican.

David's republican costumes (1794, Musée Carnavalet, Paris) are pen-and-ink
studies for respectively a people's deputy and a citizen.

In the years shortly before 1789 France had been in the process of acquiring a
formidable army and navy. As long ago as 1758 the Duc de Choiseul, favourite of
Madame de Pompadour, had become the key minister in the government. While
France's forces were being humiliated on land and sea, in Europe and in America,
by the English, Choiseul set about the work of reconstruction so that his country
would be capable of a war of revenge. He and Choiseul-Praslin, his cousin, controlled between them the ministries of foreign affairs, war and the navy. As he did
not trouble himself overmuch about finance, Choiseul was able to build up a
formidable fighting force once the war was over. By 1771, instead of an ill-equipped
fleet of some forty ships of the line, France had sixty-four ships of the line and fifty
frigates. The reforms of the army were even more sweeping. Choiseul bought many
noble officers out of the service, increased the control of the Ministry of War over
recruitment and equipment and took over arms and munitions factories. Certain of
his actions would affect the career of Napoleon. He founded the first of a series of
schools for young nobles aiming for the Ecole Militaire (itself a Pompadour project);
Gribeauval, his protégé, organized the artillery into a Corps Royal of six regiments

and introduced the new mobile rapid-firing cannon that he had invented; and in 1768 Choiseul bought from Genoa the rebellious island of Corsica. In 1771, once Louis XV understood how much all this had cost, Choiseul fell from power. His reforms proved their worth six years later. Louis XVI decided to fight Choiseul's war of revenge in support of the American rebels. When in 1781 Cornwallis surrendered at Yorktown to Washington, a French fleet under de Grasse blocked his retreat by sea and half the forces blocking his retreat by land were French. They were led by the Comte de Rochambeau, but the Frenchman who took the glory was the young Marquis de Lafayette.

Lafayette so idolized Washington that he named his first son after him. In 1789 he sent Washington one of the keys of the Bastille. He reckoned that, like his American hero, he must be the people's friend. His National Guard was a semi-military police force open (in theory) to the people, provided that the people could buy the uniform. His new institution indicated the way that the armed forces would go. In 1789 over two-thirds of the army officers were still nobles. The Assembly accordingly opened promotion to commoners. One Assembly decree of 1790 laid down that 25 per cent of all sub-lieutenants were to rise from the ranks and 75 per cent were to be chosen by competition; and another decree, of 1791, drastically reduced the numbers of staff officers.

The navy, so effective against the British in the American war, had different problems: it was more concerned with fighting the supporters of the merchant navy, who wished to join it, rather than doing down the one thousand or so noble officers on whom it relied. It won its skirmish with the civilians but lost the campaign for noble hearts. By 1793 three-quarters of the officers had deserted or emigrated; and the gunners, aristocrats among seamen, had left in large numbers to join the army. The results were predictable. From the Battle of Ouessant, which the British called 'the glorious first of June', to the Battle of Trafalgar, the French navy lost every major engagement it fought. By 1806 France was no longer in charge of her coastal approaches; she could no longer protect overseas colonies; and ocean-going trade was dead.

As the army became fashionable, so the army set fashion. At first the revolution was a citizens' cause, a revolt against the standing armies of despotic kings, but Lafayette's Parisian militia became the pattern for a new kind of army, one that always existed for the nation. To Bourbon white Lafayette's National Guard added the blue and red of Paris; and from 1791 this tricolour uniform – blue for the jacket, white from the waistcoat to the breeches, red for all piping – was standard throughout France.

In 1792 there was a drastic change in the army's fortune and status. In April Louis XVI had to declare war on his nephew, the King of Hungary and Bohemia (soon to be the Emperor Francis II); French troops were driven back from the frontier; and in June, days after Prussia joined Austria by declaring war, the King vetoed a move to bring 20,000 guardsmen from the countryside to the capital. These events were linked psychologically. If the *patrie* was in danger, the King was to blame. It was not enough that, after one invasion of the Tuileries, he donned the Phrygian cap of liberty, so a second invasion brought to an end the monarchy. Louis was a deposed tyrant: the spirit of liberty could be served only by a republic. The fleur-de-lis was removed from patriotic uniforms and by 1794 the tricolour was the national flag.

The effect on the army's appearance was quickly felt. In 1792 *sans-culottes* in trousers rushed to volunteer; and men in ripped clothes, bare feet and clogs joined up. The people's army, without a sense of style, was equal only in its blue, white and red. Arrayed in this revolutionary motley, it drove away well-turned-out Prussians from Valmy and well-turned-out Austrians from Jemappes. Dirty faces and long unpowdered hair were natural and could be the right of all peoples; and with crazy logic the Edict of Fraternity led to the overrunning of Belgium and Savoy and the defiance of Britain, the Netherlands, Russia and Spain. The era of scruffy enthusiasm perished in the defeats of 1794. As line regiments had lost huge numbers, volunteers and, from August 1793, conscripts were incorporated into the regular army as reservists, later as full members. To back them up the Convention established in 1794 a training school for republican teenagers, the Ecole de Mars. *Sans-culotte* boys, grouped into their tens, hundreds and thousands under decurions, centurions and millerions, while waiting for David to design their clothes, were rigged out in smocks, trousers and spats, while under their caps their hair was cut *à la Titus*. Their seniors often dressed with more panache. The Hussars of Death and of Liberty, with their tightly bound hair and cut-away jackets and golden stripes, or the Dragoons, with short tufts and long mops of hair trained to protrude through gilt helmets like plumes, were flamboyant representatives of the new freedom, but their glamour was the mark of a class apart, they were first among equals. War brought into being a republic and led to the execution of the King and the reign of Terror. War also meant that the eventual hero of the revolution must be a soldier.

The immediate prize of success in war was loot. Early in 1793 French soldiers occupied the whole of Belgium, then the Austrian Netherlands, but Dumouriez's defection at the front and the in-fighting between Girondins and Jacobins at home deprived the troops of their sense of purpose and forced them to withdraw. A drawn battle at Hondschoote saved Dunkirk from the British and victory at Wattignies cleared the north-east border of the Austrians, but not till the Battle of Fleurus in midsummer 1794 was the way open to the reconquest of Belgium. The Commission Temporaire des Arts set about organizing discriminating plunder; the artist Wicar was authorized to seek out the best paintings; and soon an archaeologist, botanist, antiquary and architect joined him. In the end Wicar, as friend of David and thus indirectly a protégé of Robespierre, did not go. Already, even before

Luc Barbier is said to have been the model for the god in Gérard's 'Cupid and Psyche' (1798, Musée du Louvre, Paris).

his fellow nominees could act and before the political crisis in Paris had come to its bloody head, Rubens's most celebrated works were *en route* from Antwerp to the Louvre: his *Descent from the Cross*, his *Elevation of the Cross* and his *Coup de Lance*. These altarpieces were but the hors d'oeuvre to the Rubens meal that would satiate the palates of Parisian connoisseurs in the following years. They became available through the efforts of a former pupil of David's, the hussar Luc Barbier, and one Léger, who was attached to the adjutant-general's office. For Barbier the act of pillage became a glorious activity. That autumn he told the Convention: 'it is in the bosom of free folk that the works of celebrated men should remain.' His handsome face, his youthful energy, above all his uniform, gave him the opportunity of a life-time.* He took it, and, by acting as he did, he prepared the way for the systematic seizure of other peoples' treasures by force of French arms.

*Barbier was said to be the model for Cupid in Gérard's picture of Cupid and Psyche.

When Barbier started his work, it was not yet clear that the soldiers would have the ultimate say in either politics or the arts. Robespierre was the most unmilitary of politicians, a man who had dared to oppose the policy of aggression and who, dressing as though he was still a lawyer of the *ancien régime*, was impervious to changes of fashion. For all his reputation for cruelty he always wanted any execution to be the last. In him David found the unique expression of republican probity, a Spartan straight out of Plutarch, without the crude vigour of Danton or the savage ambition of Marat. If in Marat he found the prototype of a revolutionary martyr, in Robespierre he found the lawgiver and high priest of revolution. It was virtue which gave Robespierre authority: his only power came from the power of his speeches to persuade. Throughout the early months of 1794 David was gripped by the austere insistence of that voice. Robespierre's enemies were his. When Robespierre stepped down from the tribune after defending himself for what was to be the last time, David cried out, 'If you drink the hemlock, I will drink it with you.' He had made himself a companion of his own *Socrates*. He was terrified when some of the spectators took him at his word.

On the Ninth of Thermidor Robespierre's enemies had him killed before he could kill them. It was then the turn of his accomplices; and so some Thermidoreans turned on David. Had they known the records of the Committee of General Security, he would not have survived. Investigations are decided by words not actions; and as he sought to defend himself, David became increasingly inarticulate. One result of an old duel wound in his right cheek was a stammer, which became more marked whenever he was embarrassed. It was his incoherence which saved him. He was not the only one deceived by Robespierre, he pleaded. 'I will not attach myself any more to men, but only to principles.'

At the supreme moment of his life David had shown he was no hero, just an artist who depicted heroic gestures. He was allowed to live, after he had survived two periods in prison. The man who despised female gentleness was grateful to be reconciled to the wife he had divorced. In the mirror he scrutinized his features and found nothing to be ashamed of. The painter who had painted only human action painted from his window in the Luxembourg palace a view of the gardens, his solitary landscape. He set about finding a subject that would express his wish to make peace.

Meanwhile the Thermidoreans and the Directors whom they set up to take over from them continued to fight most of the rest of Europe. It was this almost constant warfare which opened careers to talented soldiers and so to young Napoleon; and the supreme art became the military art, the art of conquest.

CHAPTER 3

The Art of Becoming a Hero

DAVID was not the only sympathizer for whom the death of Maximilien Robespierre was almost a catastrophe. One of the men whom he admired as a revolutionary hero was the victor of Toulon, Napoleone Buonaparte, who had owed his position to Augustin Robespierre, younger brother of Maximilien. At the time of the Thermidorean coup, while the Republic was fighting Italians, young Buonaparte was on a spying mission – itself a suspicious occupation – in Genoa. He was recalled and imprisoned. There was this difference between him and David. David was interested in anyone as a subject for his art – politician, soldier, *sans-culotte*, peasant – who glorified the revolutionary cause; to Buonaparte glory for himself meant everything, the arts nothing.

Buonaparte also endured prison much better than David, for he was brave, ambitious and fatalistic. Either he would be executed or he was merely being forced to put up with a small interruption to his own astonishing career in the service. It was astonishing to have been promoted from captain to brigadier-general in four months. His promotion was only possible because the revolution had opened the way for youth. In that sense, if in no other, he was a child of the revolution.

His beginnings just twenty-four years earlier had scarcely hinted at such a rapid rise in the French army. He had been born on 15 August 1769 in Ajaccio, capital of Corsica, son of Carlo Buonaparte and Maria-Letizia Ramolino. Both his parents came from families that on the island counted as minor nobility. His father's family could be traced back to Tuscany in the twelfth century and his mother's family back to Lombardy in the fourteenth century. Carlo and Letizia had a town house, a country farm and, according to Napoleon's great-uncle, the Archdeacon of Ajaccio, boasted that they had never bought oil, wine or bread. In a poor country this was true wealth. Later in life Napoleon was never allowed to forget his Corsican origins. These were evident not only in his swarthy Mediterranean features, but in the way he spoke – his first language was the Corsican dialect and, even though he become an effective user of French, he never mastered a French accent – and above all in the way he felt. He was brought up to accept the idea of the vendetta – occasionally he would pursue foreign policy as a means of revenge – and he believed in the family. When he rose to become Emperor of the French, he installed three brothers as kings, one as a grand duke, one sister as a queen, one as a grand duchess and one as a princess. The Buonaparte siblings co-operated like members of Cosa Nostra, their own Mafia; and over all of them ruled their mother, Madame Mère. Her husband had died while the children were young. She lived on, dauntless and domineering, for fifteen years after the death of her most famous child.

Corsica affected the circumstances of Napoleone's birth. In 1768, when the Duc de Choiseul had bought the island, it was in revolt against Genoa. During the last months when his mother was carrying Napoleone, she was hiding in the mountains as a refugee. The leader of the revolt, Pasquale Paoli, had been in service with the King of Naples, had returned home to lead a successful revolt against the Genoese and then was only crushed by the French a few months before Napoleone's birth. Carlo Buonaparte had been one of Paoli's trusted aides and may have thought of exile. But whereas Paoli was a lifelong bachelor who could afford to devote himself to noble causes, Carlo had his legal practice and a young wife with one child already (Giuseppe) and another on the way. He decided to make his peace with the French and to move out of the hills and back to Ajaccio. Had Carlo followed Paoli into exile, Napoleone might have been born in England, whither Paoli fled. As it was he was born a French citizen and subject of Louis XV.

He began life as a provincial in the most recent of France's acquisitions. At the age of five he went to a local mixed school run by nuns before moving on to a day boys' school, where he learnt to read and write in Italian and to calculate. Even at this stage mathematics was his favourite branch of learning; and he did sums at home, for the joy of it. Apart from the ancestry of his parents, there was little to distinguish him from any other bourgeois boy in Ajaccio, who was son of a lawyer, grandson (through his mother) of a soldier and great-nephew of an archdeacon. He was not brought up to think of himself as he might have been on the mainland, as a nobleman with social and fiscal privileges. In Ajaccio he mixed with his wet-nurse and her sons and in the countryside with farmers. He never acquired the gracious manners of a well-educated aristocrat, but he learnt one lesson many aristocrats were denied: he could talk to other people as though they were his social equals. He expected to be poor. What counted was personality – his own was combative, touchy and adventurous.

The French were resolved to bring the Corsicans into line. They determined to introduce the three orders of society – clergy, nobility and commoner – and this gave Carlo Buonaparte the chance to prove his noble lineage. He had fought persistently to recover property due to him, whether the unpaid dowry from his wife's family or an estate left by a relative to the now defunct Society of Jesus; and naturally he applied to become *noble*. His title was recognized in 1770, he took to a powdered wig, to colourful waistcoats and to elegant knee-breeches and he filled his house with books. When it was time for Corsica to send its best wishes to the new King, Louis XVI, Carlo was one of three nobles chosen to represent the island. This visit to the court may have filled him with notions of the fine life of France, but the steady growth of his family – Lucciano, then Maria Anna (known as Elisa), Luigi, Paoletta, Carolina and finally Girolamo – made the charms of a rich man's ways seem ever more remote. Once again it was the nice social distinctions of the *ancien régime* which came to his rescue. The French *intendant* of Corsica, a bonhomous Breton called the Comte de Marbeuf, told Carlo Buonaparte that noblemen's children could be educated for nothing, provided that their parents were sufficiently poor. Boys intended for the Church could go to the seminary at Aix, girls could go to the convent school at St Cyr and boys intending to try for a military career could go to a military academy. Giuseppe, placid and easy-going, would be a priest; eventually Maria Anna would be right for St Cyr; as for Napoleone, he was so self-willed that the only education for him would be officer training. Applications were made for the two older boys, supported by Marbeuf, proving how necessitous their father was. In 1778 the French government announced its decisions. Giuseppe would go to Aix at sixteen, but must first study somewhere else in France. Realizing that such schooling was beyond Buonaparte means, Marbeuf obliged again by offering to pay for Giuseppe's preliminary studies at Autun, in Burgundy, where his nephew was bishop. Napoleone in his turn was accepted for the military academy at Brienne, provided that his quarterings were aristocratic enough for the herald at Versailles. Till the great man had spoken, he too would stay at Autun with his brother. On Christmas Day Giuseppe and Napoleone arrived at the port of Marseille. Napoleon had come to France as to a foreign country, unable to speak the language. He had left behind a small, inward-looking, mountainous island for a great land, where wealthy farmland stretched away before him, rightwards to the Alps and Italy, leftwards to the Pyrenees and Spain and northwards to the Massif Central, Burgundy, Champagne, Paris and Versailles.

Napoleone spent the first three months of 1779 in the cathedral city of Autun. In the spring he moved a little closer to the capital, when he joined the academy of Brienne. Brienne was one of twelve royal schools founded by Louis XVI's minister of war, St Germain, in 1776. Before that date Brienne had been just an ordinary boarding-school, run by Franciscan friars; and despite its change of function the friars were still in charge. Napoleone soon adapted to the little austerities of institutional life. He slept in a dormitory made up of ten cubicles, where he was locked in from ten o'clock till six in the morning. Every day he went to Mass, worked for some eight hours, enjoyed two hours of recreation, had three meals and said his prayers before returning to his cubicle. The school was small – there were only about fifty boys when he arrived – but the teaching was thorough. The basic diet of learning was Latin and mathematics, still Napoleone's best subject. He read physics, history and geography, built fortifications and drew relief maps. He was a conscientious pupil, the kind of boy whom teachers approve of. Good relations with fellow pupils he found less easy to establish. He had a strange Christian name, a surname of which nobody had ever heard and he spoke with a strong Corsican accent. A boy with a less strong personality might have become more French than his fellows, but Napoleone would not bend to be popular. He became popular the hard way, by being himself. The incidents of his childhood that stand out – a refusal on one occasion to eat his food on his knees when punished and on another his curt order to stop an uninvited guest from coming to a school function – suggest an imperious nature. But he could also be sentimental about his homeland and he loved Tasso's romantic epic of the First Crusade, *Jerusalem Delivered*. He could respond to the piety of Père Charles, who prepared him for Communion, and be on good terms with the porter – later in life he made a point of visiting the priest and he found the porter a job at Malmaison. He made one or two close friends among fellow pupils. He came to enjoy life at Brienne.

There is a story that in a school game in Corsica he had cried till he was allowed to be a Roman rather than a Carthaginian. He did not like to be on the losing side. In history class at Brienne he learnt only about the victories of France – in the past there had been no Crécy, no Poitiers, no Agincourt. He believed so strongly in heroes, whom he read about in Plutarch's *Lives* and in Corneille, that when a preacher asserted that Caesar and Cato were in hell, Napoleone would not believe him. Like his father he became agnostic. When, however, his mother came to see him in 1782, he was too overjoyed to discuss with her his lack of faith.

Before he passed out of Brienne, there was talk of him becoming a sailor; and it is just possible that, as now France was at peace with the old enemy, he may have thought of training at the English naval college in Portsmouth. In the end he went to the Ecole Militaire in Paris. It was an important moment in family life. His father came over to France with Lucciano, who would follow Napoleone at Brienne, and with Maria Anna, *en route* for St Cyr. He also wished to sort out problems with Giuseppe who, despite many academic prizes at Autun, had just announced that he too wanted to be a soldier. Napoleone wrote a letter home to his uncle Nicolò Paravicini, arguing both sides of the case with inexorable logic. His conclusion is hard, but perceptive. Giuseppe would like to be in the army, just so as to strut around looking a smart infantry officer in a garrison town. Better call him home to Corsica and turn him into a lawyer. The sudden death of Carlo Buonaparte from stomach cancer in 1785 meant that Giuseppe had to go home, for he was head of the family.

By then Napoleone was installed in Paris. The Ecole Militaire, a fine building recently built to the design of Gabriel, the Neo-Classical architect of Le Petit Trianon and the two hôtels in the place Louis-le-Grand (now place de la Concorde), stands on the left bank of the Seine, in front of the large expanse of the Champ de Mars. After the rustic simplicity of Brienne, the style of life there appeared very grand. The beautiful décor, the delicious meals and the elaborate uni-forms were overwhelming. He kept to his principles. When one of his best friends, Laugier de Bellecoeur, who had come with him from Brienne, gained a reputation for effeminacy, Napoleone sent off a memorandum to the Ministry of War on the values of Spartan education. It was the year when David showed *The Oath of the Horatii* at the Salon. He wrote to his mother to comfort her for the death of his father, counselling her to calm her sorrow – he fell back on the ethics of stoicism, just like a Davidian hero.

Because the Ecole Militaire was near the open space of the Champ de Mars, Napoleone was once able to watch Blanchard prepare to ascend in a balloon. Whether out of impatience or malice, he cut the ropes before Blanchard had left, so that the balloon flew away without its pilot. Otherwise, Napoleone was a model pupil. He was proficient at mathematics and geography, a fencer with a reputation for breaking foils, an awkward dancer, a weak draughtsman, a poor German scholar. He was following the artillery class, which usually took two years and some-times a lot longer. Napoleone had finished in a year and was commissioned for 1 September 1785. He was the fourth-youngest officer to graduate.

At sixteen his formal education was over. He was an unusual kind of army officer. He had already developed a liking for authors of the French Enlightenment. At the Ecole Militaire he had studied Montesquieu, who reinforced his admiration for the Roman Republic. Soon he was deep into Rousseau, the protagonist of liberty. He defended Rousseau's belief in a civic religion, in contrast to the internationalism of the Catholic Church, in a pamphlet he wrote on 9 May 1786 at 4 p.m. When he argued this case, to clarify his opinions, he was stationed in the La Fère regiment at Valence, as near as possible to Corsica and his beloved family, for whom he was at this moment the only breadwinner. He dreamt of Corsica and of freedom. He sent to Geneva for Germanes' *History of the revolutions in Corsica* and for any other available books on Corsica. He made notes for himself in favour of the right of Corsicans to fight against Genoese or French oppressors. Like many able young men, he was planning his first book: it would vindicate the virtue of patriotism and celebrate the heroic stand of General Paoli, who had fled from the island around the time of his birth.

For Napoleone the years between 1786 and 1789 were dull. France was at peace, there were occasional riots to crush (one in Lyon in 1786) and two periods of leave at home (in 1787 and 1788). His main recreation was his voracious reading. In French translation he read classical history: Tacitus's terse accounts of weak absolute monarchs, Livy's stories of fine republicans and Plutarch's *Parallel Lives of noble Greeks and Romans*. Besides his favourite Montesquieu he read Raynal, author of *The History of the Two Indies*, and Montaigne, all three of them analysts of human society, historical relativists. He also discovered a lifelong love of one of the bogus successes of the century: Macpherson's *Lays of Ossian*. He could switch from the technical details of French high finance to the exotic world of Islam (without the religion). He turned to political theory. Plato's *Republic* was ideal insofar as its ruler acted for the good of his subjects. England he studied for its constitutional history up to the Glorious Revolution – he showed a special sympathy for the attempt of Simon de Montfort to curb the abuse of royal power. Among recent statesmen he admired Frederick the Great of Prussia, the most militaristic of the enlightened despots who ruled over the major continental countries other than France. France lacked both the English liberties and the compensations of despotic efficiency. He commented: 'We are members of a powerful monarchy, but today we feel only the vices of its constitu' tion.' He followed the political crisis that was developing as a result of government mismanagement. 'There are few monarchs who do not deserve to lose the thrones they occupy.' In May 1789 the Controller General, Necker, made a statement on the state of royal finances and Napoleone made notes on Necker's figures.

These notes were made at Auxonne in Burgundy, where Napoleone was sta' tioned from September 1788 to September 1789. While others may have been pre' occupied with events in Paris, his thoughts returned to Corsica. He wrote to Paoli in June 1789, 'I was born when my country was dying. Thirty thousand Frenchmen disgorged upon our shores, drowning the throne of Liberty in a sea of blood.'

He was determined to fight for the freedom of his island home, with his pen rather than with his sword. Whenever he could, he spent time in Corsica; and it was only after the defeat of his support for a liberal régime led by Paoli and because of the pressure of his ambitions that he was drawn away to Paris. He became Napoléon, brother to Joseph, Lucien, Louis and Jérôme, and France became his *patrie*.

Between September 1789 and April 1792 most of his energies were devoted to Corsica. It was he who drafted a public letter for his compatriots warning the National Assembly in Paris that reactionary forces still controlled the island – and his views were justified when early in 1790 Corsica became part of metropolitan France. In Bastia, then the capital, he distributed national cockades, he joined the National Guard, he worked at his *Corsican Letters*. It was not till February 1791 that he rejoined his regiment at Auxonne. He protested when he was ordered to go to Valence, possibly because he was thinking of the education of his favourite younger brother, Louis, whom he had with him; for in Auxonne he had made time to teach Louis history and mathematics and to report to Joseph how gracefully Louis behaved at social gatherings and how easily he charmed all the women in town (Louis was just twelve). In Valence his mind reverted to politics. Within a week of his arrival, he heard how the King had fled to Varennes – the news made him into a convinced republican. Soldiers were asked to take a new oath of loyalty to the constitution and the National Assembly. Buonaparte was eager to swear. On the Fourteenth of July it was he who proposed a toast at dinner in Valence to the Patriots of Auxonne, among whom were all the men in the regiment, the sergeants and half the officers.

Once more he tried his hand at writing. His hero among living writers, the Abbé Raynal, offered a prize at the Academy of Lyon. He wrote a rambling essay on education for happiness. He was himself only when he commended the systems of Lycurgus in Sparta and of Paoli in Corsica. In October 1791 he went home yet again, where he soon learnt that Corsica was no Sparta.

The next eight months put paid to his dreams of being simultaneously the perfect patriot and the perfect Corsican. A new order recalled all officers below the rank of lieutenant-colonel back to their regiments by 1 April, 1792. To escape its provisions Buonaparte decided to apply for the post of second-in-command of the National Guard; and his family made sure he was elected. He soon discovered he had made an ill-judged move. Being as anticlerical as a good Jacobin should be, he was all for dissolving useless religious houses and enforcing the civil constitution of the Church. On Easter Sunday, 8 April, in the cathedral square of Ajaccio, a National Guard lieutenant was shot dead by someone in a crowd of devout Catholics. Buonaparte wanted to use his troops to crush the demonstrators. Unfortunately the Citadel was still held in the name of King Louis by a Colonel Maillard. Maillard was as stubborn as Buonaparte. He would not let the guardsmen take refuge in his Citadel, he would not give them any ammunition, he would not disobey the municipal instruction that the guardsmen should withdraw from the city. In the end it was Maillard who won the day. Buonaparte was advised by his brother Joseph that he would have to vindicate himself at the Ministry of War in Paris, for Maillard had complained of him to the minister.

He arrived in Paris at the end of May. He was there to protect his reputation, but the most egotistical of men could not but be stirred by events in the capital. He was a witness of the attack on the Tuileries on 20 June and wrote to Joseph two days later to describe it. He approved of the way the King reacted – he had donned the *bonnet rouge* – but he worried at the precedent set by the triumph of mob violence. He was to see a more terrible example. On 10 August the crowd burst into the palace and massacred the Swiss royal guard. 'If Louis XVI had showed himself on horseback,' he told Joseph, 'victory would have been his.' He could not bear disorder.

The tenth of August led directly to the abolition of the monarchy. It followed inevitably that the school of St Cyr, royal and aristocratic, would be closed. For her safety Buonaparte took his sister Maria Anna away from Paris. By October 1792 he was back in Corsica.

In February 1793 he had his last Corsican adventure. In January Louis XVI had been executed and the new republic was at war with the kingdom of Piedmont-Sardinia. What could be more logical than an amphibious attack on Sardinia mounted from Corsica, and who more obvious to use than Buonaparte? The expedition was urged on him by Saliceti, his political mentor since the failed coup of the previous year. Reluctantly Paoli consented to an attack on the island of Maddalena, just off the northern tip of Sardinia. There was some initial success. Buonaparte captured all but a tower on the nearby islet of San Stefano and trained his guns on Maddalena in readiness for the sailors to bring their ships in to land. For two days they did not come; and then their first casualties cooled all revolutionary ardour. Furious and impotent, Buonaparte was forced to retreat. He complained to the war office, he suggested two new plans of attack, he regretted he had not been in charge. A speech decided his fate. Convinced that Paoli, after his long stay in England, was sympathetic to the enemies of France, Lucien Buonaparte denounced him to the *société populaire* of Toulon. From Paris the Convention ordered Saliceti to arrest Paoli. At first Buonaparte tried to protect him, until he found out that Paoli no longer trusted him. Offshore, Buonaparte trained his guns on the Citadel of Ajaccio, but could not penetrate its ancient walls. With his family about him he was forced to flee and take refuge in Toulon with Lucien. Behind him lay Corsica, which he would see again only once and briefly. His destiny called him from across the sea. Though it would take time for him to drop the 'u' from his surname, he had become a Frenchman.

Up to this moment, apart from his ill-judged hero worship of Paoli, there had been little to distinguish young Buonaparte from other young officers. His military ventures had been failures. He had had to renounce his island home because he had no future there. In France he counted for little. It was no great privation to surrender the privileges of noble status which his father had struggled to obtain. He lacked the refined manners of a natural aristocrat and he spoke with a foreign accent. He was without the resources of a fine house and beautiful *objets d'art*, he had no compliant mistress to boast of, he had no memory of that *douceur de vivre** which Talleyrand,

*Talleyrand spoke of the *douceur de vivre*, the sweetnes of living, as an aristocrat who was aware he would never again have as agreeable a style of life as he had enjoyed in pre-revolutionary France, when as a wealthy, well connected bishop he had never allowed religious duties to distract him from his single-minded pursuit of pleasure.

the worldly Bishop of Autun who had replaced the nephew of Marbeuf, so wist-
fully ascribed to the *ancien régime*. For him the government of Louis XVI had meant
poverty and an unsatisfying job. With the abilities and the will to be a revolutionary
hero, so far he had had no chance to prove himself one. He had this advantage over
his fellows: here on the mainland he had no past. The future opened up before him
a career based on natural gifts. He decided to write.

Circumstances in southern France made him anxious. He had barely settled his
family outside Marseille when the Midi revolted against the Jacobins in Paris.
Catholics had not approved the Civil Constitution of the Clergy, royalists had been
scandalized by the execution of the King, but the immediate cause of revolt was the
outlawry of the Girondins and their federalist sympathizers. In the name of the one
indivisible republic there was to be no dissent. Midsummer brought the madness of
civil war; and one of Buonaparte's less pleasant duties was to shoot down National
Guardsmen in the streets of Avignon. He retired to the neighbouring village of
Beaucaire to recover from the ordeal. He wished to point out the folly of resistance.
He wrote a dialogue, *Le Souper de Beaucaire*. He imagined a discussion between
travellers at an inn. Two merchants from Marseille defend rebellion. Two citizens
from Montpellier and the Nîmois listen. Their companion, a soldier, argues passion-
ately in favour of peace within France at a time when foreigners and counter-revolutionaries threaten from without. Inevitably the soldier wins the argument. His
victory brought good fortune to his creator. The pamphlet was read by his fellow
Corsican Saliceti, who showed it to Augustin Robespierre, younger brother of
Maximilien. Here was a soldier who spoke for the cause. He must be given the
chance to act for the cause.

In the last week of August the key naval town of Toulon admitted an Anglo-
Spanish fleet to its harbour. The arguments of Buonaparte were proved right. To
besiege the port, Carteaux, who had been Buonaparte's commander in Avignon,
needed an experienced regular artillery officer, so Saliceti nominated his country-
man for the post. The siege showed that Buonaparte was not just right-thinking: he
was that much rarer revolutionary, a man whose actions spoke louder than his words.
Buonaparte used his influence with Saliceti and a representative of the people called
Paul Barras. From every possible direction he commandeered guns, horses and
oxen. Realizing from his knowledge of the terrain that Toulon harbour was cres-
cent-shaped like the harbour of Ajaccio, he grasped that he must grab one of the
horns. He fretted at the incompetence, the indecision and the idleness alike of inferiors and superiors. As Carteaux was replaced by Doppet and Doppet by
Dugommier, Buonaparte despaired of implementing his bold and simple plan. Not
till late November was it adopted, not till mid-December was it effected. He was
soon vindicated, for the evening after his gunners opened fire on the British fleet Lord
Hood sailed away. Within a week Buonaparte was promoted to brigadier-general. It

was both a startling and a dangerous achievement. At the end of 1793 a special republican feast day was laid on to commemorate the glorious recapture of Toulon. In April Augustin Robespierre wrote to his brother of Buonaparte's 'transcendent merit'. Buonaparte was a Jacobin hero, a partisan.

In truth he was political in his own way – he knew how to intrigue to get his own way. For the next two and a half years the principal campaign he waged – in a difficult situation – was to further his own career. He was attached to the Army of Italy, but could not persuade the authorities to have a plan of attack. He was ordered to go to Genoa to reconnoitre. Suddenly the coup d'état of Thermidor ended the lives of the Robespierre brothers and put their protégés at risk. Saliceti arrested Buonaparte and imprisoned him in the château of Antibes. Had the expedition to Genoa been treasonable? Calmly Buonaparte occupied himself in his cell by studying past invasions of Piedmont, while evidence was collected to show that his spying mission had been official. Saliceti released him. Buonaparte was needed, for, as he had predicted, the Austrians had come to help their Piedmontese allies. With Buonaparte's aid they were repulsed. Much to his disappointment the French were then ordered to retreat. The hero of 1793 ended 1794 in a mood of frustration.

The next year, 1795, started badly. He was ordered to prepare an amphibious expedition against Corsica – it was called off – and he was transferred to the Vendée, so he resigned. He moved to the map department of the Ministry of War, he thought of joining the Turkish army, he dreamt of Cyrus and Alexander. He had ideas about Italy, which he encouraged the French to attack. The attackers lost their nerve, but, more importantly, Buonaparte's patrons in Paris lost their posts on the Committee of Public Safety, still effectively the French government, and Buonaparte was sacked. His failure to go to the Vendée meant that he was no longer needed.

This was not true for long. When the Constitution of the Year III was published, Parisians learnt that two-thirds of the existing deputies of the notorious Convention would be members of the new Legislative Assembly. Crowds led by National Guardsmen prepared to march on the Tuileries, where the Convention was planning its own continuing life. The government turned to Paul Barras and Paul Barras turned to Buonaparte. He had witnessed the invasion of the Tuileries in 1792. There would be no such happening in 1795. Positioning his cannon as expertly as at Toulon, he ordered his men to shoot at point-blank range. For the first time since 1789 civilian mob violence had been defeated by disciplined military force. Buonaparte's whiff of grapeshot in the vintage month of Vendémiaire enabled the Directory to take supreme power. The Directors knew whom to thank. By the foggy month of Brumaire he ws commander-in-chief of the largest of French armies, the Army of the Interior. He set about obtaining the one appointment that mattered to him, control over the Army of Italy.

Love won him his hero's desire. Hitherto Buonaparte had been too preoccupied with getting on to allow himself more than a little flirting. In southern France he had had an affair of the heart with Désirée Clary, who was to marry a rival soldier, Bernadotte, and eventually become Queen of Sweden. In Paris his ruthless courting of politicians gave him an entrée to the frivolous salons of their mistresses and wives. One of the most notorious beauties was Thérèse Tallien, whose lover, later husband, had dared to criticize Robespierre in the Convention. His courage had rewarded his friends, among them Rose, former Vicomtesse de Beauharnais, the imprisoned Creole widow of a guillotined royalist. Rose enjoyed her freedom by being a regular guest in the Tallien household, and, rumour would have it, the mistress of Paul Barras. She and Thérèse became leaders of fashion. Neither beautiful nor intelligent, yet exquisite, passive, lazy, easy-going and extravagant, Rose attracted the notice of the young General Buonaparte.* He insisted that she should call herself not Rose but Joséphine – one of her names was Joseph – and one night in January 1796 he made love to her. For her it was perhaps a boring encounter, for he lacked experience; for Buonaparte it was the night he discovered his deepest feelings. He demanded marriage and Barras, who wished both to be disentangled emotionally from her and to be linked politically to him, encouraged the idea. Command in Italy would be his wedding present to the bridegroom. Perhaps to gratify this embarrassingly intense young man and maybe to escape from him, Joséphine consented. The ceremony occurred in the windy spring month of Ventôse. In less than sixty hours Buonaparte departed for Italy. The opportunity for which he craved was his: he could make himself a hero.

---

*There is a romantic version of how their first meeting arose after the young Eugène had come to beg Buonaparte to let him keep his father's sword. Their most recent biographer, Evangeline Bruce, will have none of it.

CHAPTER 4

Le Style Directoire (1795–9)

THERMIDOR 1794, preserved in popular memory only because of a recipe for presenting lobster, has been seen for many years by historians as marking a decisive change in the political history of the French Revolution. It has also been seen as a cultural divide, for, as David was put into prison, Joséphine de Beauharnais was freed. Spartan austerity went out of fashion; Alexandrine luxury came in.*

The truth is less simple. The politicians who combined to defeat Robespierre were not mainly merciful men who hated the guillotine. Some were ex-Terrorists who believed that Terror was no longer useful; others had been *représentants en mission*, some of whom had been involved in the policy of dechristianization; yet others were obscure former Girondins who were only alive because they were obscure. If these men were united by any ideal, it was by the ideal of their own survival as rulers of a bourgeois republic. They did not believe that there should be a maximum price for grain, they did not believe that Catholics should be allowed to worship freely, they did not want to restore confiscated lands to royalist exiles or churchmen, they had no idea how to make France solvent, they were in no hurry to make peace. They feared *sans-culottes*, Vendéens, *chouans*, *émigrés*, generals and foreigners. All that autumn in the south, royalists or federalists took the opportunity for private revenge; in the capital there were one or two food riots; not till early 1795, when the west was pacified, the Netherlands occupied and Prussia signed a treaty, was there any news to sing about. And then for the national anthem they chose that most stirring of songs: the Marseillaise.

*In the ancient world Sparta was famous for the austere, xenophobic and militaristic attitudes of its citizens, which gave the city its prestige among the Greeks. By contrast Alexandria, founded by Alexander the Great and later the capital of the Greco-Egyptian kingdom of the Ptolemies, became the richest, most cosmopolitan of Greek cities, with a reputation as a centre of sensual extravagance that surpassed even that of older cities like Corinth and Syracuse.

Only in war did France's government achieve much. If the Constitution followed English and American precedents by creating a second chamber (the Conseil des Anciens), its key provision for the first chamber (the Conseil des Cinq Cents) ensured that there would be continuity with recent French practice. Two-thirds of the old deputies would be members of the new assembly. This had provoked the violent reaction which necessitated Bonaparte's whiff of grapeshot. What was more worrying was the pattern of behaviour this action set. However ingenious the electoral devices of the revolutionary leaders, they would never accept the results of their own schemes. Just as the Jacobins had expelled the Girondins because they found their presence unacceptable and their policies treasonable, so the centrist politicians who took over from the Jacobins never recognized that there was any legitimate alternative to their own moderation. Whether voters opted for the royalist right or the Jacobin left, in either case their choices were overridden. Under the new form of government, the Directory, it became the norm every time there was an election for there to be an immediate coup d'état. It was the only method by which mediocrity could be preserved; and in the end mediocrity fell to one coup too many.

Only one political movement had in its aims a touch of altruism: the so-called Conspiracy of the Equals. François-Noel Babeuf, who dechristianized himself by taking on the first name of Gracchus, wished to play the part of an antique tribune of the people. Long before Stalin he talked of collective farms, long before Lenin he planned a takeover of power by an activist élite. He even shared Mao's hatred of towns and had he seized control of France might have been the Pol Pot of the eighteenth century. Luckily for France the 'conspiracy of the equals' amounted to little more than the five hundred subscribers to Babeuf's newspaper, *Le Tribun du Peuple*. In spring 1796, Floréal IV, Babeuf had an apparent success, when three battalions of the *légion de police* mutinied, largely because they were frightened of being forced to fight at the front. But the mutineers were crushed with ease; and the authorities turned on Babeuf, put him on trial and executed him as a traitor. There was no conspiracy, just a dream. There was never a chance that the proletariat would dictate.

The only dictatorship France had known was the moral ascendancy that Robespierre had sometimes exercised through the Committee of Public Safety. To prevent its re-emergence the lawyers established at the centre five Directors, one of whom would be replaced annually; and in the departments they delegated to local bureaucrats. It was a system that made for indecision in Paris and torpor elsewhere. There was one brilliant minister, Talleyrand, at the Foreign Office, but the Directory had a genius for attracting nonentities. That is hardly surprising, after the holocaust of able men in 1793 and 1794. In the late 1790s many of the cleverest men left in France were intent on making money; and it is because they had money to spend that important artifacts were made and that the *style Directoire* has its place in the history of French art.

Boilly's 'Point de Convention' (c. 1798, now in a private collection) illustrates the bold freedom of Directoire fashions. The picture's title is a pun, for the young couple reject both conventional costume and the politics of the defunct Convention.

There were three principal ways of becoming rich: being a general; being an army contractor; and being the owner of *biens nationaux* (property that had been confiscated from the Church or the emigrant royalists). The first way to wealth came from plunder, the second from corruption, the third from speculation. Not till he won victories in Italy could Bonaparte afford to finance Joséphine; only when he had come to supply the fleets of France (entirely) and of Spain, could Ouvrard take on Thérèse Tallien* as his mistress; and it was only as a banker that Récamier could endure both the chastity and the frigid furnishings beloved of his wife, Juliette. Such women were expensive commodities, for they were the arbiters of taste; their menfolk merely paid. After the aggressive masculinity encouraged by the Jacobins, it was a relief to accord such respect to women. With delightful whimsy the women reversed the sequence of ancient history. The Roman manner had had its day and they

---

*Thérèse Tallien, the least inhibited of Directoire beauties, appeared in society naked or almost naked more often than her rivals.

David's unfinished 'Madame Récamier' (c. 1800, Musée du Louvre, Paris) sets
the most renowned beauty of the age on the chaise longue to which she gave her
name in the barest of salons. She did not like what she saw, so David left her as
she was.

reverted to the Greeks; and though inevitably David went back to his Spartans, he
was fashionable enough to dwell more on their gracefulness than on their toughness.

Fashion was at the heart of the *style Directoire*. Clothes dictated everything – or
rather the lack of clothes. Under Jacobin rule dress had been practical and sober, as
life was earnest. Now there was a tendency to freedom, even licence. Just as prosti-
tutes, who had been banned under the Terror, returned to the streets, so in the salons
ladies of lightly held virtue sought to reveal their charms. Ideally dresses were cling-
ing, white and diaphanous. Women wore soft Indian muslin, a very expensive
material, or cotton, but not much else. The corsets and flounces of the *ancien régime*
gave way to a Grecian simplicity. In place of the high-heeled shoes of pre-revolutionary days women liked to go barefoot – as is the case with Madame Récamier in
David's famous portrait of her – but were willing to compromise by being shod in
antique *cothurnes*, sandals tied to their legs with ribbons. Like feet, arms were often

David's Henriette de Verninac (1798, Musée du Louvre, Paris) is a portrait of
the young daughter of Charles Delacroix at the time of her marriage to the
diplomat Raymond de Verninac de St-Maur. Her 'Greek' costume is fringed
with kashmere.

bare, but for David Madame Récamier wore short sleeves. Waists went higher and
higher till by 1800, when Madame Récamier was painted, they had reached the
bust. In a woman of such exquisite taste the effect was tantalizing; and Bonaparte
was not the only rough man of action to be seduced by a society beauty. To dazzle
the men the women would deck their naked arms and feet discreetly with diamonds
or more classical jewellery, such as cameos; and to offset their monochromatic
costume they would casually drape over their shoulders fine cashmere shawls.
Joséphine was celebrated for the grace with which she wore hers. David's portrait of
Henriette de Verninac de Saint-Maur shows how becoming they could look. The

Madame Sériziat, David's sister-in-law (Musée du Louvre, Paris) is pictured
in the simple relaxed style cultivated by the wealthy who wished to be safe.

love of oriental materials was wholly appropriate to the year, 1798, for it was the year
when Bonaparte was in Egypt and the year when Henriette's little brother Eugène
Delacroix, who was to be the finest orientalist of all painters, was born.

These clothes are proof, if proof is needed, that society was reborn. The clothes
suited the fashionable soirées and balls of the newly chic part of Paris, the Right
Bank, above all the Champs Elysées, where the Talliens lived, and the streets in the
area of the Chaussée d'Antin (Joséphine lived at right angles to it in rue
Chatereine). There were clothes for everyday. Fashion magazines, like the *Journal des
Dames et des Modes*, re-emerged; and the styles favoured by the very rich were copied

by every woman who liked to think of herself as up to date. In a northern city scanty clothes would have meant chapped skin in winter and sunburn in summer, so there were also more practical fashions: delicate cotton or linen dresses and even, as the workshops of Lyon were slowly returning to production, dresses made of silk. When David was let out of prison, he went to stay in the country with Madame Sériziat, his sister-in-law, and painted her in a white cambric dress, tied with a ribbon round her waist (this was in 1795), and in a tightly fitting bonnet. In the capital women wore coat-dresses with long sleeves indoors and riding costumes and cut-away coats, *redingotes*, outside. The royalist ladies of boulevard des Italiens affected jackets with short sleeves *à la romaine*; those who had incipient Bonapartist sympathies took to crocodile bonnets in 1798. Everyone had dresses that flowed too gently to support pockets and so needed the reticule, skimpy ancestor of the modern handbag.

It was in the late 1790s that women gained the importance in fashion that they have never lost. For a time, however, some men were determined to show contempt for practicality, especially the right-wing gilded youth or *jeunesse dorée* who after Thermidor flaunted their rejection of Jacobin ideals. Instead of revolutionary hair *à la Titus*, these *muscadins* went in for long, powdered, plaited hair, turned up with a comb (an allusion, it was said, to the way the executioners prepared their victims for the guillotine) and with one long curl at either side. They went in for starched green cravats – green was thought a royalist colour – and grey greatcoats with black collars and skin-tight breeches. At the end of 1795 they faded from public view, to be replaced about 1797 by the *Incroyables*. These young men had no clear political allegiance: their one loyalty was to their tailor. They wore square-cut, tight-fitting coats with huge lapels and breeches on which they tied extravagant loops of fabric. Like the *muscadins* they went in for long hair; and Bonaparte found them effeminate. They set a fashion that did not last. Most elegant men wore short black coats, waistcoats (sometimes two of them), pantaloons (often grey) and boots. Civilians were moving towards the simple, well-cut clothes of the nineteenth century. It was only soldiers who chose an occupation that allowed them to dress flamboyantly; yet the best soldier of all preferred to be simple.

Shoes and knee-breeches were worn only at balls; and balls became a special feature of Directory society. In the winter of 1794–5 it was said that all France danced from relief. By 1799 there were 1500 dance-halls in Paris. In 1797 the waltz came to the capital and soon all Paris was dancing with joy. As partners whirled round the floor holding each other more closely than ever before, their costumes seemed perfectly adapted to the rhythmical movement of their bodies, the men controlling and controlled and the women fluent and yielding. They danced as if the business of life was pleasure.

Pleasure was also business. The progress of the revolution had caused havoc to France's luxury industries. Whereas the whims of Directory society helped to revive some branches of the textile industry, there was not yet enough wealth in circulation to resurrect the craft of the silversmith. In 1797 a public exhibition of the products of French industry was held, at which there were 110 exhibitors and not a single silversmith. Silversmiths' shops in the area of the Palais-Royal had been replaced by *patisseries* and those in rue Saint-Honoré by *marchandes à la toilette*. Although society hostesses like Madame Tallien wanted silver for their sumptuous tables, they had to make do with what was left over from the *ancien régime*. The ageing Salembier continued to make designs for silversmiths, but nothing came of them other than cheap Neo-Classical pastiches. The young apprentices enlisted in the army. Ironically it was war which preserved the traditions of their métier. During the crisis of 1792 Nicolas Boutier, a gunsmith, had established a factory to make rifles within the château of Versailles; and there locksmiths and silversmiths were employed to make sabres while jewellers made chasers and damasceners to adorn them. It was thus in the manufacture of metal for destruction that some of the skills of the metalworkers of a more peaceful past were kept intact. Not till after 1800 were those skills used again as before 1789.

It was Bonaparte who was responsible for restoring the decorative arts to their eminent position among the arts of France. What applied to the silversmiths applied also to the designers and workers at the Sèvres porcelain factory and the Gobelins tapestry factory and the Savonnerie carpet factory. Each of these institutions had been set up to serve a court and each still needed a court. From 1795 there was a court of sorts. The Directors requisitioned the Luxembourg palace, principal home of the Comte de Provence (the future Louis XVIII) till he went into exile in 1791, and renamed it the Palais Directorial. There they received in such style as they could afford. While Barras took over the main building, his fellow Directors lived in the Petit Luxembourg nearby. Unsold royal furniture was installed to fill the rooms. Servants had a uniform. The architect Chalgrin was asked to make alterations. He envisaged a new *escalier d'honneur*, but for that, as for so much else, he had to wait for the fall of the Directory.

So far as architectural projects were concerned, the Directory was a time for schemes, not achievements. In addition to an official residence for the executive, the two houses of the legislature also had to be placed. Initially both had to be in the Tuileries till the Five Hundred could be moved to the Palais Bourbon (former home of the Prince de Conde). The problem was partly how to fit a hemispherical chamber into a rectangular room, partly how to be cheap. In the end the architects, Gisors and Leconte, found a solution which was criticized for its meanness. In 1808, however, Le Breton saluted them as 'authors of the only architectural monument built in Paris during the Revolution'. There was competition after competition: how

Right: David's 'Monsieur Sériziat' (Musée du Louvre, Paris) wears male costume that is equivalent to his wife's dress.
Left: David's 'Jacobus Blauw' (National Gallery, London) dresses in the elegant manner of a Dutch diplomat, but as his face suggests, he was too intense and he was dismissed.

to erect altars to the fatherland, what monuments suited place des Victoires Nationales (place du Carrousel), how to improve place Vendôme, place de la Concorde (so named since the removal of the guillotine), place de l'Indivisibilité (place des Vosges), and places de la Bastille and du Jardin du Tuileries. There was talk of adding to the Louvre, putting up a giant column by the Pont Neuf, constructing a temple of victory on place de l'Etoile, beautifying the Tuileries, the Carrousel, the Champs Elysées. What was needed was somebody who could mastermind the arts; and for such activity David was no longer available.

From his window in his room at the Luxembourg, David had painted the gardens. A landscape, he believed, was a minor form of art; and he had been humbled. On

David's 'Caspar Meyer' (Musée du Louvre, Paris) looks more secure as a man
of the world and proved to be more durable as a negotiator.

release he went to stay with Pierre and Emilie Sériziat at Saint⁄Ouen⁄en⁄Brie and
painted his charming and gentle sister⁄in⁄law Emilie, was rearrested and imprisoned
again, this time in the Quatre⁄Nations (later the Napoleonic Institute), was let out
on amnesty and promptly returned to the Sériziats, for whom he painted Pierre. His
mood of relief is expressed in the calm attention with which he looked at his rela⁄
tive, a man who aspired only to be a country gentleman, with his riding jacket and
whip, his top hat, his buckskin breeches and his brown leather boots. He went back
to Paris and back to his wife; and the Directory held sway.

He had not renounced an interest in political figures – he painted contrasting por⁄
traits of two Dutch ministers to the Republic, the simple Jacobus Blauw and the
sophisticated Casper Meyer – but he wished to find a way of responding to the lower
emotional key of political life: he looked for a subject that would bring a sense of rec⁄
onciliation. From the moment he had been in prison, he had understood what he
owed to the wife he had divorced, he sought and gained her forgiveness, he had
remarried, he appreciated how women had the gift for making peace. For his subject
he naturally went back to early Roman history. He chose the moment when the

Sabine women, led by Hersilia, intervene to stop the fighting between their Sabine brothers (in her case Tatius) and their Roman husbands (in her case Romulus). The scene implied a change of manner, for in his early Neo-Classical pictures only men had acted, women had merely reacted. Now he found works like *The Oath of the Horatii* too histrionic. He had to change his style. In the *Horatii* he had made too obvious his grasp of anatomy. 'In . . . the *Sabines* I shall treat that area of art with more cleverness and more taste. This painting will be more Greek.'

When he began to work on the composition while still behind bars, he thought of clothing his characters. Once back in his studio in the Louvre some of his pupils persuaded him that, as Greek art revolved round the nude, he should strip the costumes off. He had no problems with naked men — they were always available in any well-attended studio — but he had trouble with the group of women round Hersilia. It was during this crisis that the two dames de Bellegarde offered their bodies to art. Through Madame de Noailles they had been introduced to the teenager Etienne Delécluze, one of David's youngest pupils, and struck him dumb by leaning over him while they glanced at his picture and so smothering his blushing face with their coiffures. This embarrassing moment had the desired effect, for Etienne was relieved to bring them to the attention of his master. David took to the look of Aurore de Bellegarde and begged to use her face for the dark-haired woman kneeling by Hersilia whose ample bosoms hang pendulously towards her infants on the ground. Madame de Bellegarde, flattered to be put in the picture, made a point of appearing at the theatre with her hair done in David's way. Her provocative presence did not detract from the tonal unity of the painting — earth colours predominate — nor from its emphasis on the maternal role.

Women were also wanted again for erotic art. In 1793, at the height of the Terror, Girodet-Trioson, David's eccentric pupil, had exhibited a *Sleep of Endymion* in which a naked fleshy androgyne is lightly caressed in sleep by the beams of the moon. His most worldy pupil, François Gérard, was currently producing a slick, sleek *Cupid and Psyche*. David, though he had adapted to the Directory's politics, could not breathe in the hothouse atmosphere that modern female fashion encouraged. He became worldly, but it was with the worldliness of a man who had known the *ancien régime*. He was invited to join the new Institute, which had replaced the old Academy he himself had helped destroy; and he accepted with pleasure. Visits to his studio by the *beau monde* became normal. Returning *émigrés* were graciously entertained. Bonaparte briefly sat for him. When David had the courage to protest against the plunder of the art of the Netherlands and Italy, he irritated the Director Barras into calling him an 'imbecile'. But the Directors were in accord with his ideas on clothing suitable for the new regime. 'The new government of the Directory,' wrote Delécluze, 'doubtless to get rid of every memory of revolutionary costume, hideous and disorderly as it was, decreed for the representatives of the people, for the

The negotiations in David's 'Sabine Women' (1799, Musée du Louvre, Paris) were conducted by women. At the picture's heart Hersilia separates her husband Romulus, one of the twins on his shield suckled by a wolf, from her brother Tatius.

members of the Tribunate and the Council of the Ancients, a costume that approximated as closely as possible to antique form, so as to satisfy and even flatter the taste of the times.

'The five members of the Directory sat on curule chairs, draped themselves in the antique manner and, in the midst of these adornments, which may have been a little theatrical, contrived to reconcile minds to support the idea of a court that was plain enough not to offend Republicans who were not Jacobins and adequate to reassure Royalists fed up with living in exile.'

Delécluze also regarded the system of revolutionary feasts, which subsisted throughout the Directory, as signs of the same tendencies. There were seven national feasts a year: those of the founding of the Republic (1 Vendémiaire), of Youth (10 Germinal), of Married Couples (10 Floréal), of Thanksgiving (10 Prairial), of Agriculture (10 Messidor), of Liberty – on the day Robespierre fell (9 Thermidor) – and of Old People (10 Fructidor). These annual festivals, which Delécluze called pagan, took place on the Champ de Mars or the Champs Elysées. The organizers put up altars or temples copied from those at Paestum; processions of singers from the Opéra, got up like classical priests and priestesses, sang choruses from something like *Iphigenia in Tauris*,* while burning pine resin instead of incense. In Paris such events had some impact, for there were enough high-minded bourgeois intellectuals to appreciate the somewhat desperate attempt to find a popular alternative to Christianity. But they left no more lasting impression on those who witnessed them than a well-staged show. The Director La Revellière was keen on the deistic cult of Theophilanthropy; and at one stage some Parisian congregations could listen to readings from the Koran, Confucius, Socrates, Seneca and Pascal until a conductor in tricolour tunic led them in the singing of the patriotic *Chant du Départ*. It was all faintly absurd. Like Comte fifty years later the Theophilanthropists could not unearth the religion of humanity. They might like the logic of the *décadi*, but the French preferred their Sundays. From 1795 women campaigned to restore Catholic rites. The west, though subdued, was not reconciled to the Revolution. The south had no interest in its cult. The Directory, not keen on persecution but resolute against royalism, tried to divide altar from throne, the faithful from the Pope. In the Renaissance Christian and Classical Rome had gone hand in hand. The Enlightenment and the revolution had divorced them. Not till Bonaparte found a way to bring them together once more were Frenchmen free to enjoy both Easter and the Fourteenth of July.

François de Neufchâteau organized the festivals – David was no longer a master of ceremonies. But his *Intervention of the Sabine Women* bore serene testimony to the powerful desire for national unity. In 1799 a younger rival caught this mood with greater, but more specious, intensity. *The return of Marcus Sextus* was intended by Guérin as an allegory of the fate of returning *émigrés*, when an aged Roman comes home to find his wife dead and his daughter distracted with grief. His sense of desolation gave his creator fame and free tickets at the theatres. Yet between David and Guérin there is no contest. Even when most vehement, as in *The Death of Marat*, David understood that saving grace of decorum which is at the heart of classicism. No restraint inhibits Guérin; and his elderly hero plays on the feelings of spectators by playing at being profound. He lacks all Davidian humanity.

There is some absurdity in David, for his naked Latins guard their modesty by letting sheaths fall at convenient angles, twisting buttocks into shadow or turning so that their front leg covers up the back leg. In private portraits, however, there is a remarkable sympathy with his sitters which nobody in Europe – certainly not Goya

---

*The story of Iphigenia in Tauris had been set to music by one of the most celebrated of eighteenth-century composers, Gluck.

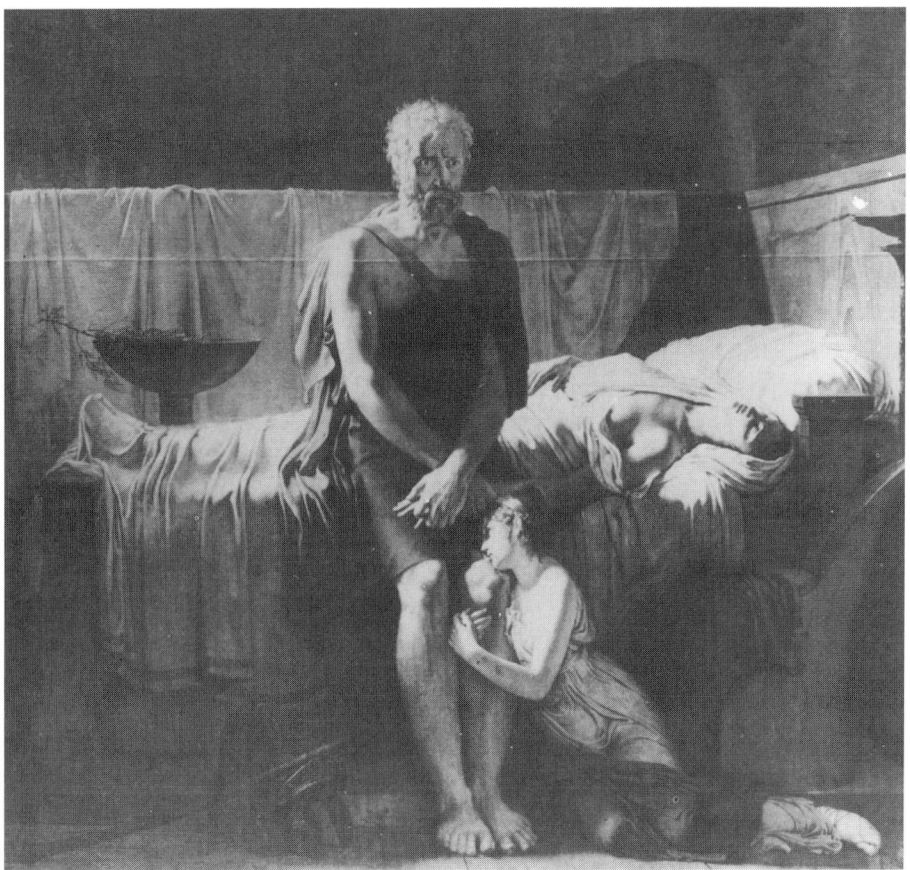

For the 1799 Salon Guérin invented the scene of the return of Marcus Sextus from exile (Musée du Louvre, Paris). He imagined that an exile has returned home only to find his wife dead.

– could then equal. His artistic practice, if not his theory, had escaped from the rigid precepts of academic thinking. Once its terrible bloodletting was over the revolution had given him freedom to be himself; and there was no more charming period in his art than the age of the Directory. No longer a dictator, he led by his example; and his ideas had some effect not only on painting, for he had a strong and beneficent influence too on the art of making furniture.

His connection with one cabinet-maker antedated the revolution, for as long ago as 1784 Georges Jacob (1739–1814) had made furniture to his designs for his studio. Thanks to this connection Jacob's business flourished at a time when the royal and aristocratic links of many craftsmen threatened the survival of their business. While Riesener never recovered from the loss of the patronage of the court, Jacob found employment with the one prince of the blood acceptable in radical circles, Philippe-Egalité, and later first with the Convention and then with the Committee of Public Safety. The abolition in 1791 of the distinction between *ébéniste* and *menuisier* may have sometimes eroded the quality of what was produced later in the decade, but, as Jacob's style was austerely Neo-Classical, it could make a virtue of the lower costs of production which lack of money necessitated. David had imbued him with a love of antiquity; the English taught him to treasure the mahogany that the French imported from Santa Dominica; Percier and Fontaine, already a team, gave him designs for the furniture of the Salle de la Convention. He felt able to retire in 1796. As Jacob frères his two sons, Georges II (1768–1803) and François-Honore-Georges (1770–1841), took charge of the family firm in rue Meslée.

The Revolution had checked the use of veneering, marquetry and ormolu. The Directoire *ébéniste-menuisiers* sought for clear lines and delicate effects. If they liked mahogany, whether dark or light, for its texture and colour, they also used native wood – yew (to be grand) or walnut, beech and lemon trees (to be modest). With light grey or white paint they counteracted the dominance of brown. Chair-backs curved elegantly backwards or inwards; they might be shaped like gondolas or palm leaves or lyres; their back feet were 'Etruscan', sabre-shaped, their front feet balust-ers that playfully ended in the muzzle of a wild beast or a bird's beak. In 1799 *The Harlequin*, 'a paper of bits and pieces', gave the first description of the goat's-leg feet and lion's-leg feet, the latter in imitation of Pharaonic furniture, which had become the fashion. It was a sign that there was more to the Directory taste than the classical influence that produced day beds with curving head-rests and chairs based on the Greek *klismos*. By 1799 Bonaparte had ensured that the cultural map included ancient Egypt as well as ancient Greece and Rome.

In every Directoire room the most common piece of furniture besides chairs was a pedestal table. There were large ones on twin pillars with pine cones at their heads, tall thin ones with bamboo-like bronze pillars, tables decorated with 'Pompeian' porcelain and marble-topped octagonal tables with tripod legs. In a decade when dressing-room tables looked like desks, the line differentiating leisure from work was blurred. While Bonaparte was in Italy, Joséphine ordered from Jacob frères a bed with a canopy like a tent and eight stools like drums – it was her gracious way of rec-ognizing how her husband made his living. She also knew her fate would be settled by war.

It was war which had given Bonaparte his chance, war which had made him famous, war which gave him power and war which made him the hero of the arts.

Before 1796 the French revolutionary armies had had some striking successes. They had repulsed invaders at Valmy and Jemappes and in the course of 1794 and 1795 they had overrun both the Austrian Netherlands (Belgium) and, thanks to the ice, the Netherlands proper. They had been lucky that the rulers of Austria, Prussia and Russia were so preoccupied with grabbing as much of Poland as could be seized that they were not unduly worried by the founding of the Republic or even by the execution of first the King and then the Queen. Though the overrunning of the Netherlands put pressure on the western parts of Prussia in the neighbouring Rhineland, in 1795, even before the Batavian republic (the former Netherlands) or Belgium had been incorporated into France, Prussia had given up fighting. Of the powers only Austria on land and Britain at sea continued to oppose.

It was typical of Bonaparte's luck that the general who might have upstaged him, Lazare Hoche, after pacifying the west and crushing the Royalists at Quiberon, urged an amphibious attack on Britain at its weakest point, Ireland; and Hoche's reputation was drowned in the wintry storms of 1796. Bonaparte, who had been senior gunner on the Italian border, argued that by striking at Austria there he would relieve any pressure Austria could impose on France's German frontier. He proved a better judge than Hoche. His Army of Italy was outnumbered two to one by the forces of Piedmont-Sardinia and of Austria. He always made sure that his enemies never combined. He led his troops up and down hills and mountains, along defiles, across rivers. He forgot the respect due to elderly opponents, he marched at a speed that was contrary to the rules of polite warfare, he never spared his own men. He combined great inventiveness with great precision. When dividing his troops, he gave them the exact time when they must reunite. He used small detachments as decoys, then hurled larger forces at his opponents from an unanticipated direction. Because he was on the attack, he risked putting himself between them and their bases. They were so afraid of the threat to their lines of retreat that they did not think they could threaten him too.

Within a month, the Piedmontese had signed an armistice at Cherasco. It took just one more month, from the end of April to the end of May, for Bonaparte to cross the plain of Lombardy. He came to view the campaign as a succession of magic moments: the troops making light of the 500-foot-wide Po at Piacenza; Bonaparte on a white horse cajoling his men across the bridge at Lodi; the ferocious assault on the hilltop of the village of Castiglione; Bonaparte falling into a dyke by the pontoon bridge near Arcola; the dogfight at Rivoli. At no time was victory inevitable. He took eight months to take Mantua. He made political mistakes. As he could not feed his soldiers, he forced local people to give them food; he held the Duke of Parma to ransom; he invaded the papal states. He made himself feared and hated. At one moment he was almost supplanted as commander, but he eventually led his men by winding mountain passes into the Austrian plains. He extracted a truce at Leoben, before retreating to Italy. There he concluded the peace of Campo Formio in October 1797 and overwhelmed the defences of Venice. Contrary to the instructions he had received from the Foreign Minister, Charles Delacroix, he organized satellite republics modelled on the Batavian Republic of the Netherlands: first the Cispadane, then the Cisalpine and later the Ligurian republics.

While his conquests gained him public glory, privately and unwittingly he was being humiliated in love. He had enjoyed scarcely two days with Joséphine before he left Paris. He went away to win battles, which she was glad to acknowledge, for being the wife of a victorious general brought her social prestige. But when in May Milan became French and at her husband's request she was given permission to join him, she was in no hurry to do so. She preferred to flirt with Murat in Paris, to announce a false pregnancy, to languish in bed. Besides, she had found Lieutenant Hippolyte Charles, 'dashing in his hussar's uniform resplendent with gold braid', to be more elegant than her awkward general, more charming and much less embarrassing. Soon she was confiding somewhat excitedly to Talleyrand that 'Mesdames Récamier, Tallien and Hamelin have all lost their heads over him, he is so handsome. And such taste! He is so superbly accoutred, I am convinced that no man has ever before known how to arrange a cravat.' While Bonaparte was moody and severe, he was lighthearted and funny. After her husband's boring monologues she appreciated a lover's banter. If Bonaparte's lovemaking was as abrupt as a military manoeuvre, Hippolyte wooed her to win her. Her pleasure at his conquest of her became a lingering one which she was in no hurry to give up. Murat had to go from Paris without her; and it was not till she had ordered clothes from the dressmakers, commissioned the redecoration of her house and gained a passport for Charles that she and Fortune, her pug, were ready to set out. They met Bonaparte in Milan, where he installed her in the magnificent Palazzo Serbelloni, for forty hours of love and a gala and a ball, till he returned to the front near Mantua. The misfortunes of war forced him to make her hurry to Florence for safety's sake, before calling her back to Milan, where he could be near her and would 'caress her so boldly' that Hamelin, a guest who witnessed one of their encounters, pretended to be looking out of the window. Once more, in the season of mist and mud, he had to leave her to confront the Austrian reinforcements and not till after the spectacular victory at Arcola could he feel sufficiently safe to recall her. She meanwhile was with her *chevalier servant* in Genoa. She sent no message with Bonaparte's urgent courier, but the lack of a reply brought some compensation when she arrived in Milan, for she brought with her her latest acquisition – an artist.

Antoine Gros was one of David's favourite pupils. Though he had not won the Prix de Rome, David had obtained a passport for him so that he could study at the

Gros' sketch of Napoleon at Arcole (château de Versailles) was made while Joséphine clasped her husband on her knee.

French school in Rome. There in 1793, as a protest at the removal of the fleur‑de‑lis from the school's coat of arms, a mob set on Basseville, the French ambassador, and lynched him. The students, Gros among them, fled for their lives; and Gros made his way to Genoa, where for the next three years he made a living painting mini‑ atures of the rich. Joséphine found his work charming. She determined that this was the man who could picture her husband, soon to be the victor of Arcola, as a hero. There was one problem. Posing, so natural to her, was foreign to Bonaparte, so she had to come up with an ingenious solution. While over breakfast Bonaparte held the tricolour, Joséphine held him. Lavallette, his aide‑de‑camp at three of these sessions, asserted that 'Gros achieved an amazing likeness of Bonaparte as he was at the time'. His secretary, Bourienne, found no artist convincing. Nobody, he said, ever captured the 'mobility' of his master's face, 'that quick and piercing eye, that lightning glance, that expression now tender, now stern, now terrible, at times even caressing'. Bonaparte himself was pleased to have the portrait and pleased to have met its maker. He had a job to do.

Ever since the 1794 campaign in the southern (or Austrian) Netherlands, a major concern of French generals had been the acquisition of loot for the nation. In 1794–5 a procedure had been established whereby books and manuscripts went to the Bibliothèque Nationale, items of natural history to the Jardin des Plantes and works of art to the Louvre. One of the first conservators of antiquities at the Louvre had been Wicar, a pupil of David's who shared his master's Jacobin views and who therefore fell with Robespierre. His task was continued by others. Among panels chosen were some of the central sections of Jan Van Eyck's *Adoration of the Lamb* in Ghent. Among canvases the principal trophies came from Antwerp, home to the most famous paintings by Rubens in the world. The French already had the wonderful Rubens series commissioned by Marie des Médicis for the Luxembourg palace, but in the churches of the painter's home town there were even greater masterpieces. They were greeted by critics in Paris with a mixture of wonder (at the painter's art) and condescension (towards his beliefs). The *Décade Philosophique* had misgivings that they had been detached from their setting. 'Can it be denied that these three paintings . . . lose overmuch of their value when they leave the temples dedicated to the suffering being whom they represent and the credulous nation in whose eyes this being is still a god?'

The author was ill at ease with Christian images. His reference to 'the credulous nation' of Belgium was the remark of an Enlightenment Frenchman, his reference to the 'temples' and 'a god' the remark of a Neo-Classicist. To such a man, or Bonaparte, Italy's famous days lay in its pagan past. Bonaparte modelled himself on ancient generals: he would plunder as they had plundered. To help him select what to take, in addition to Wicar, recently restored to favour, there would now be Joséphine's pet painter, little Gros.

The course of the French armies through Italy took them from one hoard of treasure to the next. The historical geography of the country, which had encouraged the division of the north into numerous city states, meant that at any major river crossing or on any prominent hilltop there was a palace or two, some villas, some churches. If Austria could not protect them, still less could they protect themselves. At each stop the French paused to offer the priceless gift of liberty before collecting in return a valuable tribute to their own cultural discernment. The Duke of

Piacenza and the Pope were asked for presents so that France would not treat them as enemies. Venice, the only remaining native republic of importance, was treated with special harshness; and the Doge's barge, the Bucentaur, was shattered into tiny splinters to ensure that, once a symbol of a thousand years' independence had been broken, it could never be restored. After the commissioners had gone home with their haul, which included the enormous, splendid Veronese *Feast of Cana* from San Giorgio Maggiore, some other agent arranged that the Lion of St Mark and the four horses of San Marco should be removed.

Decisions on which city to despoil were arbitrary. While Turin and Florence (till 1799), Genoa, Pavia, Brescia, Padua, Vicenza and Bergamo were spared, Parma, Modena, Milan and Bologna paid highly for their hospitality to the French. Lebrun, the husband of the exiled painter Madame Vigée-Lebrun, was disappointed with the Bruegels sent from Milan; and nobody gave a moment's thought to the wreck of a *Last Supper* that remained on a convent wall just outside that city. Much more exciting was the grabbing of Raphael's *St Cecilia* from Bologna, of Correggio's *Madonna with St Jerome* from Parma and, after a special expedition to Perugia, of Raphael's *Madonna of Foligno*. From Venice came the most famous Titian in the world, *The death of St Peter Martyr* (which in 1866 was to perish in a fire), various Veronese canvases from ceilings in the Doge's palace and Tintoretto's first masterpiece, *St Mark freeing the slave*. But nothing anywhere in Italy could equal the collection of the Popes.

One French general, Pommereul, hoped to remove from their walls the frescoes of Raphael, then much preferred to the Sistine chapel frescoes of Michelangelo, but in the end they were not touched; and nobody took much notice of his other idea, taking Trajan's column. It was much easier and much more gratifying to package marble sculptures about which every artist and connoisseur dreamt: the Apollo Belvedere, the Laocoon, the Dying Gaul, the Belvedere torso and the Cleopatra (who was really Ariadne). For three hundred years these statues had been the main inspiration of European art. Beautiful Renaissance or Baroque derivatives – David (by Michelangelo, in Florence) or Apollo and Daphne (by Bernini, in Rome) – were not taken so seriously. When the papal negotiators met Bonaparte, they found him reading Plutarch. Was he thinking of Sulla, who had staged a triumph in Rome on his return from Athens? He was always a man with a love of the grand gesture, the noble sentiment. If he had not thought of a fine rhetorical touch at the time, he developed a talent for inventing one later. It was only when he was on St Helena that he found the words for his famous order of the day which he pretended had been issued at the start of his campaign: 'Soldiers, you are naked, ill-fed; though the Government owes you much, it can give you nothing . . . Rich provinces, great cities will lie in your power; you will find there honour, glory and riches . . .'

At the time he said nothing so memorable. But his letters show that he was obsessively anxious to acquire for Paris as many masterpieces as his men could lay their hands on. It was not that he loved art for art's sake: he valued it for the fame posses-sion brought. Besides, he was acting in the spirit of the instructions he received from home. A stream of messages came from the Foreign Minister, who till 1797 was Charles Delacroix, soon to give his name to Eugène, the baby who was to be the great painter. It was in the Directors' name that a specialist commission was nomi-nated to supervise the collection of masterpieces, but it was to Delacroix that the commissioners had to answer. Sometimes Delacroix wrote from Paris in reaction to events that had happened in Italy only eight days before. He noted that he had not sent the team sooner because Bonaparte was winning victories too quickly. He con-gratulated Bonaparte for adding a clause to the terms of the armistice with Parma which insisted on the gift of twenty pictures. In exile on St Helena, Bonaparte would claim credit for his ruthless devotion to the cause of the Louvre. No artist he himself sponsored would owe him so much as Delacroix *fils*.

The transport of the booty required the skilful organization on which Bonaparte prided himself. Despite the vagaries of the weather and the bad roads, the brigands on land and the pirates by sea, the inadequate packaging materials and the inexpe-rienced packers, most of the enormous haul reached its destination safely. Some vases from the Vatican shattered but most pictures and statues survived their journeys to and (after 1815) from Paris. During the stay or stop-off in France most of the objects were well looked after, for the French had some of the best restorers in Europe and probably took more care of their prizes than the previous owners.

For Bonaparte what mattered was the show he could stage. In the latter part of 1797 he was concerned principally with the political and diplomatic consequences of his victories: setting up the new Cisalpine republic in northern Italy and nego-tiating a truce with the Austrians at Campo Formio and a peace at Rastatt. At the end of the year he was back in Paris. His reception at the Luxembourg was ecsta-tic. In half a century no French general had achieved so much. The Legislative Body put on a banquet for him in the galleries of the Louvre, to which the five Directors, the ministers, the *Corps diplomatique* and the heads of the branches of the civil service were invited. A few days later he was elected a member of the Institute. He became the most admired man in the capital, the man for whose attention all hostesses vied with one another. David, who had sworn that he would never put his trust in men, was seduced while sketching for three hours the conqueror's face. 'Oh, my friends, what a beautiful head he has . . . my friends, he is a man to whom people would have built altars in antiquity; yes, my dear friends, Bonaparte is my hero.'

This antique hero did not have his antique triumph till he was once more out of the country. The first convoy of loot arrived at the end of 1796 and the second in the summer of 1797, both very quietly. The third did not come till the summer of 1798, just too late for the *Quatorze Juillet*. On this occasion its contents became a theme for

David must have outlined Napoleon's head (Musée du Louvre, Paris) soon after he met the victor of the Italian campaign in 1797.

public rejoicing at the feast of Liberty which marked the anniversary of the fall of Robespierre. For ten days crowds had trooped to the suburb of Charenton to marvel at the boxes of treasure that had been unloaded there. On the Ninth of Thermidor an immense cortège moved slowly from the quay beside the Jardin des Plantes (near the present Pont d'Austerlitz) to the Champ de Mars, where it paraded in front of the Directors, who were stationed near an altar dedicated to the fatherland. Four groups of chariots carried first the manuscripts and books, secondly the natural history display – rare minerals (including fossils from Verona), lions, tigers, panthers, palm trees and carob trees – thirdly the Renaissance paintings and fourthly, bedecked with laurels, garlands of flowers and captured flags, the ancient statues. Each group of chariots had at its head a band, which marched along to the thump of drums before detachments of cavalry and infantry and those members of the Institute, whether scientists or artists, whose interests corresponded to the chariots' contents. At the back of each group choirs of professional singers sang hymns of joy in honour of the arms of France. The festival was self-consciously pagan, but nonetheless gratifying to national pride. Only one great painter was not impressed. A few days after the festivities David told his pupils that he regretted that all these objects had been brought from Italy. He explained: 'Remember . . . people in France do not naturally like the arts: their taste is artificial. You can be sure that, in spite of the lively enthusiasm shown at present, the masterpieces brought from Italy will be thought of only as expensive curiosities. The place a work was meant for, the distance you travel to go and see it, make it seem more valuable, and paintings especially, made as they were to adorn churches, lose a lot of their charm and impact when they are no longer where they should be. The sight of these masterpieces will perhaps create learned men, like Winkelmann,* but not artists . . .' The story of the next years was to bear out the truth of this claim. No great artist was formed in France between Marengo (in 1800) and Waterloo (in 1815).

In 1798 Bonaparte was still acting as an honest republican. Early that year the Directors continued his Italian policy: Berthier invaded the Papal States and created a republic in Rome. As long ago as 1796, while treating with the papal envoys, Bonaparte had specifically asked for the surrender of the bronze bust of Junius Brutus, who led the republican resistance to the Tarquins, and the marble bust of Marcus Brutus, who led the republican resistance to Julius Caesar. He and Berthier thought uncritically that the finest moments of ancient Rome had occurred in the years between the dates of the two Bruti. Their viewpoint was Plutarchan.

But if Bonaparte knew from Plutarch that Sulla had made a triumphal entry into Rome, he also knew that Sulla had retired into private life. He could not but be drawn to a more glamorous Plutarchan hero. In Italy he had been, like Alexander, a commander who had conquered when young. What lands now lay ahead for him to win?

While Parisians marvelled at the trophies he had won, Bonaparte had just marched into Cairo, which Alexander had known as Memphis.

On his return from Italy he had been charged with the task of commanding an army to attack the English, who alone of the major powers continued to fight on. Though at one stage sailors mutinied, the English had begun 1797 with the defeat at sea of one of France's satellites, Spain, and ended 1797 with the defeat of another, the Netherlands. During the bitter gales of February 1798 Bonaparte had walked along the coast of north-eastern France, wondering how a land power could attack a naval power across a stretch of water. It was too risky. He had a better idea. Months earlier he had written that the best way to attack the English was through India. Much of England's wealth came from India; and in Mysore France had a powerful ally in Tipu Sahib, who had a favourite wooden toy of a tiger eating a redcoat. But as so often it seems that Bonaparte was not concerned only with a doubtful future:

---

*Winckelmann (sic) (1717–68) was a German aesthete, who is regarded as one of the founding fathers of Neo-Classicism. He was one of the first to argue for a 'Greek' style, even though he had never gone further than Italy.

he also looked back to a familiar past. Alexander had gone to Egypt and founded a great centre of civilization named after himself. Pompey had sought refuge in Egypt and met his death there; Julius Caesar, after pursuing his rival to Egypt, had taken Cleopatra back to Rome as his mistress; and, having routed the fleet of Antony and Cleopatra at Actium, Augustus had finally turned Egypt into a Roman province. In Bonaparte's eyes the true successors to the ancient Romans were not the Italians, many of whom he felt were decadent and servile, but the French. They could found a new empire in the East.

France had a new Foreign Secretary, Talleyrand, who some said had replaced Delacroix in bed as well as at his post. Together he and Bonaparte planned a daring adventure in the Levant, which would bring them both to Constantinople. If Bonaparte was guilty of over-confidence in urging his ideas, then it is worth noting that Talleyrand, the shrewdest, most cynical politician in France, agreed with him.

For the arts the expedition to Egypt was to be an event of unequalled importance, possibly even more important than the Italian campaign. Delécluze, in his life of his master David, refers to the effects on French taste of the spread of knowledge of so many works of ancient art (often prompted by their transport to Paris): the translation of Lessing's *Laocoon* and of Stuart and Revett's *Antiquities of Athens* and the publication of Lagardette's *Ruines de Paestrum*. To these works which did so much to inspire Neo-Classical ideas he inevitably added the new fashion for the architecture of Egyptian temples. For this enthusiasm Bonaparte deserves to be singled out as more influential than anyone else. From the moment he thought of going to Egypt, he made plans as though he were fulfilling a mission. It was not enough that he should prepare an amphibious force to free the country by fighting its Mameluke rulers. He wanted to master Egypt's culture. There, he knew, was a civilization older than that of Greece, grander than that of Rome. But as a man who was a creature of the Enlightenment, he was aware that for over a thousand years Egypt had been a Muslim land, so on board ship he read a translation of the Koran and pronounced himself impressed.

Bonaparte liked to think of himself as chiefly a scientist. He had been elected to the Institute as a mathematician. He had once made a note of the dimensions of the Great Pyramid and he now calculated how out of its stones a wall could be built round Paris that would be one metre wide and three metres high — it was the sort of detail with which he liked to astound the learned. He was determined that one of the principal results of his expedition to Egypt would be an increase in rational knowledge. A French chemist analysed the formation of carbonate of soda on desert lakes, French biologists drew crocodiles and collected mummified ibises, French archaeologists clambered up the Sphinx to measure it. Like Pericles, Bonaparte knew that his country's mission was to civilize. Once in Cairo, he set up a French Institute to enlighten all mankind, but Egyptians first of all. French physicians suggested how to treat ophthalmia, smallpox and the plague, Frenchmen showed how to fly in a balloon and how to govern and discussed how best to rebuild the ancient canal between the Mediterranean and Red Seas. Their leader showed some sensitivity to the feelings of his new subjects (it was in Egypt for the first time that Bonaparte acted as a ruler). He convinced the muftis that he was a true friend of the Prophet. He explained how he had humbled old enemies of Islam – the Pope – and, in Malta *en route* for Egypt, the Knights of St John. He referred his successes to the mercy of Allah. He arranged for fireworks to mark the birthday of Mohammed.

Bonaparte's initial campaign in Egypt was notable in new ways. He took his troops from the vicinity of Alexandria to the outskirts of Cairo by marching straight across the sands. They grumbled more than in Italy, for on the journey they encountered not only hunger, which they had met with before, but also thirst. When he confronted the dashing Mameluke cavalry outside their capital, he was conscious of fighting near the Pyramids. 'Forty centuries look down on you,' he told his soldiers. In terms of military history the battle that followed was remarkable for less heroic reasons, for it demonstrated yet again the truth that Arthur Wellesley had recently established in India: that the bravery of a native force could not match the discipline and technology of an invading European army. It took only two hours' French cross-fire to give him control of lower Egypt. From the thirteenth century Mamelukes had mastered the area; they would do so no more. Their resistance, however, continued; and to crush them Bonaparte instructed General Desaix to pursue the defeated Murad Bey into Upper Egypt. This pursuit, not well known because it was not an action of Bonaparte's, was a feat of some skill. The French were often outnumbered and had no maps to guide them. Stragglers were liable to be killed, their stores were captured, the enemy was elusive. The French went south to Syene or Aswan and east to Kosseir on the Red Sea, hoping to cut off reinforcements from the Arab peninsula. Yet when they first sighted the ruins of Thebes, they spontaneously applauded. It made one witness proud to be a Frenchman.

By the time Desaix had returned, Bonaparte had crossed into Syria. Just ten days after the Battle of the Pyramids, off Aboukir Nelson had shattered Bonaparte's fleet and blocked retreat by sea. Talleyrand had not gone to Constantinople; indeed he had taken care to indicate to the Sultan that the French were occupying Egypt only temporarily (in law Egypt was still a province of the Ottoman Empire). If he intended peace, his words had the opposite effect: the Turks declared war on France and soon a holy war. The people of Cairo were encouraged to revolt, the British blockade tightened and the plague struck. Not even a little light adultery – Bonaparte had been told of Joséphine's affair and repaid her in kind – was enough to ease his problems. As usual, he decided on a military gamble: he would solve them by finding a new target to aim at. Learning that two armies, those of Damascus and of Rhodes, were being sent against him, he decided to meet the nearer by marching towards Syria. He was in the Holy Land as quickly as possible. There his forces won exciting battles at the biblical sites of Mount Tabor and Nazareth and he staged a courageous visit to the plague victims of Jaffa. But the garrison at El Arish held him up for eleven days; and this gave just enough time for a ferocious pasha from Bosnia, the septuagenarian Djezzar Pasha, and William Sidney Smith, an English sailor, to prepare the defences of Acre. The crusading port resisted the French for two months till they had to withdraw. With difficulty Bonaparte was able to disperse the army of Damascus, but he could not take all his wounded back, so he had immovable men killed, and with a much-weakened force dragged the remaining troops back by the desert of Sinai. He had the nerve to assert that his excursion had been a success; and yet it was with relief he heard that the army of Rhodes was anchored in Aboukir Bay, for now he had a chance to be decisive. The French cavalry led by Murat made one ferocious charge; and the French hold on Lower Egypt was made firm. Bonaparte could leave Egypt a victor. Most of the survivors, the men he left behind, had to wait two years to surrender with relief to the British.

Bonaparte's Egyptian campaign gave him a taste for political power, but otherwise it was an interlude in his career. It may not have mattered that he never got to India. There in 1799 the British defeated and killed Tipu Sahib as they took Seringapatam, his capital, and confirmed their mastery of Mysore for the next 150 years. In the story of Egypt the Napoleonic episode had effects that would last a little longer, till the fiasco of the Suez War forced a final withdrawal of both Britain and France from Egypt. But it was in the story of European sensibility that the effects were immediate.

Bonaparte was aware that on his marches to Egypt, Persia and India, Alexander the Great had taken with him learned men and philosophers. He was proud that he had thought of arranging for a small regiment of savants to accompany him to the East and proud of the work that the Institute in Cairo had done. Eventually, from 1809 to 1828, the fruits of its labour were published in the magnificent volumes of the *Description de l'Egypte*, so that all the world could know what Bonaparte had done for the land he had liberated. In the preface the reader was reminded of its ancient invaders, from Alexander to Augustus, as their missions were the models for his. He was the hero who by bringing Egypt into the modern world had restored its glory. Through France's civilizing role Egypt would be able to fulfil its destiny once more. Napoleon be praised.

By reason of the date of its publication the *Description* was a piece of imperialist propaganda. Such an achievement of French scholarship inevitably could never popularize; and by an irony of history experiences in which Bonaparte had less direct involvement did much more for Egypt's fame. They had occurred on what he regarded as sideshows. The first was the result of a lucky accident. In July 1799, while laying the foundations of a fort on the arm of the western delta near the town of Rashid (Rosetta in Greek), an engineering officer named Bouchard noticed a small slab of black basalt, some three metres long, inscribed with three different scripts. One of them he recognized as Greek. Bouchard and his companions assumed, correctly, that, whatever they were, the other two scripts must contain the same information. News of their discovery soon reached Cairo and the stone was moved to the Institute. Though nobody could read the unknown scripts, now known as hieroglyphic and demotic, the learned guessed that they were looking at two versions of the same Egyptian language. Bonaparte was shown the stone and was curious about it. He commanded that it should be copied and the copies sent to scholars throughout Europe. Marcel and Galland, two lithographers, were brought from France to make them; and in 1800 two were given to du Theil at the Institut National in Paris.

The Rosetta Stone became involved in the final débâcle of the expedition. General Menou had kept it in his house, covered with a cloth and under matting, and thought of it as his own. In the treaty of surrender the English insisted that it was to be their national property, but much further wrangling was needed before they could move it first to the Society of Antiquaries and thence to the British Museum. A Frenchman had the last word. Though Thomas Young, a British scientist, was the first person to work out that Egyptian writing consisted mainly of phonetic signs, the Frenchman François Champollion, still a child in 1799, grew up with an ability to decipher hieroglyphs. Realising that modern Coptic, spoken by the Christian Copts (Aiguptoi in Greek), was the nearest tongue to ancient Egyptian, he had learnt it and so could give meanings to words that others could not make out. In 1822, with Champollion, the sure basis for any literary understanding of ancient Egyptian art – scientific Egyptology – began its life, just one year after Napoleon had died.

The principal founder of modern Egyptomania had been on the Egyptian campaign. Joséphine had introduced her husband to Vivant Denon, hedonist, scholar, *littérateur* and engraver. Though her other protégé, Gros, would have loved to have gone to Egypt for the sake of the colourful costumes, he was not invited. By asking Denon, Bonaparte had opted for a lesser artist, but for the historians of travel and taste he had made a happy choice. Denon proved to be a resourceful, indeed a delightful companion; and he was to be a wonderful recorder of all he witnessed. In 1802 his *Voyages dans la Basse et la haute Egypte* was published in Paris and, in English, in London. It became an international bestseller and in this way an effective piece of propaganda.

By 1802 Bonaparte was First Consul; and it was tactful for Denon to dedicate his

The Rosetta stone, now in the British Museum, London, was found in the Nile delta. It was to provide the clue for the deciphering of ancient Egyptian because it records a document in ancient Greek, demotic and hieroglyphic Egyptian.

When challenged by Napoleon on the merits of contemporary Italian painters Canova singled out for praise Appiani, whose portrait of Desaix, Napoleon's helper in Egypt and saviour at Marengo, is now in the château de Versailles.

book to him. 'Europe, in learning that I took part in one of your most memorable expeditions, will receive my work with avid interest. I have neglected nothing to make it worthy of a hero to whom I should like to offer it.' All his life, he explained, he had wanted to travel to Egypt; one word from his hero had made up his mind for him; and the French troops who had gone too had given up wives and children, friends and fortune simply to follow Bonaparte and because he was their leader. But there was for Denon a figure scarcely less attractive: General Desaix. Desaix was 'a savant, a searcher for truth, a lover of the arts'. The campaign in Upper Egypt from August 1798 to March 1799, on which Denon accompanied him, was his greatest achievement. Fifteen months later on the field of Marengo he was shot in the chest and killed. 'I am plunged into the deepest grief for the man I loved and esteemed the most,' Bonaparte wrote home to his fellow consuls. Denon's account of Desaix in his book was also an elegy. Desaix was a man he admired before he had become a friend. After recalling one of their fascinating conversations, Denon had thought how many things they would have to say to each other for the rest of their lives. Fittingly one of the first objects put up in Paris in the pseudo-Egyptian style that Denon did so much to foster was a monument to Desaix.

Denon was quick to learn that there was much more to Egypt than the Pyramids. He was intrigued also by the customs of the modern Egyptians: their belly-dancing (which he found disgusting); the way all their customs tended to the state of rest; their idle habit of building as little as possible and repairing nothing – a wall soon became a ruin – and the foul-smelling rubbish outside their villages. There was also much to admire. He was convinced that the inhabitants of the Delta were the gen-tlest and most sociable of Egyptians and the Bedouin the most tolerant. He was touched by a story of their hospitality. A chief had held a French officer prisoner for some months. One night the chief had to flee to escape from a party of French raiders. In his haste to get away he lost everything except the clothes he wore and one loaf of bread. This he made a point of halving with his prisoner. 'I do not know,' he said, 'when we shall have our next meal, but no one must accuse me of not sharing the last food I have with my friend.' Then at Girge, the capital of Upper Egypt, Denon was entranced by a young Nubian prince, lively, cheerful, intense and bright, whose face expressed his character. 'We chatted with him a lot,' he noted.

Denon watched Bonaparte's two victories at the Pyramids and Aboukir. On the second occasion he was struck by Murat's daring if rash cavalry action and was asked by Bonaparte to make a plan of the battle; and he was delighted to 'give a true image of the theatre of his glory'. He made one of his careful drawings of the moment when the pasha was led as a captive before Bonaparte. Gros, then back in France, would later centre his version of the battle on the more exciting incident of Murat's charge. Denon had his reservations about the arts of war. 'O war, how bril-liant you are in history! but how horrid when seen from close to, when the horror of

Although Denon made engravings of the temples of Dendera and Edfu, he used the preliminary plates of the 'Description de l'Egypte' when supervising the making of the centrepiece for the first Sèvres Egyptian dinner service (1804–8).

your details is no longer hidden.' He would never be a great war artist. But he was the first member of the Institute to penetrate Upper Egypt.

As a man of the Enlightenment he was unmoved by the sight in the Thebaid of the caves of the first Christian monks, who were 'creatures of that contemplative system, so useless to humanity and so long respected by peoples who have been misled'. He drew a picture of a priest who was 'ignorant and drunk'. Everywhere he looked he saw there were temples. 'Temples, yet more temples and always temples,' he sighed in mock despair. 'I tried to work out if the arts had any periods and a chronology. If there ever existed a palace in Egypt, it must have been at Thebes that the remains could be traced, since Thebes was the capital . . . If there were periods in the arts, the results of the first efforts must also be in the capital. Luxury and magnificence distance themselves only slowly from such a central point, since invariably they are found alongside opulence and superfluous wealth.' He regretted that Egyptian art lacked individuality. All the same he copied down hieroglyphs with great care, though he had no idea what they might mean. When he came on a figure of a scribe writing, he was delighted. 'The Egyptians then had books.'

Denon's experience of Egypt made him aware that art had a much longer history than he had supposed. 'How long ago one must reckon for buildings decorated like these! How many centuries of civilization it must have taken to produce such buildings! How many centuries for them to fall into ruin, how many more centuries for them to serve as foundations! How mysterious, obscure, limitless are the chronicles of these lands!'

Because he knew so little about those chronicles, Denon had little sense of the long course of Egyptian history. Of the Old Kingdom the most impressive survival was the Pyramids, whose plans he had sketched. From the New Kingdom date the gigantic temples of Karnak, whose sight had overwhelmed him. What attracted him most, however, were the ruins of that postPharaonic stage of Egyptian history, when the Ptolemies ruled from Alexandria. At Tentyra (Dendera) 'nothing is simpler and better calculated than the lines of this architecture'. With Egyptians 'the idea of the immortality of God is presented by the eternity of his temple'. The temple at Apollinopolis (Edfu) in 'grandeur, nobility, magnificence and state of preservation surpassed everything I had yet seen in Egypt or elsewhere'. On returning there he realized that it was not so enormous as structures in Thebes (Luxor), but he reckoned (rightly) that its more elaborate style came from a later time. And when he got to the sites near the first cataract he was captivated by them. 'The Nile makes a detour as though looking for and embracing this enchanted island [Philae], where the monuments are separated by bouquets of palmtrees or rocks, which seem to have endured only to keep the riches of nature close to the magnificence of art.'

The rediscovery of Philae was to be of great importance for the Egyptologists, for there in 1815 an Englishman, Bankes, found an obelisk, which like the Rosetta Stone had Greek and hieroglyphs carved on it; and so the experts could work out the words 'Ptolemaeos' and 'Kleopatra'. Ptolemaic Egypt held the clues to Pharaonic Egypt. Knowledge of ancient Greek helped the unravelling of ancient Egyptian as love of ancient Greek architecture prepared the way for appreciation of ancient Egyptian architecture. Denon exaggerated when he wrote that the Greeks invented nothing. What was true was that a taste for things Greek gave a foretaste of concoctions much older than theirs.

Denon was no great scholar. He published his book because he knew that in erudition he would never compete with the authors of the *Description de l'Egypte*. He had stated that the Sphinx had African features and that Copts looked as though they came from ancient Egyptian stock, but he preferred fact to hypothesis. He had felt his feet blistered by the sun and been worried by the vultures that trailed the French soldiers; he was keen to take a crocodile home. He was a man with good stories to tell. He also knew that fame is short-lived. 'The glory of kings survives the night of time only in so far as it is preserved in the monuments raised by the arts.' That was true of Achilles,* Sesostros, Pericles, Augustus and the Medici (and would be true, though he did not yet know it, of his own hero, Bonaparte). He showed Bonaparte his drawings and was told that his mission was fulfilled. He was offered the chance of going home early with Bonaparte and he took it.

Bonaparte had been wondering how to bring his adventure to a satisfactory end, satisfactory that is for himself and thus for France (he was beginning to identify France's needs with his own). The English, to lower morale, washed papers ashore to let him know that not only they and the Turks were his enemies. The Austrians were again in arms and the Russians, having gobbled up most of Poland at the request of the great Catherine, were moving west at the behest of her mad son Paul. While Bonaparte was in the East, the Directory's generals had swallowed Switzerland, now the Helvetic Republic, and Naples, now the Parthenopean Republic. The English fleet could not do much, except to ship the Neapolitan royal family off to the island refuge of Sicily, but on the continent what mattered was whether there would be determined attacks on the overstretched forces of the French by the large armies of two major land powers.

France needed a saviour; and the Directors wished to summon Bonaparte home. Anticipating their message, he was off, skirting the shores of Cyrenaica to avoid the British fleet. On 9 October 'our hero' reached Fréjus. 'Nothing was more unexpected than our arrival in France,' wrote Denon, 'and the news spread like a flash of lightning.' A week later Bonaparte was in Paris.

It was a moment of crisis in his personal life and political career. Joséphine had made good use of his absence. While he was away, she had bought a decaying house at Malmaison to indulge her dreams of luxurious living. She could not afford the house on Bonaparte's salary – Barras claimed that it was he who made the down payment of 50,000 francs – but she determined that the buildings should become a château

---

*Denon's cultural heroes make up a mixed bunch. Achilles was a figure of Homeric legend. Sesostros I, a Pharaoh of the Twelfth Dynasty and one of the earliest builders at Karnak, was unfamiliar but Pericles from fifth century Athens, Augustus at the turn of the Christian era and the Medici in fifteenth-century Florence were much better known to Denon's readers as patrons of respectively the Greek classical and Roman classical periods and the early Italian Renaissance.

that would reflect her personality. Besides, there too she could continue her affair with Charles. If Bonaparte aspired to the role of Caesar, she was content to be a new Cleopatra – fascinating, seductive and extravagant. Even as she was planning the garden or preparing to redecorate the interior, she was aware that her fate would be settled by war. But she was not prepared for the flash of lightning – it filled her with alarm.

On the whole Joséphine was a sentimentalist who loved the nearest man to hand. She was attracted to soldiers, but a martial style meant a well-cut uniform, tastefully draped tent-like hangings and a dashing manner – not hacked bodies, raped women or abandoned children. She suggested intimacy but hitherto she had found it hard to give herself to any one lover. She was compliant and liked a tiff for the sake of the reconciliation that would follow. Suddenly she came to realize her mistake. Charles was charming and gallant, but her Bonaparte was unique. Terrified that she would lose him, she tried to meet him on the way and missed him. On his return he pointedly dealt first with the politicians and then went home and slammed the door behind him. Joséphine was distraught. With her children Eugène and Hortense she knelt outside his door, weeping. In the end he opened it to her and allowed himself to forgive her, for the time being. She had understood at last that she was dependent on him. Charles had to go; and it seems that soon afterwards he left her life discreetly for ever. Hencefoward Bonaparte was her all in all.

His principal concern was power. Annually one Director had to resign and a new one succeeded. In 1799 Sieyès came to office. Supposedly France's expert at constitution-making, in 1799 he was sure that France needed a new constitution. He had become famous in 1789 by producing a pamphlet, *Qu'est-ce que le Tiers Etat?*, in which he had argued that the true nation of France consisted of the unprivileged. What had become obvious to him during the subsequent decade was that the power of the people was not adequately represented by the people in power. He wanted a strong executive, but had no strength to execute his ideas. He looked around for a soldier to help him. Joubert had been politically ambitious but was dead. Bernadotte was suspect, Moreau and Macdonald would not listen. Bonaparte was the hero of the hour and seemed docile, yet intelligent enough to follow the thoughts of men (like Sieyès) who were more intelligent than him. Bonaparte was chosen.

The excuse for the plot was the usual one for any plotter: there was a national emergency. It was easy to get the Council of Ancients to agree that Bonaparte and Sieyès and Roger-Ducos, two Directors, should form a triumvirate. The Council of Five Hundred, the conspirators felt, would soon agree too. The method of persuasion would be an indirect use of military force, but, by trying to harangue French politicians as though they were Egyptian elders, Bonaparte stirred up a defiant demonstration and had to retire from the chamber in disarray. The president of the Five Hundred was his brother Lucien; and, though he had failed to carry the argument indoors, it was through his eloquence that Bonaparte's soldiers were persuaded to calm the fears of the deputies with their bayonets. In the manifesto issued to justify his behaviour, Bonaparte ignored his brother's help. He was intent on supreme power for himself. It turned out that Sieyès had no formula for the perfect constitution, so Bonaparte constructed one according to his wishes. He would represent the sovereign nation as First Consul. A dishonest plebiscite proved that the people wanted him – they probably did – and within days he was on the way to becoming the true monarch of France.

A few days later still the Salon opened. The major painting of the year was David's *Intervention of the Sabine Women*. Once women had brought peace to Rome. Now Joséphine and her Bonaparte were reconciled; the First Consul would bring peace to France; and the arts of peace would flourish again.

CHAPTER 5

From First Consul to Emperor

L'Empire, c'est la paix, the Empire means peace, claimed the Emperor Napoleon III. The assertion was a paradox in the 1850s, when most of France's neighbours were suspicious, even fearful of her adventurous foreign policy. In the 1800s it would have been a contradiction in terms, for as First Consul and as Emperor Napoleon I owed his position to war.

The 1799 Brumaire coup ended an effete, ineffective regime. France was beset by enemies and needed its most brilliant general to save her. If such an analysis justified his seizure of power, Bonaparte at first acted bashful. He sent off Christmas letters to London and Vienna, expressing his wish for a European peace, only to find, as he must have expected, that neither Britain nor Austria believed him. In France, however, his double dealing did him no harm. While intending war he posed as a would-be peacemaker; and in the end he could claim to have achieved peace abroad and at home. The Consulate, established and sustained by force, seemed a moment of reconciliation. The flight of the eagle was out of sight as the dove took wing.

Bonaparte's policy of pacification took many forms. After defeating the Austrians, he signed a continental settlement. He acknowledged that, as he could not defeat the British, he must live with them. In the running of France, where there was chaos he brought order. In place of religious strife he offered harmony. He laid down the principles of law, he brought stability to the finances, he set up a new system of advancement based on merit, he revived the social ways of a court. He himself became alike chief subject and principal patron of the arts.

On first seeing the head of Bonaparte, David had made out an antique hero's features. Bonaparte's new title now cast that head in an antique hero's role.

Bonaparte was impatient to achieve greatness and quick to realize that it was propaganda which could give him the air of greatness. 'The Revolution' had always been an abstract ideal and it required a bloodless pedant like Robespierre to thrill to its call to virtue. At its start the hero of the hour had been Junius Brutus, the first consul of the Roman republic, rather than modern liberal (and noble) monarchists like Mirabeau or Lafayette. At times key events – the oath taken in the tennis court at Versailles in 1789 or Louis XVI's acceptance of the constitution of 1791 – had to be immortalized in paint or print, but the revolution moved so fast that such depictions were left unfinished, as the people's heroes turned into the people's foes. In 1792 France saw the logic of its glorification of Brutus. It became a republic. The Romans had merely banished the Tarquins, but the new rulers of France put 'Louis Capet' on trial and beheaded him. Men were proud to be regicides and the most proud, most fanatical, were the Jacobins. They fostered the cult of their own latterday martyrs – Lepeletier and Marat and Barra – and had in David a great artist with an intense devotion to their cause. But revolutionary intensity threatened art. Only the Marat picture was finished; and David's politics, which led him to sign death warrants when he could have been painting, almost brought him in his turn to the guillotine.

In the feverish times of the Terror the foes of France had been spiritual, imaginary ones and its champions had been journalists like Marat. Under the Directory, which finally let David out of prison, the republicans first relaxed, then grew corrupt; the politicians and David eschewed heroics of any kind. The delights of mediocrity, however, soon palled. France was swept along by a yearning for a new kind of hero. While the land struggled against foreign armies, the sword was mightier than the pen. The most obvious kind of hero has always been an athlete or a warrior; and Bonaparte, young, handsome, vigorous and victorious, had a perennial appeal. When in addition he revealed a gift for making peace, he acquired the gravity of a statesman. Potentially he was a new Julius Caesar; and he had no intention of allowing a new Brutus, a Marcus Brutus, to assassinate him.

In the spring of 1800 Bonaparte declared: 'Because I am forced to do so, I shall make war.' He also made sure that he would take the credit for any success in it. Troops under Moreau in Germany were sent to the Italian front, since Bonaparte was to fight in the peninsula. Only the garrison of Genoa under Masséna held out against the Austrians; and Bonaparte made no attempt to save it. By crossing the Saint-Bernard under May sunshine, he planned to cut off the Austrians' escape route. He had just entered Milan when he heard that Genoa had fallen. He turned south into the land of corn, mulberries and vines that surrounds the medieval fortress of Alessandria. From there the Austrians launched an attack that he first misread as a feint. Some of his troops had dispersed to look for the foe; and his depleted forces were first halted, then driven back till by three o'clock his army, having lost half its artillery, was in full retreat. Melas, the Austrian commander, was so sure of imminent success that, when he hurt himself falling off a horse, he withdrew to Alessandria to recover while juniors finished off the pursuit. Luckily for Bonaparte

David was invited to paint 'Napoleon crossing the Alps' by Charles IV of Spain in 1800. Painted by 1801, it pleased its subject, who then had other versions made – this one is in the Musée du Louvre, Paris.

his frantic appeal for help had meanwhile reached Desaix and at five o'clock Desaix appeared on the battlefield. A rapid cavalry charge changed everything. Marengo, the village at the centre of the action, became famous for a brilliant victory; and as Desaix had been killed at the start of his action, all the glory went to Bonaparte. Even when other French armies annihilated the Austrians at Hohenlinden in Germany, Bonaparte had no words for Moreau, their able general. *Le Moniteur* meanly accused Moreau of peculation and did not let him defend himself in print. What was not a triumph for the First Consul was a triumph just for the Republic.

While Joseph Bonaparte negotiated the treaty of Lunéville which drove Austria out of all Italy except Venice, David was completing a process of elevating his brother Napoleon Bonaparte to a superior level of humanity. David had been offered certain official posts that he disliked. He had been named government painter (he

Prud'hon's 'Triumph of the First Consul' (Musée Condé, Chantilly) represents Bonaparte as a Roman warrior.

declined to be so) and made a member of a commission with Lucien Bonaparte to put up columns to dead soldiers all over France (he resigned). But he had little choice when Bonaparte asked him to paint the First Consul crossing the Alps.

The idea for the picture may have come from Charles IV of Spain, anxious to appease the French, but the impetus to achieve it came from Bonaparte himself. He had crossed the Saint-Bernard on a mule on a fine day. David suggested that he should have a sword in his hand, but he wished to be seen tranquilly seated on a rearing horse, his favourite mount. In his search for authenticity, David asked Bonaparte to pose, only to be told that the great men of antiquity had never posed, Alexander had not been a model for Apelles. It was his genius which David must capture.

To judge from the fame of his portrayal David did what he was asked to do. The horse looked like the horse ridden by Peter the Great in Falconet's statue of the Tsar, David's eldest son dressed up as Bonaparte and Gérard, his pupil, climbed up a ladder so that David could calculate the angles of vision correctly. The grey sky and the rocky landscape offset the glamorous central figure, splendidly clad, with his billowing cloak balanced by the windswept horse's mane and tail. Only on closer inspection does the spectator note that the protagonist's face is impersonal and the stance of his charger is frozen. The painting was intended to be reproduced – four versions were soon made available – and it quickly gained the status of an imperial

Ingres's 'Bonaparte as First Consul' (Musée des Beaux-Arts, Lille) stresses his civilian role.

icon. Twenty years before, David had painted a Polish nobleman, Count Potocki, nonchalantly subduing a fiery horse. *Napoleon crossing the Saint-Bernard* carries less conviction. It cruelly shows how hard it was for David to suggest movement. Unfortunately Bonaparte, who had not posed, looks as though he had. The reason is that he is not an individual so much as a type, an *imperator*, a general who will be an emperor. David knew of earlier equestrian portraits – Titian's *The Emperor Charles V at the battle of Mühlberg* (which belonged to Charles IV of Spain) and the statue of the Emperor Marcus Aurelius (which he remembered from Rome). In the foreground of his own portrait David refers to two earlier conquerors of Italy who crossed the Alps before Bonaparte – Hannibal and Charlemagne. Both the artistic tradition and the historical reminiscence add to Bonaparte's importance. He is a man of destiny.

Artists might go further than David in emphasizing links with the past. After Marengo, Prud'hon designed a picture that casts Bonaparte in a classical triumphant role. With a laurel leaf round his head, he is drawn by four horses in a chariot, with Peace and winged Glory standing at his side, preceded by naked running boys and grave women attendants, one of whom plays a lyre while another strews rushes before him. Here Bonaparte is an antique Roman leader reborn. On occasion he was content to be a modern civilian ruler. Even when he had become First Consul for life (in 1802), he was too clever to seem just a soldier, for that year, by signing the Treaty of Amiens with England, he had brought peace to the continent. In 1803 he gave the people of Liège the large sum of 300,000 francs to build the suburb of Amercoeur, which had been shattered by Austrian guns in 1794. Even before the money was given, Bonaparte had commissioned David's young star pupil, Jean-Auguste-Dominique Ingres, to provide the citizens who would be grateful with a memory of himself. As so often he allowed the painter only a brief moment to sketch him, so as in David's masterpiece Bonaparte's head is awkwardly set on his shoulders. With his wonderful sense of surface texture, Ingres lavished his art on the gold and scarlet costume that had been devised for the First Consul. Through a gap in the curtains to his right the viewer can catch sight of the cathedcral of St Lambert, which the Austrians had wrecked. Now that France controlled Belgium, the work of restoring churches could begin.

On 20 May 1802 the Legislative Body issued a medal that had relief busts of the three consuls on the obverse and the words 'Interior Peace' and 'Exterior Peace' on the reverse. They were right to place interior peace first. Victories at Marengo and Hohenlinden were nothing new in recent French history. What no one before Bonaparte had done was to bring peace to France. He had a low opinion of *The Intervention of the Sabine Women*, but he approved of the sentiment that David's painting expressed.

When in 1790–1 the revolutionaries had reorganized France into departments and communes and *arrondissements*, they had in mind a democratic ideal. 'The people' was to choose its rulers. At first the people elected men best suited to govern, like lawyers or men of affairs, but in many areas, notably Paris, elections became political; and Girondins or Jacobins or crypto-royalists seized power. From time to time there were purges of whoever at the time happened to be politically incorrect. Under the Directors purges became a part of the system, which contradicted the theory of popular sovereignty or, in Rousseau's terms, the General Will. If Bonaparte had once spoken this language, by 1799 he talked another tongue. He believed in order, which meant that he was the best judge of how to run France. The law of the plebiscite put the new constitution to the vote in December 1799. Frenchmen were reassured: the duties of the consuls and of their advisers were founded on the principles of liberty, equality and fraternity. The revolution, they were told, was over. Early results suggested that they agreed, so on Christmas Day the new constitution started operating. In February 1800 the final tally was announced: over three million in favour, only some 1500 against (the figures were false). The day before the law of 28 Pluviôse was proclaimed. The First Consul would nominate prefects for the departments and mayors for the larger towns. Bonaparte was set at the pinnacle of a pyramid. He conceded the appointment of the prefects to the Second and Third Consuls. They had their creatures; they were his creatures.

Another legacy of 1791 was the national or constitutional church. Only in the minds of its inventors had it ever inspired affection. By contrast the banned Catholic Church inspired martyrs and, worse still, royalists. Religious strife had led to civil war, which still lingered on in the west. If France was to be at one with itself, there must be a religious settlement that appealed to the conservative majority.

Whether it was, as he liked to claim, the memory of a church bell tolling in the village of Rueil (by Malmaison) or the prompting of an idea devised by his far-sighted and cynical intelligence, Bonaparte took the chances offered by the Battle of Marengo and the election of a new Pope (Pius VII) to open a diplomatic campaign. In Milan a *Te deum* gave his victory Christian significance; a conversation with a cardinal was friendly; he desisted from invading the papal states. His intentions looked good.

Once back in Paris he began secret negotiations with Rome. Not till 20 June did Cardinal Consalvi, the principal agent of the Pope, reach the French capital. Bonaparte gave him five days to bring matters to a conclusion, but he was glad that the cardinal had come and allowed the discussions to continue till well into July. On 16 July, with a sigh, the cardinal signed. The concordat was the first such document to be agreed on, for all papal agreements hitherto had been made with overtly Catholic emperors or kings. Now, though the consuls said that they were Catholics, Bonaparte granted that the Catholic Church was the religion of only the great majority of French citizens (as it probably was), not as such the religion of the French Republic. The consequences of this principle were worked out in a spirit of compromise. Those who had stayed faithful to Rome were no longer to be persecuted; those who had put the Republic first could be forgiven. Bonaparte was not worried that a few republicans and a few royalists refused to be reconciled. The great majority of French citizens and, more to the point, their wives, were happy. Almost at once Bonaparte gave the Pope and his cardinals further cause to sigh. He quickly issued Organic Articles that took back to the State rights that had been allowed to the Church. By then the faithful whose brothers and fathers had died in the scrubland of the Vendée were too weary to take up arms once more. The revolutionary calendar was doomed. Everywhere in France, in accordance with the wishes of the State, on holy days and on Sundays, the bells of the churches called Catholics to prayer.

On 4 August 1802, by a *senatus consultum*, Bonaparte was made First Consul for life and given power to designate his two fellow consuls. He was content with his present colleagues, Cambacérès and Lebrun, respectively Second and Third Consul. Cambacérès was from the south and as an ex-member of the Convention guaranteed the regime's revolutionary credentials. Lebrun, a Norman, had worked for the King – he stood for France's monarchical tradition. In their origins and inclinations they balanced one another. Both served Bonaparte well. Lebrun was glad that the First Consul's powers were increased. Cambacérès was involved in the codification of the law.

Codification was associated with the policy of Louis XIV's advisers, notably the great Colbert. After the revolution the work had to be redone. Commissions were set up in 1800, 1801 and 1802. Only one of these finished its work under the Consulate. In 1804 the Civil Code came into force. The Consulate lasted only five years; the Code it produced outlived it. An exceptional epoch provided France with its characteristic rules.

Bonaparte's hand in the framing of the Civil Code may have been exaggerated. He could not attend all the deliberations of its draughtsmen. But there is every reason to believe that what they decided met with his approval. If the lay State, personal equality and liberty, and liberty of conscience were permanent revolutionary gains, the laws of marriage and inheritance seem peculiarly Napoleonic achievements. Above all Bonaparte had wanted to restore the authority of men.

It had been the bitter experience of government during the revolution that paper money could become worthless; it was the achievement of Bonapartist rule to give paper money back its value. Since 1694, copying the Dutch, the English had had a national bank; and one reason for England's frequent success in its endless wars with France was that England always seemed able to borrow and to lend. When in the early years of Louis XV John Law, a Scotsman, tried to teach the French Anglo-Dutch finance, his system had collapsed. For the rest of the century French governments preferred to muddle on from one state of debt to the next, until all government credit collapsed and there was a revolution.

In 1789 the revolution opted for paper money and finances deteriorated. The only reason why chronic insolvency had not mattered too much was that France continued to win battles against her enemies and made her enemies pay for them. As for the Directory, that had survived by one device after another while government contractors like Ouvrard became rich at government expense. When Bonaparte succeeded the Directors, he had a dream of stability. In 1800 he set up the Bank of France. Its control of finance was none too secure – the dream was an illusion, but a comforting one. The Bank endured and in 1811, under the Empire, it moved to the buildings of the Hôtel de Toulouse by the Palais Royal, which had been the town house of one of Louis XIV's natural sons. By association it had acquired some raffish grandeur.

In the winter of 1799–1800 imperial pretensions lay ahead. One of Bonaparte's first actions on becoming First Consul had been a request to his brother Lucien, who had done so much for him during the coup of Brumaire, to erect a series of statues in the Grand Gallery of the palace of the Tuileries. They included eminent republicans of antiquity – Demosthenes, Brutus, Cicero and Cato – as well as eminent ancient generals – Alexander, Scipio and Caesar. But when it came to modern times, Bonaparte asked for fine soldiers (Gustavus Adolphus, Turenne, Condé, Marlborough, Prince Eugène, the Maréchal de Saxe, Frederick the Great) and one *ancien régime* sailor (DuguayTrouin) before moving on to a cluster of figures connected with the revolution (Washington, Mirabeau, Dugommier, Dampierre, Marceau and Joubert). This last group contains some surprising names. Mirabeau had been a liberal monarchist, Dampierre a royalist who had been lynched by a republican mob. Dugommier had fought alongside Bonaparte at Toulon. Marceau had been prominent in the war in the west, but less prominent than Bonaparte's former rival, Hoche. Joubert, one of the best of the revolutionary generals, had been killed during the Italian campaign of 1799. None of these men were as famous as Washington, the general who like Bonaparte had set his people free before becoming, also like Bonaparte, head of state.

The list is revealing. It combines the ancient worthies whom he would regard as politically correct and those whom a student of military history would revere. The revolutionary list is more personal. If it includes Washington, patron saint of revolutionary generals, who had just died, that may be because at this stage Bonaparte hoped to be the Washington of France. In one important respect he was not suited to the role. Like the Roman Cincinnatus, with whom he was frequently compared, Washington had retired to his estates when his work for his country was done. Bonaparte, in this like Alexander and Caesar, would never know when to retire. Since his work was never done, he was better adapted to playing the part of an absolute monarch on the European, even the world stage. As First Consul for life, he exercised almost unrestricted power, like Julius Caesar, and like Caesar's his authority was insecure. Instinctively he worked to establish a new, more glamorous style of rule, which would give the feel of a permanent regime. That he was ruler of all Frenchmen, regardless of their past, he showed when a *senatus consultum* granted an amnesty to all *émigrés* who returned by the first of Vendémiaire in the year 11 (23 September 1802) and took an oath of loyalty to the new constitution. What they had done could be forgotten: what counted was fidelity to the Consulate now.

Bonaparte himself stood for a system of advancement based on merit – that was the way he had got on and he wished to encourage others to follow his lead. In 1802 the decision was taken to found lycées, which would open by education a career to talented boys. Scholarships were to be given to those who would back the Consulate as officials or right-thinking members of the liberal professions. He wanted his talented boys to be sound.

Their parents, he felt, needed more obvious rewards. Three weeks after the law on the lycées, he instituted the Légion d'honneur. A legion had been the Roman division of an army. Bonaparte's legion was as much civilian as military, an army of French *notables*, consisting of fifteen cohorts numbering 250 members each. They were promised a salary, lodging and retirement homes. They would swear to devote themselves to the service of the Republic, to resist all attempts to restore feudalism and to work for liberty and equality. Old Republicans were not impressed. Elites had not belonged to the France of the *sans-culottes* and indeed the five-pointed stars and ribbons of the legionaries marked them out from their more ordinary compatriots. The kings of Bourbon France had been saddled with old aristocratic privilege; Bonaparte's France would have no such restrictions – it stood for the privileges of a new meritocracy.

Even before he invented the new privileged class, Bonaparte had revived the social ways of a court. There were still living round Paris many retired members of the court of Versailles who had been prudent enough or lucky enough to survive the revolution. A former First Woman of the Bedroom instilled good manners in the girls at the school she ran, the Institut National de Saint-Germain, where both Caroline Bonaparte and Hortense de Beauharnais happened to be pupils. In Paris the widowed Duchesse d'Orléans encouraged men to discard their revolutionary trousers and boots in favour of *ancien régime* silk stockings and buckled shoes. In 1802 she gave a reception for the marriage of Louis Bonaparte and Hortense de Beauharnais, where the valets wore livery and powdered wigs.

In the move towards grandeur and formality the First Consul gave the lead. He transferred his residence from the Palais du Luxembourg to that of the Tuileries. Within a few months, wrote his architect Fontaine, he was insisting on the 'magnificence due to his rank'. Soon his apartments were furnished in lilac-blue and yellow silk, fringed with gold and white; the walls were hung with great paintings; there were Sèvres vases on the tables; his wife was bedecked in the jewels of Marie-

In Isabey's unfinished picture of the First Consul visiting a factory in Rouen (château de Versailles) Bonaparte and Joséphine encourage the textile firm of the Sevène brothers.

Antoinette. Bonaparte made himself less approachable. Visitors were restricted to the antechambers appropriate to their rank. The English who celebrated the peace of Amiens by making the trip to Paris were delighted to notice how much magnif✗icence had returned to the capital. Compared to Bonaparte, the Habsburgs, the Hohenzollerns and the Hanoverians seemed to be homely, dull and provincial. Even if the new courtiers had to learn the lessons of etiquette that had been discarded in the previous decade, they were glad to do so. And the Paris crowd was relieved to know that once again it had its betters.

At first Bonaparte was satisfied with Joséphine's little château at Malmaison, but in 1802 he moved into Saint✗Cloud, once the home of Louis XVI and Marie✗Antoinette. There he held court as though he were a king.

As he acquired the aura of a king, Bonaparte himself became alike chief subject and principal patron of the arts. David and Prud'hon and Ingres painted him so far as the military, symbolic or civilian nature of his role was to be stressed. Isabey, the painter and miniaturist who was a close friend of Joséphine's, drew him performing one of the more tedious duties of a head of state, visiting a factory.

Bonaparte realized that such a visit was important. The revolution had disrupted the luxury trades for which France had been famous. Around Paris and Lyon, as well as in other parts of the country, there were able craftsmen who could no longer use their skills. He wished to see the tapestry workers, carpet-makers and silk-weavers at their looms again, the carpenters and cabinet-makers shaping and carving wood, the ceramicists of the porcelain works at Sèvres restored to their former fame. It made economic sense; it was socially beneficial; above all it would bring glory to France and the First Consul.

Such an artistic programme, Bonaparte well understood, would be costly; and he was loath to spend money he did not have. In 1802 for the first time for many, many years the budget was balanced. The work of redecorating and reappointing the Tuileries and Saint-Cloud was already in hand. The style that was first revealed in exquisite form at Malmaison could now be shown off in a grander manner in the former royal palaces. Of these only Malmaison survives, shorn now of its huge park with lakes, fountains, menagerie, Swiss dairy, Gothic chapel and hothouse. Joséphine had a special love of her hothouse, for as a Creole she wished to bring the warm winds and exotic flowers of her Caribbean island to her home in the cold and misty Île de France. Her husband was made of sterner stuff. Bonaparte thought dis-comfort a price well paid for grandeur. He even took to going to Mass once a week at Saint-Cloud before holding stiff receptions for the leading servants of the State. These officials soon learnt that they must dress in splendid costumes.

Only Moreau, the distinguished victor of Hohenlinden, made a point of dress-ing soberly. He had no time for the new baubles of the Legion of Honour and he wished to get rid of Bonaparte. Along with a number of royalists – Cadoudal (who had led the western rebels), Pichegru (a general who had taken part in royalist plots before) and some *émigrés*, among them the Bourbon Duc d'Enghien – he wished to destroy this regime before it mimicked the *ancien régime*.

Bonaparte reacted decisively. Moreau was tried and exiled, Cadoudal tried and executed, Pichegru committed suicide and the Duc d'Enghien, resident just outside France, was seized, tried and shot. Bonaparte had banished his brother Lucien for comparing him to Monck, the general who had restored the Stuarts. The Enghien affair made it clear that between him and the Bourbons there could be no truce.

As First Consul, even for life, Bonaparte was not a sacred monarch – not a Louis XIV reborn, not a Most Christian King of France. His authority could never be royal in the traditional sense of the Bourbons. His authority as monarch must derive directly from the people. On 18 May 1804 a *senatus consultum* announced that, pro-vided the French people agreed, their government would be entrusted to an heredi-tary Emperor. As always a plebiscite could have only one result, the correct one. First Consul Bonaparte was now Napoleon I, Emperor of the French.

As Emperor Napoleon needed to cultivate an imperial style.

PART TWO

NAPOLEON AND THE ARTISTS

CHAPTER 6

Imperial Designers

IF ANY ONE person was the author of the imperial style, that person was Pierre Fontaine. By living from September 1762 to October 1853 he spanned the whole Neo-Classical period from elegant revival under Louis XV to hefty survival under Napoleon III. He worked for Napoleon I, Louis XVIII, Charles X and Louis-Philippe; and, when he died, the idea of giving Paris the look of an imperial city, which had been conceived during the First Empire, was about to be realized under the Second Empire.

Pierre-François Fontaine was born in Pontoise, the son and grandson of trained architects who had turned to gardening, the building business and fountain-plumbing. As a schoolboy he showed his modern taste by taking the day off from school to see Gluck's *Iphigenia in Taulis*. He showed his tact and enterprise by hitching a lift to Paris from an unknown rich man who was so impressed by the boy's determination that he invited him into his coach, smartened up his appearance, gave him dinner, bought him a ticket and afterwards drove him back.

He showed a like determination when, having been taken on as a trainee builder under the architect André on the estate of the Prince de Conti at l'Isle-Adam, he slipped out one night with a friend to show off his portfolio of designs at the Academy of Architecture. Because they had no money, the boys had to walk there through the night without food. In Paris, Fontaine's plans found no favour, he had to return to l'Isle-Adam to face an irate André and he fell seriously ill. But his father was sufficiently impressed to see that Pierre deserved to have the chance to study. In 1779 Pierre presented himself at the house of Peyre, inspector of royal buildings, eager for instruction. By 1785 he was ready to compete for the Prix de Rome. The subject was a project for a tomb for kings and the princes of the blood. He imagined a whole cemetery dominating the city from the heights of Montmartre, whose crowning feature would be a massive statue of Destiny, set on a circular pyramid. His fellow students were impressed, but the professors awarded him only the second prize. He recovered from his initial disappointment and decided to go to Rome anyway, sustained by promises of family financial help. He went with a young archi-tect, Dufour, and Michallon, who had just won the sculpture prize. When they reached Rome, it was raining. The promised funds did not arrive; and, though he and Dufour won money on the papal lottery, Fontaine was soon desperate for cash. He painted little watercolours for tourists, but was only too aware of his technical deficiencies. Luckily an old French expatriate connoisseur appreciated his talent and taught him the art of perspective while they gazed at the Forum, sitting among the ruins, distracted only by the occasional puff of wind, which blew away the lines they had traced in the sand. So encouraged, Fontaine regained his enthusiasm. He begged his old friends to join him. In 1786 one of them, Charles Percier, whom he had first met in Peyre's studio in 1779, won the prize for architecture. 'I am full of joy,' wrote Fontaine. Through his father's connections he was presented to the Director of the French school in Rome. By then Percier was already installed. They soon began the key relationship of both their lives. 'We made, Percier and I, without any noise or commotion, a pact of friendship founded on respect and confidence. Together we worked out a plan of study which later became very useful to us.'

Though nicknamed the Etruscans for their love of antiquity, Percier and Fontaine soon discovered the subtle pleasure of noticing that there were two Romes in Rome. Beside palaces lying in the dust, near crumbling baths, stood the lively palaces of the contemporary Roman nobility. They sketched Renaissance Rome as well as the Rome of the Caesars. From Monte Mario, a favourite viewpoint, Fontaine drew first a reconstructed ancient Rome and then a panorama of modern Rome. In 1788 they asked if they could restore the arch of Septimius Severus. Instead Percier was ordered to perform a much more perilous task: he was to right Trajan's column. Despite a bout of ill-health he succeeded. It was July 1789.

The revolution ruined Fontaine *père*, so in 1791 his dutiful son walked home to Pontoise. Almost at once he went to Paris in search of work. He drew fluent designs for silk manufacturers and for painted paper workshops. In the same year Percier, having made the acquaintance of the sculptor Canova in Rome, made a leisurely progress home, stopping off to draw in Arles, Nîmes and Orange. A count commissioned from him an obelisk in memory of his daughter, a duchess; and Cardinal de Brienne asked Fontaine to build him a villa near Sens. Thanks to the kindness and then the departure of Dufour the two friends took lodgings in the same house in rue Montmartre. They won a competition for the National Assembly, but politics and inflation meant that nothing was done. In 1792 France became a repub-lic and the Tuileries became seat of the Convention. Again they drew up plans and again nothing came of them. But they met Georges Jacob the cabinet-maker and were asked to design furniture in republican style.

Percier was contented, but Fontaine was frustrated by the lack of practical achievement. He took ship for London, only to find that once there he was obliged to live from his designs for ornaments or frames or painted paper. A second time his father pressed him to return, for now that England and France were at war the property of families with *émigré* members was liable to be confiscated. Just as he was about to leave London, he received a request from Percier: could he join him in his new job, as designer at the Opéra? While one curtain after another fell on some political career, the Opéra stayed open; and Percier and Fontaine made their names. In 1798 they helped transform that section of the Palais Bourbon which became the council chamber of the Five Hundred. They went on producing designs which Jacob would execute. They were employed by the *riches* or *nouveaux riches* of Directory society – Ouvrard, Chauvelin, Dumoulin, Gaudin – to restore or build their houses. They were *à la mode*. They kept their drawings and prepared to publish them.

After Brumaire their first job involved working on the town home of the Marquis de Chauvelin, neighbour to Joséphine Bonaparte. Though her husband as First Consul was resident in the Luxembourg, she loved to escape to her old home in rue Chatereine, which she planned to embellish yet was loath to entrust to her current architect. She visited the house next door and was so enchanted with it that she told Isabey, who was painting her portrait. He suggested that she could invite Percier and Fontaine to rehabilitate her dilapidated country château at Malmaison. She had to see the two men straight away. Isabey came to convey the message: would they come at once to the Luxembourg? Percier said he would go, but not without Fontaine. Unusually Fontaine was hesitant. It was Isabey who insisted that they should go; and his friend David undertook to introduce them.

The interview that ensued was to be a decisive moment in the story of Percier and Fontaine. Hardly had the first polite words been exchanged between Madame Bonaparte and the architects when the First Consul entered the room and, as was his custom, ignored the newcomers and began a spirited conversation with David. Would it not be fitting if the fine works of art from Italy were installed under the dome of the Invalides, the military church? There was an embarrassed silence. David, as a mere painter, begged to be excused. Percier, as usual, was diffident. Fontaine, as so often, spoke out. Captured flags would be suitable for the chapel of the Invalides; captured masterpieces should be on display in the Louvre. Abruptly Bonaparte left the room; and Joséphine took the opportunity to show some drawings of Malmaison while everyone waited for three hours for her husband to come back. With Murat, he whisked the three artists off to the museum. Bonaparte looked at the horses from San Marco, at the Laocoon, the Apollo Belvedere and the Medici Venus – the three most famous statues in the world – and then left in silence. A few days later his decision was announced. He had accepted Fontaine's advice. Furthermore, the two architects were to be on a commission to arrange a celebration of the hanging of the flags in the Invalides. Their role henceforth would be bound up with the official plans of the head of state.

They were not yet the setters of style. For becoming so they had to thank the First Consul's wife. While her husband was on his way back from Egypt, she had acquired Malmaison, which cost him virtually all his money; and she had not cared to worry about the expenses that her purchase was bound to cause. Percier and Fontaine were asked to draw up plans. They suggested a pavilion apart for husband and wife; and there each would have a set of rooms in an appropriate style. The old château would be turned into a place in which to receive friends and family. Parallel to it, a new building would house ministers and civil servants. Near the existing stables there would be another building for guards and domestic servants and coaches and horses. Outside there would be a pleasure house, a little zoo, several hot-houses and, just for Madame, a botanical garden. 'This project,' commented Fontaine, 'simpler and less costly than any which we have worked on since, seemed then too hard to carry out, because it needed more time and money than the First Consul could afford.' In the end, he added sadly, the bit-by-bit restoration work cost more than the grand scheme would have done.

In the end Bonaparte was so enchanted with what they had done that he asked them to do more: to plant terraces in front of the Invalides and to site the four horses of San Marco there (they recommended instead that the statues should be set on top of something like a triumphal arch near the entrance to the Louvre). Then at the start of 1801 an 'infernal machine' exploded in rue Saint-Nicaise. Suspicion unjustly fell on the architect of the Tuileries, Leconte, and Bonaparte dismissed him. With equal abruptness he told Fontaine that he had become government architect. Fontaine tried to put in a word for Leconte, but Bonaparte would not listen. With a little help from Joséphine, Fontaine was able to gain official recognition for Percier as his partner.

Bonaparte was less pleased, however, when he learnt that the two friends had spent over 600,000 francs on Malmaison and anticipated spending more. He grum-bled about everything, about the tent put up to house domestics needed for a feast, about the bad smell of the drains along the road, about the excessive grandeur of the buildings at the entrance. His wife found their gardens too regular – her taste was for a sentimental, English garden, so they called in Morel, a septuagenarian specialist in such matters. Morel provided her with the winding paths, the curving streams, the asymmetrical groups of plants and above all the sentiment that was beyond the scope of their precise, logical minds to imagine.

Ironically Bonaparte found Malmaison too small for a country retreat. He wanted to use the old royal palace of Saint-Cloud, now empty and ransacked, where he had played out the last frantic moments of the Brumaire coup d'état. This time Fontaine

This is one of several paintings of the château and gardens at Malmaison by Garneray, commissioned by Joséphine and still in the château de Rueil-Malmaison.

was careful to predict expenses of at least 1,200,000 francs; and Bonaparte on check-ing was given an estimate of 3,000,000 francs. It would cost too much to restore Saint-Cloud, but the State would pay. The First Consul must live in a grand manner. That would mean that the Tuileries, his principal residence in town, would have to have extensive alterations. There in 1802 lights were lit in the arcades of the gardens beside the parterres and the château itself was illuminated to mark the signing of the peace treaty of Amiens with England. A sense of splendour had returned to France; and for that, with the approval of Bonaparte, Fontaine was chiefly responsible.

In Fontaine's partnership with Percier, it was Percier who was concerned to add delicacy and refinement in the detail, Fontaine who had the bold ideas. From 1801 till 1813 every year they issued a set of six engravings to publicize their recent designs. They seem to have started with watercolour drawings made by Fontaine, but they dispensed with any vagueness in their effects when they came to the engravings, pre-ferring the technique of crisp outlines that had been invented by the Englishman John Flaxman. The result is that they make their designs easy to follow, but they convey no hint of their feel for colour and texture. Only those who knew their real-ized designs would know of the lime greens, acid yellows, sky blues, terracotta, gilt

This engraving of the library at Malmaison is a design published by Percier
and Fontaine in their 'Recueil des décorations intérieures'.

and various shades of brown in their rooms or of the interplay of mahogany,
ormolu, marble, porcelain, gilded bronze, platinum, cotton, silk and wool in their
furnishings. Fontaine had the ideas, in collaboration with Percier he perfected the
patterns; others made the objects.

Percier and Fontaine had no problems in adapting to the new regime, when in 1804
the First Consul was transformed into the Emperor. By temperament they were
courtiers whose political convictions bent with the prevailing wind. They did not
suffer any of the soul-searching that tortured David. They were also artists whose
tastes coincided with the fashion of the age. In the 1780s David had worked in a
Roman republican manner which reached its climax in *The death of Marat*. After
the fall of Robespierre and his own frightening trial and humiliating imprisonment

he changed to a Greek republican style which found its serene realization in *The Intervention of the Sabine Women*. In the arts of design, especially as these were shown off in their published engravings, Percier and Fontaine displayed much of his later aesthetic. Indeed, they were more Greek than he was in that they based themselves on something like the pure lines of the most refined Greek vase painters. But there was a new fussiness in their details. At times it seems that they did not know when to stop, for their patrons, above all Napoleon himself, demanded displays of opulence. Spartan austerity was out; Corinthian pillars and Corinthian luxury were in.

Despite the high valuation that Neo-Classicists gave to all things Greek, it remained true in Napoleonic France that Rome was far more familiar than Athens, Sparta or Corinth. There was also a reason for emphasizing Roman connections in a new way. The Jacobins had stressed republican virtue; it was now necessary to laud imperial glory. In 1801 the Senate was installed in the Luxembourg palace. As France was still a republic, the statues to be put up in the Senate chamber were to include those denouncers of corrupt kings, Brutus and Demosthenes. Under the Empire, however, they were censored. And a room nearby was dedicated to the cult of the Emperor, in which Regnault was to paint *Napoleon marching to the temple of immortality*. Just as more was known about republican Rome than Greek democracy, so more was known of the Rome of the Caesars than Greece in the reign of Alexander the Great. Napoleon loved to plan on a grand scale, but Rome not Alexandria was his model. It was under the Roman Emperors that structures had become massive: the Forum of Augustus, the Golden House of Nero, the Colosseum of Vespasian, the Palatine palace, Trajan's column, his enlarged Circus Maximus, the baths of Caracalla and of Diocletian. Not till the sixteenth and seventeenth centuries did Christian Roman architects such as Bramante, Michelangelo and Bernini equal the pagan ancients; and Pope Sixtus V laid out a grandiose town plan.

As early as 1798 Bonaparte had asserted, 'If I were master of France, I would want to make Paris not only the most beautiful city that had ever existed but also the most beautiful that could exist.' Once the Emperor Napoleon, he regarded Paris as the capital of his empire and Rome as merely its second city. He would outdo Augustus and Julius II as Paris would be superior to Rome. France had just one classically inspired complex which already might compete with Rome: Versailles, the creation of Louis XIV and his architects. Napoleon wanted to do more for Paris than emperors and popes had done for Rome. To achieve his ambition he needed a team of architects far more numerous than Louis XIV had had. He decided that they should be led by Fontaine and Percier.

Since October 1789, after the women had brought back 'the baker, the baker's wife and the baker's son' from Versailles to Paris, the Tuileries palace had been the nominal centre of political life. There the King and Queen had lived till the palace was stormed in August 1792; and there under the Republic the Convention had held its meetings. After 1795 the Luxembourg palace had become the home of the Directors; and briefly as First Consul Bonaparte had been installed there. He wanted a grander setting in the centre of the city. Only the Tuileries could provide it.

It was in 1801 that Percier and Fontaine were made joint architects of the Tuileries; and all through the summer Fontaine was busy preparing plans to enlarge and beautify it. Joséphine wanted some alterations to her rooms and those of her daughter, Hortense de Beauharnais; and orders were given to extend the terrace by the Seine towards place de la Concorde. Next year, once there was official concord between Britain and France, Bonaparte decided that 200,000 francs would be all the money available to maintain both fabric and furnishings of the palace – a sum that would put a stop to several schemes, moaned Fontaine – and yet he put forward a number of amibitious projects. He wanted to build a road to connect the Louvre to the Tuileries, a façade in front of the buildings in place du Carrousel, the demolition of the riding school where the revolutionary assemblies had met and the extension of the road from place Vendôme to the Tuileries gardens. At the same time he was planning to construct new bridges and new quays and to provide more and better public utilities.

In 1802 Bonaparte was keen to separate the Tuileries from the houses clustered around it, so that it would be both more secure and more accessible. The place du Carrousel was cleared, the nearby buildings were being knocked down and Percier and Fontaine urged that everything as far as the Louvre should be cleared (in this they did not get their way and there were still slums round the Louvre till 1848); and work began on that most famous of Napoleonic streets, rue de Rivoli. Inside the palace Percier and Fontaine set about lightening the sombre appearance of the ground floor. When first Bonaparte had entered it, he had remarked how sad it looked. Soon the walls were covered with stucco and the cornices and coving were painted in cheerful colours that reflected round the rooms off the many mirrors. The décor was in that airy, playful style people called 'Pompeian'.

At Saint-Cloud Bonaparte began to behave in a regal fashion. Etiquette at the court of the First Consul became stiffer; like a Bourbon the unbelieving Bonaparte started to attend Mass; and the receptions became more and more elaborate. In the summer of 1804 he quietly made himself Emperor of the French and decided that he would involve the Pope in a spectacular ceremony of imperial consecration. The Pope would stay in the Tuileries, as the redecoration was complete, and Percier and Fontaine would design an imperial throne. It was they too who had principal charge of the consecration. Percier had the task of designing the imperial carriage. Fontaine was asked to put up a gigantic tent before the archbishop's palace on the Île de la Cité, to illumine the Tuileries palace and gardens, to stage the meeting of Pope and

Emperor at Fontainebleau, to rescue the tent when it had been torn by the wind and above all to make Notre-Dame a magnificent backdrop. His tent, supported by sixteen pillars, was hung with Gobelins tapestries. On each pillar there was a golden eagle and above flew the imperial flag. So vast was the tent that four coaches could simultaneously enter its four raised sides. It led to a specially constructed staircase which led to the archbishop's palace. There Napoleon was vested in an immense scarlet cloak, glittering with golden stars and edged with ermine. From there he walked under an entrance formed by four Gothic arches supported by pillars at whose bases were thirty-six statues symbolizing the chief cities of the Empire. Above the entrance were statues of Clovis, the first Frankish king to be crowned a Christian monarch, and of Charlemagne, the first Frankish emperor to be crowned by a Pope. High above, level with the towers, flew the banner of Napoleon's Empire. Inside the cathedral everywhere the eye wandered were to be seen eagles, bees and the names of Napoleon and Joséphine. The throne, which took up the whole width of the nave at its entrance, was shaped like a triumphal arch, resting on eight pillars, and was festooned with trophies. It was reached by a staircase of twenty-four steps, covered with carpets strewn with bees. The Emperor's throne was placed on a raised platform under a canopy of scarlet velvet, hung with gold fringes and buzzing with the familiar bees. Beside it, at a lower level, stood Joséphine's chair.

That day, the eleventh day of Frimaire year 13 (2 December 1804), 20,000 notables witnessed the ceremony. The doors of Notre-Dame had been open from six o'clock in the morning and the curious guests, so anxious to see what was going on, had wandered round the cathedral, disrupting the workmen who were still putting the final touches to their work. The masters of ceremonies and their assistants were not at their posts, people had been so busy planning that they were not there when they were needed and it required a few forceful junior officers to restore order. In the end all passed off in good order. And that evening the Tuileries palace and gardens were lit up, an orchestra played under the windows of the Emperor and Empress and fireworks were let off in place de la Concorde. Despite the cold a large crowd was present. The snow that had fallen at dusk covered the trees and the statues, so that the lights glistened even more brightly.

Fontaine, who recorded all these events in his diary, was so relieved that he made a mistake about the central moment of the day. He noted that 'the Emperor was crowned by the Pope's hands in Notre-Dame'. But as anyone knows who knows the story behind David's enormous canvas of the *Sacre de Joséphine*, at the key moment Napoleon seized the crown from the Pope's hands and crowned himself while before him knelt his adoring and exquisite wife, just wedded to him validly the day before. The key moment was her moment of triumph.

By the time he was crowned, Napoleon was once more at war. The peace so extravagantly celebrated in 1802 was at an end by the summer of 1803. Fontaine recorded
how the architects and other government employees offered 8000 francs to help pros-
ecute the war against England. He and Percier were asked to have made portable
wooden barracks which could be transported to Boulogne, where the gales forced
the builders to redesign the roofs before the First Consul could sleep securely in one.
That duty performed, the two friends could concentrate on the publication of their
first book, *Houses and palaces of Rome*. It succeeded so well that they were encouraged
to bring out two other books, first the selection of their interior designs and then
Pleasure houses in Rome and its surroundings. Fontaine's pre-eminence was officially recognized at the end of 1804. 'I was named architect for the Tuileries, the Louvre and
its outhouses, the imperial manufactures of the tapestries of the Gobelins and the
carpets of the Savonnerie, the marble stores and all Crown buildings within the
walls of Paris.' Nobody since Le Brun at the court of Louis XIV had cut such a
dominant figure in the arts. Fontaine protested that Percier was not recognized as his
partner. Percier reassured him. He was pleased to have no ultimate responsibility,
pleased to be able to devote more time to his pupils and, besides, he was sure that
nothing between them would change. There would just be a clearer division of
roles. Percier would stay at home, draw up the plans, carry out studies. Fontaine
would take on the official life, run the business, appear in public, manage the work
in hand. Their profits they would pool. They would live close to one another. Percier
was in a mezzanine apartment in the Louvre. Fontaine occupied a little house near
the Pavillon de Marsan by rue de Rivoli and later the Hôtel d'Angivillier.

Early in 1805 Napoleon was keen for them to carry out more ambitious projects
in the Louvre and the Tuileries. No more artists were to live in the Louvre, so poor
David had to paint his monumental *Sacre de Joséphine* in the former town buildings
of the abbey of Cluny. Napoleon wanted to have a large new chapel in the Tuileries,
to start the restoration of Notre-Dame, to house the Bibliothèque Napoleon in the
Louvre. He approved some preliminary ideas at Fontainebleau while on his way to
be crowned King of Italy in Milan. In midsummer he was back and found that
much still remained to be done. In the autumn he was off to Strasbourg to prepare
his campaign in Germany, for Austria and Russia had joined a third coalition with
England, and Fontaine hastened to Strasbourg — not even the impressive palace of
the de Rohans was adequate for the Emperor and his court — before returning to fight
his own campaigns in the Tuileries. Napoleon had other concerns on his mind: his
armies converged like the ribs of a fan on the Austrian army at the Swabian city of
Ulm, then pierced a gap between a second Austrian and a new Russian army at
Austerlitz in Moravia. He was back in Paris by January 1806, eager to find out what
had happened to his palaces. He was content, but wanted more action. A month
later he ordered that a triumphal arch in honour of the Grande Armée was to be

Percier & Fontaine's chapel in the Tuileries palace is shown in a sketch which
comes from the *Journal des Monuments de Paris* (1897).

erected between the Louvre and the Tuileries on the spot where Louis XIV and his
courtiers in fantastic costume had staged the mock battles of his carousels. Denon
would be in charge of the sculptures, Fontaine of the arch itself. Next day Fontaine
submitted a plan. He was told that the arch must be in place by 1809.

It was, he thought, the most exhilarating time of his life. He was captivated by
Napoleon's talk of glory. When asked, he hurried off to Lyon, to see if a great new
palace could be built in the second city of France. He was disappointed that the
prospective site, the island of Perrache, would be expensive to buy – the canny merchants of France's financial capital intended to profit from the presence of their
Emperor – and that it was liable to flooding and unhealthy. He came back to Paris
with three suggestions, none of which had any appeal to his master. But he had

noticed a more promising place, the Montagne Sainte-Foi, which commanded a dramatic view over the city; and he produced a fourth plan whose grandeur tempted Napoleon until he saw that it would cost 30,000,000 francs. Such extravagance would not do – he was for ever saying that Louis XIV had been ruined by his architects – but there might be an excuse. His courtiers, having no desire to leave Paris, noticed that in the capital there was a small hill where such a palace might seem well placed. Politics eventually would give Napoleon his excuse.

In 1806 Napoleon swept into north Germany to rout Prussia, which had foolishly challenged him after Austria had had to make peace, then in 1807 he turned on Russia, his last rival on the continent. In Berlin and Milan he passed decrees to close the continent to his one persistent and undefeated opponent – England – which seemed to reinforce his geographical mastery. In 1808 he took to swatting a lesser power, Spain, before in 1809 he once again faced down the dauntless Austrians. He wanted enduring peace. His Empress had produced no heir. Conscious that alone among the great rulers of Europe he ruled only by force, he craved legitimacy. He thought he could achieve all his aims if, by taking a wife from an imperial family with a long history, he found a woman who could give him a son (as he had a child by a mistress, the fault for his childless marriage must lie with his wife, not with him). He looked first to the Romanovs to find a suitable replacement, was rejected and then applied to the newly defeated Habsburgs. In 1810, after gaining the necessary divorce, he married the Archduchess Marie-Louise; and in 1811 she gave birth to his heir, Napoleon the King of Rome.

Wise historians may think that despite Trafalgar 1805 was Napoleon's finest year. But during the next six years, so far as his contemporaries could judge, he seemed to grow more and more powerful. Nobody could check him.

His self-confidence found its natural expression in grand plans. He would out-Bourbon the Bourbons with his sense of splendour. 'Napoleon,' Fontaine told his diary, 'during his fourteen years' residence, carried out in the Tuileries palace much less for his own interest and convenience than for the general harmony, beauty and magnificence of the building he thought of as the sanctuary of the monarchy.' Louis XVI's apartment on the first floor had become his. It comprised a suite of large rooms, including the Council Chamber or *le Grand Cabinet de l'Empereur* and the gallery of Diana. In 1806 Napoleon ordered that these rooms should be restored and redecorated. Two years later Fontaine produced his plans. Napoleon 'wanted magnificence, gold, Gobelins tapestries and great pictures', but he also did not like spending money. Only in 1810 did he authorize the work, after insisting that Louis XIV's decorative scheme should be retained to keep expenditure down. In other ways Louis XIV's example was followed. Inspired by Hardouin-Mansart's and Cotte's chapel at Versailles, in 1806 Percier and Fontaine built a split-level chapel. But whereas at Versailles the architects had used the graceful curves and counter-

Percier & Fontaine's *salle des spectacles* in the Tuileries palace is shown in another sketch which comes from the *Journal des Monuments de Paris* (1897).

curves of the late Baroque, Percier and Fontaine were constrained by the rectilinear obsessions of Neo-Classicism. To counteract the bleakness of the consequent severity, Percier graded his colours from the grey Portland stone used for the austere Tuscan columns of the lower floor to the white stucco found on the only slightly less austere Doric columns of the upper floor, the gilt on the capitals, cornices and ceiling, the polychromatic marble of the altar and the marble mosaic of the floor. The overall effect must have been imposing and cold.

A similarly hard rationality informed the grand staircase which Percier and Fontaine built to lead up to the Council of State: it bisected the centre of a rectangular space itself divided into smaller rectangles by massive Doric columns. But in the enormous *salle des spectacles*, reserved for the grandest of occasions, they broke up a rectangular space by means of circles, semicircles and arcs. They aimed to overwhelm the beholder.

In 1806 Napoleon explained to Fontaine his desire to unify his two chief palaces in Paris. In 1807 and 1808 Fontaine produced no less than seven plans. Their problem came from the fact that the two palaces were not aligned, partly because there was a bend in the Seine. Their solution was to construct a series of variations on a huge rhombus with one wing parallel to the Louvre and the other wing parallel to the Tuileries. Napoleon would have liked there to have been a space between the two palaces, but Fontaine argued that the difference in height between the buildings would be shocking. His view prevailed. In the end a large wing was added to the Louvre on the north side along the new rue de Rivoli. On the south side, where already the Henri IV wing stretched along quai du Louvre, Fontaine and Percier were involved in redesigning the *grande galerie*; and the grand staircase that leads up towards it was Percier's.

The two palaces had their most glorious moments when Fontaine and Percier stage-managed the second marriage of the Emperor to his Austrian wife. Scarcely had the news of the marriage been announced on 24 February 1810 when Fontaine received instructions from Napoleon as to what to do. The wedding was to take place in the *grande galerie* of the Louvre, there was to be a banquet in the *salle des spectacles* of the Tuileries, a concert on the terrace of the Tuileries, a triumphal arch at the entrance of the revolving bridge and fireworks in place de la Concorde. As so often Fontaine is a reliable guide to the ceremonies because he planned them and recorded them and eventually published his designs for them. In his dead-pan manner he told how the Emperor went to meet his bride at Compiègne, how he conducted her to Saint-Cloud, where the civil marriage took place on 1 April, how on 2 April they came to central Paris, where the religious marriage occurred at two o'clock in the *grande galerie* of the Louvre (specially lit for the occasion by Fontaine), how at four o'clock the pair presented themselves to the people of Paris on the balcony of the *salon des Maréchaux* in the Tuileries, how at seven o'clock they banqueted under the

In this photograph Percier & Fontaine's Arc du Carrousel is before the front
entrance of the Tuileries palace before that was burnt down in 1871.

domes, half-domes and arches of the *salle des spectacles*, how at nine o'clock there was
a concert and fireworks. The Emperor retired after expressing his satisfaction.

That same year Fontaine and Percier had their reward. For the Arc du Carrousel
they were awarded one of the decennial prizes for the visual arts. Officially they were
the most distinguished architects of the decade during which Napoleon had ruled
France. They were encouraged to draw up that year the grandest of all their palace
plans.

The idea of a palace on the Montagne de Chaillot had not been forgotten. It
appealed to Marshal Bessières, governor of the Ecole Militaire, opposite which it
would stand. In August he told Fontaine that the Emperor was reflecting on the
project. In November it was announced that the Empress was pregnant. In January
1811 Napoleon went to visit Chaillot in person and one week later announced that
the palace to be built there would be the palace of the King of Rome. Luckily two
months later the Empress did give birth to a son.

Fontaine has left watercolours and a lengthy description of his intended palace.
It would be, he said, as extensive as Versailles, 'occupying with its outbuildings the
slopes and summit of the montagne de Chaillot which dominates the most beautiful part of the capital with the easiest means of access' (he meant by road across the
Pont d'Iéna or by boat from the river bank). He was confident that whatever its
imperfections, it would be 'the largest and most out of the ordinary building of the

Percier & Fontaine's plan in the Bibliothèque historique de la ville de Paris makes clear how colossal the palace of the King of Rome at Chaillot was to be.

century'. What he failed to add is that, like Versailles, it would have been far too hor-izontal for its size. When the Emperor asked him what was the most beautiful palace anywhere, he answered: 'the most imposing but also the least convenient is the palazzo Farnese in Rome, the grandest are those in Genoa, the largest are those in Germany and the most habitable, those in France'. Fate intervened and the King of Rome never had his habitable palace. When in 1937 a Palais de Chaillot came into being, it was not the culmination of the urban design, for from 1889 on the same side as the Ecole Militaire there had been a much more impressive structure than any-thing possible in Napoleon's days: Eiffel's skyscraping steel tower.

Until contractors built in steel and concrete, European architects had used the tech-nical vocabulary evolved in the ancient world except in one respect. The invention of the pointed arch had led to cathedrals lighter and taller than anything Christian Romans with their rounded arches could ever have achieved. In the Renaissance its influence was felt in the way that the domes of the Florence Duomo and of St Peter's in Rome were more pointed than the pagan Roman Pantheon; and later Borromini and the Rococo architects of central Europe sought ever more dizzying effects of height. Neo-Classicists revolted against all such excess. They chose purity of form. The most imaginative among them in France, Ledoux and Boullée, designed wher-ever possible with the perfect shapes of the circle, the triangle and the square; indeed

Boullée's gigantic monument to Newton (Bibliothèque Nationale, Paris) was
impossible to realise, like many revolutionary ambitions.

Boullée's monument to Newton, had it ever been built, would have been a sphere some five hundred feet high. Napoleon's architects were less extreme, but they too wanted to adapt to the present the styles of antiquity. In this they were at one with their master. Napoleon had ambitions to build on a grand scale, but he was too prac-tical to want to build on the scale of Boullée. What the geography of Paris allowed was not the dominance of the Acropolis over Athens – the eminence of Montmartre stood outside the city wall – nor even the several climaxes provided by the peaks of Rome, but long vistas to hills in the middle distance. Napoleon grasped the impor-tance of such axes of vision: from the Ecole Militaire to Chaillot; from the Invalides to the Champs Elysées; from the Palais Bourbon past place de la Concorde to the Madeleine; and above all from the Tuileries palace through the Tuileries gardens across place de la Concorde and up the Champs Elysées to the circle of Etoile.

He did not reign long enough to establish all that he wished to do but the clear-ing away of visual obstructions and the complementary selecting of objects to control the cityscape was begun by him. It was his nephew who would make Paris its familiar self. The idea for such a city came from him.

After Sixtus V had laid out Rome as a system of straight streets that lead to squares, his successors had filled the squares with fountains and obelisks – in the case of piazza Navona both together – and led the eye from church to church and finally into the most grandiose of all piazze and to the most grandiose of all churches. In Paris Napoleon's rue de Rivoli was but a start. Another street, now named after a battle of the first Italian campaign (rue de Castiglione), connected it to place Vendôme. There was Napoleon's answer to Trajan: prominent citizens of the department of the Seine wished to dedicate a massive column to their Emperor. After Austerlitz Denon suggested that the low reliefs on it should be carved out of bronze cast from captured cannon. By 1810 it stood in place with Napoleon on top in classical dress. There were many other plans for prominent landmarks: an obelisk on the Pont-Neuf; an obelisk in parc de Montsouris; an elephant fountain at place de la Bastille; an Egyptian fountain in rue de Sèvres; and a fountain in honour of Desaix, which Percier designed, once sited in place Desaix (place Dauphine) and now far away at Riom in Auvergne. Many such ideas remained mere concepts. Of them all a couple, however, are familiar in their realized form to all modern visitors to central Paris: the Madeleine; and the Arc de Triomphe at the Etoile.

In the late eighteenth century two churches on the site of the Madeleine had been demolished. During the Revolution it was obligatory to dechristen churches with abstract names: they became 'temples' of reason or nature. Sainte-Geneviève was transformed into the Panthéon. Even when the Catholic and Roman Church was recognized as the religion of the majority of Frenchmen, the fashion had not died. Like many of his generation Napoleon was a deist. He himself had the Enlightenment fondness for general principles and had talked the language of virtue

This engraving of Vignon's Madeleine (from the Bibliothèque historique de la ville de Paris) emphasises its majesty.

with Robespierristes. In the 1790s the architect Chalgrin had suggested that the Madeleine could be used for the celebration of the national feasts and in 1802, at the time of the peace of Amiens, others put forward the idea of renaming it a temple of Concord (like the nearby square). As late as 1806 Napoleon was still thinking in similar terms. He declared that he wished to build a temple of glory to the Grande Armée. There was a competition, for which there were eighty-two contestants. The Institut gave its verdict and awarded the first prize to Beaumont, for he made best use of the buildings still existing, and the second prize to Vaudoyer, and named Vignon *primus accessit* (his plan was not what they thought the Emperor had asked for but they praised its simplicity). The results and the plans were forwarded to Napoleon in Prussia. He wrote to the Minister of the Interior and told him to ask Fontaine to ask the contestants certain pertinent questions: where would the Emperor and the court dismount, how would the public enter, how would the Emperor reach his seat? He insisted that the building should be in a severe style and must be of use at any required moment. Then he announced his decision: Vignon's plan should be followed since it alone fulfilled his intentions. Whereas Beaumont and Vaudoyer had wanted to build a church, Vignon had envisaged a temple and – this was an important point – his temple would accord with the Palais Bourbon and would not overwhelm the Tuileries. Via Fontaine Vignon was instructed to make some changes, which he agreed to, but, when the minister maintained that, since Vignon had never built anything, another architect should construct his building, Vignon was furious. He was able to convince the Emperor that he had the right qualifica-tions and he started at once.

Work progressed slowly. By 1813 the idea of a temple of glory looked presumptu-

The Maison Carrée, Nîmes, the chief source of the Madeleine, is a Roman
temple on an intimate scale.

ous even to Napoleon. It would be better if his temple was considered a Christian
church. Under Louis XVIII it was dedicated, like its predecessors, to Mary
Magdalene. Vignon had created a building that combined the baths of Caracalla
with France's most elegant peripteral temple, the Maison Carrée at Nîmes. He was
not the first to do so. The elements of Roman baths and temples had been combined
before in earlier Christian churches such as the Redentore in Venice. Inside, its
architect, Palladio, had applied the ancient distinction between the Frigidarium or
cold bath, Tepidarium or lukewarm bath and Caldarium or hot bath to the modern
divisions of a nave and apse. Outside he had broken up the rhythms of a pagan
temple façade to accommodate the taller nave and lower aisles of a Christian basil-
ica. If Palladio had adapted classicism to Christian ends, Vignon, to do him justice,
had thought that he was called on merely to revive classical pagan ideas. His temple
of glory was too rational to be changed easily to express the emotional faith of a
repentant Mary Magdalene. The Madeleine's twelve imposing Corinthian pillars
also left far behind the modest refinement of the Maison Carrée. As with too much
Napoleonic building, the Madeleine has an air of bombast. Always a familiar part
of any tourist's view of Paris, it has not inspired affection.

Napoleon did not aim so much to be loved as to be admired. His amazing military successes were intoxicating; and only planning and building on a large scale,
such as was possible to him chiefly in Paris, could symbolize his view of his achievements. There was, however, one architectural form from antiquity that had
grandiose implications but did not have to be enormous. Every cultivated man of

Chalgrin's original Arc de Triomphe (Bibliothèque historique de la ville de Paris) was more restrained and less ponderous than the present building.

the world knew of triumphal arches in Rome, whether of Titus or Septimius Severus or Constantine. In Napoleonic France, as French armies won ever more battles, triumphal arches became almost commonplace. They were more comprehensible marks of crushing victories than temples of glory, however huge.

After Austerlitz triumphal arches spread across the land. Napoleon passed under the one in Strasbourg in January 1806. Shortly after this he passed by one in Paris at the roundabout of La Villette. Next month he orderd the erection of two more: one in place du Carrousel to commemorate Austerlitz, one at the entrance of rue

Saint-Antoine to commemorate Marengo. Champagny, his Minister of the Interior, suggested a third one, a triumphal arch in place de l'Etoile, at the top of the Champs Elysées. 'A triumphal arch,' he argued, 'would close at that point in the most majestic and picturesque way the superb view from the imperial palace of the Tuileries.'

To avoid delay Champagny did not allow a competition. He named two architects to be in charge: Chalgrin, who had carried out so much work in the Luxembourg, and Raymond. They had different ideas. Chalgrin wanted isolated columns, Raymond engaged columns. When Fontaine remarked to Napoleon that 'at such an elevated spot, it was essential that this monument should be colossal', and that at a distance nobody would see the engaged columns, Raymond withdrew and Chalgrin carried on alone.

Chalgrin died in 1811 and was succeeded as architect by a pupil who had worked with him at the Luxembourg. The fall of Napoleon brought an end to work on the arch and not till 1836 in the reign of the mildly Bonapartist Louis-Philippe was it finished. By then it was the tallest triumphal arch in the world. Chalgrin's intention had been to build something simpler. His design had placed the central arch beneath a frieze and a cornice. The attic storey was added later. The present Arc de Triomphe is thus more emphatic and weighty, less pure in taste than Chalgrin had imagined it. Napoleon had his own ideas about the sculptures, but the best, by Rudé, including the Volunteers of 1792 or La Marseillaise, were not executed till the mid-1830s. As it is, then, the Arc de Triomphe is a tribute to the cult of Napoleon rather than a memorial of the Empire itself. It was up the Champs Elysées and past the Arc that Napoleon's ashes were taken one cold winter's day in 1840. Since then procession after procession has taken the same route to mark the great moments in France's history or, in 1871 and 1940, its worst humiliations. No ruler, not even Louis XIV, ever imparted such a sense of theatre to the public life of the French nation as Napoleon.

For such a self-dramatist Napoleon showed in certain ways a remarkable degree of self-restraint. Given a choice between bread and circuses as a means of appeasing his people, he often chose bread.

Napoleon was keen to improve the economic and social life of his capital. He had the elderly Brogniart build a Bourse, a temple of finance based on the Temple of Vespasian, on the Right Bank. Aware that there were some 25,000 workers involved in the building trades, he undertook to support the construction industry as an act of social welfare. His officials built over seventy streets and over a dozen quays. He wanted pavements, which came in about 1812, he wanted more bridges, so he put up the Pont d'Austerlitz, the Pont d'Iéna, the Pont de la Concorde and the iron footbridge, the Pont des Arts, he wanted to make it easier to move around the city, so names of streets parallel to the Seine were written in black and those at right angles to the Seine were marked in red on a yellow background. He wanted the city to be cleaner (Paris stayed dirty). He wanted to make it safer and more cheerful at night (it was lit by gas lamps). He wanted to cope with the water shortage, so he had the river Ourcq diverted and by 1812 eighty-four fountains played in Paris every day of the summer.

He did not forget the humble needs of everyday life. The market of Saint-Honoré was opened in 1810, in 1811 a new market of Saint-Martin was begun (it opened in 1816) and the first stone of the market of Saint-Germain was laid in 1813. In 1811 the Halles des Vins was begun in the grounds of the former abbey of Saint-Victor; and there was a new iron and copper Halle des Blés. In 1808 Napoleon made decisions about abattoirs. There should be one at Ménilmontant, a second at Grenelle, a third at Roule, a fourth at Villejuif, a fifth at Montmartre and a sixth at Rochechouart. Finally Napoleon also intended to take good care of the sick and the dead. With hospitals he had little success, but Brogniart used the former property of Louis XIV's confessor, Père La Chaise, to lay out a city cemetery like an English park.

Napoleon had great plans for Paris. Both what was projected and what was realized is preserved in the delicate, precise watercolours of Fontaine, who had more say than anyone after the Emperor in what was done. Fontaine's career as official architect lasted almost fifty years; Napoleon's career as head of state lasted only fifteen years. What outlasted both was the law of 28 Pluviôse, Year VIII (17 February 1800) which made Paris not only the political capital but also the administrative capital of France. In 1789 Paris had ended the political domination of Versailles. In 1794 the division of Paris into sections was ended. Henceforward Paris would be divided into *arrondissements* (at that stage just twelve). By the law of 28 Pluviôse two prefects were appointed to take charge of Paris: the prefect of the police and the prefect of the Seine. It was when his nephew Napoleon III appointed Baron Haussmann prefect of the Seine that the great mid-century transformation of Paris began. This was in the spirit of Napoleon I except in one respect. The first Emperor always worried about cost. He remembered how Louis XIV had had to raise taxes – in truth more because of his wars than because of his building programmes – and so nobody would ever have been able to write a satire on one of his prefects of the Seine called *Les comptes fantastiques d'Haussmann*, not only because there were as yet no *contes fantastiques d'Hoffmann* but also because there could have been no confusion about and so no pun on *comptes* (accounts) and *contes* (fairy stories). Napoleon I was not prepared to mortgage the future for the sake of the present. He had a series of plans, but no grand overall plan, lots of tactics, but no strategy. As a result, despite all his improvements, till after 1850 Paris was still essentially medieval, with clogged streets, inadequate drains and slums near the city centre. Auguste Renoir told his son Jean how in the 1840s he had been brought up in poverty in the shadow of the Louvre. Parisians grew vegetables in their little gardens, butchers killed livestock behind their shops and wine was sold in jugs. When Auguste and his urchin friends played beneath the windows of the Tuileries palace, periodically the Queen would throw sweets down to them; and he first knew that she had fled because no more sweets came his way.

In other ways Napoleon anticipated the work of later urban improvers, his nephew and Haussmann, Pompidou, Giscard d'Estaing, Mitterand and Chirac. He acted on principles that they would have recognized. 'Men are great only by the monuments they leave behind.'* 'The city of Paris is short of monuments; she must have them.' 'What is great is always beautiful.' The Arc de Triomphe, the Madeleine and rue de Rivoli set the pattern for the Opéra and the *grands boulevards* and for the Beaubourg, La Défense, Opéra-Bastille and the RER. There may have been more tension in Maire Chirac's relationship with his three presidents, all of them rivals, than in that of Prefect Haussmann with his Emperor, yet both rulers of Paris and each head of state has acted within the law and in the tradition of Napoleon.

What is notable is that Napoleon was better at fulfilling his duller objectives – providing markets and abattoirs – than at the more glamorous ones. Besides the palace of the King of Rome he wanted to build a palace of the Archives, a palace of the University and a church of St Napoleon. The three palaces never got beyond having their foundations laid and the church was never finished. Sometimes his Bourbon successors had their reasons for not pressing on with his schemes, for example the Arc de Triomphe. Sometimes there was bad luck. The Odéon theatre, which Chalgrin started in 1808, burnt down in 1818. Some of the more exciting objects – the Bastille elephant fountain and the Pont-Neuf obelisk – scarcely got beyond the stage of design. But Napoleon left the memory that in his day the architects and builders had a purpose. 'In the Revolution a vague energy had vainly woken the Nation up to the destruction of the arts. People had discussed a lot and produced nothing. After this crisis, Sire, I dare to say that Your Majesty ought to return the arts to the primitive simplicity that renders them great and impressive.'** Napoleon took the advice he was given. He was sensible enough to listen to the advice of his Ministers of the Interior or to his prefects of the Seine, Frochot and Chabrol, but in matters of taste he deferred usually to the artists. The expert on improving Paris was Fontaine.

---

*This is an extract from a letter written by Denon to the First Consul (see Biver, *Le Paris de Napoléon*, p. 350).
**These sayings of Napoleon are quoted in the English version of Guerrini, *Napoleon and Paris*, p. 61.

The Empire style was not one that Napoleon initiated but one to which he could respond. In architecture its elements may be found in previous styles. Many of their colleagues were like Percier and Fontaine in admiring a variety of different kinds of classic art.

Even if Napoleon had not gone to Egypt, there would have been a taste for Egyptian motifs. Students who had been to Rome knew how Baroque architect-sculptors had made use of obelisks; and in ancient Rome Caius Cestius had built his mini-pyramid to be his tomb. After 1798 the Egyptian taste became modern. In 1800 an architect proposed to put up an obelisk, complete with fake hieroglyphics, in the provincial town of Douai; and the façade of a house in one of the new Napoleonic streets, rue du Caire in Paris, was decorated with heads of the goddess Hathor, bell-shaped capitals and low-reliefs based on Egyptian temples. Durand, influential professor of architecture at the Ecole Polytechnique, designed a pyramid tomb; and obelisks, cornices with the sacred asps and blank walls are made into fea-tures of an ice-house built by another architect, Dubois, in the park of Soisy-sur-Etiolles. Egyptian columns gained even more prestige when they appeared in the portico of the Hôtel Beauharnais in Paris, then home to the sister-in-law and step-daughter of Napoleon himself.

But even if it was easy to assimilate Egyptian forms, which had affinities, espe-cially in their characteristic columns and statues, with pre-classical Greek art – Chateaubriand was only one writer to see Egypt as the founder of ancient art – Empire architects felt more at their ease among the monuments of classical ancient Greece and Rome and in the European buildings that had derived from them. In the late eighteenth century David Leroy, who was a professor at the Academy, had published a book on the monuments of Greece. Delagardette's *Ruines de Paestum* came out in 1803 and in 1809 there was a French version of Stuart and Revett's *The Antiquities of Athens*. There were books on ancient Rome, on Pompeii and Herculaneum, on Dalmatia, where Diocletian had had his enormous palace at Split; and Percier and Fontaine were enthusiasts for Renaissance Rome.

If the Academy had been abolished, the Institut had replaced it; and there was a strenuously academic tradition in the way young architects were trained. The French Academy in Rome, which had also had to close down in the 1790s, came to life again and in 1802 was installed in the Villa Medici. The Prix de Rome was as much sought after as it had been by Fontaine and Percier. To win it students were required to design an imperial palace, a building for the education of the princes of the impe-rial family, a home for the Légion d'honneur, a site for the University. They made a fair out of a collection of temples, gave Doric pillars to a Bourse and used a colon-nade surmounted by a half-dome for public baths. The designs in many cases were interchangeable. The peristyle of a Roman villa or a triumphal arch might be placed anywhere. But Percier's pupils won prizes as often as the pupils of Chalgrin or

Ledoux; and Percier allowed for originality. Percier was aware that there was a classical tradition. He and Fontaine could even insist in 1811 that French students in Rome should take the Renaissance as well as antiquity for their field of study. In their portico for the consecration of Napoleon in front of Notre-Dame they had gone so far as to use mock Gothic shapes.

The Empire architects are sometimes accused of monotony and the charge is sometimes just. Brogniart in his Empire old age built his Bourse as a temple, designed a theatre as a temple and a church as a temple. The projected palace of the Archives, to be placed on the Champ de Mars, would have consisted of four squares based on a cross placed at the centre of a square. In the Renaissance, Palladio had adapted a theme of proportions to innumerable variations. Under the Empire his most admired villa was the Villa Rotonda because each side of the building was like any other.

The Empire architects also tended to grandiloquence. The cavernous prisons of Piranesi, whose sons had come to Paris and made sure that their father's engravings stayed in print, and the pure geometric dreams of Boullée and Ledoux had left a fondness for sheer scale that infected both the Emperor and his architects. Napoleon had seen the Pyramid of Kheops and the Sphinx and his savants had been to Luxor and Karnak in Upper Egypt. The Colosseum and the baths in Rome were on the academic teaching syllabus. Napoleon's revolutionary administrative reforms which swept away the lumber of the past and his crushing victories alike called for large memorials. The Emperor dreamt of a Paris of long vistas. The Arc de Triomphe was to be the largest triumphal arch in the world, the Madeleine was much bigger than the Maison Carrée in Nîmes, no palace would compare with the combined Louvre and Tuileries or the palace of the King of Rome. If in the reign of Louis XVI peristyles had had four or six columns, under the Empire they habitually had ten or twelve.

Such buildings were apt to be stark. The hemispherical dome of the Panthéon and the parallelepipedal shape of temples were geometric ideals which no rich detail should obscure. On the relatively small Arc du Carrousel Percier showed his habitual skill in using the different textures and colours of bronze, granite and marble of three distinct types. For the much larger Arc de Triomphe, however, Fontaine argued that ornate columns would have been inappropriate. The friends had in mind that every building must be suited to its situation, each mass related to the next mass. For them proportion was part of the general theory of perspective. Just as they had grand views, so their views were long. Percier and Fontaine worked for a master who, like many dictatorial rulers before him, wished to control the landscape or the cityscape for as far as his eye could see and beyond. Not for nothing was the age of Napoleon the age when the balloon and semaphore were first used for military reconnaissance.

Percier and Fontaine were not just architects. Part of their approach to building was their belief that there existed a close link between architecture and decoration. On the Arc du Carrousel they were concerned with the colour effects of the different materials and the way that the sculpture fitted into the whole edifice. They were keen to create total works of art.

Different artists held different ideas about how interior decoration should relate to architecture. David sought for sturdy simplicity, Prud'hon for languid luxury. From the frescoes of Pompeii and Herculaneum came the tall, thin fluted columns in the bathroom and over the beds of the Hôtel de Beauharnais. By contrast majes- tic columns support a barrel vault above the Salle des Fêtes at Compiègne and the grand staircase at the Luxembourg; and few staircases are grander than those of Percier and Fontaine at the Louvre. They also knew how to give a sense of power to a chimneypiece, as in the Salle des Caryatids in the Louvre or in the bedroom of the Emperor at Fontainebleau, where the chimney is made into a triumphal arch. The taste for monumentality that they inspired descended even to those who designed shop fronts. 'There is no store which is not decorated in the antique manner and the lemonade seller in her cafe at the corner seems like Aspasia in her boudoir.'*

Great or small, these designs were made out of elementary geometric shapes. Walls or doors were divided into vertical and horizontal rectangular bars, sometimes subdivided into squares. Over doors or on ceilings there were semicircles and on ceilings circles within squares. Within rectangles on the ceiling there were often circles and lozenges and within the lozenges yet more circles. Even iron balustrades or stairways acquired a rhythm combining lozenges, circles and rectangles. This love of regularity affected the way the designers used some of their favourite motifs – rosettes, opening flowers, palm leaves. If a petal or part of a leaf curved in one direc- tion, a corresponding petal or part of a leaf curved in the opposite direction. Garlands of flowers and fruit were strewn from candelabras, from lions' heads, eagles, cupids, winged spirits, all equally stylized. The most delicate plants in nature were marshalled by art into agreeable arabesques.

Correct though the architects were in their use of the five orders of architecture, they felt free in their decorative schemes. They had long realized that Ionic and Corinthian and Composite columns used stylized leaves on capitals; and now they knew that there were other kinds of stylization on the capitals of Egyptian columns. They took to experiment. They produced Corinthian capitals without volutes or changed the acanthus leaves into palm leaves or made capitals bell-like in shape.

*The remark which refers to Aspasia in her boudoir comes from the *Journal des Dames* (see Hautecoeur, *Histoire de l'architecture classique en France*, tome V, p. 347).

As Napoleon's was a military regime, however, the laurel wreath of victory counted for more than other plants. Everywhere there were helmets, swords, trophies, shields and Amazons' skins, not only in the obvious places such as the triumphal arches and the Vendôme column but on the doors of town houses and their salons. If the master of the house loved hunting, then the arms became hunting weapons. They were balanced by instruments of peace: lyres, tambourines, pipes of Pan, cornucopias, torches, urns and vases. Among fauna, as they had been adopted by Napoleon himself, eagles and bees were common in his rooms; and lion muzzles looked out from the centre of medallions. Sinuous movements made dolphins and swans favourites with decorators. They often turned to mythical beasts – sphinxes and chimeras – to support chimneys. The classical gods supervised Napoleon's life. Jupiter watched over his sleep at the Tuileries, Apollo and Minerva encouraged his reading in the library at Malmaison, in the Salle de Vénus of the Louvre the presence of the goddess indicated that the arts were inspired by the love of Beauty, herself the lover of Mars, god of War. Fame and History announced Napoleon's glory above the chimney of his Grand Cabinet at the Tuileries, Victory crowned his efforts on the ceiling of the throne room at Saint-Cloud and in the Salon des Fleurs at Compiègne his Fortune bestrode the globe.

These various motifs were most of them familiar – even the sphinx was well known from the story of Oedipus long before Napoleon went to Egypt – but they were made generally accessible by the publication of many designs by Percier and Fontaine and by those of a provincial craftsman like Beunat. What the Empire designers gave them was a new clarity and artificiality. Every detail was easy to identify, every detail was remote from the natural world. But nothing was so significant for the ethos of the period as the way in which hangings were hung. It was Joséphine who in 1796 had first asked Jacob to make Bonaparte a wooden bed painted in green bronze under a canopy like a tent held up by lances and, for the same room, stools shaped like drums. The use of tents indoors was repeated in Joséphine's bedroom at Malmaison and in Napoleon's study at Fontainebleau. It was as though war was so much his métier that even at home he lived like a soldier. The tapestries of the Gobelins had fallen out of favour. Instead carefully draped materials – thick velvet, brocaded silk and embroidered satin – hung on walls and from ceilings and from the tops of beds. They added grace and warmth to the most severe of designs. The Empire style never lost its link to war but it remained a domestic style.

It has been calculated by an historian of Napoleon's Paris that between 1784 and 1815 he spent just over eight years, four months in the city, much of it once he was ruler of France, presumably in the Tuileries. At Saint-Cloud he spent some two years, four months, over ten months at Malmaison, over five months at Fontainebleau and between one and two months each at Trianon, Compiègne and Rambouillet.

Percier & Fontaine's grand staircase in the Musée du Louvre still preserves a sense of Napoleonic grandeur.

All in all he was over twelve years in Paris and its neighbourhood. As ruler of France he was there for about eight years.

For a soldier-monarch this is revealing. In terms of his allocation of time Napoleon was more a civilian than a man of the sword. This affected his view of the arts of peace.

The grand plans Napoleon had for Paris were scarcely begun by 1815. Even if it seemed as though for fifteen years the whole city had been one vast builder's yard, many of the larger buildings were far from completion when he left France for good; and the grandest of them all, the palace of the King of Rome, had only its foundations in place. In fourteen years he had not transformed Paris anything like as much as his nephew Napoleon III was to do in only four years more. His nephew's opening up of the city has given to Paris that sense of grandeur which he himself had wanted; and Napoleon III also managed to make bigger improvements to the quality of life in the city by building the great market of Les Halles in the centre and the huge sewerage system underneath. If Les Halles has been transformed, much more of Napoleon I's Paris has disappeared. Most of the markets and all the abattoirs have been demolished, of the fountains which were put up few are in their original site, all the stone bridges have been rebuilt or enlarged to cope with much heavier traffic. The Musée d'Orsay, like the railway station that was there before it, occupies the site of the Napoleonic Ministry of Foreign Affairs and a Napoleonic barracks. The proportions of the Napoleonic Bourse and Arc de Triomphe have been spoilt by enlargement. The palace of the Louvre has become much larger than Napoleon envisaged, but, now that it is just a museum, it has at last realized his idea for it. Of the Tuileries palace little remains. In an anti-Bonapartist frenzy the Communards fired the palace in 1871; and only the Pavillons de Flore and de Marsan, now the extremities of the Louvre, have survived in a modified form. The huge Salle des Spectacles under dome and semi-domes, the intimidating throne of Napoleon, the exquisite rooms of Joséphine and the imperial family, all are gone. In the Paris suburbs the palace of Saint-Cloud is also a memory – it was burnt down during the Franco-Prussian War in 1870 – except for its fine park. It was at Saint-Cloud that Napoleon had first seized power and at Saint-Cloud that he celebrated his marriage to Marie-Louise. Both as First Consul and as Emperor, he had always regarded the Tuileries as his principal residence – for Parisians it is associated with their quieter pleasures. In the geometrically planned walks of the Tuileries gardens they now enjoy an idle stroll or watch children cheerfully spinning on the huge carousel near rue de Rivoli. None of this has spoilt the grand Napoleonic vista that starts with Percier and Fontaine's Arc du Carrousel, once the entrance to the Tuileries, and ends at the Arc de Triomphe; and if they wish to experience neo-Napoleonic architecture, they can walk to the new entrance to the Louvre, the transparent pyramid by Pei.

Percier had officially retired as long ago as 1804, but Fontaine and other Napoleonic architects like Vignon carried on working for the restored Bourbons. Fontaine was no longer first architect – he had been made first architect of the Emperor in 1813 – he was architect of Paris, architect for the King and architect of the Duc d'Orléans. From 1815 to 1830 he worked chiefly for the Duc d'Orléans at

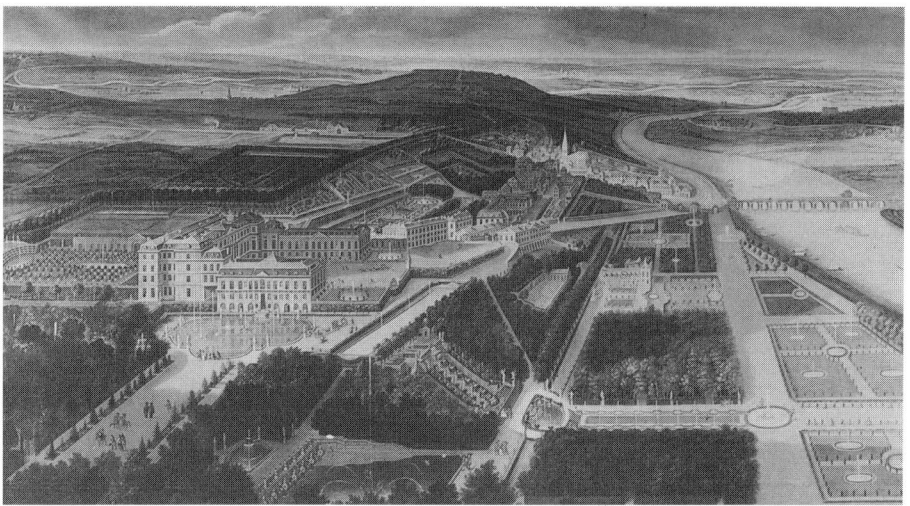

Allegrain's picture of the château de Saint-Cloud (preserved at Versailles) gives a seventeenth-century view of Napoleon's principal palace outside Paris.

the Palais-Royal and the châteaux at Neuilly and d'Eu. When in 1830 the Duc became Louis-Philippe, King of the French, this made it easy for Fontaine to carry on as royal architect. The King was a covert Bonapartist. The statue of Napoleon was replaced on top of the Vendôme column, the Pont d'Iéna got back its eagles, the Arc du Carrousel its low-reliefs; and work was begun to finish off the Arc de Triomphe. In the 1830s Fontaine was still working at the Tuileries, at Saint-Cloud and at Fontainebleau, and he was involved as consultant in the royal plans for cre-ating Louis-Philippe's historical museum at Versailles (and thus the appalling Galerie des Batailles). He survived the death of Percier in 1838 and the fall of Louis-Philippe and kept his post as architect of the Louvre and the Tuileries till 20 September 1848, the day he was eighty-six. Exactly five years later he presided over the Council of Civil Buildings for the last time. He died on 10 October 1853, and was buried in the cemetery of Père-Lachaise in the same tomb as Percier and another friend from Roman days, Bernier. In Rome the three had made a pact of friendship and vowed they would never marry, a vow they had kept. In death they were not divided. On their tomb Fontaine had a Latin inscription carved, HIC TRES IN UNUM, which for its conciseness cannot be exactly translated into English but which roughly means: Here three go (or goes) into one.

In 1821, commenting in his diary on the news of Napoleon's death on St Helena, Fontaine had written: 'It is not up to us to hazard thoughts on the causes or conse-quences of such an astonishing series of disasters. The man who was their first

Pierre Redouté worked for Joséphine at Malmaison. The best example of interior design inspired by his prints is found in the Salle des Fleurs, château de Compiègne, which was meant for Marie-Louise.

victim has finished his career on a rock, in the midst of the seas. He lives only in the memory of those who have known him and his actions belong now to the annals of History.'

For those who never knew him one way of remembering Napoleon's life is to visit the places associated with him. His glory is sensed not so much in the sombre tomb under the Invalides dome as in the palaces that still bear the impress of the *style Empire*.

Before 1810 Napoleon had spent only a few days at Compiègne. In that year he made it an official imperial palace and was there for a month. He stopped off at Compiègne *en route* for his first meeting with his fiancée Marie-Louise near Soissons, but was so impatient that in a heavy storm he took Murat and one valet and drove off through the forest in an unliveried carriage. Coming unexpectedly on his bride, he leapt into her carriage and kissed her. In a mood of slightly less impatience he had alterations made to Louis XV's château. For the sake of Marie-Louise, who had just left the noble setting of Schönbrunn, the avenue leading from the main façade was lengthened till it disappeared from view.

He spent only twenty-four more days at Compiègne, all of them in 1811. The Empire refurbishment of the palace is thus intimately connected with the first period of his second marriage, when for a brief moment Napoleon appeared to be the arbiter of Europe, defied only by Britain, which was as powerless to strike directly at him as he to strike directly at her. The dining room, painted like oyster-coloured marble, the library with its striking ormolu decorations – designed by Jacob-Desmalter – the Salon du Roi de Rome, with furniture by the same master, and the suite of rooms made for the Empress – all carefully preserve this moment. Compiègne was to have its greatest days during the Second Empire, when it became the favourite home of the Empress Eugénie. Though its forest is famed for the railway carriage where the First World War armistice was signed, Compiègne has never suf-fered from war or neglect and so preserves the glow of its resplendent past.

There is greater melancholy in the association of Napoleon with Fontainebleau. Although he thought of making sweeping changes to Versailles and was to use the Grand Trianon, Napoleon had preferred to emphasize a connection with Fontainebleau, as home to the Valois and the first Bourbon, rather than one linked to the four latest Bourbons. It was there that Napoleon first met Pope Pius VII when he was coming to Paris for the imperial coronation. It was there that after Napoleon's return from his victorious campaign in Austria Joséphine hurried over from Saint-Cloud in October 1809, only to find that the door between her bedroom and Napoleon's had been bricked in – two months later she learnt that their marriage was over. It was there finally that he abdicated on 6 April 1814; and from there two weeks later in the great courtyard he took solemn leave of the Old Guard on his way into exile on Elba. Ever since, the Cour du Cheval Blanc has been called the Cour des Adieux.

Napoleon inherited the architecture of Fontainebleau. What the Empire affected was the décor of the *petits appartements*. In Joséphine's Salon Jaune there are rectan-gular panels of gold silk and rectilinear furniture (by Jacob-Desmalter) and a rec-tangular Aubusson carpet. Her *cabinet de toilette* was fitted out with a precise attention

The château de Fontainebleau, artistically the most heterogeneous of the Emperor's palaces, contains this bedroom in pure Empire style.

to detail which reflected the Emperor's commands. Her bath was sunk so that it could be concealed when not in use by a sofa that turned into a screen when the bath was in use. Elsewhere are his bed, his camp-bed, a desk by the ubiquitous Jacob-Desmalter and the desk on which he signed his abdication.

It is, however, at Malmaison that Napoleon's presence is most intimately evoked. It was Joséphine's home, bought in his absence, and it was there that she lived after the divorce and there that she died. The attempt by Percier and Fontaine to redesign the architectural appearance of the château was frustrated by the Emperor's alarm at the thought of any more private extravagance. What they were able to do was to revamp the interior. Malmaison is not exactly as Joséphine left it. In her bedroom there are chairs from the Tuileries, probably similar to her chairs; Napoleon's famous Salle du Conseil, shaped like a tent, is a reconstruction and the chairs this time come from Saint-Cloud. The dining room, the music room and the library follow the designs of Percier and Fontaine. Although there are some incongruities – the throne of Fontainebleau is in the billiard room – the house still gives a faithful impression of its great days. The silver-gilt and enamel *surtout* on the dining-room table contains twenty-six pieces out of the 1075 given to Napoleon by the City of Paris to mark his coronation; and 'Pompeian' figures prance along the panels. In the music room are instruments that may have belonged to Joséphine and in the library are books that certainly belonged to Napoleon. Downstairs is Gérard's visionary picture of Ossian welcoming the valiant soldiers of the Emperor into Valhalla. Upstairs is a much more exact Sèvres portrayal of Napoleon and his marshals on the *Table d'Austerlitz*. Upstairs too is the bed in which Joséphine died, fittingly the work of Jacob-Desmalter, and Garnerey's watercolours of her estate.

Most of her park has gone, but what remains contains many of her roses. Percier and Fontaine were not allowed to design the garden, because she wanted not a formal French garden but a sentimental 'Chinese' (or 'English') one. Joséphine's passion for roses overrode the policy of her husband, so in 1810 the British and French admiralties co-operated to send her seeds of the new roses from China. She also employed an English nurseryman, Kennedy, who worked alongside Dupont, director of the Luxembourg gardens, to find her specimens. After her death she inspired a remarkable tribute. Between 1817 and 1824 appeared a three-volume account of *Les roses*, in which Thory's text was complemented by Redouté's coloured prints.

Possibly because Napoleon went there principally to relax, Malmaison played a special role in his life. It was while walking in the gardens that he heard the bells tolling from the nearby church of Rueil and, thinking back to his pious childhood, realized how great their impact must be on simple people and how such people must be allowed their religion. According to his secretary Bourienne, whose own hôtel in Paris is one of the finest of Empire houses, Napoleon spent some of his happiest moments there. He also experienced one of the most poignant moments. Joséphine had died while he was on Elba. Towards the end of the Hundred Days, after Waterloo, he returned to Malmaison for the last time. 'Poor Joséphine,' he said, 'I cannot get used to living here without her. I see her constantly, emerging from one of the walks, plucking one of the roses she loved so much. She was the most graceful woman I have ever set eye on.'

Fontaine was in a less sentimental mood. On 25 June he came to call on the Emperor. 'I wanted to carry out my last duties and give some token of recognition to the man I had served so long, who had been so good to me, whom I had known at the height of his power and who now, in his misfortune, was reduced to relying on the kindness of a few faithful friends. I wanted to present myself to him, but at eleven o'clock in the morning he was asleep. I came back again at one in the afternoon, but he was still asleep. As I had to hurry back to Paris, because it might be impossible for me to stay there, I left, almost relieved that I had not woken him.'

Fontaine had done his duty well. At Malmaison Napoleon had almost relaxed, softened by Joséphine's charms; and there the Empire style, which elsewhere can be grandiose and cold, was exquisitely expressed. Sentiment balanced strength.

CHAPTER 7

Imperial Fashion and the Painters' Models

VISITORS to Paris during the time of the temporary truce of Amiens were struck by the way the men strutted around like peacocks. The First Consul owed his prestige ultimately to his success as a general and he was careful to cultivate the tastes of the soldiers who had made that success possible. When in 1804 he was proclaimed Emperor, the army held first place among the ranks of his subjects; and the Empire lasted only while the lord of hosts was with it.

The change from Consulate to Empire, though instantaneous in law, was gradual in fact. Almost as soon as he became First Consul, Bonaparte had started to behave as a monarch; and as Napoleon I, Emperor of the French, he implied that he was not like the Holy Roman Emperor, soon to be demoted to mere Emperor of Austria – he was Emperor by will of the people. There was a cult of Napoleon when France was a mere republic and a cult of the great nation when France had become the heart of an Empire. All over Europe for all of fifteen years France and Napoleon were *à la mode*.

For France that was no new role, for during the eighteenth century she had set continental fashions in dress, décor and manners. Voltaire mocked the German princelings with their fancy-dress armies, the stiff ceremonial of their tiny courts and their vulgar mistresses, all of them derived from Versailles, yet Frederick the Great of Prussia and Catherine the Great of Russia corresponded with French intellectuals, in Spain the political reformers were known as *afrancesados* and even Prince Metternich, who was foreign minister of Austria from 1809 to 1848, clung to French as the language still normal in diplomacy. The prestige of all things French had been a result of the fame of Louis XIV. Now that prestige was reinforced by the fame of Napoleon. The latest fashions in Europe and even in America were set by Empire style.

The most fashionable of all those fashions was found in the fashion industry itself.

Unlike David's portrait of her, Gérard's 'Mme Récamier' (Musée Carnavalet, Paris) discloses the hostess of a famous salon as she liked to be seen.

If the appeal of Napoleon was military and masculine, the Empire line, the distinguishing feature of women's dresses, expressed the more subtle influence of Joséphine, the first and more exquisite of his two Empresses.

As Citizeness Beauharnais she had been rescued from prison by the Director Barras to become one of the three graces of Directoire fashion who cultivated an almost naked classic simplicity. The first of them, Thérèse Tallien, disappeared into social limbo after she left one lover – Barras – for another, Ouvrard the army contractor. Her fall was the work of Joséphine herself. In the winter of 1799–1800 Madame Tallien appeared at a state function at the Opéra with two friends, the three dressed as huntress-nymphs in tunics that fell just below the knee and light sandals with purple thongs. Joséphine told them such excess was intolerable – she made it clear she stood for '*bon genre*', good taste. Instinctively she was interpreting her husband's wish that French women should look decent. Morality was modish.

As the First Consul insisted on such respectability, only one person could still rival Joséphine: Juliette Récamier, the banker's wife. If Madame Tallien was notorious, Madame Récamier combined disingenuousness with diffidence, charm and sensuousness with chic. Her much-vaunted virginity, for she resisted her husband's advances if not financial, was a tease. The look of her bedroom, which was sketched by an admiring English artist, became a model to all who wished to proclaim their love in public with good taste; and she gave her name to the kind of *chaise-longue* on which she lounged. Her studied perfection is preserved in the two loveliest portraits of Consulate beauties, by David and by Gérard. As David saw her, she is ill at ease on the famous studio bed made by Jacob. Instead of the many mirrors of her apartment which reflected her refined figure there is only an antique lamp on a tripod, painted by David's young assistant Ingres, to lighten the gloom. Her *toilette*, consisting of a simple white dress, a single string of pearls and a blue hairband, is too austere. She preferred the red-cheeked, coquettish portrait by David's most worldly pupil, Gérard. As in the master's work she is barefoot and clad in a white dress with a thin strip of material just below the breasts, but this time her shoulders are uncovered and there are warm tones in the golden shawl, the russet pillars and orange-red curtain behind her – she is thus at once tantalizing and demure. Her parties, favoured by returning aristocrats and curious vistors from abroad – a more sophisticated clientèle than Bonaparte could attract – were meant to be the setting against which she would sparkle.

Madame Vigée-Lebrun, temporarily back from her stay in Russia, recalled one such occasion. 'She invited me to a grand ball, which I went to along with princess Dolgorucki, whom I had the joy of having beside me in Paris. This ball was charming. There were lots of people without any sense of disorder, there were many, many pretty women, the hôtel was very beautiful – everything was exactly as it should be. As the peace of Amiens had just been signed [the ball must have taken place in

1802] the occasion was marked by a dress sense and grandeur which the younger generation had not experienced till then. It was the first time that twenty-year-old men and women saw in Paris liveried servants in the antechambers and ambassadors in the reception rooms and distinguished foreigners, expensively dressed, decked out in their gleaming orders. Whatever you may say, this luxury was more appropriate for a ball than skirts and trousers.' In the midst of all this magnificence Juliette Récamier must have shone by reason of her simplicity.

She affected a manner that was at one extreme of a trend. Consulate ladies were reborn from first-century Rome, with a *coiffure à l'Agrippine* or *à la Phèdre*.* The bare arms, the compressed and raised bosoms, the bare throat were normal. So too was the light shift which fell straight to the knees or the feet. A corset was still rare, Engish drawers had commonly replaced underdress; and coloured satin dresses or shorter dresses in lace were held to be appropriate. Madame Récamier was a hot-house plant who needed an expensive interior. Her contemporaries took to strolling out of doors in short jackets called spencers and sometimes in sleeves and collars. They liked to wear muslin, which the First Consul disliked, for muslin came from India, now firmly under British control – Bonaparte was for forbidding the import of any products from outside France. As Emperor he would encourage the home production of cheap cotton shawls, because the fondness for cashmere that had been fostered by the Egyptian campaign had helped British trade more than French.

Under the Empire the social reign of Juliette Récamier did not last long. Late in November 1805 a panic induced by the British victory at Trafalgar caused several banks to fail, Récamier's among them. Juliette could no longer afford her snow-white modesty. Forced by relative poverty to retreat from the splendours of Hôtel Récamier to the secularized Abbaye aux Bois in rue de Sèvres, she lived out her long life largely as a widow, now the muse of the greatest writer in France (as he reassured his readers), François-René de Chateaubriand.

Even before 1806 the salon of Madame Récamier could not rank with the recep-tions of a consecrated Empress. Joséphine was unequalled in the world of fashion because fashion was made by her. The gigantic painting of the imperial coronation by David is called the *Sacre de Joséphine* (the Consecration of Josephine), since it records the moment when the Emperor, immediately after crowning himself in the presence of the Pope, is preparing to crown his wife. By his gesture and by David's brush Joséphine's dress sense was given monumental authority. While she knelt, seeming to pray, according to the Duchesse d'Abrantès, to Napoleon rather than to God, she was wearing a white satin dress, embroidered in silver, and a white velvet coat, under an immense heavy crimson velvet cloak with golden Bonaparte bees,

---

*Agrippina was mother of the Emperor Nero, Phaedra wife of the Athenian ruler Theseus and both appear in famous tragedies by Racine.

David's 'Sacre de Joséphine' (Musée du Louvre, Paris) parades Napoleon's
relationship to his wife in a setting just grand enough for him.

imperial eagles and laurel embroidered on it. Offsetting its crushing weight was her
shining, light tiara, entirely of diamonds.

Joséphine was more at ease in less formal attire. She sat for her favourite painter
Prud'hon in the park of Malmaison draped against green mossy banks, casually
wrapped in a deep red shawl, her mouth as always firmly closed to hide her poor
teeth. She made the modern concession to practicality: she wore shoes. In other ways
her Empire style was a late development out of the Consulate style. Waists were still
high, necklines were still square-cut but shoulders were now covered. She patronized the couturier Leroy, who designed gloves and shoes, fans and silk hose. She was
faithful to Napoleon's policy of wearing French fabric – tulle or gauze or silver lamé
or crêpe. Above all she favoured silk, to support the industry of Lyon, and as court
life became more elaborate she gave more scope to the embroiderers. After the
Bayeux tapestry was put on exhibition in Paris in 1806, embroidery *à la Reine
Mathilde* – Queen Matilda had been wife to William the Conqueror – was popular.
Napoleon had also been keen to revive the lace industry. At the coronation the only
lace in evidence was in the form of Alençon lace collars, but soon there were dresses
made of lace.

Because Joséphine preferred a less fussy manner than Marie-Antoinette, it was
hard for the Napoleonic fashion industry to employ as many workers as under the

Prud'hon's 'Joséphine' (château de Versailles) places the first Empress where she liked to be seen, elegant and pensive in the grounds of Malmaison.

ancien régime. But the Empire style encouraged the wearing of formal and informal dress, used a variety of textiles – all perforce native – changed with the seasons and was made familiar by journalism. *Le Journal des dames et des modes*, the *Revue du Suprême Bon Ton* and *L'élégance Parisienne* gained converts to the newest message of fashion. Nothing was, however, as effective as the appearance of Joséphine. Her immediate influence was felt at the imperial court, whether by her daughter Hortense, who adored her, or by her sisters-in-law, Elisa, Pauline and Caroline, who loathed her. When Hortense became Queen of the Netherlands, the three Bonaparte princesses ruled somewhere in Italy, Joseph her brother-in-law some time in Spain and her brother-in-law Jérôme some time in Westphalia, and as Jérôme's

In 1806 Ingres exhibited this portrait of Madame Rivière, with portraits of her husband and daughter. The three paintings, in the Louvre, reveal the glamour of Empire society.

first wife was an American who after her divorce returned home, Joséphine's style became international. Her gracious manner, which contrasted so favourably with the boorish manners of her husband, had the effect of making her look more alluring. Glittering on grand occasions in her favourite ensemble of jewels known as a *parure* (consisting of a comb, a bandeau, necklace, earrings and an ornament for the belt), she moved elegantly in her free-flowing dresses, usually white and so contrasting with the unmixed colours of her shawl, her coat or her hat. Other women might go on campaign with their husbands and take to epaulettes on their shoulders, corsets round their torsos and more solid shoes or boots on their feet. Even in her heyday other women could affect their own particular style. Madame Rivière, as seen by Ingres in 1805, looks ready to fall into the lap of the beholder like a succulent peach. Joséphine was always exotic and more remote, like one of the rarer roses in her beloved gardens. After her, Napoleon's second wife, for all her Habsburg blood, was a luscious pear, healthy and common. Before the marriage had been celebrated, it had been consummated. Marie-Louise gave him the heir he wanted but took away the sure sense of style Joséphine had given his court. If she went to Joséphine's hair-dresser, she was copying Joséphine's choice. By 1814, when she died at the age of fifty-one, Joséphine was no longer a beauty. Marie-Louise, barely out of her teens, had never been one. In her portraits she is well, expensively dressed; and the paint-ers could find in her no trace of poetry.

The tendency of women's dress to become more masculine had accomplished some-thing of a crossover in fashion in imperial France. The cut-away overcoat known as the *redingote* (a corruption of the English riding coat) was adapted to women for outdoor wear. By contrast men, having tried plebeian dress in the time of the *sans-culottes* and rejected the antique favoured by the circle of David and the actor Talma, opted for more glamour.

Among men the *redingote* had been at the height of its popularity in the period of the Consulate. In Paris the most notable change in fashion, however, was the formal-ity introduced by the First Consul, who prescribed as correct dress for men at the Tuileries palace short breeches with hose and shoes with buckles. Every government official from the First Consul down had a specially designed uniform. Ministers wore two coats, one red, one blue, with silver oak leaves embroidered on them. Councillors of State wore a dark blue coat with sky-blue embroidery. Senators had cloth or blue velvet coats with gold embroidery and vests embroidered in silver thread. The Consuls themselves cut the most splendid figures of all. For ordinary occasions they were dressed in white velvet coats with gold embroidery and blue long breeches and small boots. The dress uniform involved blue velvet coats, adorned with gold embroidery, white trousers and short boots. In Ingres's Liège por-trait of Bonaparte, the First Consul wears an embroidered crimson velvet double-breasted cut-away coat and knee-breeches.

Such frippery was as nothing compared to the costumes that Napoleon donned for his coronation as Emperor, which Isabey the miniaturist designed. For outside Notre-Dame there was a *petit costume*. It was, however, the grand costume for the interior of the cathedral which revealed Napoleon in all his magnificence. An ample red velvet imperial robe meant to recall imperial Rome was speckled with gold bees, sprigs of laurel, olive and oak leaves surrounding the letter N and lined with ermine. The robe opened at the left shoulder to reveal the imperial sword, held by a white satin sash, richly embroidered in gold braid. Underneath was a long white satin

David's 'Comte de Nantes' (Musée Jacquemart-André, Paris) enjoys the official costume of an ennobled civilian.

tunic embroidered with gold braid, white embroidered stockings and satin sandals. On the velvet of the imperial robe, underneath his lace collar and cravat, shone the grand collar of the Legion of Honour. The Emperor crowned himself with a gold laurel-leaf crown and held in his left hand a sceptre and in his right hand the staff of Justice. If David's representation of him in Notre-Dame is better known than any other, it is Ingres who most exactly conveyed the grandeur of his presence, a grandeur that his old republican friends regarded as politically incorrect and which the painter was unjustly blamed for revealing.

The inspiration for the ceremonial costume of his courtiers was the Emperor's *petit costume*: a knee-length mantle, a coat, a waistcoat, knee-breeches, a lace cravat and a plumed hat. In attendance the French princes wore white velvet, the Grand Elector (Joseph Bonaparte) poppy red, the Archchancellor of the Empire (Cambacérès) purple, the Archchancellor of State (Eugène de Beauharnais) light blue, the High Constable (Louis Bonaparte) medium blue, the marshals deep blue and the admiral dark green.

The Empire maintained its love affair with lavish costume even after the coronation. At court men wore *habits à la française* (a coat, waistcoat, knee-breeches, silk stockings, pumps). Among men at court, apart from Napoleon's youngest brother

Jérôme (who went with his wardrobe to become the King of Westphalia) and his brother-in-law Murat (who took his to become the King of Naples), the greatest popinjays were the marshals off duty – Ney spent more than 12,000 francs on each dress uniform – and their rivalries were good for the embroiderers. They kept Picot in business in Paris and Bony in Lyon.

Napoleon's whole policy aimed to encourage men to be aware of their clothes. He imposed uniforms on civilians. At the Collège Napoleon every student wore a dark, austere costume.

Those civilians who held official positions enjoyed more elaborate clothes. Though once a republican, the man who became François, Comte de Nantes and a Councillor of State took evident pleasure in the way that David painted him in his blue and silver embroidery and his magnificent taffeta sash. Away from the Tuileries others, especially young men, wanted to ignore Napoleon's wishes and were able to do so. Coats were shorter than he liked them, the head just emerged from the cravat and the collar reached to the ears. Because men still liked to show off a well-shaped calf, breeches were still as common as trousers. Boots were favoured; and around 1811 hussar boots with tight trousers became modish. Fashion followed its own whims regardless of the wishes of the Emperor. But for its high-standing collar the *redingote* began to look more like the modern overcoat. Towards the end of the Empire single-breasted *redingotes* made their reappearance. Their collars and lapels imitated the military look; and in winter collar and facings were made of astrakhan fur (a reminder that the Empire had come to dominate eastern Europe). No man could avoid the fact that the ethos of the Empire was created by soldiers.

There were subtle ways of downplaying their role. The top hat was distinctively civilian; and in 1803 silk top hats came in. Around the same time young men began to cultivate despair; they adopted a pallid expression and went around with permanently half-shaved beards. Their subtle revenge on the men of war was to aim for a feminine grace in their way of dress.

Napoleon wanted his soldiers to be smart. He had made his name directing the Army of Italy, whose troops were ill clad and unkempt; and the forces he had left behind in Egypt came back dressed in all the hues of Egyptian cloth ranging from scarlet and crimson to brown, green, violet and light blue. For the textile workers of France he wanted work: for the men of the Grande Armée he wanted uniformity and panache.

The armies of the French crown, like any eighteenth-century army, were both patriotic and aristocratic. Their infantry wore white to distinguish them from the infantry of their competitors. During revolutionary wars the citizen-soldiers felt free to dress as they pleased, sometimes with reference to the blue, white and red of the

Napoleon would have not liked to think that Géricault's 1814 'Wounded cuirassier' (Musée du Louvre, Paris) was a typical imperial soldier.

tricolour, just as they felt free to be insubordinate and individualistic. Napoleon wished to retain the revolutionary sense of initiative while restoring the sense of order. He brought back the office of Marshal which had been abolished in 1793 and created the Imperial Guard to be the army élite. What affected the whole army was first the reorganization that Napoleon carried through during the years of the Consulate and secondly the steady succession of victories between 1805 and 1812. The new enlarged army, the Grande Armée, was divided into seven corps, each made up of varying numbers of regiments of infantry, cavalry and artillery, so that each corps was a little army that could act on its own or as part of a large machine. As erstwhile enemies were turned by defeat into allies, they might find themselves fighting alongside French colleagues. In such circumstances the details of uniform were of great importance because uniform gave a soldier his identity. In 1804 Napoleon ordered a survey of views on uniform. It was decided that coat-tails and gaiters should be shorter, trousers should replace breeches, an alternative should be found to the cheap blue coat that was being issued and the infantry's hats should be changed. Of these recommendations the last two were the most radical.

The revolutionary blue colour of the coat was unfortunate. The only reliable dark-blue dye was indigo, most of which came from Bengal (British), Java (Dutch) or central America (Spanish); and all of these sources were blocked off by the British navy. In 1805 and 1806 Napoleon authorized a return by the infantry to royalist white, but this caused confusion (the Saxons wore white), made all wounds seem fatal and was mocked by republican veterans as the uniform of a clown. In 1807 Napoleon decided to keep blue coats, but it was to be some years before the supply of white ran out; as late as 1811 the Emperor had to order one regiment to abandon its white; and in 1814, when there was a scramble for any form of uniform, some infantrymen were delighted to find that the supply of white coats was not yet exhausted.

A fundamental change occurred in 1806 when the cylindrical shako replaced the *bicorne*, the two-horned cocked hat, as standard headgear. The shako might look less jaunty than the *bicorne*, which could be worn at any angle and remained popular with rakish officers, but it was made of strong felt or leather and protected the skull from sabre cuts and rifle butts. It was soon decorated with a variety of plumes – scarlet or red for the grenadiers and carabiniers, yellow, green and red for the *voltigeurs* – and an extra-tall shako was invented by aides-de-camp around 1810. The height of chic was to imitate the hussars and wear a conical shako, the *mirliton*, adorned with a huge plume and coloured *flamme* that passed through cords holding a cockade and ending in elaborate tassels.

Not all infantrymen stuck, as the light infantry stuck, to the shako: grenadiers went in for bearskin hats. Here again the economic results of Napoleonic policy spoiled artistic effects. There were not enough bears left in Scandinavia and too many bears were inaccessible because they were North American bears and therefore available only to smugglers. In 1812 the Russian bears proved even more resistant to French advances.

The cavalry also had its moments of experiment. Dragoons, who fought both on horse and on foot, traditionally wore green coats. One regiment was asked to change this to try out sky blue but after a short while the idea lost favour, leaving some impoverished officers incorrectly dressed. In 1811 a new group of cavalrymen, the lancers, was created from the dragoons. The Polish lancers were allowed to keep one piece of distinctive national costume, the *czapska* helmet.

Napoleon's most practical innovation in cavalry costume was bringing back the body armour known as the *cuirasse*. This was made from hammered steel. A large frontpiece protecting the chest was connected to a backplate by shoulder straps and a belt. Padding was used to prevent the uniform from being rubbed. The uniform of the cuirassiers proved so successful that after the Austrian campaign of 1809 Napoleon extended the use of the *cuirasse* to the Carabiniers. Both kinds of heavy cavalry had their gorgeous helmets which went through various styles. Napoleon declared that he wanted the Carabiniers' uniform to be as beautiful as their armour; and one detachment impressed one young German, Carl Schehl, so much that he called them the most beautiful regiment he had ever seen, joined them as a bugler and marched off with them to Russia – and came back.

Nobody compared in glamour with the Hussars. An officer in the Hussars put on 156 buttons of five different kinds. His costume lived up to its exotic Hungarian origins. He wore a shako, a dolman, a *pelisse*, braided waistcoats, a sash and a *sabre-tache* hanging from his sword-belt (the last was very useful, for it could hold maps and dispatches and serve as a lap-desk). Like an officer of the Chasseurs, he often wore the colback, a headpiece of Turkish origin which had passed to France from the Austrians. From 1806 a single-breasted coat with long tails, the *frac*, replaced the dolman, but some hussar regiments tenaciously held to their traditional uniform right up to 1813. Then all the glamour in the world could not stop them from being crushed at Leipzig by the superior forces of their continental foes.

The artillery, Napoleon's own branch of the army, was less flamboyantly dressed. All of them wore blue with red trim. The horse artillery wore steel grey. Similarly the military bandsmen – the trumpeters, horn players, fifers, drummers, master drummers and drum majors – were restricted by the 1812 regulations to one colour, in their case green. This regulation could not be put into force till after the Russian campaign was over.

Dating from 1804, the Imperial Guard was like a microcosm of the whole Grande Armée. From 8000 in 1805 it grew to be a force of 65,000 by 1812. Its infantry originally consisted of a regiment of foot grenadiers and one of foot chasseurs. Regiments were added: a Middle Guard of fusilier-grenadiers and fusilier-chasseurs, a Young Guard of sharp-shooters. In 1806 the Grand Cavalry got a regiment of dragoons and in 1807 a regiment of Polish light cavalry and a regiment of *chevaux-léger* lancers, then in 1813 one regiment of Guide-grenadiers, one of Guide-dragoons and one of Guide-lancers. The basic uniform was a blue coat with white facings, a plumed bearskin bonnet at eye level and tight-fitting white gaiters. The 1806 dragoons wore an eagle ornament and a green coat with white facings, the Polish light cavalry had *czapskas*, blue *kurtkas* and crimson trousers, the lancers of 1807 were in red and those of 1813 in blue. The Guide-grenadiers were dressed *à la hussarde* in a black shako or colback, a green dolman with white braid and red breeches and the Guide-dragoons wore red shakos, green tunics and grey trousers with red stripes. If the whole Grande Armée was polychromatic and ostentatious, the Guard was at its gaudy heart.

Acts of killing do not require that the killer should be well groomed or handsome; indeed, the most efficient killers have often been dirty, dishevelled, sweaty, shabby, ugly and ill dressed. At the end of the nineteenth century the British were to learn in South Africa that their beautiful uniforms hindered their guerrilla campaign against the Boers; and in Napoleon's time the French were given the same hard lesson in remote mountainous valleys of Spain and southern Italy and on the freezing plains of Russia. Fancy costume was good for morale; winning victories was even better.

The chemical technology of the French textile industry could not make dyes fast. Blue dyes exposed to sun or rain turned to green or purple; over the years yellow dyes faded away altogether; and scarlet lost its brilliance. It was hard to distinguish between shades of bright yellow, golden orange, orange and fawn. Since linen and cotton could be washed, rather oddly white was the most practical colour to wear for dirty work.

The state of the uniforms depended on the good faith and good management of the *capitaine d'habillement*. If he was unreliable, clothes might be small, short, tight, badly cut, badly sewn – he had to be able to gain the co-operation of a good contractor, who was himself subject to the pressures caused by the slow arrival of payment from the War Ministry, the slovenly methods of his workers, the sheer magnitude of the task; and there were always the incentives of fraud. Even Napoleon, who took as much interest in the minutiae of his soldiers' appearance as a modern sergeant-major, could not oversee everything.

For parades Napoleon could insist on neat and attractive uniforms. During long campaigns, however, boots and shoes wore out, clothes were taken off the bodies of dead comrades or dead foes; and only occasionally was there a windfall, as when after the 1809 Austrian campaign Napoleon was able to re-equip his men from better-made Austrian costumes.

Soldiers also had ways of treating their orders in ways that suited themselves. They discarded their woollen breeches for cotton trousers in the heat of a continental summer and tried to get them back in the cold of a continental winter. They found a use for their shakos as receptacles for booty or food or as bungs to block holes in the defensive system of a wall. In Moscow, Napoleon encouraged the Guard to grab as many fur waistcoats as they could find; some marshals authorized the seizure of sheepskins; in practice, however, the soldiers who were best prepared for the long return march to Germany and France were those who had been able to take fine nobles' furs or sturdy peasants' boots. No more than Hitler could Napoleon provide adequate clothing for a Russian winter. As in late 1812, so again in early 1814 the rules of survival overrode all other concerns. In 1815 the Emperor found that his men looked as ragged as they had done in 1796. Had he won at Waterloo, he might have had time to make them look smart again.

INFANTERIE DE LIGNE

Officier | *Deuxième Porte-Aigle*

One of Carle Vernet's 1812 pictures of military costume of the line infantry must have been more to Napoleon's taste than the reality had been.

Only the painters could make them appear as magnificent as Napoleon wanted them to be. In 1812 the artist Carle Vernet published a series of illustrations of the uniforms of the Grande Armée as they never were. Shortly after Waterloo his son Horace Vernet began to paint battles of the Grande Armée as they had never been.

The true part of the Napoleonic legend concerning military costume involves the Emperor himself. In careful contrast to the plumes and sashes and braided waist-coats and swishing cloaks of his crack troops, and above all to avoid the lavish spend-ing of marshals like Ney, Murat and Marmont on clothes, Napoleon opted for simplicity.

He was proud of the way David portrayed him in his study in 1812, dressed as a colonel of the Foot Grenadiers, in a blue uniform with white facings. This uniform he kept for Paris. On the march he preferred the green cavalry uniform of a colonel of the Chasseurs *à cheval*. Accounts for 1811 show that he had one uniform of each kind delivered to him every six months: the grenadier's on 1 January and 1 July, the Chasseur's on 1 April and 1 October. But the most famous parts of his military dress were his heavy grey calf-length overcoat, made of wool cloth at Louviers, and his *bicorne* hat, which unlike others he always wore not *en colonne* (facing from front to back) but *en bataille* (facing from side to side). It was easy for Napoleon to see that he must look distinctive. It was a sign of his acute psychology that he also realized that he should look dull.

There were grand state occasions when he knew he had to take on the style fitting anyone's idea of an Emperor: at his imperial coronation in 1804, at his royal corona-tion in 1805 as King of Italy, when he wore a gold embroidered robe of green velvet, and at his second marriage in 1810, when he was dressed in an *habit à la française* of crimson velvet with gold embroidery. In his will he left two crimson robes with waistcoats and breeches to the two brothers closest to him in age, Joseph and Lucien. Everything else went in the end to his principal heir (after the death of the King of Rome): Louis-Napoleon, the only surviving son of his brother Louis and Joséphine's daughter Hortense, the future Napoleon III. Napoleon's grandest cos-tumes can be seen in museums at Milan and Fontainebleau, but he is remembered as he would have it, swathed in a grey coat, with a *bicorne* on his head.

CHAPTER 8

Imperial Artists: Painters and Sculptors

IT MAY BE surprising that someone as uninterested in costume as Napoleon
should have such an influence on the way people in France dressed. He was
aware that the contrast between his own simple uniform and the ostentatious
style affected by so many of his marshals indicated their subordination to him. He
had insisted on more modest women's clothes in a period of his life when he was
repeatedly unfaithful to the one woman he loved: Joséphine. He was also anxious to
provide work for the textile factories in Lyon, near Paris and in the north-east, which
provided most of the clothes that his French subjects wore. But fashion as such was
of no concern to him. Fashion by its nature concerns what is passing; Napoleon
worked for what would survive.

Towards the arts of painting and sculpture, however, Napoleon had a different
attitude. Naturally he wanted to give artists work. He also wanted them to work for
him. Even if he did not have an eye for beauty, he had an eye for detail. He was also
conscious that his reputation depended on the way men and women saw him. Before
1789 the Bourbons had exercised a certain control over their artists. The greatest
Bourbon, Louis XIV, had used artists' services for propaganda, to publicize his
greatness, firstly to his courtiers and secondly to his people. Napoleon wanted his
artists to perform a similar service for him, to record his civic achievements and above
all his military triumphs – over the third coalition at Ulm and Austerlitz, over
Prussia at Jena-Auerstädt, over Russia at Friedland, over Austria at Wagram. Even
the setbacks, like the bloody drawn battle of Eylau, could be turned into examples
of Napoleon's mercy; his mistakes at Marengo became a sign of his wonderful good
luck; Trafalgar played no role in the story of the Empire, just as Acre was irrelevant
to the story of Napoleon. Bonapartist artists of the future might dwell on the retreat
from Moscow or Napoleon's farewell to the Guard in the Cour des Adieux at
Fontainebleau. His artists did no such thing – he was unmoved by pathos.

Napoleon inherited from the Directory the exhibition of the arts known as the Salon. Traditionally this event had been biennial, but under the Directory there had been Salons in 1796 (as well as in 1795), in 1798 and in 1799; and in the first years of the Consulate the Salons were annual (in 1800, 1801 and 1802) before settling back into the biennial rhythm, which lasted till the end of the Empire.

Though there were never many architects who submitted their designs or engravers who submitted their prints, the numbers of sculptors to show their statues rose towards the end of the Empire (up to sixty-two in 1812) and the number of painters rose dramatically (up to 433 in 1812). This meant that at the moment when Napoleon was suffering his worst humiliation (in Russia), his Parisian subjects were given the chance of appreciating the effects of his beneficent patronage in the form of over 150 sculptures and over 1000 paintings.

Napoleon was keen to operate a system similar to what had operated under the *ancien régime* of the arts; and he wanted prizes to be given to his artists to celebrate ten years of his rule (in 1810). Everyone (including Napoleon) knew who was the greatest painter in France: Jacques-Louis David. Oddly placed only second in the class of history painters (for *The Intervention of the Sabine Women*), David was ranked first in the class of those who had represented a subject honouring the national character. He was now the Emperor's man.

Inevitably the picture for which David was so honoured was the *Sacre de Joséphine*. David had changed a lot since he had been a fiery Jacobin. His need for heroism, which he had renounced when Robespierre his idol had deserted him, had been revived by the sight of young Bonaparte; and he had glamorized the victor of Marengo in the various versions of his hero crossing the Alps. In 1789 he had painted Rome's first consul Brutus sacrificing family to the *patrie*; and in 1799 he tolerated the seizure of power by a First Consul in France. 'We are not virtuous enough to be republicans,' he sighed. Though David might have lost his personal taste for ruthless behaviour, he was no liberal. If he had had the courage to express his disapproval of the wholesale rape of the art treasures of Italy, which had become a fixed policy with the Directors and Napoleon, that was less on moral than on aesthetic grounds. He was weary of the strains of the revolutionary years. He wanted to be free to paint and free to be rich.

On his return from Egypt, Napoleon had come to visit the painter in his studio and had commented on the canvas of the almost-finished *Sabine Women*. According to his grandson and biographer, Jules David, Napoleon had remarked that David's soldiers did not fight as modern ones fought, to which David replied that he had painted heroes of antiquity. Napoleon was not impressed – he mimicked a bayonet thrust to prove his point – and advised David to make changes. When he left, David

Leonidas and his soldiers at Thermopylae faced certain defeat and death at the hands of the Persians. The picture (Musée du Louvre, Paris) enabled David to paint as men had lived at Sparta. Napoleon did not want to know.

told his students 'these generals understand nothing of painting', but his grandson makes clear that he was hurt. Napoleon did not soothe David's feelings when he next came to see him, in 1800. By then David was about to try out his new 'Greek' style on a Greek theme: *Leonidas at Thermopylae*. Napoleon told him on this occasion that it was a waste of time painting a group of defeated men; and David protested that these men had died for their *patrie* and helped to repel the Persians from Greece for a thousand years. Unlike the First Consul, he could see dignity in defeat. Fifteen years on, it was an attitude that would sustain him in exile abroad with better grace than Napoleon showed on St Helena. Besides, when he was asked to work for Napoleon, he did not abandon his work on *Leonidas*.

According to his grandson, David was invited to have a seat on the Council of State or in the Senate. According to Fontaine he was invited to give his opinion on architectural projects. Both offers he declined: he was determined to be just a painter. Now he no longer aspired to be a dictator of the arts. In 1800, without consulting him, the First Consul announced that David was to be government painter. David turned the post down. He much preferred to devote himself to *Napoleon crossing the Saint-Bernard* in the footsteps of Hannibal and the Emperor Charlemagne. The first version was done for Charles IV of Spain, but the copies were made at the express order of Napoleon, who had been reluctant to pose but was delighted with his new image. David's reward was to be named Chevalier de la Légion d'honneur in 1803 and in 1804, soon after Napoleon became Emperor, First Painter. Delécluze says that he wore his Legion of Honour medal for the rest of his life. In 1808 he was granted the right to bear arms. By then he had made it plain that he expected to be well paid.

In 1803 he wrote to ask for 24,000 francs for the two copies of *Napoleon crossing the Saint-Bernard*. In 1805 he wrote to ask for 94,000 francs for a great succession of projects: the *Sabine Women* (which, oddly, he thought Napoleon would like to own), a portrait of the Pope (with two copies) and an advance on the great work he had started, his life-size portrayal of the imperial coronation. Eventually he expected 100,000 francs for the last painting. It was to be the first of a series of four scenes, the others of which would be an *Enthronement*, the *Distribution of the eagles* and the *Reception at the Hôtel de Ville*. He would be willing, he conceded, to accept 100,000 francs for each. In the end the commissions for two of them were cancelled and he finished only the coronation picture and the *Distribution of the eagles*. Napoleon liked to be glorified. He also liked to save money and David never got all he asked for. What upset him more, perhaps, was his failure to become to the Emperor what Lebrun had been to Louis XIV, the overseer of all art. He was the most distinguished artist in Napoleonic France, but Napoleon did not accept his argument that David should glorify him by running the arts in France. In this Napoleon was wiser than David understood, for he forced the painter to concentrate on doing what he did best: glorifying Napoleon by painting him.

Before working on his coronation painting, David was told by Napoleon to paint two preliminary portraits of the principal actors at the ceremony: the Pope, Pius VII, and (for Genoa) the Emperor in his new finery. David was no Christian but he had fond memories of Rome and during the sittings with Pius he came to have a warm affection for the Pope. The Emperor's portrait, of which only an oil sketch survives, he assigned to an assistant – it seems to have been a routine exercise, stilted, lifeless and dull. Napoleon did not like it and would not send it to Genoa. As usual, he had not been willing to pose for David – it was his fault if the work had lacked any sense of personal presence.

David took much greater care with his grand scene. His ex-pupil Gérard probably suggested to him that the crowning of Joséphine by her husband would be the most suitable moment to record; as she and Napoleon had just made their vows again in a private religious ceremony of marriage the day before, Napoleon's public investiture of his wife as Empress had a special poignancy for her. In Notre-Dame

David was commissioned to paint Pius VII. They liked each other enough for the arch-anticlerical to paint the Pope with sympathy (Musée du Louvre, Paris).

her mother-in-law had not been present; in the painting she is a prominent witness. In Notre-Dame her sisters-in-law had sulked at the thought of carrying her train; in the painting they stand behind her, tranquil and demure. David did not mind falsi-fying history. What he aimed to capture was the spirit of the occasion as Napoleon might conceive it. The austere background of the huge bare flats, put up to conceal the Gothic architecture of the chancel, the precise studies of the faces, whether of the Bonapartes (but not of brother Lucien, who was self-exiled in Italy) or of the Beauharnais, of ladies-in-waiting like Madame de la Rochefoucauld and of courti-ers like Talleyrand and even of David himself (painted by Isabey), the wonderful skill with which David conveyed the diverse textures of military and civilian male dress and of female fashion, including the sparkle of the jewellery, and above all the organizing power that subordinates the manifold activities of a large crowd to one central action – these characteristics of the *Sacre de Joséphine* give it an epic quality. Here was history made permanent. Napoleon was delighted. 'It is good, Monsieur David, I am well pleased.' The painter had given him an almost feminine grace as he raised the crown tenderly above the kneeling Joséphine. Napoleon told David he had understood his thoughts: 'you have made me a French knight'.

Technically the *Sacre de Joséphine* is one of David's most brilliant works, yet it also lacks the histrionic conviction of the revolutionary works painted between *The Oath of the Horatii* and *The death of Marat*. David was no convinced monarchist. He had seen too much to be taken in by glamour, nor was he carried along by a surge of

David's 'Distribution of the eagles' (château de Versailles) records the cere⁄
mony after the coronation that was staged to ensure the army's loyalty to its new
Emperor.

emotion. He was only too aware how careful he must be not to offend his sitters'
susceptibilities. Louis Bonaparte was angry because he was obscured by Joseph, so
David had to paint more of him into the picture. The *Sacre* is not a pure documen⁄
tary nor does it transcend the role of anecdote. Magnificent though it is, it is too
literal⁄minded to be moving.

A similar judgement can be made on the other enormous painting, less well
known, that commemorated an event which occurred three days after the coronation:
The Distribution of the eagles. On the Champ de Mars in front of the Ecole Militaire,
sumptuously decorated by Percier and Fontaine, in the presence of the imperial
family, the Army and National Guard of the Empire took an oath of loyalty to
Napoleon. As symbols, eagles were carried by colonels of the regiments (for the
Army) and the presidents of the departments (for the National Guard). 'Soldiers,'
Napoleon declared, 'these are your standards, these eagles help to rally you. They will
always be where your emperor will judge them essential for the defence of his throne
and his people; you will swear to sacrifice your lives to defend them and contribute to
maintain them by your courage and the road to victory. You swear it, we swear it.'
Racing forward, the soldiers with one voice shouted out, 'We swear.'

Once again David was painting an oath scene and he felt able to revert to classical allusions, so in his first version of 1808 he included a Winged Victory showering laurels on the serried ranks of oath-taking soldiers beneath. The Emperor asked him to remove it. He also instructed David to remove Joséphine, for by 1810, when the picture was completed, she was no longer his wife. Instead of developing his earlier coherent design David was more intent now on emphasizing the lavish military costumes – the plumes in the hats, the cut of the jackets, the gold braid, the shining brass – and the bustle of the deputies reaching forward with extravagant gestures. Above them, serene and remote, Napoleon extends his hand, acknowledging, even blessing his men. No longer just their supreme commander, he had become the focus of their life. This was the last of the rhetorical pictures of the Emperor that David produced.

There was to be one last, more subtle encomium of Napoleon. In 1812 David portrayed *Napoleon in his study*. This time he aimed at intimacy. Napoleon stands alone in his study, his right hand in his waistcoat over his portly belly, in front of his desk, where the low-burning and extinguished candles indicate that it is night. The clock against the wall is set at 4.13 a.m. Papers tumble on to his chair, on which his sword dangles, its strap hanging from the handle. Rolled up on top of the pile is a scroll headed 'CODE', referring to the Napoleonic codification of the law. Behind the Emperor, to his left, his quill pen is prominent on the desk. He may be wearing green military dress, with decorations, but he is also the civilian ruler of his people. 'You have understood me, my dear David,' he told the painter, 'in the night I am occupied with the happiness of my subjects and during the day I work for their glory.'

The Emperor was glad that the painting had been commissioned by '*un anglais*', Lord Douglas, and liked it for exemplifying his idea of the role of art – the skilful representation of physical objects – and must have noticed how cleverly David was indulging in flattery, unless he was already losing his cool sense of reality. The painting is a masterpiece of political theatre, a soliloquy involving the protagonist and his audience without the intervention of the chorus. But so adept is David at planning the setting and lighting of his hero – consequences of his Neo-Classical training – that such terms seem inappropriate. *Napoleon in his study* looks as contemporary as any figure from a chronicle of the times, though the Emperor's face shows no trace of fatigue. His watchfulness had left him serene, clear-eyed and alert.

David knew that all was not well. Delécluze remembered that at this period he sometimes criticized the Emperor to his students, thinking his hero had too warlike a temperament and that, as head of a new dynasty, he was at least as absolute in his intentions as the heads of the old one. Besides, for all his worldly success David had not forgotten his ideal of 'painting as men lived at Sparta'. In 1814, after Napoleon's abdication and at the same time as the Salon, he showed privately *Leonidas at Thermopylae*, his tribute to noble men who were about to die for an ideal of freedom.

'Napoleon in his study' (National Gallery, Washington) pleased the Emperor more than any other portrait of himself by David. It emphasised his hard work and his calm.

He was now unhappy working in the Neo-Classical mode; and the saga of his one truly Spartan picture ended in an artistic defeat as decisive as the military defeat of his own Leonidas. The picture, beautiful though it is as a study of the male nude and clear in its organization, has about it the air of the studio where he exhibited it. It is mannered and frigid. By then such an exercise was out of date. At the Prix décennal in 1810 the *Sabine Women* had been harshly judged, yet David persisted with his 'Greek' style. Itr was a sign that he was ageing. He could not adapt to change, above all to political change.

The change that he found hardest to accept was the Bourbon Restoration. When Louis XVIII came back in 1814, David lay low. But during the Hundred Days, when Louis had fled to Belgium, Napoleon came to visit him. David was touched and took an oath of loyalty to his Emperor. The 1815 Restoration seemed to him the end of his era in France. He had approved the death of Louis XVI, the new king's brother; he had been a Jacobin and, with reservations, a Bonapartist; he was ban-ished and, after chatting to his students for one last time, took his leave. Pope Pius VII, who received so many Bonapartes and Bonapartists in Rome, was willing to accept him, but the Pope's allies would not allow him to go there. The King of Prussia begged him to come to Berlin as director of fine arts, but he preferred the invitation of the King of the Netherlands to live in Brussels. Some friends, like Madame Récamier, and artists and students, above all Gros, tried to help him to return to Paris. He could not, would not come. He urged Gros, who had made his name painting contemporary scenes, to attempt 'history' painting, the classical themes. He thus encouraged Gros on a way to artistic failure. His own history paint-ing became ever more coldly erotic: only in portraiture did he remain a great artist. The huge, now embarrassing Napoleonic pictures remained in France, yet a greater work, *The death of Marat*, is housed in a Brussels gallery, not the Louvre. That one picture gives Belgians more evidence than Frenchmen that in response to events he had once painted great art. His judgement was often unsound, but he had a certain ideal of what a hero was like.

It was Jean-Antoine Gros, David's most faithful ex-pupil, who best captured the movement and dash that Napoleon wished to emphasize. He had been born two years after Napoleon, in 1771, and he belonged to the same generation. His father was an artist from Toulouse, he was the docile sort of boy who followed a family tradition and he became David's pupil in 1785 and then a student at the Academy two years later. Like all ambitious young artists he hoped to win the Prix de Rome, but he failed to do so and did not know what next to do in France as the progress of the revolution made a normal artistic career impossible. He turned for help to his former master, who was preoccupied with politics, as it was about the time that

Louis XVI was guillotined. David prided himself on loyalty to his students. In later years he was to regret his failure to do anything to save his republican pupil Topino-Lebrun from execution for designing the daggers with which conspirators planned to knife the First Consul. What Gros asked on this occasion was obtained with ease; and immediately he had a passport, he set out for Italy.

It was not the best moment for a young Frenchman to arrive in Rome. The tactless behaviour of the French students in the city, the anticlerical violence of the republicans back home and then the murder by rioters of Basseville, the French representative, meant that all Frenchmen except for enemies of the revolution hurried to leave. Gros was not interested in politics, but he wanted to save his skin, so he based himself on Florence and then on Genoa, where life was quiet. He had not had time to be seduced, like David before him, by the lure of Roman antiquity and Raphael. In Genoa he could study some Flemish masterpieces, for there young Rubens and young Van Dyck had painted nobles in stiff, formal, black attire, had rendered the costumes with panache and brought their sitters to life. Gros loved sparkling textures, flamboyant gestures and bold touches of paint. From 1794 to 1796 he had to concern himself with portraits, many of them miniatures, of anyone he could find. Then in 1796 Bonaparte swept into Italy and, once his success was assured, asked his wife to join him. Joséphine came by sea and landed in her turn at Genoa. Introduced to Gros, she rapidly decided that he was the man to paint her husband. Gros considered her as 'his fairy godmother, the good fairy of my future', but Bonaparte he found cold and severe. His famous portrait of the general, made possible only because Joséphine clasped Bonaparte on her knee, convinced even the reluctant subject that there was something to be said for art. Bonaparte also thought that Gros would do as an agent in the pillaging of Italian art treasures. So Gros stayed on in Italy, often witnessing warfare at its most exciting and most ferocious, often having the chance to see great works of art at first hand (he was in Milan in 1797). Eventually he found himself once more in Genoa, trapped this time with the troops of General Masséna, till the French soldiers had to surrender. He was back in France in 1800; he had missed the Terror, the street fighting, the dissolute parties in Paris; instead he had thrilled to the sight of Frenchmen at war, in gleaming brass and with waving plumes.

In the Salon of 1801 he showed his *Napoléon à Arcole*, but nobody took much notice. He attracted more attention the following year, with an equestrian portrait of Napoleon on a white charger, decorating a grenadier after the Battle of Marengo. The free handling of paint, the brilliant satin-white colour of the horse and the glamorous subject-matter intoxicated young artists who had been drilled in the hard, learned manner of the Neo-Classical style. Gros became famous just when it suited him; he was not courted like his master, he was Napoleonic by instinct. He won a competition to paint the Battle of Nazareth. Though he had not been to Egypt or

Syria, he spoke to an artist who had been, Denon, he got the battle plan from General Junot, he made first a geometric plan of it and then a perspectival plan. Napoleon shelved the painting, probably because it would reflect too much glory on Junot. It was as well for Gros that in 1804 he showed a work that gave greater glory to his god. His picture of *Napoleon visiting the plague-victims of Jaffa* was an artistic revelation.

It revealed a Christ-like general in Christ's own land. In March 1799 the plague had broken out in Jaffa, which the French were occupying. The British told how on capturing the city Bonaparte had ordered the massacre of 3000 Turkish prisoners, and Bourienne, his secretary, speaks of him lightly kicking the sick, but Gros preferred to follow the story of the surgeon Desgenettes, who reported how Bonaparte demonstrated courageous compassion to his men by choosing to visit the pesthouse to comfort them. Gros used an accurate composite view of Jaffa for the background, he put classsical nude and half-clad men to the fore, but in the middle and at the focal point of his painting he set Bonaparte in modern uniform. His simple French costume stands out against the exotic dress of the Arabs around him; the light that illumines him makes them glow with colour; his tender gesture, for he reaches out his hand to touch the underarm buboes of a victim, brings hope to those who lie in the shadows and despair. Once French kings had had miraculous powers to heal; so now too had the Emperor of the French. Christ had stretched out his hand thus to raise Lazarus from the dead and Doubting Thomas to find belief. Delécluze recalled: 'The memory of the expedition to Egypt was still fresh in people's minds, and the glory of the young artist, who had made sacred the memory of one event in this campaign, was as it were involved with the hero who had directed it. The sincere admiration which this composition excited was so general that painters from all the respected schools united to carry to the Louvre a great laurel wreath to hang above Gros' picture.'

The painting met favour with the political classes. Denon wrote to Napoleon, 'You are represented in it in a noble fashion, with the serenity of an exalted soul . . . Your costume is admirable, your appearance spirited and accurate. Round you everyone is so moved with confidence and hope, that there is no feeling of the horror such a scene could inspire by its represention of all that is most disgusting in nature.' Even Fouché, the lupine chief of police, was touched. 'It is the Emperor's most beautiful action.'

Gros regretted that he had not been invited to go to Egypt. 'I would have painted oriental costumes,' he wrote to his mother, 'mamelukes, janissaries, pashas, Arab and Turkish horses, I would have mingled with the French army, and maybe I would have gained my own victories in painting Bonaparte the victor. Just as Charles Le Brun [Louis XIV's painter] painted the old Alexander, I should have painted the new one.'

In 'Napoleon visiting the plague-victims of Jaffa' (Musée du Louvre, Paris)
Gros revealed Christ-like qualities in Napoleon that others had missed.

One of Bonaparte's commanders, Lejeune, was also a painter, who under his
works inscribed the words 'I have painted what I have seen'. Few artists could claim
as much. Just like Le Brun when painting battles that Alexander the Great had
fought, Gros usually had no direct experience of most of his subjects. If Le Brun
relied on ancient historians, Gros used modern eyewitness evidence – in each case
the artist's imagination alone reconstructed the excitement of combat. For the Salon
of 1806 Gros went back once more to the Egyptian campaign of 1799, this time to
the Battle of Aboukir. The battle had been fought just inland from the shallow
waters of the bay where Nelson had annihilated the French fleet while a boy, son to
the French admiral, stood on the flagship's burning deck. Bonaparte had extricated
himself from Syria, only to be confronted by an army of fresh Turkish troops who
had rushed to defend their supposed subjects, the Egyptians. Between Muslim and
Europeans the contest would always be unequal, but the issue was decided in spectacular fashion by a single charge, when Murat and the cavalry drove the Turks
towards the sea behind them. Many were killed, many were drowned and some,
among them their leader, Kincei Mustapha, Pasha of Romelia, were lucky to

surrender. Murat, who ordered the picture in 1805, chose for it the moment of triumph: 'the Pasha, surrounded by the bodies of his most faithful followers, is sup-ported by them and his son, who seeing him disabled for further combat, surrenders his weapons to General Murat.'

Again Gros had before him the sketches of Denon, who had drawn both the site and the battle itself. On an oil sketch now in Detroit the names of the battalions have been added. The picture had to be authentic, but it is raised above the level of docu-mentary art by Gros's sense of occasion: the drama focuses on Murat on his pranc-ing horse.

Something nobler was needed for Napoleon. The animal vigour of Murat was not enough. Gros confronted a more complex challenge in the story of one of Napoleon's less than overwhelming victories. After relentlessly pursuing the Russians in Poland in December 1806, the French had taken up winter quarters when Bennigsen, the enemy commander, took them by surprise and so Napoleon felt he had to launch an attack at Eylau on 8 February 1807 in a snowstorm. One French corps ran away, others barely contained Russian counter-attacks and Napoleon could claim a victory only because at the end he was left on the field of battle, before he withdrew. To reassure those at home he dictated his version of French success (translated, he said, from the German) and published the dying words of a French captain: 'I die content, since victory is ours, and I expire on the bed of honour.' He also sent to France specially prepared pictures to reinforce his message. Gros would be more convincing. For the 1808 Salon he prepared his most subtle work of propaganda since *The plague-victims of Jaffa*. He chose the morning after the battle when Napoleon, riding out with his marshals to survey the horrors of the previous day, raises his right hand to bless while his upturned eyes indicate his pious pity for the slain, and grateful Poles and Lithuanians kneel as in prayer and at the front a dying common soldier lifts his arm to greet his saviour. Napoleon has been transformed into a Christ-like cavalier, braving the snowy landscape – for all his white silk, which tones in with the background, he is very well wrapped up – to bring the benefits of Napoleonic warfare to central Europe. In 1808 his own clemency was much on Napoleon's mind. At the same Salon Guérin exhibited *Napoleon sparing the rebels of Cairo*. In 1798 the Mamelukes in Cairo had staged a rising against the French, which had left 12,500 Egyptians dead. When order had been bloodily restored, Napoleon had gone through a public demonstration of his mercy to the remaining leaders. Guérin places him at the left of his picture, stand-ing near the back, the soul of mild reasonableness, but Guérin cannot equal Gros's panache (there exists a lively sketch of the same event by Gros). Guérin's Napoleon would have had no energy to have stopped the killing.

In 1810 Girodet returned to Guérin's theme – *The revolt of Cairo* – with some-thing of Gros's intensity; and as for Gros himself, not much inspired by Napoleon's

In Gros' 'Napoleon at the battle of Eylau' (château de Versailles) even after a
bloodthirsty battle the Emperor has time to bless the dying.

most recent pyrrhic victory at Wagram or the capitulation of Madrid, he returned
for the last time to the Egyptian campaign, at the request of the Senate. The full title
of his picture was *Bonaparte haranguing the troops before the battle of the Pyramids – 21 July,*
1798. Jean-Antoine Chaptal, one-time Minister of the Interior, whose portrait Gros
painted, wrote of the profound impression the Pyramids made on Napoleon; and
the official catalogue states that it was then he cried out, 'Soldiers, remember that
from the height of these monuments forty centuries look down on you.' Delacroix
says Gros was very pleased in general with this picture, which he was forced to add
to later (so spoiling its proportions), and especially proud of his portrayal of
Napoleon's face. 'I have made him a human trophy,' he said.

Nobody else had such empathy for the Napoleonic idea of war. There were
plenty of battle scenes at every Salon: in 1806 eighteen pictures of the Austerlitz
campaign – the most famous, by Gérard, appeared in 1810; nine Wagram pictures
in 1810; and in 1812 the taste ran riot. Whereas Gérard produced society portraits
of Napoleonic grandees, sleek in shiny uniforms, at his best Gros can invest a single
figure with matchless glamour. Fournier-Sarlovèze digs his sword into the ground
to show he will not surrender Lugo. Marshal Victor is content to be superbly smart.
Leaning his right elbow on his resting horse, Lieutenant Legrand is languidly aware
of his glistening helmet and cuirass, his long dark boots and light-coloured trousers.
As Delacroix said, Gros 'knew how to paint the sweat on a horse's crop in the midst

In 'Napoleon pardoning the rebels in Cairo' (château de Versailles) Guérin portrays a conqueror who has compassion on the conquered.

of battle and almost the fiery breath from their nostrils. He makes you see the glint of the sabre at the moment when it is plunged into an enemy's throat.'

There was a sad consequence of Gros's self-surrender to his hero: he could not live without Napoleon to inspire him. Gros was always a trifle lazy and would stop painting when his watch indicated that he had done enough for the day – he did not like work to interfere with his pleasures. He needed to be galvanized and after 1815 nobody could give him the charge. He wrote to David in Brussels and was told to give up painting modern events in favour of pure history taken from Plutarch; and one enormous, dud picture succeeded the next. At last he could stand it no longer; and in 1835 he dressed up in the uniform Napoleon had given him forty years before in Italy, walked to the river and drowned himself. The Bourbons had made him a baron, but he had lost his soul.

Compared to Gros, most of the military painters are dullness visible. As early as 1800 Napoleon had started ordering pictures of his campaigns; and if in 1801 Gros exhibited his sketch of the First Consul as he had been when mere General Bonaparte at Arcole, his rivals were more up to date – David in the same year glamorized his hero crossing the Alps in a more recent Italian campaign (that of

lessly outshone an equestrian portrait of Murat by Gros which had the look of a fashion plate. Denon, the Director of the Musée Napoléon, reported on Géricault as a promising young artist who would become a fine battle painter, but nobody bought his work and Géricault kept it with him till he died.

The years 1812–14, which marked the decisive years in the defeat of Napoleon's dream of domination, saw the emergence of this keen young horseman as poet-painter of the cavalry. The *Charging Chasseur* was followed by a Polish lancer on his horse, trumpeters of the Polish lancers and of the Imperial Guard, trumpeters of the Hussars and two Carabiniers (one a half-length and one a head and shoulders). He also sketched cavalry battles and Napoleon giving orders to an officer in battle. None of these splendid evocations of the Napoleonic ideal were exhibited. Rather for the 1814 Salon he produced a wounded cuirassier staggering home leaning on a curiously squashed-up horse, a less accomplished picture than the 1812 *Chasseur* and also disillusioned. Unlike his friend Horace Vernet, in the end he had not fought for the Empire.

Before there was a Napoleonic legend there was a Napoleonic myth. One of the more bizarre tastes of the late eighteenth century was the taste for the lays of Ossian. A young Scots cleric, James Macpherson, sought subscriptions to enable him 'to make a search in the Highlands and Hebrides', says James Boswell, 'for a long poem in the Erse language which was reported to be preserved somewhere in those regions.' The sceptical philosopher David Hume was among those who gave money; and the subscribers were delighted when Macpherson returned from his travels with an epic in six books, which was ascribed to a bard named Ossian. It was an oral poem, claimed Macpherson, who was without a manuscript, but the best judges of literature in Britain, Thomas Gray and Samuel Johnson, were not convinced. Still, the high-flown feeling, improbable names and turgid diction of the work – it was in fact Macpherson's own unreadable prose – turned *Ossian* into first an English, then a European bestseller; and Napoleon, who would have liked to have thought himself as sceptical as Hume (who came to repent of his belief), was as gullible as any of his contemporaries and more in thrall than most.

Delécluze, writing in old age, claimed that Napoleon's cult of Ossian made the fake poet as influential as Homer. It is said that Napoleon took *Ossian* in his pocket on his first Italian campaign and Alfred de Musset says he had *Ossian* with him when he made the crossing of the Beresina during the retreat from Moscow. In 1804 Napoleon and Joséphine were in the theatre for the first night of Le Sueur's opera *Ossian or the Bards*. He said that, as Alexander had chosen Homer and Augustus Virgil, so he had settled on Ossian. To forestall his entry into Padua the citizens sent Cesarotti, the Italian translator of Ossian, to greet him. The French translator of

In 'Ossian summoning the spirits' (château de Rueil-Malmaison) Gérard treats with becoming gravity the bogus epic which was Napoleon's favourite book.

Ossian, who rejoiced in the portentous name of Pierre-Marie-François-Louis Baour-Lormian, was treated as a semi-offical court poet and wrote about the Concordat and the Emperor's second marriage and the birth of his son the King of Rome. Napoleon took *Ossian* with him to St Helena and on the journey told the Scots surgeon of the Northumberland, 'You have a writer whom I greatly admire – Macpherson, the author of *Ossian*.' It is the only time that Napoleon gave a hint that he knew the poems might not be authentic. If he did, it was not a question that bothered him. What he cared for in *Ossian* was the sentiment; and his painters had to care for it too.

In 1800 a medallion portrait of Ossian was painted on to the walls of the library

Girodet's 'Ossian receiving the spirits of French heroes' (also at Malmaison)
appropriates to France the Celtic fantasies invented by Macpherson.

of Malmaison alongside the other great authors. It was a signal to some of David's
younger pupils, especially *les barbus* (the bearded), those in the circle of the now forgotten Maurice Quay. Quay, whose early death has left no trace of his skill, was mag-
netic, an archaizer and an eccentric who once walked through the streets of Paris
dressed up as Agamemnon and who encouraged David to adopt his 'Greek' style.
He was also an enthusiast for Ossian and his friends listened to him. At the Salon
of 1800 one of those friends, Paul Duqueylar, exhibited the first major Ossianic

painting, *Ossian Singing a Funeral Hymn*, and in 1801, under the direction of Fontaine and Percier, Gérard, a finer pupil of David's, painted for Napoleon his first Ossianic picture: *Ossian evoking the Shades with his Harp on the Banks of the Lora*, a picture whose original was eventually given to General Bernadotte, who became Crown Prince, later King of Sweden, and whose son was named Oscar after Ossian's son. In Gérard's painting Ossian in his desolate, blind old age comforts himself with the memory of the dead Oscar, his dead daughter-in-law Malvina, his dead father Fingal and his dead mother Roscrana, while bards and warriors flit about in the moonlit clouds around him. Mist and moon and melancholy were to be the standard features of the Ossianic manner.

Girodet's *Apotheosis of French Heroes who were killed in the service of their country –* this is not the original, long, title – was exhibited at the Salon of 1802, dedicated to the First Consul, and is now at Malmaison. It is the most strange of the Ossianic paintings. It portrays an Ossianic apotheosis as an alternative to a classical Elysium or a Christian heaven, as Ossian leads his Celtic followers from 'Morven' to greet Kléber, Desaix and Caffarelli-Dufalga, who had been killed on the Egyptian campaign and who here are supported by uniformed soldiers of the cannoneers, sappers, grenadiers, dragoons, chasseurs and hussars. Above, Victory holds a sheaf of palm, laurel and olive leaves; above the sheaf is the Gallic cock, which shields a dove of peace from a rapacious Habsburg imperial eagle. In the context of 1801 the activities of the birds refer to the Treaty of Lunéville which had just been concluded between France and Austria. Not every spirit welcomes the dead Frenchmen, for there are also figures from 'Lochlin', the traditional enemies of the men of Morven – the British – who did not make peace with France till 1802, shortly before the picture was on display. This weird allegory is acted out against ghostly Ossianic clouds suffused in a cold white, lunar light.

The other notable Ossianic picture, by Ingres, has sharper forms, otherwise it sticks to the ghostly format. For most of Napoleon's reign the most dignified of David's pupils, 'Monsieur' Ingres to Delécluze (compared to 'Maurice' Quay), lived in Rome, paying his bills by painting the sharply pencilled features of elegant French officials, the director of posts, the controller of forests, the chief of police. For an official commission he had to wait till the Emperor deprived the Pope of the civil government of Rome in 1808. Napoleon wished to make his presence felt on the Capitol from which Rome was ruled, at whose apex stood the Palazzo del Quirinale. In 1812 General Sextus-Alexandre-François Miollis, governor of Rome, asked Ingres to illustrate two themes. One picture, *The Dream of Ossian*, was meant for the Emperor's bedroom. Right at the front the lonely old Ossian leans forward in sleep, propped on his harp, his pink cloak the one object in the light that is not coloured cold green, cold blue or cold white. On the nearest ice-packed cloud, floating above an improbable sea, with a lance in his right hand and his face hidden

Ingres's 'Dream of Ossian' (Musée Ingres, Montauban) has a glacial quality that distinguishes his painting when his head but not his heart is involved.

In 'Romulus Conqueror of Acron' (Ecole National des Beaux-Arts, Paris) Ingres was treating a subject familiar to a pupil of David yet that interested him only as an archaeological exercise.

in shade behind the shield in his left hand, Oscar, Ossian's son, stands poised to fight. Behind, the spirits, as if frozen in rocky sleep, encourage him to heroic deeds. Rome's new King had been born in 1811.

In the other picture Ingres turned to a more familiar story. He was asked to paint *Romulus, Conqueror of Acron* for the salon of the Empress. Romulus, the founder of Rome, had killed King Acron and dedicated to Jupiter the trophies he had won. As David's pupil, Ingres is careful to be correct in archaeological details and to place his figures parallel to the picture plane, so giving his composition the air of an antique frieze. In the context of 1812 he justifies the Emperor's pillaging of the art treasures of Europe, just as his own art 'loots' the art of the past. But his treatment of the subject is curiously mechanical. There is none of the disturbing poetry evident in other classical pictures he painted in Rome, for example *Oedipus and the sphinx*. Ingres could express primitive feeling when emotion touched him. Romulus and Ossian left him unmoved.

He had his reasons for being cautious. He had tried out a 'primitive' image in 1806 when portraying *Napoleon on the Imperial throne*. It is an awe-inspiring icon. Napoleon stares straight ahead from his throne, holding in his right hand the sceptre of the Emperor Charles V and the hand of justice in his left hand and with the

Despite his debts to Greek vases, in 1808 Ingres treated the myth of Oedipus
and the sphinx – the picture is in the Louvre – with a primitive savagery.

sword of Charlemagne hanging by his left leg – Ingres fits the objects into a geom⁄
etry of diagonals and verticals. In the upper middle section of the picture the painter
describes two great arcs, one forming the top of the throne, the other, in reverse, the
ermine front of the Emperor's cloak; and between he places the Emperor's head,
made to look circular by the crown of laurels above and the ruff at his neck. On the
carpet at his feet is an imperial eagle; and to his left and right signs of the zodiac refer
to the coup of Brumaire which brought him to power as First Consul and the date
when he was proclaimed Emperor.

What sort of Emperor he was, to Ingres, is hinted at by the pose and the style.
The face of Napoleon is like a cameo of Augustus, first Emperor of the first Rome.
The way Napoleon looks at the spectator derives from a more exalted source, the
figure of Christ at the top of Van Eyck's Ghent altarpiece, then in the Louvre; and

the suggestion of a halo implies that he too is a sacred ruler, for emperors normally seen in such a Christ-like way were the Byzantine Emperors, the Emperors of the Second Rome. Ingres has united familiar Neo-Classical vocabulary, via late Gothic Flemish devotion, with the language of liturgical Greek. He shocked critics and was hurt by their shock. But in the dimly lit part of the Musée de l'Armée where the portrait is now hung the rich colours, the pure lines and the dazzling technique combine to convey a sense of Napoleon's overwhelming power. Ingres had raised his ruler to a superhuman height.

The vision of splendour was too tiring to sustain. Men cannot easily live with aspirations to greatness. There was always a touch of bombast in the Empire. The cultivation of perpetual virility induced fatigue. A sickly exhaustion had its own nemesis when David's wild pupil, the Gascon Broc, went homo-erotically Greek in his *Death of Hyacinth*; and in Guérin's *Aurora and Cephalus* and *Iris and Morpheus* it is the sleeping males who are the objects of desire.

Broc's painting dates from 1801, Guérin's paintings from 1810 and 1811. Their cult in Napoleonic France of masculine languor had a revolutionary pre-history. In his 1794 oil sketch of Barra, a Jacobin adolescent who had been killed for refusing to hand over two horses to counter-revolutionary Vendéens, David conceived his hero as a naked hermaphrodite. Such sexual ambiguity was shown even more clearly by his most daring pupil. Anne Louis Girodet's *Sleep of Endymion*, exhibited in 1793, exposed the naked body of a beautiful young man to the desires of the absent goddess of the moon. As for Girodet it was a matter of good taste not to show how vulnerable Diana herself was to the love of a mortal man, it is only her light which caresses him. The one other figure present, shadowed by trees, is the teenage Cupid, who opens the branches so that the moonbeams may shine on Endymion's hips and chest. By a generation Girodet has anticipated the Keatsian response to Endymion's myth:

> A thing of Beauty is a joy for ever:
> Its loveliness increases; it will never
> Pass into nothingness; but will still keep
> A bower quiet for us, and a sleep
> Full of sweet dreams, and health and quiet breathing.

This romantic sensibility, with its emphasis on loveliness, sleeping and dreaming may seem remote from the stark and Spartan code of David. His favourite pupil, Drouais, who had died young, had painted pictures whose heroes draw and lose blood and tense their muscles. In *The death of Marat* David had produced the revolutionary masterpiece to honour a martyr to Jacobin virtue; and, if Marat's sore-

Girodet's 'Sleep of Endymion' (1791, Musée du Louvre, Paris) set a fashion
in languid naked young men that became popular in the time of the Empire.

ridden, botched-up body was far from the beautiful body of an ideal athlete, David
had done his best to hide the fact. Jacobin virtue was manly. But as virility was a
soldier's value too, old Jacobins fathered young Bonapartists. The upraised arms of
David's Horatii reappear both in the sketches of the tennis court oath and in the
painting of *Napoleon distributing the eagles*. In his revolutionary phase David had
reduced women's role to grieving or encouraging at the side of the stage. If during
the Directory, through the influence of Joséphine and her peers – Juliette Récamier
and Thérèse Tallien – women reminded men of the charms of the salon and the
boudoir, under the Empire Napoleon reasserted the power of men.

War separated the sexes and for many years men lived in an all-male society, to
which women were only adjuncts, as camp followers, casual lovers or victims. In
their tents and by their camp fires men's feelings of tenderness were focused on their
companions. To convey in art this almost feminine refinement became the special
achievement of Girodet. Never again so overtly homo-erotic as in his *Endymion*, in
The revolt of Cairo (1810) he takes sensuous pleasure in the act of death. There is

Girodet's 'Revolt at Cairo' (1810, château de Versailles) makes the moment of death look beguilingly beautiful.

glamour in the French officer who dashes across the front of the picture plane towards the damascened daggers of a naked Nubian and a naked Mameluke warrior; and to counterpoint the violence Girodet places at the front to the left a semi-nude dead Egyptian and to the right a dying, pallid pasha in gorgeous robes gently supported by his naked guard. Gros could convey the excitement and the glamour of war, but not same-sex love. So too, when his favourite Spartans in *Leonidas at Thermopylae* prepare to meet certain defeat and death from Persian invaders, David implies such love, but not even the date of the picture's showing (1814), when France's enemies occupied France, gives it a prophetic meaning. The poses are frigid and the gestures mannered. High seriousness has become absurd.

Girodet was more modern, because he implied an alternative to bellicose art. After the Napoleonic *Ossian Receiving the Spirits of the French heroes* he turned to the romantic vision of one of Napoleon's principal critics, François-René de Chateaubriand. Chateaubriand was a minor aristocrat from Brittany who rejoiced in the fall of the absolute monarchy, left the royal army to explore the north-east of the infant American republic (in 1791) and then, after a brief return to France in 1792 when he heard of the fall of the liberal monarchy, ran from the worst excesses of the Republic to live as an emigrant refugee in Belgium and England. In sceptical

Girodet's 'Funeral of Atala' (1808, Musée du Louvre, Paris) is one of the first
pictures to take its subject from early Romantic literature.

Paris he had lost his Catholic faith; abroad he was reconverted to the faith but not
to truthfulness. All his life he treated fiction as fact. Because in his mind he had trav-
elled down the Mississippi, he wrote of the vast region of Louisiana as though he
knew it from personal experience. This gives a special poignancy to his rhapsodic
account of the love of two savages, the Christian Atala and her pagan Chactas.
Their story he inserted in the initial, English edition of his aesthetic analysis of the
Catholic religion, *Le génie du christianisme*, but when he went back to France in 1800,
convinced of Napoleon's noble intentions, he published the idyll as a separate book.
It appealed to the newly fashionable sentimental religiosity; and it found in Girodet
the fitting illustrator of its saddest moment. Having chosen to kill herself because
her virginity has been violated, Atala is laid to rest in a cave by a hermit and her
lover, himself wrapt in grief, before he will cover Atala 'with the earth of sleep'.
Death is sleep eternal. Chateaubriand describes how before the burial Chactas has
watched by the light of the moon, itself white as a vestal virgin; and the burial occurs

Like Chateaubriand's remains, Girodet's 1807 portrait of the teller of Atala's tale is now in St-Malo (the portrait in the museum, the author's remains in a grave looking out to sea).

as 'a golden beam forms in the east'. Her innocent and deadly whiteness is contrasted with his bare, dark brown muscular body entwined with a large scarlet loin-cloth.

The Entombment of Atala dates from 1808. Next year Girodet painted a portrait of Chateaubriand, his hair blowing in the wind, as he meditates on the ruins of Rome. Napoleon did not like what he saw – he said that Chateaubriand looked as though he was a conspirator who had come down the chimney. Whereas Chateaubriand made a cult of emotion, Napoleon liked to believe he was a plain, blunt man. Girodet, after the success of the colourful *Revolt of Cairo*, had a more public triumph in a decennial award (1810). The Michelangelesque *Scene from a Deluge* – a painting about impending mortality – was given first prize in the class of history painting ahead of anything by David. If Napoleon took favourable note of the judges' verdict, he responded in a way Girodet must have regretted. In 1812 the painter was ordered to produce thirty-six identical full-lengths of the Emperor. One sketch of Napoleon, now in Chateauroux, shows him seated, stout and top-heavy. For the official version he was to look majestic, standing in imperial costume, but the mechanical way in which Girodet and his pupils had to work encouraged banality. Twenty-six dull paintings had been manufactured by the time Girodet gave up in the year in which Napoleon himself abdicated (1814). Distinguished by an original imagination and a mercurial temperament, Girodet was the one impressive pupil of David who had found it hard to be an Empire artist.

Girodet's 'Scene from a deluge' (Musée du Louvre, Paris), a heavy-handed
attempt to give Michelangelesque dignity to a disaster, was prized above any
of David's recent Neo-Classical productions in the 1810 decennial exhibition.

Not even Napoleon could control men and women of letters. But he must have
hoped that the new museum culture that he fostered would regenerate French art in
ways of which he would approve. Girodet might have kept a certain independence,
yet the school of David, as a whole, was determined to learn from the art of the past
so helpfully on display all over France because throughout Napoleon's time the army
had looted all over Europe. Napoleon, however, could not make contemporary
artists equal to the artists of the past. Besides, like all dictators what he encouraged
most was sycophancy.

The easiest way to please a ruling class has always been to portray it; and with a
large imperial family, which included two empresses, and a large court, which
included men in all sorts of colourful uniforms, there was a steady supply of
commissions. Gérard fulfilled many of them with the adroit flattery that his immac-

'Joseph Bonaparte' (dating from 1808–13 and now in the Musée Napoléon in the château de Fontainebleau) is a skilful act of flattery by Gérard.

ulate technique could provide. His Madame Mère, Napoleon's mother, affects imperial restraint. She sits confidently beside a bust of her son, dressed in a white satin
dress and a green velvet cloak, which is sewn with precious stones, pearls and a gold
border, in front of columns and curtains and a wood in the background. Joseph
Bonaparte, being King of Spain, is more splendidly arrayed. He stands before his
throne, inscribed with a 'J', in ermine and blue velvet robes, decorated with the
castle towers of Castille and the lions of Leon, his sword of honour by his side, his
sceptre in his left hand, leaning on the table that carries his crown while in his right
hand he holds his hat in the casual style of Henry IV. Joseph's wife and two daughters are much less flamboyant – she sits serenely in front of a window while the girls
stand in simple dresses, the younger glancing up at her mother, the older looking out
at the spectator. Nobody can deny that Gérard has the skills a court portraitist needs
as well as some of the defects. His picture of the Emperor's entourage is of handsome and distinguished men stylishly turned out and of sweet-natured, beautiful
women dressed in the height of elegant fashion. But his most attractive portrait was
not of any one of these people and not from the Empire period.

In 1796 he had painted his friend, Jean-Baptiste Isabey, with his daughter and his
dog. Though in state portraits Gérard was never to equal the glamour of Van Dyck,
in this painting he manages to capture some of the Flemish artist's sense of graceful
ease. Isabey has the fine figure of a cultivated gentleman, neatly turned out in under-
stated clothes, serene in manner, gracious in gesture. While he leads the awkward
Alexandrine down a staircase in the Louvre to the gardens below, he pauses on the
landing, casually bending his left leg, and gazes steadily into the middle distance. The
portrait's aristocratic air caused comment; and the Dutch ambassador bought it.

Isabey had the discretion and taste of a natural courtier. Three years later a
Consular court was set up; and so began Isabey's long public career. For the next
half-century he was to serve Bonapartes and Bourbons with polite efficiency, designing costumes for the imperial coronation of Napoleon I in 1804 and responsible for
the imperial palaces of Napoleon III in the 1850s (he did not die till 1855).

He was a born decorator; and besides the Emperor's study, he designed sets at the
Opéra and other imperial theatres. For the Sèvres factory he painted on porcelain the
top of the famous Table of the Marshals which is now at Malmaison. His sense of
style made him especially attractive to Joséphine de Beauharnais; he taught her
daughter Hortense painting; in 1805 he was appointed first painter to the Empress.
He had a delicacy of touch that made him along with the austerer Augustin the best
master in France of the exquisite art of the miniaturist. Once the Empire was established, there was a constant demand for tiny pictures of Napoleon – Napoleon in
the academic costume of the Institute, Napoleon in the uniform of the National
Guard, Napoleon in red court dress, Napoleon as a chasseur *à cheval*, Napoleon
wearing robes of state (one of the finest of them all) – which Isabey and his studio

In 'Jean-Baptiste Isabey and his daughter' (1796, Musée du Louvre, Paris) there is a gentle poetry far removed from the technical brilliance of Gérard's routine portraits of the great.

worked diligently to supply. Isabey could catch the thick curls of a smiling Murat (Joachim, King of Naples) or the fine gauze of Joséphine's veil or Queen Hortense at her most dreamily seductive. He could even give a faintly poetic air to the farm-yard features of the naïve, plump face of the Empress Marie-Louise cuddling her son, baby Napoleon, the King of Rome, his golden curls set against her brown curls, his blue eyes matched with her blue eyes, his blue suit toning in with her white dress.

It was Prud'hon not Isabey who produced the most sensitive image of the Empress Joséphine. Pierre-Paul Prud'hon, born as long ago as 1758 in the abbatial town of Cluny, had won a Burgundian Prix de Rome in 1784, when David was

The 'Table of the Marshals', at Malmaison, is one of the happier results of co-operation between designers and craftsmen. Brongniart, director of Sèvres had it made (1808–10), following Percier's ideas, Thomire worked at the bronze, Isabey painted the top, Gérard modelled the columns in biscuit porcelain etc, etc.

working in Rome with his favourite pupil, Drouais, on the intense *Oath of the Horatii* for next year's Salon. During his three-year stay in Italy (1785–8) Prud'hon was never drawn to that self-sacrificing devotion to the death which gives power to heroic poses. While living off the wealth of David's father-in-law, they were exalted in the primitive virtue of republican Rome; while struggling to keep a family, he was seduced by the sensuous idylls of Greco-Egyptian Alexandria. His imagination was stirred by Leonardo's smoky outlines, the dreamy expressions of the saints in early Raphael and the soft lighting of Correggio's darkened scenes. Back in Paris, he was carried away by Jacobin rhetoric – he was given a room in the Louvre for planning *Truth coming down from heaven led by Wisdom* – and he fled when Robespierre fell. He took refuge in the countryside of Franche Comté and provincial portraiture, but returned to Paris in 1796. Under the Directory, Alexandrine luxury, so remote from his impoverished domestic situation, was in fashion; under the Consulate he acquired a mistress and his art took wing; under the Empire he made portraits erotic.

Only one important painting celebrates the public, masculine values of Napoleon: *Divine Justice and Vengeance pursuing Crime*. The allegory owes something

to the story of Cain and Abel, for a bearded man in darkened shadow is hurrying away from a more youthful man he has slain – once again a young, beautiful naked body is bathed in light – only to find that in the sky above he is chased by Vengeance holding a torch for the even sterner figure of Justice clutching her sword. This severely moral picture makes it an ideal emblem of the harsh penal enactments of the Code Napoléon: rebels were to be imprisoned for life and those guilty of murdering their fathers were to have a hand cut off before execution. Nor was this all. In seeking to crush dissent, Napoleonic France had become a police state. Arrest and imprisonment at will, once vilified by the cartoonists as an abuse of the *ancien régime*, had returned; and the Minister of Police, Fouché, an ex-priest who had once zealously dechristianized during the Terror, now used spies to check on all who disliked the Empire, until in the end he betrayed Napoleon as ruthlessly as he had betrayed all he had served before.

Such ironies were beyond Prud'hon. He preferred to please rather than to alarm his spectators. Despite his melancholy temperament he aimed to give visual delight. It is his picture of the Empress Joséphine which stays in the memory, dressed in her imperial finery, but seated in the gardens of her beloved Malmaison, languid, pensive and alone. Prud'hon was more at ease with Napoleon's wives than with Napoleon. He painted mythological love scenes with a poignancy that escaped the awkward emotion of David – where David's *Sappho, Phaon and Eros*

Isabey was a master of miniature painting. The Walllace collection, London houses three of his master‐pieces: the large grisaille of Napoleon and the enticing images of Joséphine and of Marie‐Louise with her son.

looks merely coy, Prud'hon's *Venus and Adonis* conveys the slow, lingering regret for a love that is fated to end shortly in violent death. Prud'hon was a sensualist; and this made him as adaptable to the healthy appetites of the jolly Habsburg Marie‐Louise as to the darker mood of the rejected, exotic Joséphine. For the baby King of Rome, the son of Marie‐Louise, he was invited to design cradles; and on one occasion, when designing a cradle that was crafted by Odiot and Thomire in silver gilt, mother‐of‐pearl, velvet, tulle and silk, he produced an infant's throne for the heir of one emperor and grandson of another. An eagle perches at the foot of the bed, Fame crowns a canopy over the sleeping Caesar with a wreath of laurel (meaning glory), while the river gods of Tiber and Seine are carved on the outer sides. Prud'hon was equal to the demands of an Empire artist: he knew how to be grand, to order.

Sculpture has always been recognized as a more public art than painting. Not only are its materials, such as marble and bronze, more enduring, they are also more expensive, so that only a very rich man or a group of rich men can afford the services of a sculptor. But the results are rewarding. Statues, being three‐dimensional, look more lifelike; being adaptable in size, they can fit into any niche or on to any plinth; being usually made by a team, they can be remade by any member of the team.

Prud'hon's melancholy streak tackled in 'Venus and Adonis', also in the Wallace Collection, London, a theme that might have suited Joséphine: an ageing goddess tries to hold onto her young lover, in vain. The picture, however, was for Marie-Louise.

Rulers find that statues make their subjects familiar with their appearance. No image of the first Roman Emperor was as frequently copied as the Augustus of Primaporta. Louis XIV pranced on horseback all over France. Napoleon wished his features to be even more easy to recognize. He needed an army of sculptors and preferably one who could be their general.

One fine veteran sculptor had survived the revolution. Jean-Antoine Houdon had captured the spirit of the *siècle de lumières* with the wide range of his human sympathy. He had sculpted a youth who could have come from ancient Rome, a playwright (Molière) and an admiral (de Tourville) who step out of Louis XIV's Versailles, a

Prud'hon was capable of the grand manner, as in the cradle of the King of
Rome, that followed him into exile in Vienna – it is in the Kunsthistorisches
Museum.

formidable Tsarina (the great Catherine), a composer of noble *opere serie* (Gluck), a
set of smiling, beguiling countesses and charming, innocent children. One of these,
Alexandre Brongniart, would grow up to manage the Sèvres factory for Napoleon.
Above all Houdon had captured the values of fashionable Enlightenment: the wry
smile of Voltaire (whether bewigged or with his natural hair), the simplicity of
Rousseau, the plain common sense of Franklin, the grand idealism of Washington
and the brooding intensity of Jefferson. He sculpted the early heroes of the revolution – Lafayette, Necker, Mirabeau and Barnave – but after 1791 he contributed little
to the Salons. David did not approve of him and he received few commissions. He
did not take easily to doctrinaire Neo-Classicism. When he showed off his Diana in

In this bust by Houdon (in the château de Versailles) for once Joséphine is given a middle-aged appearance.

1802, she was ridiculed for being too French. Still, in 1806 there were portraits of Napoleon and Joséphine, probably in terracotta; and from 1808 there survive marble busts of the Emperor as a colonel of the cavalry, unostentatious, young and thought-ful, and of the Empress in a Greek tunic, with a band round her curls; and from 1812 there remains a commanding statue of Joubert, the brilliant general who had died at Novi in 1799 – like Hoche and Desaix, he was safe to glorify because he had died before he could outshine the glory of Napoleon.

Houdon was a figure from the past, whom Napoleon was kind to remember. There were competent successors whose style was more modern, like Chaudet and Bosio, who could manufacture the images that could be dispatched wherever they had to be copied. Hundreds of these were processed every year, once the French had mastery of the quarries of Carrara. But this was not enough for Napoleon. He wanted a great sculptor, who would be to him as Michelangelo had been to Julius

II and the Medici Popes. Such a man was not available in France. There was one, however, in Rome, the second capital of the Empire. Napoleon had good reason to seek immortality in the hands of the papal sculptor, Antonio Canova. In the end he did not receive what he would be truly thankful for.

The story began with a sculpture of perfect love and ended with statues of Venus, goddess of love, and Mars, her lover. In 1802 Joachim Murat, who had recently married Napoleon's youngest sister, Caroline, bought Canova's Cupid and Psyche, the most famous of Neo-Classical erotic statues, for their grand apartments in the Hôtel de Brionne, to the north of the Tuileries palace. Thus, with a hint of restless sexual desire (for the lovers do not eye one another), began a close connection between the Bonapartes and Canova. So sure were some of his English admirers that he was a Bonapartist that they could not bring themselves to ask him to sculpt monuments to Nelson or to Pitt: inferior British patriots were preferable to devious Italians of doubtful allegiance. In this they were unfair to Canova. For all his courtly ways he valued freedom and was devoted, if to anyone, then to the Pope, Pius VII, whom Napoleon had made his prisoner.

In 1810 Canova came to Paris and there, in the Tuileries, had a series of eight conversations, which he recorded, with the Emperor. As he presents himself, this peasant's son from the Veneto showed no fear of a lesser nobleman from Corsica. He was tactful enough to refer to the ancient history of the Bonaparte family. 'Aren't you a Corsican?' interrupted the Empress (Marie-Louise). 'Yes,' replied Napoleon, 'but of Florentine origin.' Canova then told him that the president of the Florentine Academy, Senator Alessandri, had married off one of his daughters to a relation of the Bonapartes. 'As a result you are an Italian, Sire, and we are proud of the fact.' 'Indeed I am,' said Napoleon. Canova quickly seized his chance to recommend to Napoleon the said academy.

Being tactful by nature or nurture, Canova also dared to defend the Pope. 'Why does Your Majesty not make peace with the Pope?' 'Because priests want to be in charge everywhere, to involve themselves in everything, to be in charge of every-thing, like Gregory VII.' 'But now nobody need fear that, since Your Majesty has supreme power everywhere.' 'The Popes have always stopped the Italian nation from raising itself up, even when they were not masters of Rome . . .' Napoleon conceded that Popes had failed to dominate Italy. Canova suggested that the shepherd's crook was just as much a cause of the greatness of Rome as the sword. Napoleon talked of the greatness of Caesar and Titus, Trajan and Marcus Aurelius and how it was always the Popes who had sowed discord. 'You are so great, Sire, that you could well allow the Pope a place where he could be independent and exercise his ministry freely.' 'He has even pretended to excommunicate me.' Canova persisted. As he

Canova's 'Cupid and Psyche' – this version is in the Louvre – was the key early nineteenth-century image of young love; and so it seemed to Caroline Murat and her Joachim.

would soon become a father, the Emperor should reconcile himself with the Pope, preserve beautiful temples in Italy and Rome and be respected rather than feared. 'That's what I want,' snapped Napoleon, as he broke off the conversation.

However impressed he may have been by the achievements and the personality of Napoleon, Canova remained faithful to his Italian, his Roman heritage. Napoleon wished him to move to Paris. 'Here is the capital of the world,' he said; 'you should stay here, you would be fine here.' 'Sire,' replied Canova, 'you can make decisions about my life; but if Your Majesty is pleased that my time is devoted to your service, allow me to return to Rome after I have done the work I have come to do.' Napoleon smiled. 'Here you would find your home; here are the principal ancient works of art, everything except the Farnese Hercules – but we'll have that soon.' 'Would it please Your Majesty to leave something in Italy. These ancient monuments form a chain or collection with so many others which cannot be taken away, either from Rome or from Naples' – Naples was the home of the Farnese collection. 'Italy can compen-sate itself by excavating. I want to excavate in Rome. How much does the Pope spend on excavation?' Canova explained that the Pope had very little money, but his intentions were good. What were the Borghese family doing? Canova explained that they usually invested alongside other families. 'I paid fourteen millions for the Borghese statues . . . How much does the Pope spend on the fine arts? 100,000 écus?' 'Not so much. He is extremely poor.'

These conversations show Napoleon at his most arrogant and *nouveau riche*. If he reveals any saving grace in them, it is his respect for another great man. Napoleon admired an artist who like him had struggled from humble beginnings to reach a position of eminence. Antonio Canova, born in the small Venetian town of Possagno in 1757, became apprenticed to a minor local sculptor with whom he moved to Venice in 1768. There he received little formal education before he started to work independently in 1775. What changed his career for good was a journey to Rome and Naples in 1779, for he settled in Rome the following year and scarcely left the city till he died in 1822, when his remains were moved back to the gigantic Doric temple church that he had had built in Possagno. In Rome Canova fell in love with the antique or, rather, with a modern idea of the antique, pure and ideal.

Canova's vision of ancient art gravitated between two extremes – the strong and the sweet – but though he made his name with arabesques of violent action, such as the Hercules and Lichas (1795–1802), what won him clients among the connoisseurs was his highly polished pathos. In 1787 his pensive monument to Pope Clement XIV was installed in the Church of the Holy Apostles in Rome and his reputation was made. Instead of the tense spiritual drama of Bernini there was a restful, even bland acceptance of human mortality; character had given way to thought, contortion to calm.

He was invited to Russia by the Tsarina Catherine the Great and to Vienna by Kaiser Francis II, but, in spite of a visit to Austria and Germany in 1798, he could not be lured away from Rome. Napoleon had a little more luck, for Canova was in Paris in 1802 and 1810, but he was determined to remain an international artist and, however willing he was to be commissioned by Napoleon and the Bonapartes, he would not commit himself to them. There were dignified portraits of Madame Mère, of Grand Duchess Elisa as Concord – since she had control of the Carrara quarries, she had to be appeased – and, later, of the Empress Marie-Louise in a similar pose. Napoleon was keen enough on Canova's statues to confiscate Perseus and Venus Italica, but it was above all the women to whom Canova appealed.

Joséphine was an avid collector of his statues. She owned Hebe and Paris in addition to a version of Cupid and Psyche. It was for her in 1813 that Canova undertook to sculpt the Three Graces, but she had died before the group was ready in 1816 and the work passed to Tsar Alexander I. Meanwhile, when in 1814 Napoleon's first abdication had opened Rome to English tourists, a second version was ordered by the Whig grandee, the sixth Duke of Bedford, for the Temple of the Graces at Woburn Abbey (the complementary Temple of Liberty proclaimed his

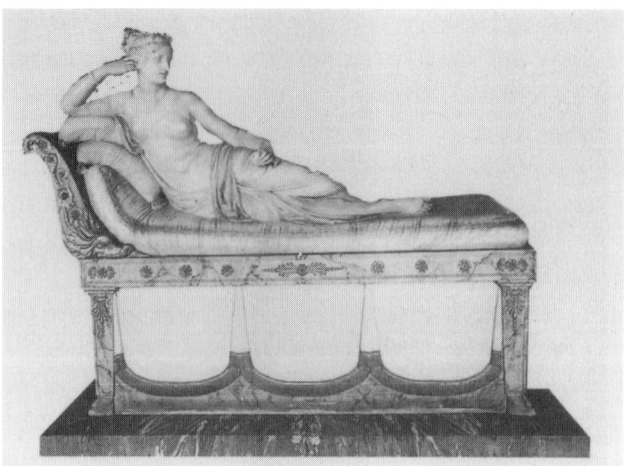

Canova's 'Pauline Bonaparte as Venus victrix', which adorns her husband's
Villa Borghese in Rome, pays sensitive tribute to her louche reputation.

Francophilia). The public life of masculine politics held no interest for Joséphine.
Her sphere was the private, feminine world of personal feeling, to which the statues
of Canova made a direct appeal. In this world Venus was preferred to Mars.

This seemed to be Canova's instinct. Of his Bonapartist sculptures the most celebrated involved the goddess and the most derided the god. In 1808 Napoleon's
favourite sister, Pauline, Princess Borghese, invited Canova to portray her as all-con-
quering Venus, Venus Victrix. Canova had suggested that she should pose as
Diana, but Pauline, who was scarcely famed for her chastity, knew what was
appropriate; and the master sculpted her reclining on a day-bed, naked down to the
waist. In the story of Empire day-bed art the sculpture lies midway between David's
Madame Récamier and the *Grande Odalisque* of Ingres, being half a portrait and half
a nude. When gossips wished to know if Pauline had posed as she was represented,
she replied archly that the room was warm.

Posterity has enjoyed her charms more than it has revered the grandeur of her
brother. When Canova was in Paris in 1802, Europe was at peace and he wished to
praise the First Consul for his part in making the peace. By the time he began to
work on the statue, Napoleon was Emperor and any European peace had to be on
the terms of the god of war. An enormous standing nude represented this ideal. It
was not the way that Napoleon liked to imagine himself. In 1810 he told Canova
that he would have liked to have been sculpted in the French way, that is with his
own clothes on, but Canova insisted that heroic images of art were based on the
naked human form. For once Napoleon was the sounder judge. There is something

Canova's 'Napoleon as Mars', captive of the Duke of Wellington in Apsley House, London, is monumental enough for the hero but too far from the original to be convincing.

faintly ludicrous about this idealized version of the Emperor, which lacks his distinctive broad forehead, squat figure and large belly: the modern Mars was no beauty. The fortune of the statue was also bathetic. Whereas the Pauline is still found in her husband's Roman home, the Villa Borghese, among the Borghese treasures, Napoleon fell into the hands of the Duke of Wellington, who also bought Pauline's Paris home to be the British embassy. Napoleon he kept for himself; and Canova's statue stands by the stairs in Apsley House at No. 1, London. Symbolically as well as actually, the Emperor ended up a captive Mars.

NAPOLEON'S FAMILY TREE

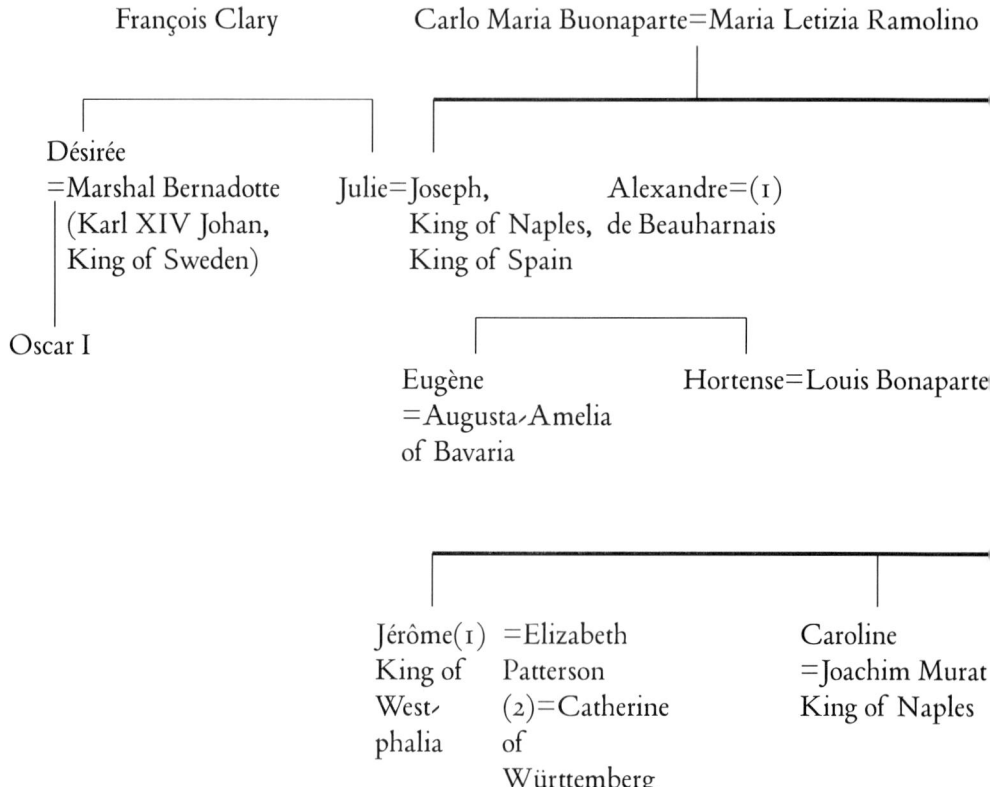

François Clary   Carlo Maria Buonaparte=Maria Letizia Ramolino

Désirée
=Marshal Bernadotte
(Karl XIV Johan,
King of Sweden)

Oscar I

Julie=Joseph,   Alexandre=(1)
     King of Naples, de Beauharnais
     King of Spain

Eugène   Hortense=Louis Bonaparte
=Augusta-Amelia
of Bavaria

Jérôme(1) =Elizabeth   Caroline
King of   Patterson   =Joachim Murat
West-   (2)=Catherine   King of Naples
phalia   of
       Württemberg

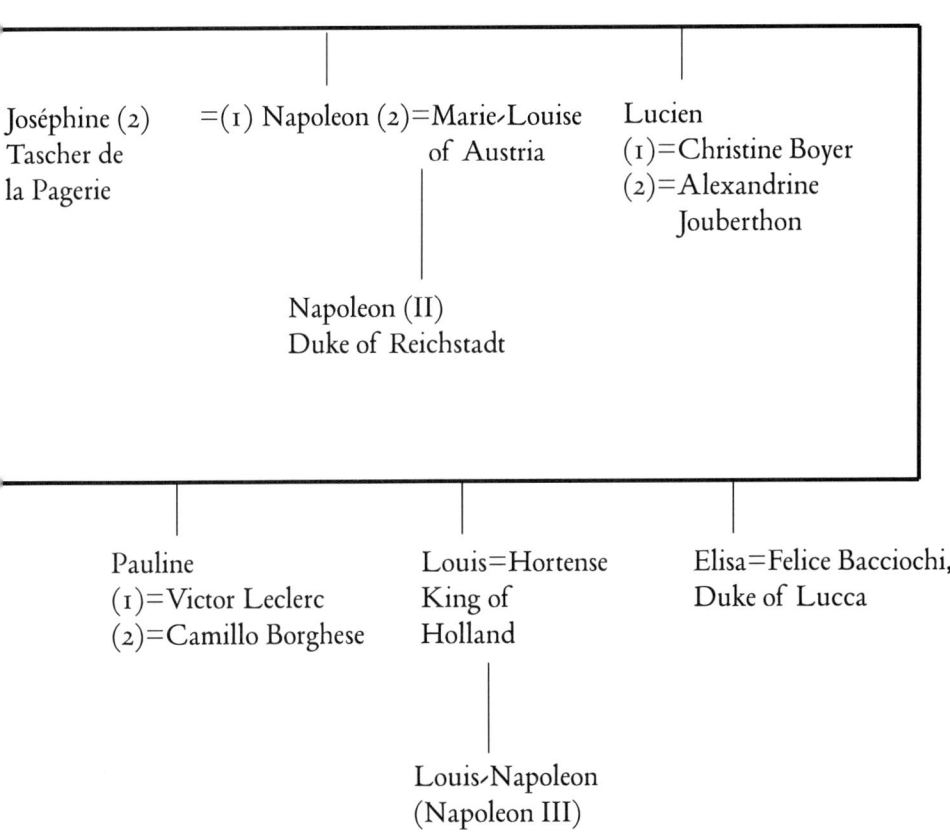

Joséphine (2)   =(1) Napoleon (2)=Marie-Louise   Lucien
Tascher de   of Austria   (1)=Christine Boyer
la Pagerie   (2)=Alexandrine
                                                    Jouberthon

Napoleon (II)
Duke of Reichstadt

Pauline   Louis=Hortense   Elisa=Felice Bacciochi,
(1)=Victor Leclerc   King of   Duke of Lucca
(2)=Camillo Borghese   Holland

Louis-Napoleon
(Napoleon III)

CHAPTER 9

The Napoleonic Empire and the Diffusion of Empire Décor

FROM THE YEAR when his Cupid and Psyche was acquired by Caroline Murat to the time when he began to design the Three Graces for Joséphine de Beauharnais, Canova was aware that being an Empire sculptor meant working for a family, a clan, whose fate depended on the destiny of one man. Napoleon may have ended his days defeated, but he and his family had enjoyed many years of power with a relish that only the once insignificant can savour. Art had added spice to their power.

The Buonaparti had arrived in France almost destitute, cut off from their Corsican roots by the accidents of war, almost friendless in their new country, dependent for their survival on Napoleon's success. In Corsica, after the death of Carlo Buonaparte, Joseph had been the head of the family, but in France he was to have a political role only because Napoleon found him one. The other brother nearest to Napoleon, Lucien, had proved himself a fiery orator and on his own might have made a tempestuous career for himself. As a tribe, however, the brothers and sisters came to realize early that without Napoleon they were nothing. They were not pleased when they found that they had to share him with his wife and her children. Not one of them liked her. Letizia Buonaparte overlooked the failings of her own daughters – for a pious woman she was remarkably tolerant of Elisa's pride, Paulette's sensuality and Caroline's scheming nature – but she would not forgive the easy-going morals of Joséphine. Joséphine could never be one of the family. She was a Creole, she had been married to a French aristocrat, her Beauharnais children, Eugène and Hortense, were irritatingly clever, attractive, good-looking and loyal, and she proved to be incapable of bearing a Bonaparte – everything about her was wrong. Napoleon thought he would heal the rift when he persuaded his favourite brother, Louis, to marry Hortense de Beauharnais, but the marriage proved a dis⁄aster and Napoleon could not prevent Louis from harassing Hortense with his doubts about her fidelity nor Hortense from justifying them by being unfaithful. Because as yet he had no legitimate children, he made the sons of Louis and Hortense his heirs. And even when from his second marriage he fathered a son, Napoleon (II), King of Rome and later Duke of Reichstadt, he did not forget Louis and Hortense. Louis⁄Napoleon, their one surviving son, remained the 'Eaglet's' heir and long after both his uncle and his cousin had died he became the Emperor Napoleon III.

Napoleon saw himself as a dynastic ruler. The Wittelsbachs had been rulers in Munich since the twelfth century – he arranged that Eugène de Beauharnais should marry Augusta⁄Amelia of Bavaria. The Habsburgs had ruled in Vienna since the thirteenth century – he himself married Marie⁄Louise of Austria. He had consid⁄ered a Romanov relation, but the Tsar would not agree, and perhaps he had taken away too much land from the Hohenzollerns to marry a Prussian princess. Towards the Bourbons he was relentlessly harsh. He executed a French Bourbon prince, the Duc d'Enghien, to show that he still sided with the executioners of Louis XVI. He drove Spanish Bourbons from their thrones – Charles IV and Ferdinand VII from Spain, Ferdinand IV from Naples. It was the Hanoverians, however, who were first among his enemies. He was able to snatch Hanover from them, but the British Isles were beyond his reach. He merely contented himself with imitating one of the worst follies of the King of England. Without having grasped the emotional and political problems George III had caused himself and his family by the Royal Marriages Act, Napoleon determined that he too should dictate the marital choices of those closest to himself. Whereas George III had made a catastrophic attempt to control his sons and daughters – his inferiors – Napoleon set himself a much harder aim, the domination of brothers and sisters – his equals. He was to find that even he could not manage the people who knew him best.

Each relationship was different. In 1794 Joseph married Julie Clary, elder daugh⁄ter of a rich merchant of Marseille – money would always rule Joseph's heart – and his prudence as well as his seniority made him the brother to whom Napoleon would turn for comfort or, but rarely, for advice. Lucien was neither so calculating nor so accommodating. In Corsica he had told Joseph he believed that Napoleon had the temperament of a tyrant. Once the family was in Provence, he was typically defiant. Without a word even to his mother he married Christine Boyer, penniless daughter of a local innkeeper, and the following year became the first brother to be a father. He supported the Jacobin cause with vehement speeches and was lucky that, when the Robespierre brothers fell, he had in Napoleon a brother who had the political skill to rescue him from the trouble he had created for himself. Soon Napoleon had troubles of his own. A tepid affair with Julie Clary's naïve younger sister Désirée, who was to become Madame Bernadotte, evaporated when he met Joséphine de Beauharnais. Nothing his mother, brothers or sisters could say would stop him from becoming her lover and her second husband. Napoleon found Joseph a consular appointment, Lucien a post in the Army of the North and, when Joséphine helped him gain command of the Army of Italy, he took Louis with him as a lieutenant, then his aide-de-camp. He left Jérôme behind at school at his expense and found another job in the Army of Italy – purveyor of supplies – for his mother's half-brother, Joseph Fesch. When he got his mother to write a charming letter to Joséphine – 'I already consider you one of my daughters' – his happiness seemed secure.

By April 1797 he was holding court in Milan and called his family to him. Joseph and Louis, whom some mysterious illness had forced to go home, and Paulette came from Paris. From Marseille, Letizia brought Elisa and Caroline and Jérôme. Elisa was twenty and anxious to marry anyone – Letizia persuaded Napoleon to let her marry a dull Corsican captain, Felice Bacciochi. Paulette, whom a member of her brother's staff described as 'the prettiest and most unreasonable person imaginable', was in love with Fréron, an unsuitable journalist in his forties – Napoleon moved quickly to marry her off to one of his favourite companions, a young general, Victor Leclerc. Caroline showed a keen interest in Joachim Murat, the most swashbuckling soldier around, but was first taken off by Joseph, the new ambassador there, to Rome, before being taken back to Paris to continue her schooling at Madame Campan's alongside the hated Hortense. For some time Hortense's mother, Joséphine, had been unwisely, casually involved with Hippolyte Charles and the Bonapartes smarted at the thought that their Napoleon was an unwitting cuckold. It was not till he was in Egypt that Napoleon was told what everyone else had known for some time. 'I have great private unhappiness,' he wrote to Joseph, 'the veil has at last quite fallen from my eyes.' His first act was to take revenge by taking a mistress, the first of many. When he was home, he would divorce her. In his absence the Bonapartes had begun to enjoy their riches. Joseph acquired the country estate of Mortefontaine for 250,000 francs, Lucien Plessis for 60,000 francs and Joséphine was charged 225,000 francs for Malmaison. The crisis came when Napoleon arrived home. In their Paris hôtel, Eugène and Hortense had to join their tears to their mother's to effect a reconciliation between Joséphine and Napoleon. The pleading worked. Each gave up their lovers. She never dared to offend him again. Napoleon became even more dominant. He would allow her, with occasional protests, her little extravagances like Malmaison, but it was clear to her that her only protection against his family would be her husband.

His immediate concerns were political. He wished to seize power and to use it against his country's enemies. During the foggy month of Brumaire 1799 he almost bungled his takeover by seeming to bully the Council of the Ancients, but was saved by the timely eloquence of Lucien, luckily the president of the Council of Five Hundred, who at this crucial moment persuaded the Guard of the Councils to intervene to protect his brother. In his first official bulletin as First Consul, Napoleon made no mention of Lucien's help, but he rewarded him with the Ministry of the Interior. Meanwhile Joseph was nominated as one of the commissioners who were to negotiate with the United States, Louis was raised to the rank of colonel of the dragoons and shortly afterwards Caroline was allowed to marry her Joachim, now made the commander of the Consular Guard. The family had arrived.

It was during the Consulate that the tensions between its members became evident. Lucien continued to be headstrong. In 1801 his office published a 'Parallel between Caesar, Cromwell, Monk and Bonaparte', the parallels hinting that Napoleon ought to found a dynasty. For his pains he was sent off to Madrid as ambassador, taking his brother-in-law Bacciochi with him, only to return prematurely with 1,000,000 francs, a set of Spanish paintings and a Spanish mistress. Napoleon forgave him again and made him one of the Tribunes. What he would not forgive was his marriage plans. In 1800 his first wife had died in childbirth. Two years later he fell in love with and made pregnant Alexandrine de Jouberthon, a bourgeoise whose bankrupt husband had disappeared in Santo Domingo and was presumed dead. Wishing to legitimize his son, within a day of the birth Lucien had married Alexandrine in a religious ceremony. Napoleon had planned that Lucien should marry the notoriously ugly Queen of Etruria. Instead he found that Lucien had produced a child who could be his own heir from a most unsuitable womb. His mother, who regarded Lucien as her favourite, told Napoleon, 'He is no more obliged to ask your permission to marry than you have any right to tell him to marry whom you choose.' Warning Joseph that he should not try to make peace between himself and Napoleon, Lucien set out for Rome in a sulk. Soon his mother had followed him. The break seemed complete.

Napoleon wanted to prevent any more disasters. He had reckoned without the most irresponsible of all his brothers. Jérôme had no memory of hard times. He had been at the same school as Eugène de Beauharnais and was jealous of Eugène's abilities and energy, jealous that Eugène had been called away to Italy and Egypt. He sought compensation by squandering money he did not have. Early on he found that there was always someone from whom he could borrow money – he had a talent for being rescued. At one stage Joséphine had thought that he would make a good match for Hortense, but Napoleon wanted to make a man of him and sent him to sea. Taking advantage of the temporary peace with the British, Jérôme arrived in the United States, where his good looks, his charm and his free spending made him a rapid social success. Americans still had fond memories of French help against the British. Jefferson, who had drafted the Declaration of Independence and helped draft the Declaration of the Rights of Man and the Citizen, was now President of the Union. It was smart among the rich to be Francophile. In these circumstances it was hardly surprising that Jérôme captured the heart of the belle of Baltimore, the wealthy and beautiful Elizabeth Patterson. Jérôme did not care that he had broken the law, which decreed that every Frenchman under twenty-five must have the permission of his father or mother to marry – he was in love. Despite the efforts of the Consul-General to frustrate him, Jérôme was married in the presence of the Catholic Bishop of Baltimore on Christmas Eve, 1803. The news did not reach Napoleon till January 1804.

Sternly Jérôme was warned of Lucien's fate. For a time he resisted his brother's bullying, but in the end his usual difficulties overcame him. He was short of money, so he decided to appeal to his brother's good nature by coming back to France with his now pregnant wife. They arrived in Lisbon in April 1805, where soon they parted in sweet sorrow so that he could go to Milan to see Napoleon and plead their cause while she took ship for Holland. They were to see one another again only once, many years later, in Florence. On that occasion they did not say one word to each other, for Jérôme was with his second wife – according to his elder brother, his first.

Jérôme, in the end, had done his duty, for the Emperor, as he now was, needed to use his family to further his plans. By the end of the Consulate, most of the necessary connections had been made. Early in 1802 Hortense was married to Louis. Late in 1802 Paulette accompanied her husband to Santo Domingo, where he died of yellow fever, and the following year, after threatening suicide for a while, she decided it was more becoming to become a princess. The man she chose was Prince Camillo Borghese, who was not only by descent a Romano dei Romani but also enormously rich. To mark her new status, which placed her in rank above her mother and both her sisters, Paulette renamed herself Pauline. In 1804 she lost the little boy she had had by Leclerc. She was unable to replace him. Like her sister-in-law Joséphine and her brother Louis, whose psychological and arthritic suffering has been ascribed to syphilis, she may well have had some venereal disease. She did not allow it to prevent the steady procession of men to her bed.

There were two more marriages to be made and one to be unmade and replaced. In 1806 Eugène de Beauharnais married Augusta-Amelia of Bavaria and found that soon he and his bride were deeply in love with one another. In 1807 Jérôme was found a suitable bride in Catherine of Württemberg and he would love her with as much faithfulness as he could manage (which was not much). In 1809, in the presence of Louis, Jérôme and Murat and their wives Hortense, Catherine and Caroline, Napoleon divorced Joséphine – this time Bonapartes seemed to have triumphed over Beauharnais. But when Napoleon married Marie-Louise of Austria, it was clear that what he craved above all was to give the Bonaparte name imperial legitimacy. He wished to be above the Hanoverians and the Hohenzollerns, up with the Habsburgs and the Romanovs. To achieve his aims, his brothers, his sisters and indeed the wider family had to help him set up an empire that was not purely French. What he had in mind was an empire that stretched from Spain and Naples in the west and south to the Netherlands and Germany in the north and east. Although

Eugène was just a viceroy, Elisa became nothing more than a grand duchess and Pauline nothing more than a princess, his brothers, except for Lucien, were to be kings and Caroline, through her Joachim, a queen. More distant relations married old nobles – a Murat niece became a princess of Hohenzollern-Sigmaringen, a Bacciochi niece became princess of Salm-Salm, a male Tascher de la Pagerie (from Joséphine's family) took as his bride a Princess von der Leyen, a female Tascher de la Pagerie became Princess of Arenberg, Stéphanie de Beauharnais, herself a princess because Napoleon had adopted her, became Grand Duchess of Baden-Baden. Finally in 1810 Charles Bernadotte and his wife Désirée, sister-in-law of Joseph Bonaparte, were invited to be Crown Prince and Princess of Sweden, with the right of succession to the childless Swedish King. All these members of the extended family – to whom must be added the Pattersons of Baltimore – drew their greatness from their connections with Napoleon. The family would have courts like him, they would patronize the arts like him – in short, they would spread the Empire style wherever they went.

In 1804 First Consul Bonaparte became Napoleon I, Emperor of the French. To naïve observers the Consulate had stood for peace. To everyone it was clear that the Empire meant war. Whether the British or the French were to blame for the breaking of the truce of Amiens did not matter, for by 1804 both governments were committed to the renewal of conflict till one or the other or both were exhausted. Napoleon hoped to invade Britain. The British response, a crushing naval victory over the combined French Mediterranean and Spanish fleets off Cape Trafalgar, made the idea obsolete. By then it was obvious both to Pitt and to Napoleon that the next stage would unfold on land. In the third coalition the British were allied with Austria and Russia, but could do nothing to prevent Napoleon's defeat of an Austrian force at Ulm and a joint Russian and Austrian army at Austerlitz (both events occurred in 1805). Belatedly Prussia intervened, only to be crushed at Jena-Auerstädt (1806). Russia tried again in 1807 and had to make peace at Tilsit. And when Austria, seemingly resurgent, was overrun in 1809 and its Emperor felt obliged to marry off his eldest daughter to his conqueror, there seemed nothing much any of Napoleon's enemies could do. Britain could secure the Bourbons in Sicily, but could not keep them in Naples, could keep a foothold for the Braganzas in Portugal, but had to watch while the Bourbons were driven out of Spain.

Between 1805 and 1809 Napoleon was able to dispose of Spain and to redraw on the map the boundaries of the Low Countries, Germany, Austria, Italy and Poland. In 1806 he ended a thousand-year reich when he dissolved the Holy Roman Empire. He gave to Germany and back to Poland a sense of national cohesion when he founded respectively the Confederation of the Rhine and the Grand Duchy of

Warsaw. He seemed to continue revolutionary policy by incorporating more and more Netherlandish and Italian land into France. He deliberately gave a taste of separate identity to the Illyrian provinces which Austria had ruled, by accident not purpose he divorced Spain from its American colonies – he had already sold the huge French colony of Louisiana to the ex-colony of the United States – and he took over the Papal States. Everywhere French influence was felt, in matters of law, civil and military administration. A class of Francophile enthusiasts or camp followers or quislings emerged in every country where the French armies marched. They depended on the Napoleonides, as Napoleon's closest relations were jokingly called, who in their turn depended on Napoleon (which was no joke), who made his point by making them add the suffix Napoleon to their Christian names.

When Napoleon made himself Emperor of the French in 1804, he made each of his brothers, except for Lucien, imperial highnesses and called his mother 'Madame Mère'. His uncle Fesch, as Cardinal Archbishop of Lyon, was a prince of the Church. At this stage the Beauharnais sisters-in-law, Joséphine and Hortense, were also imperial highnesses, but of the sisters only Pauline was a princess. Elisa and Caroline were still only Mesdames Bacciochi and Murat. Caroline was furious. When Napoleon remarked sarcastically that she behaved as though he had deprived her of her family inheritance, she fainted. The stratagem worked. He allowed all the Bonaparte women to be imperial highnesses, but he soon exacted his price. In December, at the imperial coronation, Elisa, Pauline and Caroline were obliged to join their sisters-in-law, Julie and Hortense, in carrying Joséphine's train. The broth-ers too made an issue of the ceremony. If the embarrassing Jérôme was out of the way, Lucien and his mother refused to come, Joseph recalled his republican ideals and, when David painted the official painting of the scene in Notre-Dame, he was told to insert Madame Mère and sought to appease Louis, who grumbled that he was blocked from view by Joseph. Each one of the tribe longed to be influential. Soon Napoleon's dramatic victories gave all of them their chance of promotion to grand-ducal, even to royal, rank.

The first to profit was Eugène de Beauharnais. In April 1805 Napoleon was crowned King of Italy and straight away he made his stepson his viceroy. After Austerlitz Austria made peace, ceased to exercise overlordship in Germany – the Holy Roman Empire was finally defunct – and ceded Venice, Istria and Dalmatia to Napoleon's new kingdom. The French then turned south. After Murat had driven the Bourbons from the mainland – the British controlled the sea – much to his disgust Napoleon gave the kingdom to his elder brother Joseph (in February 1806). He turned his thoughts to Germany. For a decade Belgium had been part of France and now Napoleon thought of doing the same to the Dutch or Batavian republic. To appease the King of Prussia, whom he had allowed to take Hanover from the British, he made the Netherlands a kingdom and Louis its king (and so

Hortense its queen). The accord with the King of Prussia did not last and soon Napoleon was annihilating the most respected army on the continent. He had already created the Confederation of the Rhine, which made France rather than Austria or Prussia the arbiter of Germany. In October 1806 Napoleon was in Berlin, but he did not have time to make political rearrangements till he had beaten the Russians the following April. He decided to push Prussia to the north-east. North-west Germany became the Kingdom of Westphalia and the wastrel Jérôme, who had been ruling the frontier region of Berg, became its first and last king. The final kingdom to go Bonapartist was Spain, where Napoleon intervened in person, in 1808. As this was the most senior of the satellites, Napoleon handed it over to Joseph. Naples went to Murat. Caroline was at last a queen.

She had done better than her sisters. Political power meant nothing to Pauline. She was content if she could live in Paris, which was hard for a Roman princess, spend a lot of money, for which she needed her husband's wealth, and entertain amusing lovers, for which she needed an agreeable setting. Elisa had the opposite problem. So easily could she dominate the boring Felice that she wanted further scope for her organizing abilities. When she was given the former republic of Lucca as her duchy, she found herself constricted, and she worked hard to become Grand Duchess of Tuscany. She transformed Lucca and reconciled the Lucchesi to monarchical government, but her rule in Tuscany was less popular. She was acutely aware that she had no final authority. She sought consolation in the company of men and women of talent. Like most of the family she had a series of lovers. Only Louis, who was neurotic, and Eugène, who was honourable, tended to be chaste. What distinguished her from the others was her ambition to patronize the arts, maybe as Paganini's mistress, certainly as his muse.

Elisa Bonaparte had the family penchant for building. She had some five palaces when she was at Lucca. Her architect Bienaimé transformed one of her official residences, at Marlia, and modernized another, in Lucca itself. When she came to Florence in 1809, she set about redecorating a number of apartments in the Pitti Palace, including the columned music room, the Sala dei Tamburi, and two bathrooms (ingenious bathrooms were an Empire speciality). From Paris she summoned the *ébéniste* Jean-Baptiste Youf, so that he could make designs for the local cabinetmakers, and she filled the new sections of her palaces in both Lucca and Florence with his furniture. She had to conform to Napoleon's favouring of French craftsmen by putting Savonnerie carpets on the floors, hanging silks from Lyon on the walls and listening to the chiming of clocks that came from Lapaute. In one way, however, she could exploit a local advantage her lands gave her over the French. She had control of the Carrara quarries, from which Michelangelo had taken his marble

This architect's desk (Galerie Camoin, Paris) was probably designed by Youf
in Lucca for the pleasure of Napoleon's eldest sister, Grand Duchess Elisa.

slabs. She went in for the mass production of busts and statues of the Emperor,
which she exported all over Europe, at great profit to herself. It was pleasant to be
called the Semiramis of Lucca, after the Assyrian warrior-queen, but Elisa was altogether modern in her business sense, her easy arrogance – 'I have the best composed
court it is possible to have' – and her enlightened self-interest. Having blundered into
a dull marriage, she insisted that her lovers should be interesting and amusing.
When a courtier was asked by the Emperor how the Grand Duchess was occupied
at Piombino, the reply was frank and succinct. She was occupied 'in making love'.

If Elisa seemed an eighteenth-century despot of the kind the Bonapartes had
swept away, Jérôme was instinctively the most parvenu member of the family. Had
he known his father well, he would have been the '*fils à papa*', for he remained all his
life a spoilt child, a ne'er-do-well, a rake. He found himself a king in 1807, his power
centred on the former principality of Hesse-Kassel, where he lived at the grandiose
palace of Wilhelmshohe, which he tactfully renamed Napoleonshohe. Whereas
Elisa was at home among Italian-speakers, Jérôme never bothered to learn German,
so that his courtiers were forced to learn French. He prided himself on seducing

The throne of Jérôme, King of Westphalia in Kassel is only slightly less grandiose than the throne that Percier and Fontaine designed for the Emperor's use in the Tuileries palace.

most of his wife's ladies-in-waiting – his principal mistress was the wife of his chamberlain, Prince Löwenstein – and he made pleasure rather than politics the chief concern of his style of government. Among the arts he valued nothing above the art of the tailor. When he left for the Russian campaign in 1812, he took seven wardrobes with him, eighteen different uniforms and sixteen crates of eau-de-Cologne. To be shown off at their best the royal costumes needed a splendid setting. When he arrived in Kassel, the castle was empty, so he had to order furniture not only from Paris but also from local craftsmen such as Friedrich Wichmann and Karl Lauckhardt. For King Jérôme's throne in the Palace of the Estates in Kassel, Grandjean de Montigny devised a severe throne – in geometrical terms a circle placed above a rectangle – set on a dais which was reached from either side by seven deep-cut steps. Above the throne hung an enormous crimson velvet canopy, lined with gold. Besides the new abolition of the legal distinctions between nobleman and commoner or between Christian and Jew there was little substance to Jérôme's achievement, but it was a magnificent show.

In intelligence Jérôme could not equal the brothers whom Napoleon favoured the most, Louis and Joseph. Louis, like Elisa, was asked to take over a republic with long republican traditions. He started off ruling at The Hague, but there the Princes of Orange had lived in the Mauritshuis, so he chose instead to settle in Amsterdam. The old town hall in Dam Square was converted into a royal palace. It was a large building, but not a huge one, and it suited the manner of a man who liked the idea of being a citizen-king. Louis set about learning Dutch – he was proud to show off his skill with the written word – and he replaced his former French advisers with Dutch nobles. He kept the Orange collection of art open to public view. The City of Amsterdam bought Rembrandt's *Night Watch* and *Syndics of the Cloth Trade*, once the centrepieces in the royal collection and from the late nineteenth century the Rijksmuseum's proudest possessions. At his château of Saint-Leu in France Louis had employed an architect, Jean-Thomas Thibault, who was Roman-trained. Thibault was now invited to come to the Netherlands to direct the labours of three Dutch architects – Zocher, Posth and Ziesenis – in the refurbishment of Dutch palaces, such as the Castle of Soestdijk and the Huis ten Bosch. Inevitably Louis looked to Jacob-Desmalter for furniture, to Biennais for *objets d'art*, to the Paris firm of Simon for wallpaper and to Percier, Fontaine and La Mesangère for decorative motifs. He also continued to like the flattering portraits of Gérard. Yet he took care to encourage Dutch craftsmen and Dutch entrepreneurs. He was as popular as a foreigner could have been. Before the French were ejected, King Louis had so made his taste into a national fashion that, when the Prince of Orange became King William I, he demanded that in The Hague his royal apartments should be furnished, as the first Dutch king himself would have insisted, in the Empire style.

Joseph had been the first brother to become a king. He was content to be in

Naples, but Napoleon regretted that the best country he had on offer was a mere half-kingdom, since Sicily, thanks to the British navy, had remained under Bourbon rule. Worse still, Joseph was instinctively a liberal. He was for the Code Napoléon, but wished to bring it in gradually. He liked to compensate those who would lose their feudal privileges. He closed down religious orders but most of the clergy obeyed him and he was faced with clerical terrorists only in the brigand country of Calabria. He was more at his ease when commissioning works of art, for he was by nature as cultivated as he was charming and as sensuous as he was indolent. Naples had its art treasures to cherish. Thanks to the marriage of Elizabeth Farnese to Philip V of Spain, there were Farnese sculptures and paintings (including many Titians and the antique Farnese Hercules). More recently, objects had been unearthed at Pompeii and Baia or confiscated from the monasteries. Joseph established a museum to make these works available to the people. He also set up an Academy of History of Antiquity in 1806, which acquired in 1808 sections concerned with literature and fine arts – but his work then ended, for his brother had decided that he should be King of Spain.

To rule from Madrid was a more prestigious occupation and a more dangerous one. In Spain there was a class of *afrancesados* who were anxious to rid their country of the relics of Black Spain, which included the Inquisition, but other liberals were not sure that subjection to a foreign power was an appropriate price for freedom from clerical domination. It took a whole day of savage street fighting to subdue the capital and there were never enough troops to hold down the countryside. Napoleon came to think of Spain as a running sore, an ulcer. The French never learnt how to lance it. Their experience of fighting in Spain brought a new word into European languages – *guerrilla*, a little war – which was not mentioned in any of the military textbooks that Napoleon had studied at school. The Peninsular War also initiated a new stage in the depiction and the experience of the horrors of armed conflict.

For a time Francisco Goya, like his friend, the writer Meléndez Valdés, was content to be at the court of King Joseph. Joseph thought of opening the Prado as a museum and invited Goya to be its director. The King wished to encourage the national pride of his new people. He commissioned busts of the dramatists of the golden age, Lope de Vega and Pedro de Calderón. He lived surrounded by the wonderful paintings collected by the Spanish Habsburg kings and may have been amused that the most recent Spanish Bourbon king, Charles IV, whom his brother had deposed, was the man who first asked for David's masterpiece of *Napoleon crossing the Alps*. He would have noticed that the family of Charles IV, as Goya had portrayed them, was the ugliest royal group in Europe. In 1810, less than two years after the terrible massacre had occurred there, Goya finished an *Allegory of the City of Madrid*, in which Joseph's head and shoulders were depicted on a shield. His handsome face is no longer there. When the French fled, Goya substituted for it the words

'*Dos de Mayo*', because it was on that day that the Madrileños had risen against the foreign oppressors. The liberal Goya had to become a Spanish patriot.

The most beautiful example of the Empire style is to be found in the park of the Palace of Aranjuez, outside Madrid. There for the Casa del Labrador, French craftsmen made in France a 'platinum study', which was then transported to Spain. They worked to the plans of Percier and Fontaine, who proudly published a plate of the room in the *Recueil des décorations intérieures*. On the walls mahogany panels are inlaid with platinum. The panels are enlivened by Pompeian motifs and frame little landscapes and pictures of the four seasons by Girodet. The floor is laid out in geo-metric patterns of marble and coloured stones, many of them from Granada. Probably the room was once filled with furniture by Jacob frères, but it is now no longer there. In the early years of the nineteenth century large quantities of French furniture were brought to Spain by Jean-Demosthène Dugourc, lured to the country by the Duchess of Alba, whom Goya was to love and lose. Elsewhere in the Casa del Labrador some rooms are lined with Lyon silk, worked to Dugourc's designs. This exquisite small building was not one of King Joseph's triumphs. Rather it is a monument to the Empire taste of Charles IV and it passed to his descendants. Joseph had no long-term interest in his second kingdom. On his way out he tried to take away many of his favourite works of art, but at Vitoria the English caught up with him and he had to leave everything behind. The pictures and *objets d'art* were appreciated by his conqueror and have stayed ever since in the homes of the Duke of Wellington.

The last of the Bonapartist kingdoms was the one where Empire influence was perhaps most enduring. When Joseph went to Spain, he was replaced in Naples by Murat. Napoleon, eager as ever to be awkward, told his brother-in-law and sister that they must surrender their French homes. Whether he was prescient or not about their unreliability, he forced them to invest their energies wholly in their new palaces. In Paris, Murat had exercised his fondness for display in the Elysée, where he asked the architect Etienne-Chérubin Leconte to work for him. Once he was in Naples, Leconte was invited to come too. Leconte carried out alterations at the San Carlo Theatre and, with the help of the Italian Simone, at the Palace of Capodimonte, perched on its hill above the Bay of Naples, and at Reggia di Caserta inland. Caroline went on weekly visits to Pompeii and Herculaneum. Murat was more interested in the abolition of feudal rights. They were united, however, in their love of luxury. On festive days Murat wore a plumed hat and a red velvet costume embroidered with silver. Royal pages had a red and gold livery, chamberlains were in red, equerries were in dark blue. The richest silk hung on the walls of the royal apartments. Chandeliers sparkled on the ceilings of the principal rooms. Everywhere there were coloured marble floors and white marble reliefs and friezes picked out in gold or blue or red or white. When the court needed a painter, Murat

Percier & Fontaine's celebrated platinum study of the King of Spain was planned in Paris and installed, for Charles IV not Joseph Bonaparte, at Aranjuez.

Jacob-Desmalter's furniture from the silver salon in the Elysée palace may fit the style of the present French head of state. The Elysée was occupied by the Murats till they had to give it up in 1808 on becoming king and queen of Naples.

could call on the leading Neo-Classical painter in Rome, Vincenzo Camuccini. When the city needed a main straight road, Murat would set about demolishing the buildings that got in the way. The Foro Napoleone, later the Foro Murat, provided a clear space before the royal palace. A spectacular adaptation of the Arch of Constantine was set up to glorify the King and the Queen. Its message was received. When the Bourbons returned, they too were impressed by the lavish refurbishment that their homes had undergone. 'Oh, papa,' exclaimed the King's youngest son, 'if only you had stayed away another ten years!' By contrast, for the young Murats life would never again be so good.

Paris was the sun of the Bonapartes' world and, if they had to go away and make their way in some country where few people liked the French and fewer people spoke the French tongue, they felt as if they were out of their natural orbit. For some of them perhaps – for Madame Mère, for Lucien, for Elisa – Italy was a second home,

At Reggia di Caserta de Simone had begun to decorate the Sala di Marte for
Joseph Bonaparte. He continued with the work for the Murats.

since several of them regarded an Italian dialect as their first language, but not even
Rome, where as in pre-revolutionary times there was a French community, was an
adequate substitute for Paris. Like the moon, Rome's cultural light was a pale,
reflected one. The gossip, the intrigues, the fashions that were important came from
Paris. The Bonapartes tried to make their new or renewed palaces look as Parisian
as possible. They imported French architects, French furniture, French fabrics,
French tableware. They asked their workmen to follow French designs. At their
courts their subjects imitated the etiquette of the Tuileries. Pauline persuaded her
brother to concede that she should be allowed to base her life round her home in rue
du Faubourg Saint-Honoré, at the Hôtel Charost, rather than on the Villa Borghese
in Rome with her prince. Hortense de Beauharnais was too unhappy with Louis to
linger long in Amsterdam. Because her brother was acting the role of viceroy in Italy
or the role of general on some campaign, it was she who was the hostess of the Hôtel
Beauharnais. While their husbands were away, each could entertain lovers with

scant social inconvenience. In the case of Hortense only one affair mattered. Her graceful dancing had been too enthusiastically applauded by the Comte de Flahaut, Murat's aide-de-camp. He came to see her to apologize. His charm made her ask him to come again. By the time that Louis had forbidden him to call, Hortense was Flahaut's mistress. One of her children at least, the future Duc de Morny, must have been his.

Something of the exquisite taste of Pauline Bonaparte and of Hortense de Beauharnais is preserved in their gracious town houses, with the light-reflecting, colour-filled rooms, each room brightened and made spacious by mirrors, each room given its own scheme by the dominance of one or two colours – blue, white, red, green, gold – and of one or two motifs – swans' necks, the head and shoulders of sphinxes, eagles' wings. The clocks glistened with gilt. The carpets were thick with pile, the chairs were comfortable and the beds – so simple in their shapes – were made grandiose by gold patterns on their mahogany bases and sumptuous by the curtains draped above them. The stage was always perfectly set for any new discreet affair.

The wealth of Pauline and Hortense did not outlast the Empire. To give financial assistance to her brother on Elba, in 1814 Pauline sold her hôtel to the Duke of Wellington, who made it the British embassy, which it still remains. After Waterloo, Hortense had to give up her hôtel too. In 1818 it became the Prussian embassy, therefore later the embassy of the German Empire and more recently the embassy of the German Republic. These democratic regimes have preserved without any sense of incongruity the memory of a dictatorial past, made beautiful by art.

The Bonapartes never straddled the continent, nor, though Lucien lived for a time in England and Jérôme in his youth and Joseph in middle age lived in America, did the family ever dominate these two English-speaking countries which were closed to French rule, if not to French influence. Napoleon did not exercise direct authority over many countries which yet were careful not to defy him, at least until it was safe. Similarly, even where approval of the Empire style was not official policy, its prestige was enough to ensure that patrons, architects, decorators and craftsmen knew its principles and followed its designs.

Percier and Fontaine were famous throughout Europe because they provided patterns for others to copy. Their fame was founded on the precise use of antiquity. In 1798 they issued their *Palais, maisons et autres edifices modernes dessinés à Rome*. Long years of study had given them an exact archaeological knowledge of ancient buildings and yet they also loved Renaissance Rome – in short they were intelligently eclectic. They followed up this success with the *Recueil de décorations intérieures comprenant tout ce qui rapport à l'ameublement*, which was issued over a period of more

One of the many splendid rooms in the Hôtel Beauharnais is the bedroom of
Queen Hortense, Napoleon's stepdaughter, sister-in-law and the mother of the
only other Bonaparte to rule in France, Napoleon III. The bed and the alcove
are by Jacob-Desmalter.

than a decade in twelve instalments of six plates each and finally in 1812 as a book. In this way anyone could learn what vases they planned for Maître B in Paris, what porcelain table-top would be made for him at Sèvres, what the differences were to be between the bedrooms of Monsieur and Madame G, what sort of desk Monsieur V would have, what *bergère*-type armchair was to be made for Monsieur de D, but then also the look of the library at Malmaison, of the ceiling of the guardroom of the Tuileries palace and of the cabinet of the King of Spain at Aranjuez. No wonder, when he was restoring his castle, the Count de Z sent from Poland his order for a bedroom. Percier and Fontaine provided an international standard of contem- porary design. If in France Fontaine had the ear of the Emperor, Percier knew Robert Adam and Thomas Hope in England. The Empire style was more cos- mopolitan than the Empire itself.

They had many imitators. Jean-Demosthène Dugourc, who was more famous for his work in Spain, drew many patterns for furniture and silks. François Grognard worked both for the Garde-Meuble Impérial and for the Duchess of Alba. Pierre de la Mesangère was a laicized priest who propagated the style with evangelical zeal. From 1802 to 1835 his *Collection de meubles et objets de goût* suggested inventive ways of using materials to *tapissiers* and their clients. As director from 1797 of the *Journal des dames et des modes* he was at the centre of the fashion industry, defender of the Empire line to French and so to European bourgeoises. Although after the wars were ended, England set the style for men, for women there never could be any substitute for France. What La Mesangère favoured mattered in every pro- vincial town from Moscow to Madrid.

The Empire style had its lowly practitioners. About 1813 Joseph Beunat pub- lished his *Recueil des dessins d'ornements d'architecture*. He announced that he had a factory of sculptured ornaments in Sarrebourg, not far from Strasbourg, and in Paris, rue Napoleon, no. 11. In his preface he cryptically refers to 'several well- known architect-decorators' who have contributed to his designs – he neither names them nor makes clear how they have helped him. From his book it is obvious how thoroughly Beunat had absorbed the manner of the day. He is up to date with the discoveries at Herculaneum, he makes play with the arch mood of David's master Vien – in his painting *The seller of Cupids* – and yet he always shows his grasp of the restrictions imposed by middle-class finances. 'These ornaments,' he writes, 'can be had in smaller or larger sizes . . . may be painted in distemper, oil or varnish . . . they can even take gilding that imitates gilt bronze . . . These ornaments can be worked like wood . . .' 'The use of these ornaments offers the advantage of a combination of beautiful decorations at a very modest price, which will always make them the choice of architects, artists and connoisseurs of art. Monsieur Beunat offers archi- tects and *amateurs* the service of executing their designs as quickly as possible at the same prices as those established for ready-made objects. A suite of rooms can be dec-

Pauline's Paris hôtel in rue du Faubourg Saint-Honoré, Hôtel de Charost, has been added to since it has been the British residence. The Blue Salon boasts a fine clock by Manière (c. 1810) that illustrates the proverb 'Ars longa, vita brevis' (art is long, life is short).

orated in 7 to 8 days.' Beunat may or may not have done well, but he was exactly the sort of person who helped to make the Empire style much more than just a preoccupation of the Empire's courts. If Napoleon's artistic policy had worked as he hoped, then France and its satellite kingdoms would have become nations full of shopkeepers like Beunat.

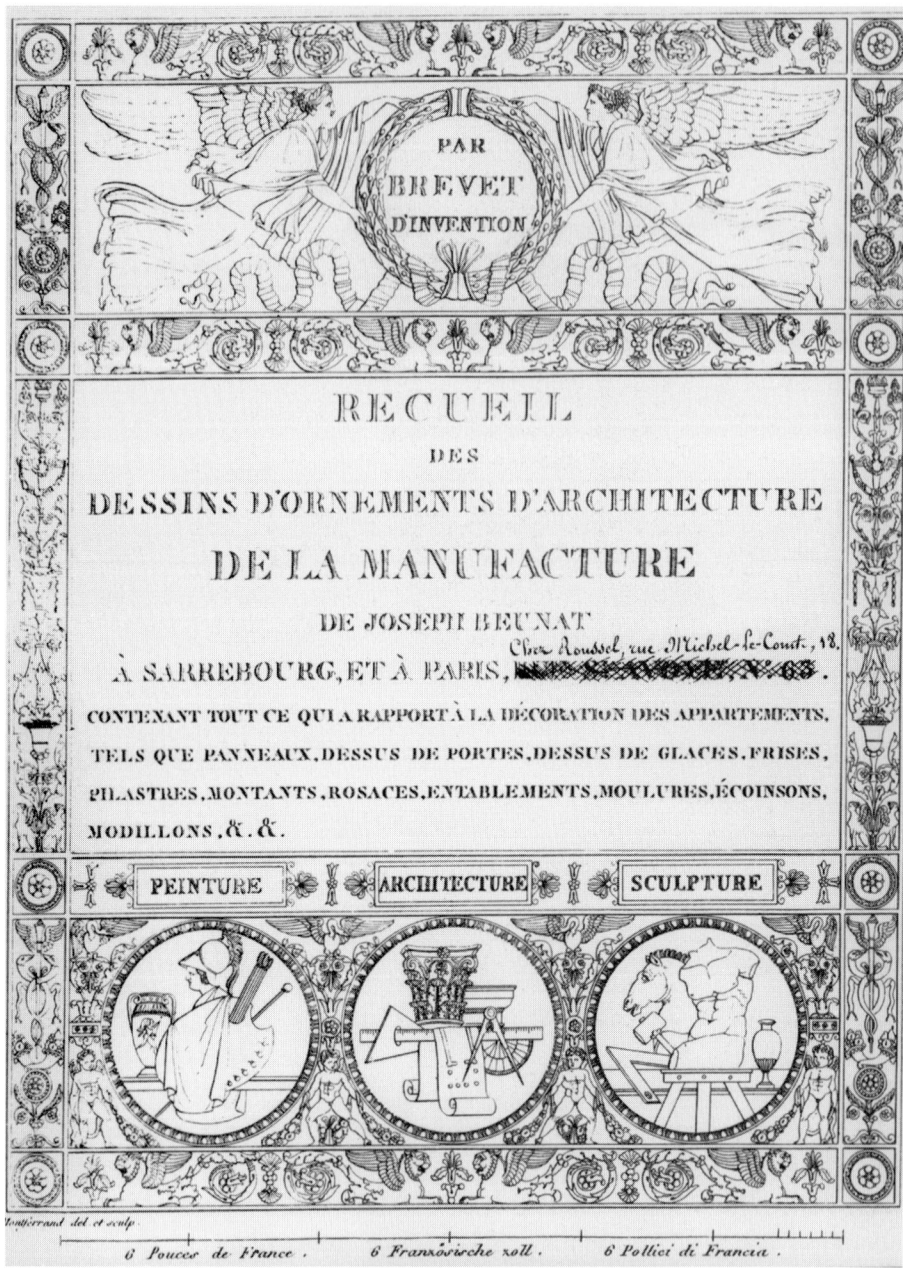

Beunat's frontispiece to his book of decorative motifs stresses his debt to the three arts of painting, architecture and sculpture, whose symbols he places at the foot of his design. Unfortunately, when the plate had been prepared, he changed his address.

The figures on Claude Galle's clock, bought by the Prince Regent in 1809 and now in Buckingham Palace, were once David's revolutionary Horatii, but they have become mere pieces of gilded bronze.

Only monarchs – whether emperors, kings or German princes – and great nobles or very wealthy commoners could afford the Empire style in its true form. Napoleon had a love of magnificence to which Napoleonic artists responded. He convinced his rivals that they should strive for magnificence too. The playfulness of Rococo decoration which had wound its whimsical way round the palaces and churches of central and eastern Europe gave way to the new imperious manner, and in lands like America or England with little Rococo tradition classic simplicity surrendered to classic grandeur. The Empire style had surprising admirers. The Prince Regent, later George IV, had collected much eighteenth-century furniture for Carlton House with the aid of Dominique Daguerre, and when in 1806 he started on his oriental folly at Brighton, he was bitterly disappointed that he could not fill it with more modern pieces of French furniture till after the wars were over. In silverware as in porcelain or in interior decoration the mood of contemporary British art was to move

The table of the great commanders, Buckingham Palace (1806–12) was made at Sèvres with mounts by Thomire. As the central commander is Alexander the Great, perhaps neither its eventual donor, Louis XVIII, nor its eventual recipient, the Prince Regent were bothered that Napoleon had commissioned it.

on parallel lines to the developments in France. Josiah Wedgwood and Robert Adam breathed the same intellectual air as Brongniart (at Sèvres) or Percier and Fontaine. Only Thomas Hope seems to have copied their work directly, but when in 1802 there was a temporary peace between Britain and France many thousands of milords and gentlemen and their ladies, many connoisseurs among them, hurried over the Channel to see what was fashionable in France. The cabinet-makers William and Edward Snell produced work in the Empire style which found a ready market, but nobody equalled the enthusiasm of the Duke of Wellington, who filled Apsley House with Empire furniture, or of the Prince Regent. In 1809 Claude Galle's clock, based on David's *Oath of the Horatii*, entered the royal collection, and in 1812 George bought a great vase in gilt bronze by Thomire. When war ended, Louis XVIII, conscious of the Prince of Wales' tastes, presented him with the

Table of the Great Commanders, which the Emperor had commissioned in praise of military genius (cameos of the commanders are grouped round Alexander). In Britain Empire arts appealed to the men who were Napoleon's conquerors, the one a general who fought the Emperor in a fitting style, the other a prince whose only battles were about what style should fit a king.

In America there could be no question of court art. Much as the Virginian dynasty – Jefferson and Madison and Monroe – favoured France, America stayed true to its republican roots. It is true that when planning a civic centre, Americans called on Frenchmen. Clérisseau helped Jefferson plan the Virginian State Capitol in Richmond, and L'Enfant brought clarity of design to the new capital city named Washington. During the Federal period, which lasted till about 1810, interior décor still owed much to publications by the Englishmen Hepplewhite and Sheraton, but Percier and Fontaine were also studied and some French *ébénistes* crossed the ocean to practise their craft. Around 1800 Honoré Lannuier came to New York and began to advertise his 'new fourniture' in the papers. Some joined him there – Alexandre Roux, Emmanuel Leprince-Ringuet, Joseph Brauwers. Others went to Boston and Philadelphia. In the latter city Michel Bouvier worked for a rich banker, Samuel Girard, and for Joseph Bonaparte, who sought refuge from Europe at Point Breeze. Bouvier's rival, Antoine Quervelle, worked for the White House and for the Blue Room there Monroe ordered Empire seats and an Empire clock. In Baltimore, where Jérôme Bonaparte had once found his true love, painters decorated their clients' houses with rosettes and leaves from Percier and Fontaine. For a time American Empire was light. Furniture was made of painted wood, tables had tops painted with delicate scenes in the Hudson River school style, arm-rests were thin and scroll-back chairs used the American not the Napoleonic eagle. Gradually the artifacts became more and more ponderous, till the Empire style looked out of place in the rougher world of Jackson's democratic America.

From 1812 to 1815 the United States was at least Napoleon's faithful friend. In Europe former allies became treacherous foes. For Napoleon himself the worst case, at least till his brother-in-law Murat stood out against him, was the Crown Prince of Sweden. Jean-Baptiste Bernadotte was brother-in-law to Joseph's wife. He was married to Désirée Clary, whom Napoleon had thought of marrying long ago. He had been a suspected Jacobin, who had disapproved of Brumaire – and yet Napoleon had made him a marshal immediately he became the Emperor Napoleon in 1804. He had intrigued with Madame de Staël, Napoleon's least favourite blue stocking – Napoleon hated and feared clever women, especially this one who talked as much as he did – and yet in 1806 he made him Prince of Ponte-Corvo. Bernadotte had given up his principles for a title and an income of a million francs. At the end of the year he did something even more advantageous for himself. When he captured some Swedes at Lübeck, he treated them with kindness and then released them. After the victory at Wagram in 1809 he caused offence once too often, for he made a point of telling his Saxons how much they were responsible for the triumph. Napoleon, who claimed all victories as his own, was not amused. He dismissed Bernadotte from the Grande Armée. It could have been the end of his career had not his detachment from Napoleon come to the notice of the Swedish leaders. They remembered his treatment of their troops, they had heard how well he had governed in Hanover, they had no heir to their throne and they wanted him. He guessed that they were desperate for a general to recapture Finland for them but he was unwilling to challenge the Russians who now owned it. In 1810 he became Crown Prince of Sweden, in 1813 he used the Swedish army with great skill in the Leipzig campaign, in 1814 he destroyed the Norwegian forces and in 1818 he became King Karl XIV Johan.

When Bernadotte arrived in Sweden, the Castle of Rosersberg had already been decorated in Empire style by Gjorwell. As King of Sweden, he made his Summer Palace at Rosendal a private sanctuary devoted to the cult of the Empire style. Like Louis Bonaparte he made use of local painters, cabinet-makers and upholsterers, and yet the decorative ideas, as well as the candelabra and the clocks, were imported from Paris. In the pages of a book dating back to 1801 – Krafft and Raisonette's *Plans, coupes et élévations des plus belles maisons et des hôtels construits à Paris et dans les environs* – Swedish craftsmen could study some features of modern French buildings that dated back only to the Directory and the first years of the Consulate, like the famous bedroom of Juliette Récamier, where the King had once been one of the most assiduous attendants. It was at her house, during the interlude of Amiens in 1802, that he had met Lord Charles James Fox and Lord and Lady Holland, the most aristocratic and articulate supporters of Anglo-French *rapprochement*. Now in his favourite palace he had his own grand bedroom, in green and white and gold, based on Percier and Fontaine. He lived in Empire splendour till his death in 1844 and was peacefully succeeded by his son Oscar, whose name had been picked by Napoleon from Ossian's lays.

French influence had its most spectacular effects in Russia. Under Catherine the Great the creation of Neo-Classical St Petersburg had begun. Her son, the mad Paul I (1796–1801), used an Italian designer, Vicenzo Brenna, and an elderly Russian architect, Bazhenov, whom his hated mother had neglected, to build a fortress, the Michael Castle, where he could feel safe. The Tsar ended up with an eclectic building, which would have offended Catherine's purist tastes, and it did not even protect him. Three weeks after he had moved in, Paul was murdered in his bedroom. His son Alexander I seems to have felt guilty about his father's death, but he had the good judgement to continue his grandmother's work. He developed her project for the capital, often under French direction.

Immediately after his accession he asked Thomas de Thomon to design the stock

The bedroom of Karl XIV Johan, Rosersberg Palace, is a fine example of how one of Napoleon's bitterest enemies copied and adapted his style.

exchange, which like the Paris Bourse became a temple of lucre. The Academy of Mines and the Admiralty were designed by Russians who had been taught by French architects, and another French architect, Auguste Ricard de Montferrand, built St Isaac's Cathedral. Alexander's love of Empire style was not ended by the fighting from 1812 to 1815. A year after Waterloo he placed a French engineer, Béthencourt, in charge of the co-ordination of building in St Petersburg. Even seventy years of Communism and three years of Nazi bombardment have not destroyed Alexander's dream 'to make Petersburg more beautiful than any other capital he has visited'. Beside his achievement Napoleon's Paris, with its meagre collection of grand buildings – the Madeleine, the Bourse and the Arc de Triomphe – and unrealized plans – the Palace of the King of Rome – and missing centrepiece – the Tuileries linked to the Louvre – looks remarkable only in principle. It is true that Alexander reigned longer, for twenty-four years, and true that his successor, Nicholas I, continued with his schemes. But in St Petersburg heaviness was avoided by the steady adherence to Greek rather than to Roman models. During the whole year a cool northern light cast sharp shadows on the shining structures that rose on the Neva's banks and in many dark months crystals of ice and snow made them glitter. Nothing that survives in France is as resplendent as the Malachite Room in the Winter Palace – and yet de Montferrand, the man responsible for it, was a pupil of Percier's. What Alexander's Russia enjoyed it owed to Napoleon's France. Alexander also encouraged one of the more unfortunate legacies of the French Emperor, a love of huge objects for their size alone. The removal of a granite monolith from the quarries of Lake Ladoga and its erection in Winter Palace Square in 1829 may have been one of the engineering triumphs of the age after the end of the wars. Unfortunately the Alexander Column, though it was more massive than anything in Paris or Rome and so adequately fulfilled Alexander's vision of himself as the guardian of Christian autocracy, never equalled its models in beauty. Luckily for Alexander's reputation as a new Augustus, he was already four years in his grave.

Napoleon and his subordinates impressed his sense of scale on every area where it was possible. In 1806 he ordered the laying out of a Foro Bonaparto in Milan, he had Frenchmen plan but could not have them execute the construction of the Piazza del Popolo in Rome, and there was a slight Napoleonic emendation of the Piazza di San Marco in Venice. The prestige of France meant that, though every country from America to Russia and from Spain to Sweden had its own architects and decorators, only Frenchmen were able to find work everywhere. Denmark had its own distinguished architect, Hansen, who designed the chief church of Copenhagen in 1808–10, and an internationally renowned Neo-Classical sculptor in Thorwaldsen, who produced statues for the interior, but culturally as well as economically and politically Denmark was subordinate to France. Perhaps only one continental land, Germany, and within that land one country, Prussia, opted for something like artis-

Since the destruction of Saint-Cloud and the Tuileries the Malachite Room, Winter Palace, St Petersburg gives one of the finest examples of the splendour at which Empire style aimed. The room was designed by Montfried, one of Percier's pupils.

tic independence. Even there French ideas left their mark.

Napoleon would have been glad had he understood how profound would be the effect of his creation of a school for engineers, the Ecole Polytechnique. There the professor of architecture was Jean-Nicolas-Louis Durand, a pupil of the most visionary of Neo-Classical architects, Etienne-Louis Boullée. In 1802–5 Durand published a textbook that summarized his lectures. Although a theorist, he had the practical turn of mind of a good teacher – he wished to provide models that could be used. His examples were drawn from many sources – classical, early Christian, Romanesque, Renaissance (only sometimes) and even Gothic (quite often). He knew what had been awarded the Prix de Rome in recent years. He was familiar with Boullée's plans. Some of his pupils worked within the Grand Empire, for example Bienaimé, who was architect to Elisa Bonaparte, but more interesting work was achieved in Germany, where his eclectic spirit mattered more than his detailed prescriptions.

Leo van Klenze had studied under Durand in Paris before he was called by Jérôme Bonaparte to be court architect in Westphalia in 1808. In 1814, when that kingdom had foundered, he was summoned to Munich by Maximilian of Bavaria, who also owed his kingship to Napoleon and had kept it. There in his dull way Klenze built the Munich Glyptothek, a sculpture gallery whose plan (in spirit) and sections (in detail) were derived from Durand. So under French inspiration began the plodding Munich classicism that Hitler was to think characteristically Teutonic. It was in Berlin that there was more sign of German originality. Before his early death in 1800 Friedrich Gilly had outlined a monument to his royal namesake, Frederick the Great, with all the starkness that French revolutionaries would have loved. Karl Friedrich von Schinkel, who was named state architect in 1815, was lucky to live longer, till 1841, by which time he had created a national as well as a regional style. To call Schinkel an Empire architect-designer would be unwarranted chauvinism. Whether as designer of stage sets for *The Magic Flute* or as painter of fantasy Gothic cathedrals, Schinkel had stylistic resources far beyond those available to Durand or Percier and Fontaine. But every so often he betrays his debt to Empire style. In his Altes Museum in Berlin the rectangular attic, which looks so four-square from outside, masks a Durandesque central domed space, such as were convention-ally used to provide a setting for classical statues. In the Charlottenburg palace in Berlin and in the Charlottenhof palace outside it, in Potsdam, Schinkel uses pure Empire decoration in a mood of refined austerity in the shape of a bed, in the motifs on a chandelier or on the walls of a Roman bath or in the tented hangings of a bedroom. He created a kind of Protestant Empire manner, which looked authentic in 1830s Prussia.

Napoleon had given the Empire style the immense authority of his blessing. Other rulers, almost as autocratic as him, but also more artistic, above all more legit-imate than him, whether through the affection of his subjects (in the case of King Karl XIV Johan of Sweden) or through the religious aura of his position (as in the case of Tsar Alexander I of All the Russias), encouraged variants on that style often long after the French Empire had disappeared. The style outlasted the regime that had created it. But it was also true that the style's longevity was a persistent reminder of Napoleon's former greatness, and its eventual demise was presaged by his fall.

CHAPTER 10

Continental Blockade and the Defeat of the Empire Style

THE LOGIC of Napoleon's victories from 1805 to 1809 and indeed of much European history for 150 years was the Grand Empire. Since the accession of Louis XIV to personal rule in 1661 it had seemed natural that France should dominate the continent. Set between Spain, Italy, Switzerland, Germany and the Low Countries, and with long coastlines on the Mediterranean sea and the Atlantic Ocean, France was the largest country of western Europe in surface area and it had the largest population. Unlike Spain or Switzerland, France had a land-scape that was both fertile and varied. Freak weather conditions had induced a severe and politically critical shortage of bread in 1787-9, but, though only parts of France had as yet been touched by the changes in farming techniques that had trans-formed Dutch and English agriculture, France could normally feed itself. In the north the plains were suited to cereal production and the undulating hills to the rearing of dairy herds. Many areas, like the old provinces of Champagne and Burgundy and the new department named after the estuary of the Gironde, were centres of large-scale vine-growing. Besides the rivers flowing into the Gironde, the country had three other river systems that were conduits for internal trade – the Loire (leading to the Atlantic), the Seine (leading to the Channel) and the Saône-and-Rhône (leading to the Mediterranean). In the eighteenth century a boom in interna-tional commerce brought prosperity to Bordeaux and Nantes and Marseille. France had a thriving textile industry, most of it in the north-eastern cloth towns and the silk-producing city of Lyon. Strict apprenticeship laws had maintained the quality of the luxury goods in furniture and porcelain, which were manufactured chiefly in the Paris region. Its jealously guarded West Indian islands of Martinique and Guadeloupe gave France the benefits of a sugar and slave economy that only England could match.

France's economic development had been hindered by weak financial structures and by an obsolete tax system, by legal restrictions on the movement of trade and by a social disdain both of peasant proprietorial aspirations and of bourgeois commercial values which was typical of the *ancien régime*. In 1789 the tax system and the legal restrictions were swept away. Peasants had succeeded in grabbing much of the land, but that was an end in itself – in remoter regions they delayed improvements for almost 150 years. Among Parisian bourgeois politicians the Jacobins were too high-minded to concern themselves with creating wealth – they preferred either to take away the property of counter-revolutionaries or to keep down the price of grain (an admirable but finally unattainable goal). Under the *ancien régime* only a few royal ministers had grasped the need for sound finance and most of the privileged classes resisted the very thought of it. While the Netherlands had had the Bank of Amsterdam (since 1609) and Britain the Bank of England (since 1694), in 1789 there was still no Bank of Paris or Lyon or France. No revolutionary minister understood finance. Cash flow problems would go away, Talleyrand implied, if Church land was nationalized and sold off. No one foresaw that inflation would follow and that the paper money of the new regime would soon be more worthless than government bonds at the worst moments of the old. When the Directors came to power in 1795, they knew how to make themselves and their friends rich, but not how to make France rich too.

When he became First Consul, Napoleon was determined that France should be financially stable and that Frenchmen should go back to work. Even if the Bank of France, founded in 1800, could never tap the resources available in Amsterdam and London – Napoleon was as obsessed with the idea of Dutch money-lenders as with the idea of English shopkeepers – the principle of cautious loans appealed to the *nouveaux riches* who wanted to hold on to their money. What Napoleon did not encourage was the spirit of free enterprise. It was not in his nature to approve of it and it was not traditional in France. What the Bourbons had developed, especially under Louis XIV, was 'Colbertism' (named after Louis' ablest minister). Businesses were set up by the State, their directors chosen by the State, their standards set by the State, their products often made for the State. Such a policy implied royal patronage of the arts. Colbert had directed the building of the extensions to Versailles, had masterminded the establishment or re-establishment of the various academies – including those of painting and architecture – and had watched over the textile factories of Beauvais and Abbeville as well as of the Gobelins, famous for its tapestries, and of the Savonnerie, famous for its carpets.

Under the Consulate and still more under the Empire this policy was revived. The Emperor tried to put the best people in charge. David was made his chief painter, Fontaine was made his chief architect, Denon became the director of the Louvre museum and the younger Brongniart became the director of the Sèvres manufactory. Napoleon ordered his silk from Lyon, his carpets from Aubusson and the Savonnerie, his costumes from factories in French Flanders, his porcelain from Sèvres, his furniture from Jacob-Desmalter, his silver from Odiot or Biennais, his bronze mounts from Thomire. Whenever possible he, his wives, his brothers, his sisters, his ministers, his marshals, his courtiers, the City of Paris bought beautiful objects that were made in France. The high finish that they demanded meant that once more artistic skill was in fashion and those who could not afford works made in the imperially patronized workshops looked for goods produced more cheaply elsewhere. Even though the Napoleonic Institute brought back a system of artistic approval similar to that once exercised by the academies, the deregulation of the arts brought about by the revolution remained partly in place. Jacob-Desmalter was not trained as an *ébéniste*, yet he was the most important of Empire cabinet-makers. Around Lyon and Paris many small and medium-sized firms made fabrics, furniture and *objets d'art* for an open market. All France lacked was any equivalent to Josiah Wedgwood, his heirs and the Wedgwood family business.

Soundly bourgeois though he was at times, Napoleon viewed life as a soldier. He wanted to make France great at the expense of her neighbours, and, if this meant marching and counter-marching through other countries and the confiscation of defeated enemies' lands, the billeting of soldiers on alien landlords and the taxing of other rulers' subjects or his own non-French subjects, he was not perturbed. Just as he wished that what was disagreeable in his regime should not be felt at home, so he intended that subjects or allies abroad should have their interests, including their commercial interests, subordinated to those of France. The Grand Empire existed for the greater glory of Napoleon and the greater good of France.

From the Directors Napoleon inherited one form of warfare that he himself could never win, namely war at sea. At the end of the American war of independence in 1783, which was marked by the signing of a treaty at Versailles, it seemed that England was reduced to the role of a second-rate power. Shorn of all his mainland American territories, except for the cold Canadian colonies that had been taken from France some twenty years before, and hanging on to a handful of West Indian isles (only after Rodney's late victory at the Battle of the Saints (1782)) and the rock of Gibraltar only after a three-year siege, George III no longer counted as a world power in the class of the Kings of Spain, Portugal or France, for, oddly, the largest areas under English control, in India, were run as a commercial venture by the East India Company, over which the English Crown had merely indirect control. The first British Empire was at an end. England had meanwhile reinforced the Bourbon family pact between the Kings of France and Spain and by its aggressive interception of neutral shipping had added the Baltic naval powers to its formidable list of foes. While Louis XVI had triumphed in his first serious foreign policy challenge, his brother of England could no longer afford to fight.

Ten years later the positions of George III and Louis XVI had been reversed. The English won their first diplomatic counterblow when in 1787, together with the King of Prussia, they stifled another Patriot and Francophile movement, this time in the Netherlands. By then his finances made any foreign adventure impossible for the King of France, while across the Channel the younger Pitt was busy restoring the credit and credibility of George III. George III went mad, or so it appeared, in 1788, but neither he nor Pitt lost their heads. In 1793, however, Louis XVI was executed and England went to war with France. Although in the previous century the English had treated their king in a similar way, the thought of republicanism now appalled them – and there was a good reason for going to war. The new French republic was at war with Austria, whose Emperor was nephew of the imprisoned Queen Marie-Antoinette, and set about invading Belgium, the Austrian Netherlands. It proposed to break France's treaty obligations by opening the Scheldt to trade. This river had originally been closed so that Dutch ports would no longer have to cope with the rivalry of Antwerp, which stood on the Scheldt, but England thought that preserving the closure was a means of guarding against the danger that Belgium would be dominated by a power that could threaten invasion. In 1794, when the French armies overran Belgium, English fears were justified.

For twenty of the twenty-two years between 1793 and 1815 England fought the French. During much of this period England helped finance whatever other powers were at war with France. There was an obvious reason for this. When the British army intervened directly on the continent, its generals had an unhappy tendency to opt for amphibious landings which failed – and not till the Peninsular War (1808–14) did England find an area where one fine general, Wellington, could succeed. England's principal military asset was always its navy. During the American war the Earl of Sandwich had invested in copper-bottom boats and after it the feats of the one able admiral of that war, Rodney, inspired a younger generation of naval commanders, of whom the finest was Nelson. In France, however, most naval officers were royalists and they would not serve a regicide cause. As a result the war at sea took a course very different from that on land. Every major naval battle that the British fought they won. They defeated the Dutch, the Danish and the Spaniards, whenever they were reluctant allies of France, as well as the French themselves. The British blockaded France or other countries at will. While the East India Company's soldiers gained more land in India, British ships picked off French or Dutch colonies one by one, cut links between Spain and Latin America and quietly dumped convicts at the newest British colony, at Botany Bay.

Though he had good reason to ignore English soldiers, Napoleon was obsessed by the need to defeat Britain. In 1797 and in 1801 England was the only power to stand against France, when Prussia, Austria and Russia, with much larger armies, felt it prudent to be at peace or to make peace. It was England which had wrecked the Egyptian expedition and French attempts at counterblows in Ireland and India had come to nothing – in 1800 England incorporated Ireland into Great Britain. The only time when there was a respite from British disruption of Napoleon's plans occurred in 1802–3, when the peace of Amiens enforced a temporary truce. But when George III had urged Parliament to call up the militia and Napoleon had shouted in public at Lord Whitworth, the British ambassador, the international stage was set for a renewal of war. The cartoonist Gillray was to imagine Pitt and Napoleon carving up Europe between them. Trafalgar and Austerlitz confirmed that the division was made between one man who controlled the sea and one man who controlled the land. For Napoleon this division was unsatisfying. What he wanted was to control both, that is he intended to control the sea from the land.

It was obvious at the beginning of 1805 that without a naval victory France could not invade England and by the end of 1805 that France did not have the fleet to do so. Napoleon had to find another way to do down the English. The import of cotton from England had quadrupled in two years, so in 1806 he prohibited the import of cotton or muslin. This was perhaps just a normal nationalistic act in support of his country's merchants, for simultaneously he pleased the silk firms of Lyon by allow, ing Piedmontese silk firms to export to France only by sea at a time when the English had effectively closed the sea from Genoa to Nice. Later that year, after the defeat of Prussia, he determined to use his new strength to act more harshly against England. Immediately after Jena he ordered the impounding of British goods, once Hamburg was taken he made their merchants surrender British goods – with only limited success – and in Berlin he issued decrees to blockade Britain. The English cartoon, ists treated this action as a joke, but Napoleon was in earnest. By further decrees issued at Fontainebleau and Milan he specified that no merchant ship from Britain or its colonies, including merchant ships that had docked in British ports and mer, chant ships that had been searched by British warships, was to be allowed to dock in ports belonging to the Grand Empire. In his struggle against the United Kingdom and its colonies Napoleon would allow no neutrals. When he made peace with the Tsar at Tilsit, the Tsar undertook to persuade the English to return the colonies they had seized and again to allow free sailing on the high seas. Were this to fail, then Sweden, Denmark and Portugal would be forced to join Napoleon's 'continental system'.

The English were not impressed. By their own orders in council they blockaded the continent – they would allow no neutral country to trade with Napoleon's land, locked Europe. Their own merchants had trading connections that allowed them to continue exporting their own goods, for example via Heligoland, which was briefly the European centre of contraband. As gradually the two blockades were more tightly enforced, the great docks of Europe grew still, whether in the old ports of the Hanseatic League like Hamburg and Lübeck or of the province of Holland like Amsterdam and Rotterdam or on the French Atlantic coast like Bordeaux and Nantes. In an age when roads were often pitted with potholes, when there were too few canals and when too few rivers were navigable, Napoleon had tried to set up a continental economy that was deprived of the most reliable of all methods of transporting goods, by boat over the sea. With the same logic he threatened to cut off the continent of Europe from all other continents, from India, from the islands of the East and West Indies and above all from the American mainland. It was as if he wished to reverse the process by which world trade had developed since Spain first grew rich on New World silver and Portugal on the spices of the East.

The continental system was an extension of war. Napoleon never professed to understand trade, only to understand traders. He was sure that by hitting the profits of the English traders he would bring the English government to treat for peace. He drove them to seek markets further and further afield, in the eastern Mediterranean via Malta in the ports of the Levant and even in French-held Trieste and Fiume, across the Atlantic in Caracas and Buenos Aires, where Creole rebels set up republics that were independent of Spain, and in New York and Boston, even though the American government tried to keep out of the quarrel between one European power to which it owed its freedom and another which was its chief trading partner. Meanwhile the British navy resumed its steady warfare against the colonies of France and its so-called allies. In 1806 the British took over the Cape of Good Hope, in 1807 Surinam, Curaçao and Madeira, in 1808 Gorea, in 1809 French Guiana and Martinique, in 1810 Guadeloupe, Réunion, Madagascar and Java, till it seemed that only one European nation would be a world power. This had implications for the future balance of power in Europe. Immediately it affected the arts of peace.

French women loved Indian muslins, French cabinet-makers loved mahogany, French textile firms needed indigo as a dye and Joséphine needed more flowers. Neither government could afford to allow no trade at all and each government did not want to trade at any disadvantage to itself. The British would license the export of coffee and sugar from Martinique and Guadeloupe and the import of cereal from anywhere, the French insisted on the export of silk and wine and, without paying any attention to either government, their traders sent lace, pictures, jewellery and *objets d'art*. What France could not survive without were the raw materials of industry to which only the British now had direct access – dyes, spices, skins, sulphur, potassium, gum – and the products, which only British industry could produce in sufficient quantity, made of cotton, wool and canvas. As late as 1811, however, it seemed that Napoleon had created grave problems for British industry.

With its rapidly growing population, which, despite its improving agriculture, Britain already had problems in feeding, and with the advanced technology of its modern industries, Britain needed to export. For its merchant shipping there was a wide world outside Europe, but the journeys were long and dangerous and the countries willing to trade were not sufficiently rich to receive all England had to offer. Britain needed to break Napoleon's blockade.

Similarly, even within the Grand Empire Napoleon made life hard for the artisans he intended to help. In 1801 he had given his blessing to the Society for the Encouragement of National Industry, which set up competitions for the invention of new machines for knitting and combing wool, for spinning cotton and for spinning silk. At the same time he knew that modernization might increase unemployment, so he liked industries that were labour intensive. This created problems, for the largest employer of workers was the textile industry, but it was precisely in the textile industry that English firms had gone over to new technology. Without the special conditions created by the continental system, France's factories were bound to suffer if there was a freeing of trade, as had happened after the pre-revolutionary Vergennes commercial treaty in 1786. What France could offer the world was the excellence of its luxury industries, where despite the interruption caused by the revolution France retained a skilled workforce. At Sèvres, Brongniart used his skill as a chemist to improve the methods used in his porcelain factory. It was Napoleon's policy to invest money in these factories by making generous orders for his palaces and official buildings. Early in 1807 he decreed that 1,400,000 francs should be spent on silk, 5000 on crystal, 1,550,000 on locks. From Tilsit in July that year he directed that 1,206,980 francs should be spent on furniture, bronze, porcelain, fabrics and lace for Compiègne and Versailles. For the same reason he laid down that his servants should wear uniforms that shone with gold and silver braid, to force them to spend money on their clothes. When it came to the wedding of his sister Caroline to Murat or of Joséphine's cousin to the Duke of Arenberg, he was generous with the trousseaux he offered the brides. There was unfortunately a limit to the number of Napoleonic parvenus who would spend extravagantly on adopting an Empire style of beauty in their clothes and in the décor of their houses or palaces, but with each striking victory and each harsh treaty Napoleon seemed to advance the cause of French luxury industries. After Tilsit a former sugar plantation owner from Santo Domingo who lived in Normandy wrote that he anticipated that the new treaty with Russia would give opportunities to Paris, Rouen, Brussels (which was offically French), Saint-Quentin, Lyon and other French towns to win the trade that formerly had been won by London, Birmingham, Manchester and Bristol. There was inevitably a downside for the industrial towns that France conquered, for in every case their interests were sacrificed to the needs of their French rivals. In certain cases this was disastrous. Naples and the Netherlands had maritime economies and they depended on trade with the English. The continental system quietly offered them nothing but ruin, unless they could change their trading habits. It was for this reason that Louis, King of Holland protested so stubbornly against his brother's plans. When he had patronized the Empire style, he had been careful to look to Dutch architects, artists and artisans. Now he was told by his overbearing brother that 'the Dutch have energy all right – for smuggling'. Napoleon was right and Louis had to go.

Napoleon's policy had linked architects, artists and artisans. The Empire style favoured by Percier and Fontaine, by Jacob-Desmalter, by Denon, by Prud'hon and by David affected alike the construction of public buildings – the Arc du Carrousel, the Arc de Triomphe and the Madeleine – and the work of the factories. It was the artists who provided the designs for the fabrics, tapestries, curtains and painted paper, who created for Beauvais its flowers and blue birds on a white back-gound. From 1800 Huet was the director of Beauvais. For the textile factory of Oberkampf at Jouy he invented delicate hues of lilac and gold and from old favourites like the *Fables* of Fontaine or new ones like *Paul et Virginie* he invented new pictures. The silk weavers of Lyon relied on a whole school of local flower paint-ers. Thomire made bronze candelabras, clocks, vases, sugar bowls, inkwells for the Emperor after the designs of Percier. Biennais and Auguste made gold-plated objects in the spirit of antiquity.

All this was luxury for the luxurious, but the existence of a journeyman designer like Beunat showed that the Empire style could be adapted to the *bourgeois moyen*. Had the Empire remained stable, the Empire style and French luxury industries could have formed the visual culture of the continent for a generation. Ironically it sub-sisted in countries that ultimately rejected Napoleon – Sweden and Russia – and was appreciated by men who became his bitterest enemies – the Prince Regent and the Duke of Wellington. But the economic policy that bolstered the Empire style had to cope with severe economic results in 1810–11 and severe military results in 1812–13.

François-Honoré-Georges Jacob, known in the trade as Jacob-Desmalter, was among artists the most spectacular casualty of his master's misfortunes.

Born in 1770 as the second son of Georges Jacob (1739–1814), a celebrated joiner (*menuisier*), François-Honoré-Georges had begun to learn his skills in the family workshop in rue Meslée at the age of five. There he had absorbed his father's love of English-style mahogany chairs with open backs, his father's flair for working with painters – first the landscapist Hubert Robert, then Louis David – and his father's modern, that is to say Neo-Classical, taste. Georges Jacob made 'Etruscan' chairs for Queen Marie-Antoinette's dairy at Rambouillet and similar furniture for 'Philippe-Egalité', the radical Duc d'Orléans, before providing David with the more austerely classical tables and chairs he wanted for his studio. His friendship with David was a passport to his survival during the worst days of the revolution. He was further helped by the revolutionary abolition of the distinction between the 'middle-class' *menuisiers* and the 'aristocratic' *ébénistes* or cabinet-makers. Riesener, greatest of *ébénistes*, was a relic of the *ancien régime* when he ended his days forgotten in 1806. Georges Jacob, with a less brilliant and much less extravagant talent, retired in 1796, assured that his firm and his style would survive under the republic.

For seven years the firm was known as Jacob frères, while it was directed by François-Honoré-Georges and his older brother, the second Georges Jacob. In 1803, however, Georges junior died, so Georges senior came out of retirement to help his surviving son, who took on the now familiar double-barrelled surname. When the two brothers had been working together, François-Honoré-Georges was responsible for the artistic decisions. In the years of the Directory (1795–9) a taste for luxury had returned, but the franc was unstable and the *nouveaux riches* wanted to make cheap materials look expensive. When Récamier, the ageing banker, bought the former Hôtel Necker at 7, rue du Mont-Blanc to be the showcase in which he could place his beautiful and famously chaste young wife, he gave Jacob frères a chance to reveal that they had a sense for the grandeur appropriate to her fame. Her boudoir, her bathroom and her bedroom were the parts of the house that were most frequented. Percier's pupil Berthault, an architect who later worked for Joséphine de Beauharnais at Malmaison, was asked to design some improvements and the Jacob frères to help execute them. Others produced the silk hangings on the walls and the glistening mirrors in which Madame Récamier and her visitors admired themselves, the Jacobs provided mahogany for the doors, the bedside tables, the pilasters that framed the mirrors and the focus of attention, the bed. This commission led to an even more useful commission, for they were asked to furnish the Bonaparte Hôtel in rue Chatereine.

Their father had made furniture for the Assemblée Nationale to the designs of Percier. The sons were able to continue the association as they realized Percier's ideas to the delight of Napoleon and Joséphine. When Napoleon eventually gave the house to his equerry, Joséphine was careful to take with her her favourite pieces, including a commode now at Fontainebleau and a desk now in the Grand Trianon, Versailles. In his diary Fontaine praised the 'rare intelligence' with which François-Honoré-Georges Jacob planned and executed the woodwork of the library at Malmaison. As Percier and Fontaine published the successive plates of their *Recueil des decorations intérieures*, they advertised the achievement of the younger Jacob. In 1801 they printed an engraving of the first boat bed, for the wife of General Moreau. In 1802 Jacob made it. When next year his older brother died, he started to use the stamp 'Jacob-Desmalter'. If his father had prepared the way for the Empire style, he became its principal exponent. As his own son, Georges Alphonse, was to be one of Percier's pupils and was to direct the business from 1825 to 1847, the name Jacob with or without its addition became as important to Neo-Classical furniture as the name Boulle had been to the marquetry of the Baroque and early Rococo periods. Boulle was for ever linked to Louis XIV and Jacob-Desmalter for ever linked to Napoleon.

Under the Empire he became chief supplier to the royal furniture repository, won the gold medal (and a commendation by the jury for his 'superior talent') at the 1806 industrial exhibition and was granted the ponderous title of 'carpenter, cabinet-maker, manufacturer of furniture and bronze for their Imperial and Royal Majesties'. In every Napoleonic palace or in every Napoleonic suite of rooms, at the Louvre, the Tuileries and the Elysée, at Fontainebleau, Compiègne, the Grand Trianon and Rambouillet, there was lots and lots of Jacob-Desmalter. No rival factory produced so much as his. None was so influential. His fondness for geometric shapes, his eclectic use of winged Asiatic Chimeras, of Greek caryatids and terms with Egyptian heads, his sense of the monumental – each feature of his art empha-sized the grandeur of the Empire. Ironically for a furniture-maker who aimed to glorify a ruler whose power depended on military might, there is no more impres-sive example of this pompous and ceremonious manner than the enormous jewel case known as the *Grand Ecrin* which was ordered for Napoleon's first wife and which became the property of his second. A cabinet, all of whose drawers and compartments have their locks concealed behind tiny bronze ornaments, stands on eight legs. Each small section is divided by rectangular bronze frames and the three main parts by engaged pillars with bronze capitals and bases. The cabinet is carved out of yew and ebony and mahogany and inlaid with mother-of-pearl (for necklaces and diadems) as well as the ubiquitous bronze. In the centre Venus rises from the sea, where dolphins play, and Cupids dance attendance round her. Although over 270 centimetres high, 200 centimetres broad and 60 centimetres deep, the *Grand Ecrin* proved too small for the Empress Marie-Louise, so two lesser jewel cases, box-like in shape, were made to put on either side of it. Meanwhile the supplanted Joséphine slept and in the end died in a massive bed with swans' heads at its head and an eagle above the canopy. The delicacy that Madame Récamier and Joséphine herself had once favoured was out of fashion. Jacob-Desmalter created a manner, sober and splendid, to fit a dominion that dominated a continent. He worked for Eugène and Hortense de Beauharnais, for Murat, for Marshal Davout, for Marshal Soult. He also did not disdain the custom of the bourgeoisie or foreigners, but churned out bookcases, desks with mechanical devices and roll-top desks and flat desks and writing desks (up to 8000 francs), pedestal tables, bedside tables (console tables could cost 6000 francs), screens for the fire and screens for the dressing room,

Joséphine's huge bed at Malmaison was made by Jacob-Desmalter, the carpet came from Beauvais and the furnishings were redecorated by Berthault in 1812.

stools, armchairs from thirty-six to 1200 francs, *chaises-longues*, beds.

Furniture was big business. In 1808 Jacob-Desmalter et Cie employed more than 300 in subordinate workshops and as many in the main workshops in and around Paris. When Napoleon was crowned and when he married, Jacob-Desmalter et Cie had a workforce of 800. What happened to his company was as much a sign of the health of the French economy then as the state of the car industry in a First World country now. In 1807, when the continental system was imposed, the number of workers fell to fifty or sixty and in 1812, when it was in crisis, to seventy.* The British navy ensured that mahogany was in short supply. Whereas in the financial year 1806–7 Jacob-Desmalter paid more tax to the Seine prefect than any other manufacturer, in the first crisis of 1807 he borrowed more than 50,000 francs from the State. When the second crisis hit him in 1812, he could not keep up his repayments. During the winter of 1813–14, while more than 2000 redundant furniture workers froze, Jacob-Desmalter declared himself bankrupt. The shock killed his poor father, who could not know that the firm's creditors would refloat the company with François-Honoré-Georges still in charge. The act re-establishing Jacob-Desmalter et Cie became official on 18 February 1815, just over a week before Napoleon left the isle of Elba. For the last hundred days of the Empire François-Honoré-Georges was once again the principal furniture-maker of France. When Louis XVIII came back after Waterloo, François-Honoré-Georges lost his pre-eminence. Everyone knew he had been the Emperor's man. Though he lived on till 1841, after the Emperor's ashes had come back to Paris, he felt like an exile from court. In 1825 he handed over the business to his son.

The crisis of 1811–12, which almost overwhelmed Jacob-Desmalter, was the worst financial crisis to afflict Napoleon's France. The Emperor had always maintained that the cycle of crises during the revolutionary decade of 1789–99 was the result of poor financial management. The Directory had coped with some of its lack of funds by means of military victories, especially those of Napoleon himself, for the losers were made to pay the cost of fighting. In this way France had avoided the horrors of high taxation. She had also never been made to endure a policy of financial retrench-ment like that which the younger Pitt imposed on Britain between 1783 and 1793. In 1809 Crétet, the Minister of the Interior, went so far as to predict that there was less need than in the past to worry about the good fortune of industry. Montalivet, his successor, was less sanguine, but early in 1810 there was a boom. Like many booms it was based on feelings of optimism rather than on optimum conditions, for there were still problems about importing raw materials from former colonies, and in May there were the first signs of trouble. Those who had bought colonial prod-ucts at exorbitant prices could not sell them and those involved in shipping could not occupy their boats. Bankruptcies followed in the region of Nantes and in some of the principal towns of Brittany – Morlaix, Rennes, Brest and Vannes. In September the ancient house of Rodde, burgomaster of Lübeck, failed and in

*The initial impact of the continental blockade led to some contraction of the business of Jacob-Desmalter in 1807. The business recovered and was able to expand in 1808–11. When therefore it was hit by the economic crisis of 1811–12, the second subsequent contraction, which still left the firm employing more workers than in 1807, was more serious, as it involved more debt and almost led to the collapse of the firm.

October the Amsterdam bank of Smeth. The Bank of France reacted cautiously and turned down several requests for loans, insisted on repayments within seventy days and cut down on loans it issued at its provincial outlets in Lyon and Rouen. At Frankfurt interest rates rose from 3 per cent to 7 per cent and then to 9 per cent. At Leipzig the volume of trade at the Michaelmas fair was 33 per cent below the level of the spring fair. The continental system meant that France had to endure the economic effects of Germany's problems. Early in 1811 the problems became those of the banking houses of Paris and Lyon and soon those of many businesses in provincial France. From the ports – Bordeaux and Nantes, Caen and Rouen – the news was especially bad. When Oberkampf was allowed a loan for three months, people were amazed by the news, puzzled by whether it was a sign of the entrepreneur's weakness or of his luck. The worst troubles for industry and high finance seemed over. In the summer, however, there were poor harvests and the winter was very cold. Hunger rather than unemployment had become the most serious economic concern of Napoleonic France.

Unemployment had undermined many of the luxury industries. The first to suffer had been the silk firms in Lyon. In three months the number of looms went down from 14,000 to 7000. Production, which had stood at almost 50,000 kilos in October 1809, went down to less than 24,000 kilos in October 1811, and there was a further decline in November. As many as 20–25,000 workers were thrown out of work and there was no hope of a quick recovery. There were similar stories elsewhere. Cotton production held up longer and crashed further. In Rouen the production of cotton handkerchiefs fell by 33 per cent, that of painted linen by 50 per cent. The numbers of 'rouenneries' (cheerful and colourful cotton goods for which the city was famous) fell from 66,000 to 40,000. In Amiens firms were left with piles of unsold cotton goods. In Strasbourg the number of Crompton's mules in use declined from 12,000 to 10,600. Beauvais, Senlis and Jouy, partly thanks to Oberkampf's loan, survived intact, but there were so many textile works all over France that bosses laid off workers in the Pas-de-Calais, in Picardy, Normandy, Champagne and Alsace. The wool trade, which had not experienced the dizzy heights of success achieved in the cotton industry, also did not experience similar depths of despair. But an inherently more exclusive trade like lace-making was badly hit. In Chantilly production declined by one-third, and at Le Puy the figures tell the same story. On the eve of the Russian campaign even the cannon-making foundries of Le Creusot were oddly silent.

In a time of near-universal bad news, bad news for luxury industries was to be expected, since by definition they produced what was not strictly necessary. For the silversmiths, jewellers and cabinet-makers of Paris, 1811 was a terrible year. 'The sky in France was cloudy everywhere during this period,' lamented the Duchesse d'Abrantes, 'it was no use the Emperor laying on festivals.' At Mont-Cenis the imperial crystal manufactory shone with its habitual splendour, but the tapestry works of Aubusson, which employed 1000 workers, and the porcelain works at Limoges stagnated, and the perfume factory at Grasse laid off 420 of its 500-strong workforce. While peasants carried on with their harsh life, neither much better nor much worse, bankers, industrialists and skilled workers looked to the Emperor for a miracle; 1812 would be a critical year.

Napoleon decided to copy the English. They had always made some exceptions to the blockade. He would do likewise. He would allow Frenchmen to export their goods under licence. He was worried by the case of Lyon, where place de Bellecour was being rebuilt as the yet more grand place Bonaparte. He had made a point of patronizing Lyon silk, not just for his coronation, but also for the hangings of his palaces and the dresses of his court ladies. Now the Tsar had restricted French imports, the French would have to export to Turkey, America and England. Montalivet suggested that France would import English sugar, which included the sugar from France's former colonies that was surplus to English requirements, only if the English imported French wine and French silk. The plan did not work: captains often jettisoned their cargo of silk at sea because they knew that the English customs would never allow it in. The silk merchants were satisfied, because their warehouses were no longer full up. France's allies were not, because the licence system seemed to make a mockery of the cessation of trade which Napoleon had demanded without pausing to consider the effects on his allies' economies.

In other ways too Napoleon failed to satisfy French business interests. Just as the upper classes resented their lack of pungent coffee and white cane sugar, so the cotton manufacturers and the fashion houses lamented the lack of raw materials which only colonies, all of them lost, could provide. Napoleon revived a policy that had been traditional since the time of Louis XIV – privateering. Surcouf of Saint-Malo and Mordeille of Marseille achieved exciting personal victories, but they could not compensate for the 120,000 French sailors who were imprisoned on English pontoons. More important for the future was the scientific quest for sugar beet, which Napoleon was pleased to grow at Saint-Cloud, but when licences were given to allow the import of West Indian sugar, the sugar beet developers faced ruin. Scientists were also involved in the search for suitable plants for producing dyes, Georgians were brought from the Caucasus to try to grow cotton in southern France and it had become fashionable for Joséphine to have her flock of merino sheep at Malmaison or Chaptal his at Chanteloup or Talleyrand his at Valençay, so Napoleon set up huge flocks near Perpignan, Arles, Puy-de-Dome, Villefranche-sur-Saône, Nantes, Trèves, Aix-la-Chapelle. The imperial flocks, above all that at Rambouillet, became the most successful of all. Possibly Napoleon's one lasting achievement for the national economy was that after 1815 France replaced Spain as the principal provider of the woolliest sheep in Europe.

In other ways Napoleon anticipated later ideas for galvanizing an economy. He was persuaded he must make his subjects spend more money. On 6 January 1811 he ordained that apart from servants nobody should present himself at court if he was not dressed in silk, that is except on the grand occasions when velvet was correct. He also implied support for the silk industry when he laid down that no cotton should be used anywhere in his palaces. Then he told Mollien, the Minister of Finance, that something must be done to help the cotton industry too, so Mollien organized secretly that huge quantities of the product should be bought. On the first day in Rouen 600,000 francs were spent, but for all its good intentions this action, even if it emptied some warehouses, did not revive the French cotton industry. Even if that industry no longer had to compete in a free market against English industry, the French factory owners had to pay too much for the cotton they still had to import – and now they were threatened by a rival within the continental system. As Richard Lenoir, one of the most eloquent of French factory owners, commented in a report he submitted in June 1811, 'In chasing English industry from the continent, Your Majesty has called on French industry to replace it, but this advantage is about to elude us and only Germany will have profited from the rigorous measures taken against English commerce.'

Every economic expert whom Napoleon consulted agreed that it was the State alone whch could remedy the condition of industry. Talleyrand had proposed a moratorium on debts, only for Mollien to argue that this proposal would make the situation worse. The General Council of Commerce suggested that the unsold colonial goods could be used as collateral against long-term loans. A director of the Bank, one Vital Roux, dared to argue that the whole idea of the blockade was flawed. He wished to see Adam Smith's unseen hand helping efficient firms. If Napoleon ever read this argument, he ignored it. It was unthinkable that the man who, as an unknown general, had once quelled a crowd with a whiff of grapeshot could allow thousands of workers to remain for long without work. Napoleon tried to save the bank of Simons by lending against the famous vineyard it owned, at Clos Vougeot, the government lent also to Richard Lenoir, one third of whose 1500 strong workforce was based in Paris, and all the more willingly to larger enterprises like Gros, Davilliers, Roman et Compagnie, cotton producers in Mulhouse, Alsace, and Tassin, wool merchant from Orléans. These loans, of which Mollien, as Finance Minister, did not approve, only delayed final collapse and hampered the future government of Louis XVIII with unpaid debts.

Napoleon also wanted to provide more workers for public works. He grumbled that too few people were involved in building his Parisian abattoirs – only 130,000 francs had been spent out of the 1,220,000 allotted – and in building the Bourse. He urged on plans in Paris for a fountain at the Bourse and another at the Bastille, for a continuation of work on the Temple of Glory – the future Madeleine – and for the

MARÉCHAL DE L'EMPIRE.

Tenue de Cérémonie.

Among Carle Vernet's 1812 uniforms none shone more brightly than those of
the marshals.

construction of the Pont d'Iéna and Pont d'Austerlitz. In Lyon he hoped for more work on the palace of the île de Perrache. He wanted engineers to work on locks and barrages at Le Havre, Dieppe, Fécamp. The solution to the problems of the economy must lie in the arts.

Just before it failed, the continental blockade almost brought the English economy close to disaster. England experienced an industrial depression in 1811 and in 1812 some of the workers in Nottingham and Yorkshire, the so-called Luddites, blamed their unemployment on the use of new technology – in the freer economy of England profitability counted before social welfare. The bosses were suffering in their own way. They had fewer outlets for their products. The contraband trade with Holland had come to a virtual stop. In the case of one key trading partner, the United States, the English continued to insist that all neutral shipping should be intercepted and the Americans that they should keep out of all European conflicts. A little skilful diplomacy could have soothed national pride, but the Francophile tendencies of Madison and his mentor, ex-President Jefferson, the expansionist enthusiasm of westerners like Clay who wished to capture Canada and the rigidity of the English turned a difference of principle into a cause of war.

There never was such an impressive display of military uniforms as that made by the enormous force with which Napoleon began to cross the Niemen on 24 June 1812. His force of more than 500,000 men included Germans from north and south, especially Saxons and Bavarians, plus Danes, Norwegians, Dutch, Swiss, Neapolitans, Croats and Dalmatians, Poles in their national colours of red and white, even some Portuguese in light brown and scarlet, all troops subjects of the Grand Empire or of the allies of France. There had never been such a dashing display of the various cuts and colours of military uniforms and Carle Vernet took an artist's delight and some artistic licence in recording them. Against them was ranged an army whose crack troops, the Cossacks, were, according to Madame de Staël, 'without order or uniform, with a long lance in their hand, and a kind of grey dress, whose ample hood they put over their head'. If looks could kill there would be no contest. No more than Xerxes when he had crossed the Hellespont did Napoleon imagine that he might not be victorious.

Napoleon's objective was the normal Napoleonic aim, the destruction of the enemy's army, but the sheer size of his own army made any advance painfully slow. Large numbers spread disease and ill-discipline. By the time he reached Vilna, 20,000 horses were dead, among the men a pattern of desertion was already well established and every time the French tried to trap the Russians the Russians slipped away. Tsar Alexander knew that in the Iberian peninsula Wellington had used the tactics of retreat to lure Marshal Masséna into a barren wilderness and Napoleon knew that one reason why Wellington had never been crushed was that he always had supplies for his soldiers. What the Tsar could not have expected was that his generals would be forced to retreat so far. What Napoleon could not have expected was that he would have to advance so far. The Russians eluded him at Vilna, modern Vilnius, their entrenched camp at Drissa was found abandoned, they failed to join up to stand at Vitebsk. At Vitebsk his faithful stepson Eugène and his most trusted marshals, Murat and Berthier, begged him to give up. For a time Napoleon hesitated. 'I have made my generals too rich,' he snarled. 'They think only of plea-sures, of hunting, of rolling through Paris in their magnificent coaches. They have grown sick of war.' He regarded risk-taking as a moral duty. 'The very danger pushes us on to Moscow.' At Smolensk he thought that he had the bear at bay, but Junot's enveloping move did not trap them, turning the city into rubble did not crush them and even the mauling of the rearguard by Murat and Ney did not stop them. It was late August and Napoleon had left a force of only some 160,000, too few for a decisive engagement. He also found that he had a new general to cope with, the sixty-seven-year-old Kutusov, whom Tolstoy was to immortalize in the pages of *War and Peace*. Because he was old, Kutusov was inclined to do nothing other than to rely on the size and the climate of Russia. He knew that space and time were not on the side of the French. He was made to fight before Moscow was surrendered. On the heights of Borodino, while 700 Russians were taken prisoner and there were 50,000 Russian casualties, the French lost 30,000 men and over forty generals. On St Helena Napoleon would describe Borodino as the most terrible of all his battles. He had won, but the Russians had not lost. They abandoned the gilded domes of the ancient capital of Muscovy to the French, yet no Russian del-egate came to sue for peace and when part of the city was fired, probably on the orders of the city governor, the French began to feel uneasy. Though in St Petersburg the Tsar was coldly received at Kazan Cathedral, no more than Kutusov would he give way. He published an appeal to his people in which he prayed God to 'look mercifully on His Sacred Church and redeem the independence of nations and kings'. Meantime Kutusov proposed to lull Napoleon and not disturb him in Moscow. Napoleon still had grandiose schemes for Russia – he would issue a proclamation to emancipate the serfs – but in the end it was he who cracked. On 18 October a sudden attack on Murat ended in a local Russian victory. Next day, while Mortier was ordered to blow up the Kremlin, the main French force left Moscow by the Kaluga road. In the event the French engineers botched their job, the Kremlin was only damaged not destroyed, the Tsar's prayers had been heard and Holy Russia was saved.

Napoleon never saw his epic career in such Christian terms. It makes more sense to talk of his heroic hubris and of the nemesis that overtook him, to cast Kutusov in the role of Fabius Cunctator and Napoleon himself in the role of Hannibal. It was as a second Hannibal that David had seen him in the most often copied of all Empire icons, the portrait of Napoleon seated on a prancing white horse on the Saint-Bernard pass. After Marengo Napoleon had been proud of the comparison, but now the parallel between his achievement and Hannibal's had a bitter similarity. That year at the Royal Academy, London, Turner had shown his *Snowstorm, Hannibal crossing the Alps*, in which a vortex of snow that the painter had witnessed in Yorkshire seems to overwhelm the puny Carthaginian soldiers and their beasts beneath it. This picture was more apt than the painting that was the hit at the Salon of 1812 in Paris, Géricault's optimistic *Charging chasseur*. The horrors of a Russian winter were as vivid to the French that year as they would be to the Germans 130 years later. In the art of the Napoleonic legend the retreat from Moscow would have its poignant moments to stir the heart – the figure of Ney dashing here and there inspiring like a latter-day Roland the resistance of the rearguard, the chaotic crossing of the Beresina, the lonely death of the stragglers by the slash of a Cossack sabre – but in 1812 Napoleon had no time to indulge feelings of tragic sensitivity. For as long as he could he concealed the truth and, when it became painfully obvious, he decided to fight and fight again. His public announcement of his defeat, which he blamed exclusively on the Russian weather, concluded with the words, 'His Majesty's health has never been better.' He would never surrender.

God, he had always maintained, is on the side of the big battalions. In 1813 and 1814 he learnt the truth of his own dictum. The vultures were soon gathering in strength. One by one his former allies deserted him. In February 1813 the King of Prussia, Frederick William IV, made a treaty with the Tsar and Eugène, who was now in command of the troops who were left over from the Russian campaign, retreated behind the Elbe. Emperor Francis II of Austria may still have wanted Napoleon to stay in power, but, as Napoleon insisted to the Austrian Chancellor Metternich that he could not give up the idea of the Grand Empire, and as Metternich made clear that Austria would not fight to preserve either Napoleon's Confederation of the Rhine, which was hated by the Prussians, or his Duchy of Warsaw, which was hated by the Russians, the unlikely union between the upstart Emperor and his legitimist imperial father-in-law could not be sustained. Napoleon used negotiations only so that he could build up his troops. From Spain, however, news came that his brother Joseph had been routed at Vitoria and Metternich was convinced that the French could be defeated. Because Napoleon had refused to give up virtually anything, the rulers of old Europe began to think of stripping him of everything. By rejecting all compromise with them he made them uncompromising too.

By losing the diplomatic battle, he put himself at a military disadvantage when he advanced into Germany. Old personal foes came to plague him. Moreau came back from the United States of America to offer advice on how to defeat him and, after Bernadotte had brought the Swedish army into play, there was a second general trained in Napoleon's methods who had a small, good army to attack from the north, while Prussia took the centre and Austria the south. Prompted by Moreau at allied headquarters, France's continental rivals showed that they had learnt their lessons in the art of war. Even though Napoleon himself won a dazzling victory at Dresden, by attacking French armies smaller than their own or led by Napoleon's sub-ordinates, they won important minor victories. In the past Napoleon had been too quick for his opponents, but several times he failed to catch up with the Prussian general Blücher. In the past too he had always fought major battles with superior forces or else fought them in such a way that at critical moments and critical places he had local superiority. But when he was caught at Leipzig he had 160,000 against 300,000. Men called it the battle of the nations. It was intended by Napoleon to be a holding operation, so that he could retreat from Saxony in good order, but he was deserted by the Saxons and the rearguard was trapped. Immediately afterwards he was deserted by the Bavarians. Even if he reached France in safety, he had with him only 60,000 men and there was no disguising the fact that he had been defeated in the most important pitched battle he had ever fought.

The coda to the Napoleonic story was a bravura display. In 1814, while the English closed in from the south-west and the Russians, Prussians and Austrians from the east and south-east, Napoleon was determined, as he told Berthier, to 'repeat the campaigns of Italy'. He was referring to the campaign of 1796 and the thought seemed to rejuvenate him. As in the south his brother-in-law Murat and worse still his ungrateful sister Caroline had deserted him in the hope of keeping Naples for themselves, the ever-faithful Eugène could rely on the Army of North Italy, which was now ordered to fall back towards Lyon. Outnumbered four to one, Napoleon defeated Russians under Prussian command at Champaubert and Montmirail and Austrians at Vauchamps and Montereau. If this had been 1796, the allies would have given up. Instead, at the prompting of the British Foreign Secretary Castlereagh, they agreed to sign the Treaty of Chaumont which com-mitted them to making no separate peace with France and to fighting France if nec-essary for twenty years. The exaggerated pose was not held for long. In the safety of Bordeaux the standard of Louis XVIII was raised on 12 March. By the end of the month Paris had capitulated. There Joseph had no will to continue the struggle, Talleyrand took care to see that he himself gave the allies the information to encour-age them to demand the capitulation and to flatter Marmont, the marshal in charge of the garrison, till he was anxious to sign the act. Marmont had been Napoleon's friend since the siege of Toulon in 1793. Now Napoleon regarded him as a Judas and in circles loyal to the Emperor Marmont's title as Duke of Ragusa, that is Dubrovnik, gave rise to a new verb – *raguser*, to betray. In April 1814 Napoleon was nobody's Messiah. Bluntly Ney told him that the army would not follow him, so on 6 April he abdicated.

The one art of which Napoleon was supreme master was the art of war. For all his concern with the arts of peace, he was certain that his survival depended on continual success in war. This view was a grave mistake, for in 1813 he might have preserved his political control of France had he been willing to give up his Grand Empire for the sake of peace. By preferring to gamble he lost everything. He also caused terrible suffering to the people he served. The extraordinary run of victories over almost twenty years meant that the French had seldom known what it was like to have enemy soldiers on their land. When provisions had been needed on campaign, the Italians, the Spaniards, the Germans, the Russians had provided them – not the French. As it was they who had determined the treaties or truces that ended campaigns, it was not the French who paid for the cost of waging war. Until 1814, too, Napoleon had called on many adult Frenchmen to fight for him – in 1814 he had to call on boys. Between 1812 and 1814 France was forced to experience something like total war. In 1945, when Germany was to endure a much more terrible version of the same experience, Goebbels, who enthusiastically encouraged Germans to embrace it, yet took away 100,000 men from the eastern front to be extras in his final movie, by chance a story of heroic German resistance to the French in the period of Napoleon. Napoleon himself was more practical. He sacrificed everything and everyone in order to win. There would be a time for celebrations later.

The military crisis had an inevitable effect on the arts. The plans for the colossal palace of the King of Rome were put on one side and with them went any further idea of embellishing the capital. It also gradually became clear with aftersight that the Salon of 1812 would be the last Salon where Napoleonic artists would glorify the Emperor's victories on the fields of Europe – the next Salon, in 1814, took place under the patronage of the restored Louis XVIII. It was at that moment, while the Emperor was in exile on Elba, that David exhibited privately his lament on lost causes, *Leonidas at Thermopylae*. This was a picture that he had thought about for over a decade. Now the subject of a small group of heroes waiting to die at the hands of overwhelming Persian hordes took on a new pathos. The ancient Greek idealism was depicted in painstaking imitation of a Greek style, which aimed to show how men lived – and died – at Sparta. But the carefully balanced composition and the even more carefully structured nudity, from which penises were ruthlessly excluded, was an inappropriate comment on the reality of the sufferings of French men in the past two years. Straining after heroic nobility always runs the risk of absurdity. As an artist the great David had lost his way. It was only as a man that he could regain his dignity, when, unlike Gros or Fontaine or Jacob-Desmalter, he chose to die in exile.

Napoleon did not accept defeat lightly. He had scorned the subject of David's painting and he did not like the thought of being forced to adopt the style of life of a little
islander. The terms of the Treaty of Fontainebleau were generous enough.
Napoleon was made sovereign of Elba, with an acceptable income, and allowed the
title of Emperor. His wife, Marie-Louise, who had fallen into the clutches of her
father, was to be Duchess of Parma with the right of reversion to her son. The other
Bonapartes would be given pensions. Napoleon accepted the terms and then tried to
commit suicide. The attempt failed, because the poison that he had kept by him since
Russia no longer worked, and he never tried again. For a time he seemed reconciled
to his fate. In the Cour des Adieux at Fontainebleau he took a tearful farewell of the
Old Guard which was to become one of the most famous scenes in his legend. 'The
happiest occupation of my life,' he said, 'will henceforward be to tell for posterity
your great deeds, and my only consolation will be to know all that France is doing
for the glory of her name.' He then set out for the south, unwisely passing through
the ultra-royalist parts of Provence, and felt it wise, if demeaning, to dress in
Austrian uniform to avoid detection. He was cheered by meeting his favourite sister
Pauline on the way and was relieved to find that he could chat amiably about naval
warfare with the English captain Ussher, who took him to take command of his tiny
island principality.

On Elba Napoleon insisted on behaving in the grandest possible manner. He
hoisted a flag of Bonaparte bees, he maintained court etiquette as if he were in the
vast setting of the Tuileries, the Empire style was *de rigueur*. Soon he was joined by
700 of the Old Guard, by his mother and Pauline and briefly by his Polish mistress,
Marie Walewska, and their son. He was obsessed by military matters and began to
plot his return to the mainland. To help him Pauline sold her jewels and also her
lovely Paris home, the Hôtel Charost, to the British ambassador, the Duke of
Wellington. Wellington accurately described her as a 'heartless little devil', for the
languid Pauline proved herself ruthlessly energetic in support of her brother's cause.
Napoleon kept himself informed and waited till the moment was right. Thirty thousand officers of the Imperial Army were put on half-pay and *émigré* nobles who had
never seen a battle were given high command. At court, though his wife was aristocratic, the gallant Ney was snubbed. Bourbon propaganda put it about that
Napoleon and Pauline were incestuous lovers. As the Bourbon government would
not pay him the money promised by the Treaty of Fontainebleau, he found that he
could not live within his income and could not even pay the Guard. His mother
urged him to take just one more chance.

Though the British Commissioner, Sir Neil Campbell, had warned Castlereagh
that if Napoleon were left too short of cash, he might invade the mainland,

The Cour du Cheval Blanc, château de Fontainebleau, dating from 1528–40, has been known as the Cour des Adieux ever since Napoleon's tearful farewell from the Old Guard in 1814.

Campbell himself went away to Italy on 16 February. When he came back twelve days later, he found that Napoleon had gone. This time Napoleon avoided the royalist Rhône valley and went by the mountain route to Grenoble. From the moment he arrived in Grenoble his adventure turned into a magic tale, in which old soldiers cheered him, Ney joined him and the fat king hurried away panting towards Brussels. David came out of sullen retirement to be imperial painter once more. Against the combined forces of four great powers there was never much chance that Napoleon could carry on winning. In the event the British and the Prussians were the first to be ready. Napoleon almost beat them, but, though he defeated Blücher at Ligny, Ney was held by Wellington at Quatre-Bras. The allies were divided but not separated, so when Napoleon and Ney turned on Wellington Blücher was not too far away. For the first time Napoleon had to cope with the defensive tactics that Wellington had perfected in Portugal and Spain and even the Guard could not break the British squares. By not defeating the British, Napoleon had lost, but, once the Prussians came on to the field of battle, his army was routed. The only course open to him was resignation to whatever fate others had in store for him. His only choice was whom he would allow to dictate his future – he chose the British. Perhaps because he had liked Ussher, he embarked on a British frigate, the *Bellerophon*, named after the mythic Greek hero who had flown on the winged horse Pegasus to slay the Chimera. For Napoleon there would be no more magical escapades, only a fight to weave legends to keep boredom and death at bay. To this end a whole new school of French painters, some even in his remaining short life, would come to provide him with aid. But the one Napoleonic figure in the arts who in late 1815 still had stomach for a struggle was Vivant Denon, keeper of the Musée Napoléon, the nearest he ever had to a minister of the arts.

CHAPTER 11

Denon and the Art of Conquest

D ENON WAS to Napoleon what Colbert had been to Louis XIV and what Malraux would be to de Gaulle. As with them it was his role to run the artistic policy of his master, but whereas Colbert was in charge of France's finances and France's navy as well as royal household expenses (among them the money spent on Versailles), and whereas Malraux was world famous as a novelist and as a fighter against Fascism long before he became France's Minister of Culture, Denon never aspired to be more than the director of the Louvre. He was not eminent as either a painter, like Louis David, or an architect-decorator, like Pierre Fontaine, and his learning was light compared to the erudition of the compilers of the *Description de l'Egypte*. He had one salient quality that made him the ideal servant of a dictator – the easy adaptability of a natural propagandist. He was not an evil genius like Goebbels, but then the Napoleonic Empire was not an evil empire like the Third Reich. Denon served an adventurer and he enjoyed it. Indeed, but for Napoleon he would have been a minor *littérateur*, a mediocre engraver, a suave diplo-mat and connoisseur who was admirably fitted to the intrigues of some little court left over from the *ancien régime*. In 1798, however, at the age of fifty-one, he went to Egypt. Egypt changed his life and gave him his part in history – he was right to call Napoleon his 'hero'.

Napoleon had a special affection for those who had been with him in Egypt. There was a complicity between them, for in purely military terms the expedition was an appalling disaster. Napoleon lost his fleet and, after he had deserted it, his army too. While he was away, the Russians overran much of Italy and the Austrians much of Germany. By his campaign in the Middle East he turned the Turks against France and, far from dislodging the British from southern India, he could not stop them from humbling France's one ally in the area, Mysore. Denon was like Napoleon, an optimist. He too saw the journey to Egypt in exciting terms. He had returned with a monkey who could seal letters and some island birds, all of which, tactfully, he gave to Joséphine. Among the Egyptian curios that he kept he prized a mummified foot. He was soon to have more important matters on his mind. When General Bonaparte became First Consul Bonaparte, Denon was asked to advise on the purchase of statues, pictures and antiquities. He frequently accompanied the First Consul to the Louvre. At fashionable dinner parties he was as agreeable as ever, but he retired home alone to engrave and to write. Eventually in 1802 Dido l'Aîné published the *Journey in lower and upper Egypt during the campaigns of general Bonaparte in Egypt*. Chateaubriand's *Le Génie de Christianisme*, which also appeared in 1802, was the only book that year to rival Denon's in international sales. The *Journey* went into four French editions and three English versions in 1802, came out in Dutch and German translations in 1803 and in an Italian translation in 1808. He was only too aware that his book was not a permanent achievement in the class of the *Description de l'Egypte*. He knew his designs could not compete with their two volumes containing 839 copper engravings (3000 illustrations in all), he could not equal their expertise in so many topics and yet he had one gift denied to the whole company of his rivals – he was a popularizer. All the same he felt the need to justify the way he had beaten them into print. 'When I left Alexandria, the members of the Institute were still in Cairo. When I came back to France, I did not know if they had been able to carry out the journey into Upper Egypt commanded by general Bonaparte before his departure. The circumstances of the war could have stopped the march of this learned society or prevented us from bringing back to France the precious results. In this case I could have found myself the only person in a position to write about this country, above all the only person who had put together a large number of designs.'

With the publication of his book Denon became a celebrity. He became the chief protagonist of the Egyptian style. Even before his book came out, one of his pictures was the source of the Egyptian temple that was planned in 1800 by Chalgrin for place des Victoires to honour Desaix and Kléber, the two 'Egyptian' generals who had just died, one at Marengo, the other in Egypt. The monument itself was never executed because it was too large for the space available, but the picture that had inspired it had a powerful effect on the decorative arts. This picture, Denon's somewhat fanciful version of the temple at Dendera (Tentyris), is based, as he explains, partly on the temple at Philae, for when he had sketched at Dendera, the lower part of the façade was covered in sand. When the French forces had arrived there, they had been so amazed that 'without orders issued or received, each officer made a detour, hastened to Tentyris, and spontaneously the army remained there the rest of the day. What a day! How happy we are to have braved it all in order to experience such rapturous delights.' These delights were conveyed by some remarkable crafts-

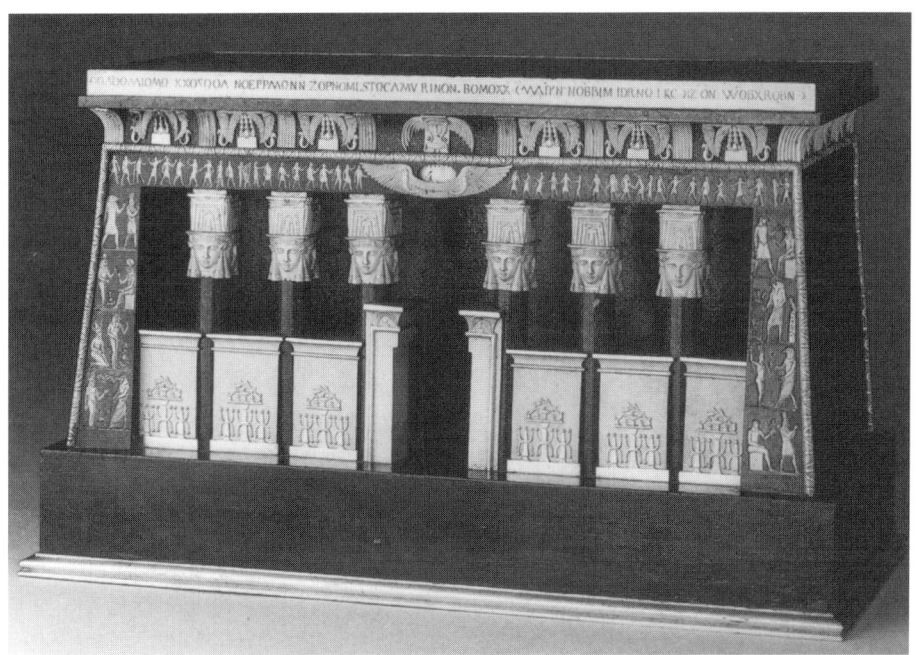

Lépine's Dendera clock, c. 1806 (private collection in Paris), is based on Denon's engraving of the temple in his 'Voyages in Lower and Upper Egypt'.

men. Around 1806 Lépine placed a clock, made of chased and gilt bronze, in the midst of Denon's temple. It was advertised as 'derived from Monsieur Denon's celebrated work . . . 18 inches long, 8 wide and 12 high . . . entirely painted in granite grey, and the ornaments, friezes and capitals are in matte gilding. The movement is arranged so as to display the ornamentation in the centre of the frieze. Without movement 1200 francs, with movement 1500 francs.'

Denon meanwhile had in train a much more ambitious plan, a huge and wholly 'Egyptian' dessert service, consisting of the dessert service itself, with motifs derived from the plates in Denon's *Journey*, and two coffee and tea services, also decorated with Egyptian themes, and, as *pièce de résistance*, an enormous *surtout* or centrepiece in biscuit porcelain. At one end was the kiosk of the temple at Philae, with four obelisks covered in hieroglyphs, at either side were the temples of Dendera and Edfu, each linked by colonnades to a pylon, in front of which stood two colossi of Memnon set behind an avenue of ram-headed sphinxes (from the Temple of Karnak). This potpourri of Ptolemaic and Pharaonic architecture was remarkably accurate in its archaeological details, and to this end Denon insisted that the Sèvres craftsmen involved, whose names are known, should consult plates later used in the

Description de l'Egypte, which did not begin to appear till 1809. Denon sought the help of Baptiste Lepère, who had been in Egypt and who was a member of the *Description* team. He wrote to Alexandre Brongniart, director of the Sèvres factory, to express his concerns about the technical problems of the enterprise. He knew that the Emperor was intent on advertising the skills of Sèvres. 'If something can be done, that is reason enough for the Imperial Manufactory to do it. If you never attempted this type of project, you would be no different from the others, and Sèvres would no longer be the foremost factory in Europe.' As always, Napoleon was more direct. 'Advise the director that if within a year the factory's performance does not improve, especially in its designs, it shall be closed. It must rank not second, but first.'

Napoleon had at first intended that the service should be his own possession, but, when he was negotiating diplomatically with Alexander I in 1807, he learnt of the Tsar's enthusiasm for the Egyptian expedition. Never averse to a fan and anxious to impress an emperor more legitimate than himself, he was persuaded to give the whole service away. He was also to give away a second Egyptian service but that time he had no control over its eventual destiny.

Part of his deal with Joséphine over their divorce was that she could have a gift of Sèvres porcelain of her choice to the value of 30,000 francs. In 1810 she made her order for a dessert service and in 1812 she received it. As so often she exceeded the specified allowance, so she volunteered to meet the cost of the centrepiece and a matching breakfast set herself. As in the first service Denon's pictures, reproduced in grisaille, decorated the various plates. There was his happy mixture of ancient and modern scenes, so that, besides a view of the entrance to the ruins at Luxor or a slightly comic view of French mathematicians perched on top of the Gizeh sphinx to measure it, the diner could feast his eyes on camels before the ruins of Hierancopolis, on a celebration in a harem or a meeting of Arab sheikhs or the signs of the zodiac. Even the jam jars and an ice-cream bucket copy his designs. For some reason Joséphine changed her mind and sent most of the set back. She told Brongniart that she found the designs too severe. Her artistic tastes may have changed or maybe she remembered that it was in Egypt that Napoleon had first learnt of her infidelity – at any rate she kept only the breakfast set, for which she had paid. Some of the plates were lost before in 1818 the remainder were presented by Louis XVIII to the Duke of Wellington, to 'keep friendship alive'.

Even if, as seems likely, his 'Egyptian' medal cabinet in the shape of a pylon derives only its scarab doorknobs from his own engravings, Denon was the key figure in the dissemination of the Egyptian style. Several small Sèvres 'cabarets' (tea or coffee services), one of which was to go into exile with Napoleon, and imitations of Egyptian statuettes or *ushabtis* and designs for printed handkerchief borders and pylon clocks resting on sphinxes and an Egyptian slave with shaved head carrying

One scene from Denon's second Egyptian dinner set, now in Apsley House, London, shows some of Napoleon's savants measuring the sphinx.

a bowl for fruit on his head — all drew on the engravings of Denon. Few picture-makers, for as an artist Denon was only a journeyman, have ever been so fruitful. In the 1920s the rage for Tutankhamun inspired yet more Egyptomanic art, but most of the art deco objects that were produced then look tawdry beside their Empire predecessors. In Napoleon's France there were so many supremely skilful artists and artisans in the State-run factories that rich and erudite connoisseurs could enjoy the glamorous vision of Egypt to which Denon, like his hero the Emperor, was always true.

The most impressive testament to this vision is not found in anything that Denon produced but in the famous *Description de l'Egypte*. This massive work, born of collaboration between some 400 engravers and over 150 men of learning drawn from the Commission of Arts and Science which was formed to accompany the expedition, was based on the research collected in some three years at the Institute of

Denon's cabinet (Metropolitan Museum, New York) seems to have been based
on a design by Percier. The work on the wood was carried out by Jacob-
Desmalter and on the silver by Biennais (1809–19).

Egypt in Cairo and published over a period of almost twenty years between 1809
and 1828. It was so successful that Louis XVIII commanded in 1820 that a second
edition should be made, so that in the end there were almost 900 plates in eleven elephant folio volumes and twenty-six volumes of text. There had never been anything
like it before, apart from the *Encyclopédie* of the *philosophes*, and there could never be
anything like it afterwards, for Napoleon's savants and engravers belonged to the last
generation of men who believed that it was possible to summarize human knowledge comprehensively.

The *Description de l'Egypte* is divided into three sections, dealing respectively with

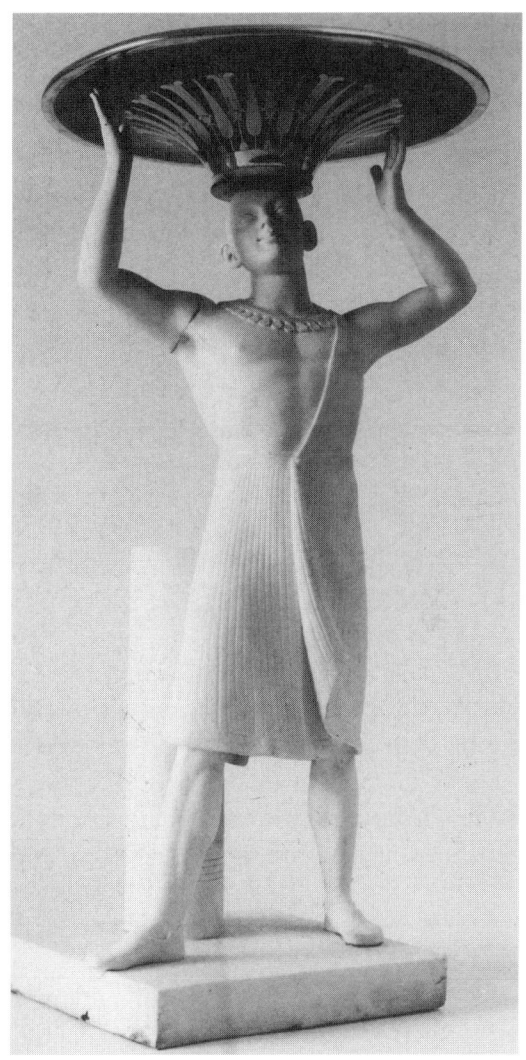

The Egyptian carrying a bowl
(1806, Moscow State Museum of
Ceramics), in Sèvres hard-paste
and biscuit porcelain, was derived
from a drawing of Denon's made
in a 'tomb of the Kings of
Thebes'.

antiquities, modern life and natural history. Because at that stage nobody could read
the ancient Egyptian language, in the interpretation of ancient monuments the
scholars relied on classical sources. They talked of Ozymandias, Shelley's king of
kings. They knew that outside Cairo stood the remains of Memphis and that Luxor
was on the site of ancient Thebes, but because the remains of Ptolemaic Egypt were
more readily available than those of Pharaonic Egypt, these assume in the *Description*
the prominence they have in Denon's own writing. It was in recording these temples
that certain of the engravers had their most obvious success, for the training of architectural draughtsmen made some expert in their handling of plans and elevations.

The ruins of Philae and Tentyris (Dendera), which inspired one of Denon's most imaginative designs, that for the centrepiece of his second Sèvres Egyptian service, were shown at their most magnificent. For much the same reason, because they could not read hieroglyphs or the cursive demotic, in some copies made from stone tablets or papyrus fragments there were mistakes. They described mummy-cases as idols and Rameses II defeating his enemies became merely 'a military scene', but then they recorded with enlightened accuracy an ithyphallic Amun*. It is precisely because they lacked the knowledge essential for the understanding of the civilization whose artifacts they recorded that their achievement has stood. In 1822, the year in which the volumes of antiquities were published, Champollion laid out his decoding of hieroglyphic writing, based on the collation of inscriptions found at Philae and on the Rosetta Stone – and Edme-François Jomard, who was then in charge of publica-tion, refused to accept his conclusions.

In turning to the subject of modern Egypt, the scholars could give the artists sounder advice. The geographical volume, which systematically divided the area from Sidon in Lebanon down to the borders of Sudan into forty-seven rectangular maps, had a key not only to several sorts of measures of distance, from modern metres and old-fashioned leagues to ancient Roman miles and Greek stadia, but also to the Arabic language. The artists observed their reluctant Egyptian hosts with a mixture of fascination and condescension, secure in the knowledge that in matters of technology Europeans were more advanced but also keen to preserve the memory of a way of life that would pass away. Some scenes of Egyptians at work, whether making tapestries or drawing water from the Nile, are valuable as sociological docu-ments, but there is more artistry in the portraits of a sheikh from Cairo or a mer-chant from Alexandria or in the exact depiction of Egyptian musical instruments.

Science and art are most happily combined in the final set of volumes which are concerned with the flora and fauna of the country. The most compendious tome on natural history written in the eighteenth century was the work of a Frenchman, Buffon, and the artists who set out to celebrate the additions to his studies which they were revealing delighted in the ravishing display of the world around them. They are at their most delicate in their drawings of flowers, they catch the shapes of innumerable beetles, of sea urchins – one takes up a whole page – and of the dreaded crocodile. By the time these plates appeared, they should have understood why Louis XVIII had declared on the front page of the second edition that he 'com-mands that the description of Egypt should carry on and that editions of it should multiply'.

The first edition had begun to appear under the Empire. The frontispiece had shown an imaginary Egyptian scene, a 'caprice' that brought together in one loca-

*The French as yet knew nothing of the sexual role of the sun god Amun in the work of creation.

The frontispiece of the *Description de l'Egypte* is a 'caprice' which brings together many sights that could be seen in Egypt but not together.

tion all the principal monuments that tourists voyaging in their mind's eyes expected
to see – an obelisk, well-known temple façades and pylons, the statue of a goddess,
seated sphinxes and, in the distance, some pyramids – but the scene was given its
meaning by the frame. At the top Napleon drives his chariot in pursuit of the fleeing
Mamelukes, the same theme as in the painting of Rameses II in his chariot, but the
engravers of the *Description de l'Egypte* were more at home in the visual language
which turned Napoleon into a Roman conqueror. In the preface he is implicitly
compared to the Roman generals who had preceded him – Pompey, Caesar, Mark
Antony and Augustus. For all the thrills that the discovery of Egypt gave to the
imagination of European artists, most of them were still by instinct Neo-Classicists.
This was true even of Denon himself, who owed his fame to Egypt.

It was probably because he had seen service in Egypt that Denon was promoted to
the highest office that Napoleon could give him. Almost three years after the coup
d'état of Brumaire 1799, Denon was named director of the Central Museum,
which, it was explained, meant that he would control the museums of the Louvre,
of French monuments and of the French school at Versailles as well as being director of the galleries of government palaces, of the medal mint, of the engraving and
mosaic workshops and of the acquisition and transport of works of art. Thirty years
before, he had been put in charge of Madame de Pompadour's engravings by Louis
XV. Now he was returning to his first love. Running museums brought together all
his gifts – his enthusiasm, his knowledge, his connoisseurship, his social charm, his
drive. With the help of two principal assistants, Visconti and Lavallée, he was to be
in charge of the Central Museum till 1815. He was to be the first great museum
administrator in French history, perhaps the greatest of all.

At the heart of Denon's concerns was the Louvre itself. In his day the Louvre did
not include the great wings that were added by Louis-Napoleon, but it was still a
large building, incoherent and inconvenient. It contained the national printing press,
the collections of Doctor Charles, the offices of Chappe the telegrapher, the Stock
Exchange, the Institute and numerous apartments for officials and artists, including
David, who had several studios there, his pupil Gérard and one survival from the
frivolous world of the *ancien régime* to whom David had extended his protection –
Jean-Honoré Fragonard. As a museum the Louvre dated back only to the early years
of the revolution, voted for in midsummer 1791, inaugurated in the late autumn of
1793. David had quickly established himself as its manager. In this, his fanatical
Jacobin stage, he allowed workmen to deface the woodwork of the doors and apartments, wreck the royal portraits of Rigault and Lebrun, efface the names of the
rulers, tear the tapestries covered in fleurs-de-lis. The artists living in the buildings
were allowed to spread themselves wherever they wanted to be in the vast sets of

rooms. Nobody appeared to care if the pictures were dispersed. During the bad old days the Pompadour's brother, the Marquis de Marigny, had treated some of the antiquities as suitable decorations for his country house and d'Angiviller had incorporated many royal drawings into his own collection. From 1794 onwards the trophies of war started to arrive and the new rulers and their families treated them as their private acquisitions. Joséphine expected to be able to have what she wanted for Malmaison. As First Consul and still more as Emperor, Napoleon, however, demanded that Denon bring order where before there was only chaos. As director, Denon had his own reasons for acting in a dictatorial manner – he longed to show that he was no mere dilettante. Less than six months after his appointment he wrote to Chaptal, Minister of the Interior, 'This most precious monument to the glory of our armies is now, thanks to the new arrangements that have been made for it and the innumerable works of art it contains, the most beautiful institution in the universe.'

His concept of French cultural eminence was Napoleonic in its arrogance. 'The French Republic, by its vigour, its superior enlightenment and finer artistic talent, is the only country in the world that can give inviolable sanctuary to its masterpieces.' That was another way of saying that other people's masterpieces ought to be the possessions of France – only conquerors had rights.

Denon was an accomplished looter because, as in Egypt, he continued to have unbounded enthusiasm for the task he was set. He was prepared to go further than Napoleon himself. He suggested that the French should pillage the gallery of Dresden – it did not after all contain the most famous Raphael panel painting in the world – but Napoleon wanted to keep on good terms with the Saxons, who did not desert him till 1813. Napoleon also resisted Denon's ingenious plan to seize some of the Uffizi sculptures because they had been transferred from the Villa Medici in Rome after the will of Anna de' Medici had left the entire collection of the family to the city of Florence. Denon was not with Napoleon on the Austerlitz campaign, so that the Viennese collection escaped his attention in 1805. He did not make such a mistake again. Armed with his sketch pad, he followed the armies in 1806, 1807, 1808 and 1809 in Germany, Russian Poland, Spain and Austria – the Emperor had to order him to leave the Battle of Eylau in 1807, when he was sixty – and he swooped down with Napoleonic zeal on the galleries on his way. Princes and princelings hid what they could before the French soldiers arrived. Wilhelm I of Hesse-Kassel had bundled up forty-eight pictures in his hunting lodge, only for General Lagrange to find them and hand them over to Joséphine, who was for once a camp follower. Denon's haul was even greater, for he took just under 300 pictures to the Louvre, including at least sixteen Rembrandts. He took almost as many works from neighbouring Brunswick. He was only slightly less rapacious when he came to the best collection of all, the Prussian holdings in Potsdam and Berlin. There could be found the most important group of Watteaus outside France, but Denon, who himself loved the painter and who at the time owned the poignant painting of the sad pierrot-like clown *Gilles*, came away with none of them. In the early nineteenth century Watteau was out of favour in France. His wistful, delicate portraits of friends and acquaintances in the guise of the characters of the Italian comedy, in their day a reaction to the heroic posturings of late French Baroque, meant nothing to people who favoured a new heroic style. Denon went away with over 100 paintings, but the finest works of the French artist of the early years of Louis XV were left behind.

Denon found he must be tactful. He seems to have been in Spain for only a few weeks and as he had a taste for Velázquez, he must have wanted to plunder the Prado. Unfortunately, Joseph Bonaparte was now King of Spain. As he wrote to Napoleon from Valladolid in January 1809, 'if any prince but the brother of your majesty were occupying the throne of Madrid I should have begged for orders to add to the collection of the museum 20 pictures of the Spanish school'. Joseph seems to have taken the hint, because he decreed that a gallery should be set up in Madrid to send pictures to Napoleon. Eventually in 1813 a small selection of Spanish art arrived in Paris, including just one Velázquez, the early classical work *Joseph's coat*, but nothing in the class of three fine Murillos brought back by Marshal Soult and nothing like the masterpieces that came much later to the Louvre from the collection of the exiled Duc d'Orléans, the future King Louis-Philippe. When King Joseph was chased out of Spain, he lost most of the pictures in his baggage train to the Duke of Wellington, who gave them back to the Bourbon King Ferdinand VII, but five Raphaels from Spain were briefly on show in Paris. Not till the age of Merimée and Bizet and Manet did French writers, composers and painters fall under the spell of bull-fights, mantillas and castanets.

Denon was equally frustrated in Vienna. The Habsburgs knew the value of what they had and even if they did not appreciate Bruegel the Elder's landscapes of the seasons – the cowherds returning their beasts from the fields, the peasants cutting wood on a dark day and the most poetic scene of all, *The Hunters in the Snow* – they took care to crate up what they considered the best pictures and sent away forty-eight cases in 1805 and fifty-four in 1809. Denon received 401 pictures, but only because their owners or the curators considered them second-rate.

All the same, during the last few years of its existence the Musée Napoléon was unsurpassed by any other European gallery or museum before or since. There were the most famous antique sculptures of Rome, from the Vatican Palace, the Borghese Gallery and the Capitol, which the taste of the time ranked above any other works of art in the world. Denon's museum contained almost everything that could be moved by the hand of Raphael and Rubens, the two most admired painters of recent times. It contained the most celebrated altarpiece of Titian's, *The death of St Peter Martyr*, since destroyed by fire, and the chief examples of Veronese's splendid feasts, but, as it was always easier to loot from churches and convents than from palaces, the religious pictures far outnumbered the mythologies and the portraits. Inevitably and ironically the museum was a repository of the taste of the *ancien régime*, partly because the collections that were raided fitted the canon of the eighteenth century. Denon himself had an enthusiasm for the Florentine art of the fifteenth century — for Botticelli, fra Angelico, fra Filippo Lippi and Domenico del Ghirlandaio – and Visconti loved Greek sculpture of the fifth century BC. In this they were ahead of their time, but Denon was the more successful in satisfying his passion. Whereas Visconti was unable to acquire the sculptures from Bassae or Aegina for the Louvre, in 1811 Denon went on his last hunt for pictures in Italy and returned with some remarkable scalps. He even came back with works by Cimabue and Giotto and, when he produced a catalogue of the new exhibits, apologized for his failure to have found a Masaccio. His museum did not go on show till Paris was occupied by foreign troops and Napoleon had left France, yet Denon still had work to do. However much he loved the past, he had always been aware that he must live in the present. Napoleon had not only wanted to bring France the best museum culture in Europe, he had also been anxious to encourage Frenchmen to be the best of European artists. For this end too he had come to rely on Denon.

For Denon there was no nobler role than that of a courtier-administrator. A few weeks after assuming his functions, Denon wrote to Napoleon, 'I pass my days concerning myself with everything you have entrusted to me, so that I can master it and maybe justify to posterity your decision in choosing me, and every time I notice some improvement to be made I ascribe it to you and am grateful to you for deciding that I should carry it out.' He was aware that he had to be diplomatic in his dealings with artists. He told Chaptal, 'Sir, the poor artist is hardly known. For the two hundred talented painters and sculptors in Paris, at most a dozen live well, others live from one day to the next.' Greuze, the sentimental moralist who had been so popular before the rise of David, was struggling with the problems of failing skill and growing poverty – Denon helped him and had Greuze paint his portrait. He ensured that Gros, Guérin and Gérard were comfortably off, he protected Prud'hon, who painted the familiar portrait of himself, and he encouraged Isabey. When Benjamin West, the American President of the Royal Academy, took the opportunity of the peace of Amiens to visit Paris and show his *Death on a pale horse* at the Salon that year, Denon made a point of showing him round the Louvre. West could not help contrasting French official enthusiasm for the arts with what happened in England. He laid on a dinner for Denon, the curators of the Louvre and several artists, including David. Thanks in part to Denon he was impressed by Napoleon and when he returned to England he said so.

The Salon of 1802 was the first Salon that Denon was in charge of. The most talked-of painting was Guérin's *Phaedra accusing Hippolytus*. The subject was earnest enough for the most serious Neo-Classicist, derived as it was by Racine from Euripides, and there was much applause when the actress Mademoiselle Mars claimed to her audience to be able

> ... *par l'illusion de ce tableau divin*
> *Entendre encore Racine en admirant Guérin*

(by the illusion of this sublime painting to hear Racine once more while admiring Guérin). France was returning to the mood of the *grand siècle* (the seventeenth century). Sophisticated society no longer pretended to adhere to the egalitarian ideals when the great actor Talma had dressed like a *sans-culotte*. If the next Salon did not occur till 1804, that was because Denon insisted that there should be a return to the pre-revolutionary habit of biennial Salons – he too had an instinct for the aristocratic habits of the past. He laid down precise instructions for would-be exhibitors. They must be rigorously realistic in matters of detail and historical fact. Portraits must be faithful, costume must be carefully researched and yet Napoleon must be seen as a certain kind of hero. Gros's *Plague-victims of Jaffa* conformed perfectly to these ideas. The result is a curious mixture of disparate elements. The buildings are topograph-ically accurate, the soldiers' uniforms and the oriental cloaks and turbans are authen-tic but the nudes derive from the studio and the message of the painting is that Napoleon's compassion is Christ-like. The painting had a modern subject and meaning under an ancient manner. At the following Salon, in 1806, Gros again caught the eye of the critics, with his colossal painting of *The Battle of Aboukir*. As Denon had watched what had happened seven years before, he showed Gros his sketches of the scene – the battle picture was exactly the sort of art he thought the Emperor would approve of, even if the dashing general whose charge settled the issue was Napoleon's raffish brother-in-law, Joachim Murat. Denon was not always so prescient. When he urged that Girodet should be awarded the Legion of Honour for *The Deluge*, his advice was ignored. Just before the 1808 Salon, however, he was sure of an impending triumph. He wrote to Duroc, 'The Salon fixed for 14 October this year will be the most impressive that there has ever been. The artists charged with works for His Majesty have fully justified the confidence with which they have been honoured. Others have made new efforts to be called on in the future and by their great talents everyone will place His Majesty's reign in the front rank in the arts, as it is in warfare, science and literature.' When Napoleon saw the great number of pictures that illustrated with panache the years of his reign, he was well pleased. David's massive *Sacre de Joséphine* dominated the Salon, but there were other key moments in the Emperor's life that were celebrated – *The deputies of Vienna surren-dering the keys of the city to the victor* (by Girodet), *Napoleon at the battle of Eylau* (by

The high point in the life of the comte Saint-Jean d'Angely was his presence at the meeting where Napoleon's divorce was announced. As portrayed by Gérard in 1808 (château de Versailles) he is gravely handsome.

Gros) and *The morning of Austerlitz* (by Carle Vernet) – and there were the usual chic portraits by Gérard, this year of the Empress Joséphine, Caroline Murat and Talleyrand. There was only one hitch. Girodet, so often the nonconformist, had painted a portrait of Chateaubriand, by then a critic of the regime, which master-piece had been accepted by Denon in the spirit of a noble courtier and then quietly put on one side. With a hint of malice Napoleon asked where it was – on seeing it, he made his famous remark about Chateaubriand looking as if he were a spy who had come down the chimney, for he did not appreciate the tousled hair and pensive look of the great Romantic, who thought that Napoleon was the only man of the age who equalled himself.

In 1810 Napoleonic themes still dominated the major Salon entries, as in David's *Distribution of the eagles*, Gérard's *Battle of Austerlitz*, Girodet's *The Revolt of Cairo* and Gros's *Battle of the Pyramids*. The previous September, when Napoleon was in Vienna, Denon had written to him, 'The Salon in future will take the place that the Olympic Games had in the past, as far as the arts of painting and sculpture are con-cerned.' By 1810 he was not so kind in his reaction to yet another of Guérin's Neo-Classical machines, *Andromache calling on Pyrrhus not to give up her son Astyanax to Orestes*. He complained of Guérin's premature success 'for which people have paid too dearly and to which the public and above all his colleagues react harshly'. Denon had none of the rigidity of either Guérin or David. The man who had so much pro-moted the Egyptian taste also loved the 'troubadour' style which devoted itself to pic-turing the factual and fictional Middle Ages and Renaissance. But Gérard's fourteen portraits, two more than in 1810, showed that their modern experience still gave Frenchmen a sense of self-worth. Napoleon had married his Austrian empress and all was well with the world. Denon was sure of his team. Gros was 'the first colour-ist of the history painters', Girodet in his *Revolt of Cairo* 'has shown that pride in design which distinguishes him' and Gérard has revealed 'the talent which he sug-gested fifteen years ago and which in the last six years I have accused him of not using'. In the last Salon of the Empire, that of 1812, Gérard was prominent again, with his portraits of Marie-Louise and the baby King of Rome, Gros had gone back to the times of François I and Charles V and Prud'hon was lingeringly sensu-ous in his *Venus*. Of these established artists only Prud'hon perhaps, because he tended to avoid the epic style, appealed to artistically sensitive souls. Had he been present, Napoleon might have sensed that the one new note in the seemingly cease-less reiteration of would-be heroic tunes was sounded by the young Theodore Géricault. His *Charging chasseur* had movement and fire. Most older artists, like the Emperor himself, were getting tired of fighting. The rhetoric of glory was no longer persuasive and it was time to retreat.

Denon was by nature a fighter. He had for too long had to cope with the petty jeal-
ousies, the greed – in the case of David the monstrous greed – and insecurities of
artists to be put out by bad luck. In 1806 he had written to Napleon to explain the
sort of world in which as museum director he had to live. 'It is a strange world, built
at once on pride and on inventiveness. You must understand a group of childish
adults, help and guide a class of men of imagination, who are easy to upset and hard
to govern and who are kept going only by the thought of fame – fame is their most
pressing need.' He had had his moments of satisfaction. In 1810 he had told
Napoleon, 'Your Majesty will find a collection of sixty paintings where the events
of your reign are represented with the severity, simplicity and truth of history.' He
himself thought of putting together a massive work on the Emperor's campaigns in
Italy and Germany to rival his previous book on Egypt. A budget of 630,000 francs
was allotted to this project till Napoleon put it off. That this amount was hardly
excessive is shown by the fact that for all Denon's efforts at economizing David went
on haggling till in the end he got 179,000 francs for the paintings of the *Sacre de
Joséphine*, the *Distribution of the eagles* and a sketch. Besides, Denon was able to turn
his scheme to good use by making his sketches available to other artists whose subjects were Napoleonic. He wanted to make his museum in every way a monument
to his hero.

In 1806 a list was drawn up of which scenes were to be painted by which artists,
on what scale and for what prices. Some well-known works were commissioned on
this occasion – Gérard's *Battle of Austerlitz* and Guérin's *The emperor pardoning the
rebels of Cairo at place Elbe-Keir* – but there were never enough artists of the first rank
working to the top of their form. *The Emperor haranguing the army on the bridge of Lech
at Augsburg, The captive Austrian army leaving Ulm, filing in front of the Emperor at the
moment when he was talking to the conquered generals, The entry of His majesty into the town
of Munich at the moment when the Bavarians came before him* or *The passage of the isthmus of
Suez* and *His Majesty visiting the fountains of Moses* have not been immortalized by
artists of note. Denon was able to tell Napoleon that haranguing troops on a bridge
had antique parallels with actions of Caesar, Trajan and Marcus Aurelius.
Napoleon himself may have had some say in choosing some of the topics. He seems
to have liked the idea of being seen visiting the bivouacs on the eve of the Battle of
Austerlitz, which was to be realized by the soldier-painter Lejeune, who was on the
staff of Marshal Berthier. Denon often thought up the more moving themes, like the
funeral of his old friend Desaix at the great Saint-Bernard pass and even the death
of Nelson (naturally he wanted to concentrate on the brave man who killed the
enemy admiral), and it was Denon who saw how precisely what had been decided
on was carried out. In a report of 1808 he noted that of the eighteen pictures

proposed in 1806 thirteen had been finished already and there was hope that others would be finished eventually. Gérard had been occupied with portraits of patrons he was bound to please but he had started on the *Battle of Austerlitz* and Gros had been ordered to concentrate on *Napoleon at Eylau* – a commission dating only from 1807 – rather than on the duller *Meeting of His Majesty with the Emperor Francis II*. By then Austria had been put in its place by the French victory at Wagram in 1809 and, while he was in Vienna with the winning army, Denon drew up a list of five large pictures for 12,000 francs each and seven medium-sized ones for 6000 francs. This time none of the great Empire artists was asked for a picture, maybe because Denon was trying to increase the number of painters who were capable of becoming military specialists. In the end nobody tackled the central subject, Wagram itself, and it was not till 1836 that Horace Vernet, son of the Napoleonic artist Carle Vernet, dramatized Napoleon's last triumph for the Salon. In the 1810 Salon, therefore, the most important Napoleonic pictures referred to earlier days, David to the oath of the army on the Champ de Mars, which had been taken after the coronation of 1804, Gérard to the Battle of Austerlitz (1805) and Gros to the Battle of the Pyramids and Girodet to the revolt of Cairo, which looked back to the remoter days of the Egyptian campaign. Denon excused himself for not having anything distinguished based on the most recent campaign with a sanguine comment. 'Without comparing myself to Boileau [the famous poet of the late seventeenth century] and the Emperor to another monarch [Louis XIV] I shall tell you in the words of that poet, *Grand roi cesse de vaincre ou je cesse d'écrire* [Either the great king should stop conquering or I writing].'

What made Denon so useful to the war artists was his dedication to recording battle scenes while they were happening. In Egypt he had sketched while soldiers fought around him. This coolness under fire made him the equivalent of a modern war photographer and as such exceptionally useful for Napoleonic propaganda. In February 1806 he returned from travels round Italy and Germany to see the sites the artists needed to know and wrote to the Emperor. 'The collection of drawings of my travels in Italy and Germany draw together all the places marked by some happenings relevant to your story. I have added, for Italy, all the monuments that Your Majesty could see which illustrate and make memorable the areas which you went through on your marches. I have taken great care to make sure that the places Your Majesty wished me to see in Germany are recorded . . . with more precision . . . I could get only a rough idea of most of the sites in Austrian states. I am certain, however, that I have covered those which especially concern Your Majesty . . .On my way back from Italy I wanted to come back to France by the river at Genoa and to sketch there the views that relate to the start of your first campaign, when I was recalled to your side, Sire, and followed in Germany the movements in your latest victories.' The campaign to which he refers at the end of his note started in 1806 and

went on till 1807. In August 1808 he was able to state that he had built up a collection of his own drawings and drawings by other artists working under him amount-
ing to 100 for that campaign, fifty for that of Austerlitz, fifty for that of Marengo and
110 for the first Italian campaign of 1796–7. The purpose of these drawings was to
'give painters the information they needed' and to furnish the decorators at Sèvres
with scenes for their plates. 'It will become in the future', he wrote, 'the reference for
the subjects of historical paintings to be given every year to the painters.' It was in
this spirit that in a letter of 16 April 1809 he wrote to ask permission to be on his
way from the moment the first cannon-ball was shot. He had been in Spain the previous year. Now he would be in Austria.

Though his travels were on official business, it was not easy to cover his expenses.
In 1810 he wrote over-optimistically to say that the Spanish campaign was as good
as over and yet he still had not been paid for his engravings. He was confident of the
usefulness of his work. 'Of the sixty pictures of modern history in this year's exhibition fifty have taken their subjects from my collection and every time that there is a
plan to do something at the factories of the Gobelins or Sèvres it is again this collection that people consult.' So thorough was he that he apologized to the Emperor for
the fact that one month in Napoleon's military history still had not been covered,
namely the Ligurian campaign (near Genoa) from Savona to Cherasco. Always he
thought that what he had done in Egypt was only the start of a great scheme, to illustrate the story of the military achievement of Napoleon from the early days till the
Salon of 1812, where an enormous number of canvases treating Napoleonic themes
was shown, while their hero was on his way to Moscow.

In 1810 Napoleon suppressed all convents in the kingdom of Italy and confiscated
their goods, including all works of art that they had owned. Only Denon, he
thought, would be able to say how much they were worth. Since his early years as
a diplomat, when he had visited Sicily, studied its antiquities and begun his lifelong habit of collecting, Denon had been fascinated by the treasures of Italy.
Already at the end of 1808 the Borghese antique statues, which Napoleon had persuaded his brother-in-law to part with, had arrived in Paris. Denon wanted still
more. It was not enough that the Laocoon and the Apollo Belvedere had come from
the Vatican and the Medici Venus from Florence – Denon wanted to add the
Farnese Hercules from Naples. But even before he had time to catalogue and
exhibit these celebrated statues he was told to leave for Italy. He left at the end of
August 1811 for Genoa and, accompanied everywhere by a secretary, a draughtsman and a painter called Benjamin Zix, went from town to town till he reached
Rome. Zix had become a friend of Denon's since he had portrayed him seated with
his quill in his hand, writing on a sheet of paper headed 'Director of the Musée

Napoléon' while at his feet are piled his great two-volume work on the Egyptian journey, his book on Sicily, his works on the Italian and German campaigns, a scale model of the Vendôme column and other monuments he had had built (including the Pont Neuf obelisk, the elephant fountain at place de la Bastille and a bust and a statue of Napoleon). It was Zix who also produced an ink-and-wash portrayal of the marriage procession of Napoleon and Marie-Louise in the long gallery of the Louvre. There, in front of paintings by Poussin, Claude, Lesueur, Rubens, Raphael, Perugino and Leonardo, was assembled the core of the Napoleonic court, all the family queens and princesses, only two of the Emperor's brothers, Louis and Jérôme (Joseph was far away, unavoidably detained by the Duke of Wellington in Spain, and Lucien still sulked in exile), Camillo Borghese and Joachim Murat (brothers-in-law), the grand dignitaries (including Talleyrand, Berthier and Cambacérès, Napoleon's former fellow Consul), then a motley entourage of heralds, pages, masters of ceremonies, officers, stewards, chamberlains, aides-de-camp, governors and chaplains. The painting of this picture was to be Zix's moment of glory, for in Italy he died.

Denon took care to take advantage of every stage of the journey. In Genoa he sketched the sites of Napoleon's campaign there, put the least valuable works of art into local churches and sent the best home. As he went south the breadth of his tastes became more remarkable. In Pisa he took a low-relief marble by Giovanni Pisano (from the thirteenth century), in Florence he took paintings by fra Angelico, Gentile da Fabbriano and Domenico del Ghirlandaio (from the fifteenth century). In Rome he took part in the plan to design the gardens of the Pincian hill. What was more unusual was his delight in the art he found in Perugia, at Assisi, Perugia and Foligno. He was one of the first critics who deserved to be called a Pre-Raphaelite. If he had read carefully his Vasari, whose sixteenth-century lives of the artists of Italy had formed the judgements of connoisseurs for 250 years, he would have had some bookish knowledge of the art he encountered, but there was a refreshing originality in his reactions to what he saw. In Milan he renewed his acquaintance with Prince Eugène de Beauharnais, now Viceroy of Italy, who as a teenager had been in Egypt with him. He visited the Brera museum and noticed several painters who were not represented in Paris. In exchange for some Lombard and Venetian pictures he acquired a Rubens, a Van Dyck and a Jordaens ('colourist painters who are essential for the school of Milan').* By the time he had come home, at the end of January 1812, he was able to tell the Minister of the Interior, Montalivet, that what was lacking to the Musée Napoléon was a collection of the artists of the Italian Renaissance from Cimabue to Raphael (almost Vasari's range). He took more than

---

*Though the Flemish painters Denon mentions worked in the seventeenth century, he thought of them as essential for the sixteenth-century 'school of Milan' in so far as they had learnt from the Milanese painters.

4000 pictures and introduced his compatriots to no less than sixty artists whom hitherto they had not known. One of the direct consequences of his work was to expand the canon of acceptable taste first in France and ultimately in other European countries.

Denon's last trip abroad seemed to be a triumph, but the triumph was short-lived. Even though the pictures from Savona and Parma came respectively in February and June 1812, the majority of works did not arrive till the Russian campaign had been fought and lost. Denon carried on unperturbed. He supervised the careful restoration of work after work. Problems arose. The Academy objected to the deal he had made with Prince Eugène, especially as one of the pictures the Brera was to surrender was its only Boltraffio, one of Leonardo's best followers, so Denon had to offer another seventeenth-century picture, this time by the Bolognese painter Domenichino. Well into 1814 he continued to work at making the Musée Napoléon the greatest museum in the world. In that year he spent more than ever on the work of restoration. When the allied troops were on the point of entering Paris, Denon's one thought was to put together his collection of Italian primitives, which he wanted to put beside the Flemish and German paintings of the fourteenth and fifteenth centuries. On 25 July, he announced, there would be an exhibition of 'the primitive schools of Italy, of Germany and of several other pictures from different schools' in the grand Salon — and here he had to change the wording of his announcement — of the *Royal* Museum. It was almost two months since the abdication of Napoleon.

Denon reacted as an experienced courtier should — he would carry on his work. Well before it was clear that the Bourbons would be restored, Denon had made his peace with the new regime. In April he sent the provisional Secretary of State, Baron de Vitrolles, a memorandum on his idea for a medal to be struck in honour of the return of the King, Louis XVIII, to France. 'We can represent France by the seashore, holding out her arms towards the approaching ship which brings the king back with the inscription "He brings the peace of the world", and mention the date of His Majesty's return and the name of the port where he disembarked.'

Soon he had a better idea. The King should offer France an olive branch, France should hold out her arms towards him and the inscription this time would say simply 'First Kindness'. This time as well as the date of the King's return there should be the heads not only of Louis XVIII himself but also of his most famous Bourbon ancestors, Louis the Great (Louis XIV) and Henri IV. If this seems shocking in an avowed Bonapartist, then it was the action of an artistic nationalist. Denon was dedicated to his museum, whether it was Napoleonic or royal, and at this stage it looked as if he might succeed. The victorious Austrian, Prussian, Russian and

English troops were allies of Louis XVIII and they could not very well despoil the collection that it was his good fortune to have acquired along with his throne. If a sovereign wished to visit the Louvre, Denon would accompany him, and he sent a record of the occasion to the royal court. He issued appropriate medals for such events. That of Tsar Alexander was commemorated by reissuing the medal that had been struck for the visit of Tsar Peter the Great. Alexander was debonair and delightful, unlike the Emperor of Austria, who was disliked for his treatment of his daughter, now the ex-Empress Marie-Louise. Louis XVIII was shrewd enough to offer his guests something in return for their help. Confiscated works that were not on show at the Louvre or the Tuileries would be sent back, so ten Cranachs, one Bruegel triptych and two Correggios left France early on. Denon's response was to try to exhibit as many works as possible, in order to keep them in France, but he could not stop the departure of several paintings by Rubens, two Altdorfers, some Italian majolica, some Limoges enamels, some ivories, the wax masque of Frederick the Great of Prussia and some unspecified erotica.

In November he was involved in the organization of the 1814 Salon. Apart from David, who gave private showings of his picture of King Leonidas and the Spartans on the eve of their defeat by the Persians at Thermopylae, all the well-known artists exhibited. For a little while Denon may have thought himself secure. Privately Louis was preparing to replace him with the Comte de Forbin, whom he took with him when he and Denon looked round the pictures on display. He made a public point of asking each of them his opinion, but Denon was not fooled. Immediately Napoleon came back from Elba, Denon offered his Emperor his service. He and his museum were indissolubly attached to the Emperor's cause. The defeat at Waterloo inevitably meant the destruction of his dearest plans.

By the end of the Hundred Days the mood of the conquerors had hardened. When Louis XVIII appealed to the Tsar to help him save the Louvre, he was brusquely told, 'Since you have kept the provinces which we wished to take away from you, allow us to take away some pictures and some statues.' For Denon there was nothing left to do except to carry on fighting a rearguard action, which would be like Napoleon's 1814 campaign in France. He knew that in the end he could not win, but he would try to draw out the time it took to defeat him and he might have one or two local victories. He kept a thirty-seven page manuscript record of this last battle for his museum, which he carried on from 7 July, when the allies first entered Paris, to 7 November.

On 7 July Denon had a visit from Ribbentrop, general administrator of the Prussian army, who came to claim works that had been taken from Berlin. He wished to teach the French a lesson – never again would they be able to impose their

will on the rest of Europe – and in a letter on the following day he demanded
immediate restitution. Duplicate copies of this letter were sent to the Duc de
Richelieu, Minister of the Royal Household, and to Talleyrand, the Foreign
Minister. Talleyrand suavely agreed and suggested that the only problems were practical – where the objects were to be found. Ribbentrop was not so easily put off. On
10 July at ten o'clock in the morning an officer arrived at the Louvre with twenty-
five men. If Denon did not give way by next morning, he would be seized and put
in prison in East Prussia. Denon did not flinch. He had no authorization, he said,
from the French government and pointed out that the Prussian officer had no authorization from his own. Later came a fierce letter from Marshal Blücher himself. His
emissary, one de Groote, asked the Louvre caretakers to take a Rubens off the wall
and, when Denon forbade them to help, had to tell his soldiers to do the work. By
this time officers of the French National Guard had turned up, alerted by Denon,
and interposed themselves between de Groote and the pictures. Not till a tactful
message from the director of the royal household arrived was the tension relieved and
the possibility of a fight over the Rubens avoided. Meanwhile Blücher had made off
with a Rembrandt and a Leonardo from Saint-Cloud, and other pictures disappeared from Compiègne, Fontainebleau and Rambouillet which had never
belonged to Prussia. It was just a question of hostage-taking, explained Blücher.
Denon felt that during this fight he had been abandoned by his king. Louis had little
choice but to yield. Prussian guns were trained on the Tuileries, Prussian troops did
their washing in the palace courtyard and hung it up on the wrought-iron gates,
Prussians slaughtered cows and sheep under the Arc du Carrousel. 'Let the
Prussians dishonour themselves,' was Louis' advice to Denon.

Denon used what delaying tactics he could, but when the Prussians wished to
take away the ten marble columns from Aix-la-Chapelle, he was furious. Such an
action, he knew, would endanger the building, so he wrote to the King of Prussia
to tell him. After only two days he had his reply from Frederick-William III. 'If
national honour and the interest that I take in the progress of the arts in my states
have caused me to ask back what has been taken by force of arms, it is equally one
of my principles to prevent anything that would result in the irreparable damage of
a building which contains all the most precious objects that we have received from
antiquity. I shall give orders that nobody should ask for any of the columns which
hold up the building's roof.'

There were some cases where it was not clear who had the right to what. In the
case of Belgium, which had been ruled by France since 1794, and the Netherlands
when Louis Bonaparte had been King of Holland, some works of art had been
brought to France in exchange for others. The Comte de Pradel wrote to Denon to
tell him that all resistance was useless, but Denon was unimpressed. In his turn he
wrote to the Minister of Police in September, 'The allied powers had treated the

museum in a way which shows that there is no provocation to fear.' Two days before, on 21 September, the Austrian commissioner had laid claim to the works of art belonging to the Italian states and then Prince Schwartzemberg sent his aide-de-camp to ask for the treasures of Venice, Piacenza and Florence. 'When I observed that I had received no instructions relative to this demand,' said Denon, 'he said he knew that but would like the act of repossession which he had been told to accomplish to be sanctioned by me.' Two days later the aide-de-camp came back with instructions that the four horses of San Marco should be lowered down from the top of the Arc du Carrousel. Denon said that such a matter was outside his competence, so on the night of 26 September workmen and Austrian soldiers in disguise came with the key to get inside the monument and started to move the bronze base and to chip away at the stone that held the balls under the horses' feet. They made so much noise that a crowd of local people soon assembled and the National Guard was called out. The following evening the Austrians appeared in strength, but military force was not enough. They could not find an engineer to help them, so they appealed to the Duke of Wellington, who was delighted not only to provide the technical aid but also to supervise the operation himself.

Meanwhile, with much less commotion, the Spaniards came to take back home some eighty-four paintings. Denon could not even save private collections, like the one Marshal Soult, Duke of Dalmatia, had built up by a combination of gifts, purchases and confiscation. The King's rule was that only art exhibited at the Louvre should not be surrendered. Denon protested that Murillo's *Saint Elizabeth caring for the sick* had been given freely by the city of Seville to Soult and by him to the King – in vain.

The final battle involved the Papal States. Denon told Pradel that he wished the papal statues and paintings to be treated as a special case and he was furious that the Protestant English were the most vocal supporters of His Holiness. His last enemy was the Under-Secretary of Foreign Affairs, who like Denon had been a career diplomat, having served as secretary to Lord Elgin in Istanbul and then having helped arrange the transport of the Elgin marbles from Athens to London. Like Denon he had published a book on Egypt, which was projected as the first of a series of books on the Ottoman Empire, and he had copied the Greek text on the Rosetta Stone and translated it into English. Possibly because Hamilton, though a generation younger, had so much in common with Denon in both his interests and his career, the fight between the two of them was especially fierce. He was given instructions by Wellington to support all that the papacy asked for – or rather its plenipotentiary in the arts, who turned out to be Canova.

The papal works – the Hellenistic sculptures and the Raphaels chief among them – were considered the prize exhibits in the Louvre. For Wellington it was imperative that they should return to Rome, so that the French people would not remember that once they had owned them and want to revive their militaristic spirit. When the Duke approached Denon directly, Denon said that he would never give up the pictures from the gallery of his own free will. A troop of British grenadiers took over the Louvre. Denon was beside himself with rage, but then thought of trying argument – it made no sense that the British should help the Pope. When Canova arrived in Paris in late August, he did not expect to succeed, for after he had contacted Baron Humboldt, the Prussian ambassador, he found that even the most vehement supporter of the principle of restitution did not believe that the Pope would win his case, for by the Treaty of Tolentino he had given many of his possessions to France. There was an attempt at bribing Wellington, for he soon acquired Canova's statue of Napoleon as Mars, and Canova allowed some works to stay, such as Flemish primitives and paintings by Cimabue and fra Angelico from the Albani collection. Just as Veronese's enormous *Marriage Feast of Cana* from San Giorgio Maggiore in Venice stayed, so too a further hundred paintings, twenty-one antique statues, the Pope's cameos, some Etruscan vases, all the Albani low-reliefs and 800 drawings from the Este collection in Modena were kept in the Louvre. Most of them were bought from the original owners. Cardinal Albani was embarrassed by some of his family's works of art and was glad to shed them. The former Musée Napoléon lost permanently 2605 paintings, 130 statues, 150 low-reliefs, 289 bronzes, 16 Etruscan vases, 76 other vases made of precious materials, 105 ivory vases, 37 wood sculptures, 471 cameos, 271 drawings and 1199 enamels and majolica plates. The Duke of Wellington took away a haul of trophies of which any one of the Napoleonides, if not Napoleon himself, would have been proud, and nothing elsewhere had quite the prestige of the restored papal collection.

On 3 October 1815 de Pradel wrote to Denon. 'I have had the honour to inform the King, *Monsieur le baron*, of the action you have taken to try to preserve for the Crown the paintings and other works of art that have been taken away by the commissioners of the allied princes. His Majesty is very pleased with it. I can only be equally satisfied with the punctiliousness with which you have acted in accordance with the instructions I gave you and I am pleased to assure you that this is so.' Denon replied with dignity. 'I am honoured by the evidence of His Majesty's satisfaction. Please be so good as to hand him the following request' – his resignation. Denon was about to enter his seventieth year. By June 1816 all the Empire officials had left. Lavallée, Denon's assistant and successor, was replaced at the Louvre by the Comte de Forbin, while already Baron de Puymaurin was in charge of royal medals. Denon's main work in life seemed over. He was glad to know that some had appreciated him. In November 1815 he received a generous and unexpected tribute from von Ribbentrop, the former chief administrator of the Prussian army. '*Monsieur le Baron*, I could not leave Paris for my native country without telling you of the personal admiration which I have for your qualities. However disagreeable our working relationship has been, as far as you were concerned, it has only served to heighten my appreciation of a learned man whom I regard myself as lucky to have known. To the feelings of respect I have for the pleasant moments I passed in your company I add the similar feelings of the civilised world, which owes you the preservation of its masterpieces, and I ask you to accept that this is the case.'

Denon lived on till 1825. He went back to his engraving and to his collecting. From his hôtel on quai Voltaire he had to walk only a short distance to the Louvre. He had six apartments devoted to his private museum of pictures, medals, bronzes, drawings, antiquities, curiosities from Egypt, China and India. In 1829 Didot published a great tome, illustrated by Amaury-Duval, one of the most faithful pupils of Ingres, which catalogued the whole collection. Despite his lack of private wealth Denon had been lucky and assiduous. Besides Watteau's *Gilles* he was the owner of a Jacob van Ruysdael waterfall, a Parmigianino head and 56 Italian primitives. He had 81 Flemish paintings and 53 French ones and a vast quantity of drawings – by Parmigianino, Dürer, Rembrandt, Poussin, Claude, Fragonard (29), Guercino (80), Raphael (10), Giulio Romano (10). He even claimed to have a set of unlikely secular relics, of the Cid, of Héloïse and Abélard, of the royal mistresses Agnès Sorel and Inès de Castro, of Henri IV's moustache, of Turenne, Molière, La Fontaine, Voltaire (a tooth), Desaix (some hair) and Napoleon (a drop of blood from St Helena). He also had the death mask of Robespierre.

In 1826 the collection was sold at public auction. Denon had died on 27 April 1825, himself a relic of the *ancien régime*, who had served in Louis XV's embassy in St Petersburg, who had called on Voltaire at Ferney, who had been secretary to the ambassador and chargé d'affaires in Naples, who was elected to the Academy of Beaux-Arts in 1787, who passed the first four years of the revolution in Venice, Florence and Bologna. When he had come back to France during the Terror, Denon had been glad of the protection of David, then a ruthless member of the Committee of General Security and at one time its president. 'I attest, Citizen Minister,' wrote David, 'that I knew citizen Denon in Italy, that I saw him exercise the arts there with success and that he has never inhabited neutral countries. We are now together working on an engraving of the picture of the tennis court oath. He is doing the engraving. He could not do so were he not a good patriot.' Denon was a good patriot in his way, not in the manner of the painter of the Horatii, of the First Consul Brutus and of the dead Marat. He was no fanatic, except insofar as he was unwaveringly true to the sceptical spirit of the sage of Ferney and by instinct a believer in benevolent despots. He found his hero in young General Bonaparte before he found in the Emperor Napoleon his ideal enlightened ruler. Bonaparte's expedition to Egypt in middle age prepared him for his own great work at the Louvre, where ever since 1857 a part of the collection has taken his name.

CHAPTER 12

The Failure of the Napoleonic Epic

NAPOLEON had been born on an island and he would die on an island. For Denon there was to be a restful ending to life, a gentle autumn before the onset of a wintry close. There was no such coda to the life of Napoleon. On St Helena he was exiled not only far from all his family, with his wife in Parma and his son and heir a virtual captive in Austria, but he was also remote from the places in which he had made his career. More than any Frenchman before or since he had dominated the European continent, which he had almost sealed off from the only important insular Europeans, the English. It was the English who had charge of his last days and they forced him to be, like a true Englishman, a man on an island.

Although he tried to behave like an emperor till the day he died, insisting on a certain remoteness from his entourage, he was stripped of the grandeur that had attended him. Without making the long trail to a distant Atlantic isle, the modern sleuth can gain some idea of Napoleon's material circumstances during this period of his life from the small museum in the Parc de Bois-Préau, just opposite the château of Malmaison. Briefly Napoleon enjoyed an agreeable time with the Balcombe family at 'The Briars', but by December 1815 the remote and damp Longwood House was ready for him and he lived there till he died. Even though it is not possible to reconstruct Napoleon's final home exactly as it was, the change in his circumstances was obvious enough. The pomp permitted him on Elba was gone. There were some memorials of his wars, like a map of North Italy, which must have been an *aide-mémoire* for the story of the first Italian campaign, which he dictated to the Count of Las Cases. He had a telescope so that he could know in advance who was about to visit him, a Chinese chessboard bought in the capital, Jamestown, to while away the evenings, and a supply of books sent to him by the Whig hostess, Lady Holland (in 1817 her husband raised awkward questions in the House of Lords about the conditions of Napoleon's detention). There were camp beds that he had used on his campaigns and which now served him for his afternoon naps. Much of his furniture was from England, such as his cane and lacquered Regency armchair and another Regency armchair in black wood, which was decorated with gilt bronze. He also had furniture with some Chinese connections. He had an elegant Chinese screen and some attractive garden chairs which were made for him by Chinese servants. He acquired a Spode tea set. Of the wonderful works of art with which he had been surrounded for fifteen years little remained to him. There were two miniatures by Isabey of the King of Rome, which he proudly showed to the teenage Betsy Balcombe, and a round gilt snuff-box, whose lid was decorated with tiny oval portraits of Joséphine, Louis, Hortense and Eugène. He also had brought with him from the Tuileries an enamel box with portraits in profile of Louis XVI, Marie-Antoinette and the King's sister, Madame Elizabeth (in his hurry to escape from Paris early in 1815 Louis XVIII had left the box behind and Napoleon had found it). To hang on the walls Napoleon had cut out flower pictures from the *Description de l'Egypte*. His most valuable possessions were his silver, including pieces by Biennais, much of which he had to sell, and various examples of Sèvres porce-lain, which he was apt to give away to people he liked. At Bois-Préau there are three dessert plates from a service that illustrated some of the places associated with him – Aboukir, where he had defeated the Turks, Fréjus, where he had landed on his return from Egypt, and Malmaison. Among clothing and coverings he had one fine cashmere shawl that Pauline had given him as long ago as 1797 and which was on his bed when he lay dying, but there was nothing fine about his bed linen or his nightshirts and for the most part his clothes looked shabby. In his final, as in his early, years Napoleon was poor. When he died he was buried quietly in the Vale of Geranium under a plain slab of stone which the governor fenced round with a metal railing to keep the vandals out.

The Empire style outlived Waterloo. Oddly it was most enthusiastically copied by some of Napoleon's personal enemies – Bernadotte, soon to be King of Sweden, and the Prince Regent, soon to be King of Great Britain, who was now in effect his gaoler. The King of France expected that all Napoleonic emblems, such as the ubiq-uitous 'N' and the Bonaparte bees, should be removed from carpets and hangings and houses, while work on the Arc de Triomphe was stopped. There was no attempt, however, to change the fashionable style.

Changes were first noticed in the studios of the younger painters. Some who had read their Chateaubriand and who supported Bourbon propaganda which linked throne and altar may have felt that the troubadour style, which anyway had begun under Napoleon, was more suited to reminding the people of France of their glori-ous past – some painters enjoyed putting François I in Renaissance costume and

This oval snuff-box (*tabatière à portraits*) shows the people whom Napoleon at different times valued most: Joséphine, her children and his brother Louis. His stepchildren never let him down.

Henri IV in his ruff (they were easily the most popular of French kings) and others went further back to medieval times, to kings like Charles V, who had won battles against the English (now a safe subject). As a literary source Homer was gradually demoted in favour of Dante, for there was nothing in the Greek to stir tender emo-tions like the tale of Paolo and his adulterous love for Francesca of Rimini. At the 1812 Salon Marie-Philippe Coupin de la Couperie exhibited *The tragic love of Francesca of Rimini*, a representation of the moment just before her jealous husband killed her and his younger brother, her lover. Joséphine bought the picture and it passed with her daughter, Hortense, to Arenenberg in Switzerland, where it still is today. The troubadour style had richer resources to draw on than the painters who had pleased Napoleon by illustrating Ossian, and unlike Ossianic art this more authentic medievalism became part of a European phenomenon. Blake was inspired by copying the tombs in Westminster Abbey but, long before the English had their

Hortense de Beauharnais took Coupin de la Couperie's troubadour painting of 'The tragic love of Paolo Malatesta and Francesca da Rimini' to Arenenberg in Switzerland, where it remains.

most eloquent champion of the Gothic style in Pugin, young Germans, in whose country many medieval towns were still untouched by the destruction of the Napoleonic wars, went wild about Germany's pre-classical past. As early as 1808 Franz Pforr began to paint *The entry of Rudolf of Habsburg into Basel in 1273* (Rudolf had been the first Habsburg to be Holy Roman Emperor) in a self-consciously archaic manner. Soon he and his 'Nazarene' friends, of whom Friedrich Overbeck was the most influential, had firmly turned their backs on the insidious influence which they saw as emanating from those Hellenistic statues that Napoleon and Denon had been so keen to filch from the Vatican. To sculpt was pagan and sensual, to paint Christian and chaste. Pforr and Overbeck were horrified by the carnality they found in Correggio and Titian and they turned back to Raphael and also to Dürer, to the Germanic tradition of the printers of woodcuts, to good honest crafts-men. The next generation would read the German medieval literature that their pro-fessors had rediscovered, but to the pious the texts proved to be double-edged, for besides the improving tale of Parsifal they learnt of the adulterous story of Tristan and the wild legends of the Nibelungenlied. In 1813, in the year of Leipzig, Richard Wagner was born.

During the last years of Napoleon two German medievalists showed a touch of genius. In 1807-8 a devout Protestant from Swedish Pomerania, who unlike Pforr and Overbeck refused to train in Rome in case the culture of the city would corrupt him, painted a solitary crucifix on a mountainous rock against a radiant sky. He meant it for the King of Sweden, a fellow Lutheran, but in the end his picture was bought by a Catholic nobleman and placed on the altar in a chapel. Without nec-essarily intending it, Friedrich had invented a new religious art for the Romantic age, in which nature took on a role of spiritual healing. In the cold, clear colours of the North he depicted visionary churches which blend in with the misty, icy forests where they are found, rocky paths that lead across crags to the heavens, paths deep in woodland that face towards the moon ahead, ships marooned in ice, ships sailing in a boundless expanse of sea, while over and over again his men and women, singly or in couples or in small groups, turn their gaze from the viewer towards horizons that seem to have no limits, as they yearn for eternity. Friedrich's symbols are found in nature itself or in the nature of the objects that are man-made. The rocks refer to the hard life of the Christian, the ship that is awaited in the dawn gives birth to hope and a man who can stand without crutches finds strength only in God. While for almost twenty years Friedrich was at the height of his powers, he painted as though there had never been any political or social shocks by the Baltic shore from which he came or in Dresden where he made his home.

The other original was Karl Friedrich Schinkel, who supplied Berlin with many of its most famous Neo-Classical monuments and who invented a credible Egyptian setting for a production of Mozart's *Magic Flute*. At the same time as Friedrich was

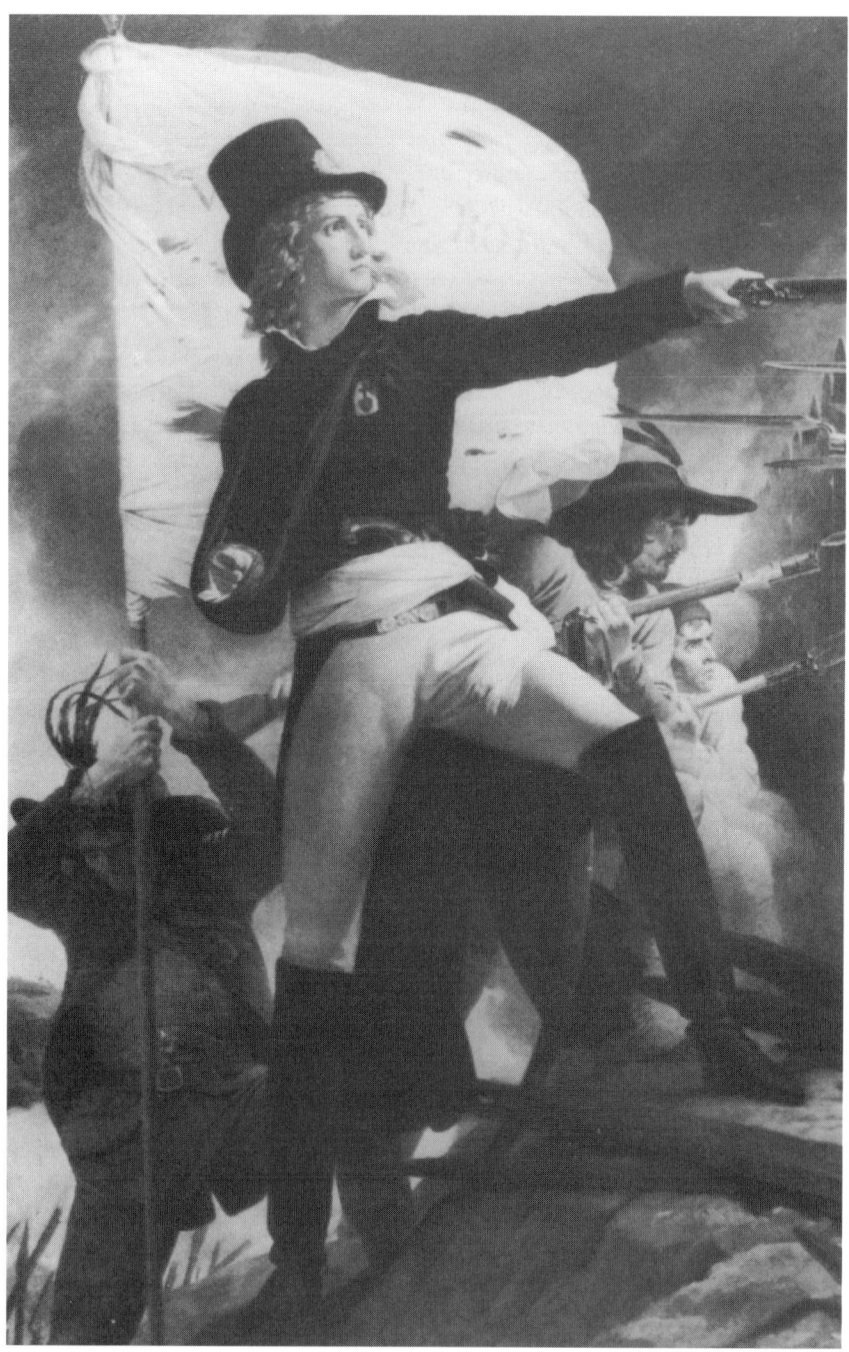

Guérin's gallant counter-revolutionary, Henri de la Rochejacquelin, is in the
Musée Municipal, Cholet.

inventing his new form of religious art, Schinkel made a lithograph of a Gothic church hidden by trees 'to express the sweet yearning melancholy' the listener feels when he hears the music of a religious service resounding from a church – and soon he was painting oils of soaring cathedrals, as though his Neo-Classical mind needed to be free from the mundane architecture he built to soar into a world of inner fantasy. This was not like the bogus world of Ossian on which Napoleon's mind was set even when he was travelling out to St Helena. Europe had been so long at war, Germany had been so deeply humiliated by Napoleon – its two major powers, Austria and Prussia, comprehensively defeated by him at Ulm and Austerlitz and Jena, its Holy Roman Empire brought to an end by him and many of its minor states reorganised by him into the Confederation of the Rhine – that many Germans found it much more pleasant to sidetrack the modern world, like Friedrich, or return to the past world, like Schinkel. Schinkel was too intelligent to live for ever in the past – when he went to England he was fascinated by the achievements of the Industrial Revolution – but he expressed in his 'Gothic' pictures a love of traditions that revolutionary and Napoleonic wars had swept away.

Napoleonic painting at its most impressive had rested on the bedrock of antiq-uity, but Napoleon himself preferred things to be factually accurate and thus modern. He had objected to David's heroes because they would never have been able to wield a weapon. He had liked Gros, who painted battles or intervals between battles the way he liked to see them, with himself in command, whether directing victories in Egypt or like a modern Messiah touching the plague-ridden in Jaffa and caring for the wounded on the field of Eylau. Napoleon's dominance of French and to some extent Italian art had been so complete that for a decade thousands of paint-ings, like hundreds of statues, had aimed merely to glorify him. Now David had left to paint the good burghers of Belgium and the lascivious loves of the gods, and his school was without direction. Gros was a lost soul and never recovered from the departure of his two masters, Napoleon and David. Girodet had gone into a decline and Prud'hon, Joséphine's favourite, was suffused with melancholy. Others were more resilient. Gérard had been Napoleon's court portraitist and he became the court painter of Louis XVIII. Guérin, a Neo-Classicist not of David's school, turned from showing Napoleon's mercy to the Arabs in Cairo to painting the young handsome General de la Rochejacquelin, his right arm in a sling, pointing his Vendéen troops onwards into battle with his pistol in his left hand, the emblem of the Sacred Heart sown on to his jacket, while the White Bourbon flag flies behind him. Guérin would end up directing the French Academy in Rome.

The most gifted of David's pupils, Jean-Auguste-Dominique Ingres, had taken refuge in Rome when there had been an outcry over his archaic portrayal of the Emperor in his coronation robes, seated like a Byzantine Basileus on his throne. There he had made a career painting French officials and their friends, he got to know Lucien Bonaparte and, apart from being asked to paint for the Quirinale, he managed to survive without working for the Emperor again. He entered some pictures in the Napoleonic Salons and sent to Paris the most beautiful naked back of the early nineteenth century, belonging to the bather of Valpincon (so called because she was at one time owned by the Valpincon family, who let young Degas see her). In 1814 for Caroline Murat he painted his most beguiling nude, the *Grande Odalisque*, with two or three extra vertebrae to make the curve of her back even more sinuous. He stayed on in Rome, drawing beautiful family sketches for the tourists who had come back, painting his own *Paolo and Francesca* in the troubadour style and waiting perhaps to make his peace with the restored regime. In 1824 he returned to Paris at the same time as he submitted to the Salon a dull pastiche of Raphael exactly appropriate to the mood of the new King, Charles X, a repentant roué. Ingres took as his subject Louis XIII dedicating France to Our Lady. He painted with great technical skill and without any emotion and he was hailed as the saviour of French art. Three years later he produced *The apotheosis of Homer*. He was dedicated to reaction.

Other painters were legitimists by conviction. During the Empire, Madame Vigée-Lebrun, who so long ago had painted her charming portraits of Marie-Antoinette alone or with her children, had briefly returned to Paris, but for most of Napoleon's reign she had mixed with *émigré* and anti-Bonapartist friends and had even spent a long while in Russia. After 1815 she was back in Paris, conducting a salon as sought after among the artistic fraternity as Gérard's. Once she had made it ladylike to be artistic – Napoleon like the Jacobins had wanted to make art virile – she taught younger men their good manners – Napoleon had never cared for politeness. Her great days were over, but she had her memoirs to write and she had the satisfaction of knowing that her royal portraits no longer faced the wall at Versailles, as they had in the time of the Empire. She was untroubled, not a little bland.

Among young artists psychological suffering became the norm. Several of the best emerged from Guérin's studio, among them Theodore Géricault, Ary Scheffer, who painted yet another *Paolo and Francesca*, and Eugène Delacroix. Politically they were probably all Bonapartists or liberals, which curiously came to the same thing. Géricault had briefly fought in the royalist cavalry, but he took to sketching and painting Napoleonic soldiers, which he never showed, and in 1818 he caused a sensation by depicting the terrible privations of the crew of the *Medusa* who had been cast adrift by their royalist officers to die on a raft. Delacroix devoted much of his time to anti-Bourbon caricatures – caricature was once more, if reluctantly, allowed and, when the second heir to the throne was murdered in 1822, Delacroix made an engraving of the assassin, with his hair flowing in the wind, a Chateaubriand of crime. In the 1820s none of these artists was of international importance in the way that David had been. The Pope, who offered asylum to many of the Bonapartes, also

Canova's 'The three graces' was planned for Joséphine. This was another version, that the duke of Bedford bought and that is now shared between the Victoria and Albert Museum, London and the National Gallery of Scotland, Edinburgh.

offered it to David. In the 1820s the Pope's wishes still counted in matters of art, and the most famous artist in Europe was proud to work for him. Antonio Canova had achieved an eminence no other sculptor had had since the days of Bernini 150 years before.

Though the English had believed otherwise, Canova had never put Napoleon first. As he told Napoleon, he was the Pope's sculptor and he was not happy till the Pope was back in Rome. In 1814, at the same time as its ruler returned, Rome became again an international centre. English *milords*, who had not been abroad since the failure of the truce of Amiens, appeared in the studios of Rome to see what they could buy. The Duke of Bedford as a Whig was Francophile and he had been in Paris in 1802. Now he came to Rome, where he was drawn by Ingres. He bought antique sculptures and some large vases, which had been intended for Malmaison, he was given a statue from Pompeii by Caroline Murat, who in her anxiety to keep the throne of Naples would court anyone sympathetic, he bought the Achilles relief of the Danish Neo-Classical sculptor Thorwaldsen and he commissioned a Priam from Canova. His contact with Canova was to have momentous consequences for them both. The following year Canova came to London to see the Elgin marbles and to see the Duke at Woburn, for the Duke wished him to make for his country seat a new version of the Three Graces – an earlier version had been ordered by Joséphine – for a Temple of the Graces that was to match the earlier Temple of Liberty. This episode was symptomatic of the international turn Canova's career took in his final years. While Joséphine's Three Graces made their way to St Petersburg, another of Canova's Napoleonic sculptures went to the arch-Tory Duke of Wellington, so that Napoleon as Mars now stands in the stairway of Apsley House, No.1, London. When it came to an address, however, Canova had proved that in cultural terms Rome was still the best address of all.

One of the places that Canova had to visit after Waterloo was Paris, where he came in search of the papal works of art. All those who could sent delegates to take back home what they could. The Prussians were first in the field and the most vindictive. When Denon resisted their claims, he was threatened with prison in East Prussia and in the end had to give way to the bayonets of Prussian soldiers who were sent to the Louvre. The Prussians, who gained more territory than any other signatory of the Vienna settlement, now saw themselves as the leaders of North Germany, so they also took the works of art belonging to Hesse-Kassel, Mecklenburg-Schwerin and some states in the Rhineland. Taking courage from Prussian success, the first ever King of the Netherlands asked that his troops, who were commanded by

Wellington, should also turn up at the Louvre. Soon they were followed by envoys from Parma and Piacenza and Tuscany and then by Canova. Finally came the Austrians, to whom the Vienna settlement had allotted Lombardy and Venetia, so that it was they who took away the four horses of St Mark's from the top of Percier and Fontaine's Napoleonic masterpiece, the Arc du Carrousel. This difficult task was achieved only with the aid of British sappers, but at least it was not as nearly disastrous as the treatment that almost wrecked the lion of St Mark, as he was being lowered from a plinth on the Esplanade of the Invalides. He fell into the water below and broke into twenty pieces, so that the Countess Potocka predicted that he would cease to exist. In fact he was restored and with virtually new wings and legs has ever since perched happily on top of his column in the piazza from which he had come.

Most of the diplomatic activity for the process of restitution was centred on Paris. Even though Canova had a weak case in international law, no soldiers and at first not even an inventory, he got back most of the papal treasures. Those he left behind, like the Tiber and Melpomene and Augustus, were large or second-rate or both. Other delegates made more surprising choices. The Tuscans were so keen on getting back the marble-top tables of the Pitti Palace that they were prepared to renounce Giottos and fra Angelicos and fra Filippo Lippis, which stayed behind in France to stimulate the troubadour style. Other decisions were more illogical. The little pre-della of Mantegna's San Zeno altarpiece stayed in Paris, while the chief panel of the same painting went back to Verona. The vast *Marriage-feast at Cana* was arguably too fragile to be taken back to San Giorgio Maggiore in Venice, but then other pic-tures by Veronese which made no sense away from the ceiling of the Doge's Palace were also kept in the Louvre or, in one case, sent to Brussels.

The works that stayed in France often stayed because nobody knew where they had been sent or because the French civil servants would not reveal where they had gone. One magnificent Rubens, a crucifixion from the Capuchin church in Antwerp, is now in Toulouse and an early Rubens, a *Madonna and saints*, is now in Grenoble. A famous painting by Raphael's master Perugino, *The mystic marriage of St Catherine*, is now in Caen. Unknown provincial museums in France have retained quite a lot of their Napoleonic plunder to this day. A French scholar esti-mated that just over half the 500-odd paintings to come to France from Italy went back to Italy and nine disappeared. Along with the Etruscan vases from the Vatican and sculptures from a collection as important as that of Camillo Borghese, Pauline Bonaparte's obliging second husband, much of quality, if seldom of the highest quality, stayed in France. By then other peoples, especially the Prussians and the British, had learnt the art of plunder from the French and the victors of Waterloo proved as rapacious as Napoleon had been in acquiring for their new national collec-tions the artistic treasures of the world.

The fall of Napoleon meant that some artists had to make quick adjustments to their work. Of nobody was this so true as of Francisco Goya, who had been stranded in Madrid during the French occupation and who had attached himself to the court of King Joseph. By conviction an *afrancesado*, he was one of those Spaniards who initially welcomed the arrival of the French, for they were enemies of his enemies, the Inquisition, superstition, bad dreams – all those facets of Spanish life that he had satirized in the plates of his *Caprichos* (or Caprices). Joseph, who appreciated fine painting and fine writing, was a cultured liberal with a handsome face, a fine subject for a portrait. While one of Goya's friends, the poet Meléndez Valdés, was caught in the capital, his former patron, Jovellanos, a civil servant of enlightened ideals, made good his escape, so that Valdés wrote odes in praise of Joseph and Jovellanos scorned the *afrancesados* as collaborators. Goya was himself in two moods, in favour of Joseph's decrees and in favour of the liberal constitution voted by the purely Spanish Cortes of Cadiz in 1812. His own act of artistic independence was to declare war on war itself. Between 1808 and 1812 he painted a Colossus striding though the countryside while terrified peasants and their animals ran in various directions in the hopeless aim of getting away from him. Slightly later Goya started on a series of etchings of the *Disasters of War*, which show bodies hacked to pieces and stuck on bushes, women being raped by soldiers, soldiers being knifed by women, Spaniards starving while a well-fed girl compatriot walks past them to meet a French soldier, a child abandoned while her mother is dying, a foolish priest balancing on a frayed rope before one crowd in darkness, a wolf dictating terms to another crowd quivering in fear. The subjects seem unrelated, but they have a relentlessly monotonous message:

> My friend you would not tell me with such high zest
> To children ardent for some desperate glory,
> The old Lie: *Dulce et decorum est*
> *Pro patria mori*

(it is sweet and honourable to die for your country). Goya was no Wilfred Owen, for he had a living to make. He had to convince the returning Bourbon King, Ferdinand VII, that he was an honest patriot. While he kept his etchings to himself, so that they were not published till the 1860s, he painted two grand oils to celebrate the rising of the Madrileños against the French on 2 and 3 May 1808. Among any paintings they rank as major works, not so much the first, which shows the common people cutting down French cavalrymen, including Mamelukes in their turbans, as the second, which raises those shot to death outside the city by night to the role of national martyrs (the leading victim, with his arms raised in a cruciform shape,

Among Goya's engravings of the 'Disasters of War' no. 32 (Why?) is one of the most horrific.

shows on one hand the sacred wound of Christ). No French painter of the age ever painted anything as savage as *The Second of May* or as moving as *The Third of May*. And yet Goya was uneasy in Restoration Spain and went to Restoration France to die.

For the two most original artists in England the ending of the Napoleonic wars came to have widely differing meanings. In 1815 Turner was still preoccupied with the analogy between France and Carthage and that year he showed at the Royal Academy his *Dido building Carthage*, a sombre depiction of a grand and futile act. He valued peace chiefly because it freed him to travel and in 1817 he went to Italy for the very first time and fell under the sad spell of decaying Venice sinking into the waters of its lagoon. The painter whom modern taste, but not the taste of his con- temporaries, rates alongside Turner, also found freedom, but in a more domestic way. At the advanced age of forty, John Constable was at last able to marry his Mary, the woman he had loved so long. In recent years he had collated innumerable small pencil and watercolour sketches of scenes along the river Stour near his riverside

In the Waterloo chamber, Windsor Castle, a shrine to the memory of the soldiers and statesmen who defeated Napoleon, Lawrence excelled himself when he came to paint 'Pius VII'.

family home in Suffolk. Now in his married home in Hampstead he put on canvas his visions of a rural England at peace with itself, where by tranquil waters boys fish or lead the horses that draw barges down to the sea or are perched for ever on a cart crossing a ford. To some, Constable's art seems a vision based on a callous Tory disregard of the rural poor, to others it is simply sentimental, but in the late 1820s it was aesthetically disturbing, as the artist had put green where he should have put brown, he had used modern labourers in place of ancient shepherds and instead of a far-off Arcadia he had painted his land as he remembered it from childhood, when there was no sound of distant offshore cannon to disturb the tranquil barges as they put out to sea.

If Constable painted as though Napoleon had never been, one able English painter was asked to paint the leaders of Europe as if he counted only by his absence. Over a period of about a dozen years Sir Thomas Lawrence, the most fluent and flamboyant of English society painters, was asked by the Prince Regent to commemorate the conquerors of Napoleon in a series of individual portraits which would be hung in an enormous room in Windsor Castle. The Prince himself, soon to be George IV, and his father, George III, and his successor, William IV, are placed on one side of the room opposite Tsar Alexnder I, Kaiser Francis II of Austria and Frederick-William IV of Prussia. Around them are their statesmen, like Metternich, and generals, like Wellington and Blücher, and the unlikely hero of the bunch, Pope Pius VII, whose unpretentious piety moved Lawrence as much as it had moved David, though his only claim to fame was passive resistance to Napoleon and though at the time he was trying to have his former enemy's conditions of captivity improved. The Waterloo Room, as it is known, is a fine tribute to Napoleon's conquerors and it may have fed one of George IV's favourite delusions, that he had been present at the battle too.

One monument to allied achievement has a peculiar irony to it. Fires in 1812 left parts of Moscow in ruins. Kazakov, the Neo-Classical architect of Moscow, died in the year of the 'great patriotic war'. Though his Kremlin and his Senate withstood the French, his University was partly damaged by fire. After 1812 the Tsar intended that Moscow, like St Petersburg, should be a monument to Tsarist absolutism. He and his brother Nicholas I commissioned works on a grand scale at a time when in France the building programmes of Napoleon had come to a halt.

In 1821, when Constable exhibited *Landscape Noon* (*The Hay Wain*), in which he imagines a rural scene only a short distance from the mill where he was born, Napoleon died far away from any familiar sight. If he was buried in the Vale of Geranium, that was because the British would not accede to the request in his will. 'I desire', he had written, 'that my ashes should repose on the banks of the Seine in the midst of the French people whom I have loved so much.' His body had to wait for another revolution, the three glorious days of 1830, before his wishes were honoured by the citizen-king, Louis-Philippe. As he would not be served by the legitimist supporters of his cousin Charles X, he had from the first cultivated the Bonapartists, especially when the former King of Rome died in 1832, for then there was only a clown called Louis-Napoleon as head of the family, who showed a knack for being captured and even, the second time round, for getting away. In the 1830s Louis-Philippe ordered that work should be continued on the half-built Arc de Triomphe. He set up a gallery of battles in a part of Versailles, where battles fought under the Empire must have their place. Finally in 1840 he sent his son, the Duc de Joinville, to collect Napoleon's ashes from St Helena and bring them home to their final resting-place in a red porphyry tomb on a base of grey granite behind and below the high altar of Louis XIV's military hospital, the Invalides. All round the walls the words and deeds of the Emperor are inscribed and carved in white marble. The memorial is cold and grand and in its pomposity it mars the noble architecture of the Louis XIV building where it is set.

It is fitting that in death Napoleon should be linked to the Grand Monarque, for more than anyone who ruled France since the seventeenth century Napoleon had fulfilled the dream of Louis XIV to reign with absolute power over France, not that is as a twentieth-century atheist dictator, like Hitler, Mussolini, Stalin or Mao Zedong, who treated their subjects with contempt, but as a man whose word had authority and who centralized authority on himself. The propaganda with which Louis XIV and Napoleon had surrounded themselves represented in part an aspiration, so that things always looked better than they were, but in part also a comfort, for after the civil wars of the mid-seventeenth century and of the revolution France had need of a sense of direction. Napoleon had been more of a soldier than Louis XIV, who liked to think of himself as a warrior, yet who in fact spent most of his life working hard at his desk, but then Napoleon had devoted more time to the governing of his empire than he had to the winning of it.

Napoleon was unlike Louis XIV in two principal ways. Whereas Louis had been King of France, the owner of his country, Napoleon was Emperor of the French, a man who depended on the support of the people. When Louis was defeated, he was still the King and he kept most of his conquests. When Napoleon was defeated, he lost everything. Madame Vigée-Lebrun noticed how during the Hundred Days many of her compatriots greeted the Emperor sullenly. After his defeat she commented, 'Without insulting the memory of a great captain and the brave generals and soldiers who helped him win such fine victories, one must ask where these victories got us and if there remains to us one scrap of land which has cost us so much blood.'

What was left by Napoleon, apart from the memory of those victories and the

One Napoleonic project was not completed till the 1990s: the transformation
of the whole Louvre palace into an art gallery. To this Pei's modern Pyramid
makes a fitting main entrance – it would have pleased Denon.

achievements of the Consulate, such as the concordat with the Pope, the reform of
the administration and the reform of the law, was what his artists had achieved for
him. He reigned just before mass production by machine took over from the individual's manual skill, so that the look of a chair, a porcelain plate or a portrait still
depended on the hand and eye of one person. In terms of aesthetic delight there is
no comparison between much that was made in the Empire style and the sorry, banal
productions foisted on their countries by twentieth-century dictators in the name of
the Aryan race or the new Roman Empire or the industrial or peasant proletariat,
just as Napoleon was never as cruel as them and lacked the means and the desire to
be as destructive as they have been. Besides, Napoleon was planning for a better
future, at least for France, to which his artists would contribute.

The second way in which he was unlike Louis XIV was in his devotion to Paris.
Louis had turned his back on his capital and ruled from the Château of Versailles
and it was not till 1789 that the Bourbons came back to Paris and ruled from the
Tuileries palace. Napoleon opted for the palace in preference to the château and,
though he was at Versailles and Fontainebleau and Saint-Cloud and Rambouillet
and Compiègne and Malmaison, he habitually ruled from the Tuileries. He had

great plans for Paris, which for the most part were left for others to complete. Louis-Philippe did something, Louis-Napoleon much more, and one project, the Palace of the King of Rome, has been replaced by the Palais du Chaillot and the gardens of the Trocadéro. He wanted a city with grand vistas, which Paris now has, above all the vista from the Arc du Carrousel past the place de la Concorde and up the Champs Elysées to the Arc de Triomphe at the end. So far as his artists were concerned, however, the most important project was the Louvre. Much of the Musée Napoléon has been dispersed, but much since has been acquired and, just after the second centenary of the revolution, the Louvre has become what Denon hoped it would be, a building devoted wholly to the arts. If that building is reached through a modern pyramid, that is in the spirit of Denon and his master, who took a special pride in his Egyptian expedition. The grand staircase of Percier and Fontaine and their Hall of the Caryatids are still there, the sculpture is shown with a panache of which they would have approved, and outside, their elegant Arc du Carrousel is a reminder of the Tuileries palace to which it was an entrance. Inside are most of the grand pictures of David and other Napoleonic works of the highest quality, like *Napoleon visiting the plague-victims of Jaffa* by Gros. There are also rooms that show off much of the finest examples of Empire interior decoration, besides the furniture, silver and porcelain. What gives the Louvre its special importance, however, is that finally it is true to Napoleon's ideal, that France possesses at the heart of its capital the principal museum of the arts in western Europe.

Appendix

The list is alphabetical
*refers to foreign artists

Architecture
Brongniart (1739–1813)
Chalgrin (1739–1811)
Durand (1760–1834)
Fontaine (1762–1834)
Percier (1764–1853)
Poyet (1742–1824)
Vignon (1763–1828)

Painting
Appiani *(1754–1817)
Boilly (1761–1845)
Broc (1771–1850)
Charlet (1792–1845)
David (1748–1825)
Gérard (1770–1837)
Géricault (1791–1824)
Girodet-Trioson (1764–1824)
Gros (1771–1835)
Guérin (1744–1833)
Ingres (1780–1867)
Prud'hon (1758–1823)
Carle Vernet (1758–1836)
Horace Vernet (1789–1863)

Vigée-Lebrun (1755–1842)

(miniaturists)
Augustin (1759–1832)
Isabey (1767–1855)

Sculpture
Bosio (1768–1845)
Canova* (1757–1831)
Chaudet (1763–1810)
Houdon (1741–1828)

Cabinet-makers
Georges II Jacob (1768–1803)
François-Honoré Jacob-Desmalter
    (1770–1844)
Thomire (1751–1843)

Silver-makers
Henry Augustin (1759–1816)
Biennais (1764–1843)
Odiot (1763–1800)
Thomire etc.

Porcelain manufacturers
Sèvres, under Brongniart fils (1770–1847)

Centres for furnishings, costume etc.
Aubusson
Gobelins
La Savonnerie (carpets)

Oberkampf at Jouy-en-Josas (cotton)
Lyon silk factories:
Camille Pernon
Grand frères
Bissardon, Caron et Bray
Chuard et Cie.

P.S. Many of the most interesting artists spanned several fields of design, among them David, Prud'hon, Percier, Fontaine, Thomire and above all Vivant Denon (1747–1825), who belonged to almost all areas of activity in the visual arts and yet to none in particular.

Select Bibliography

Age of Neo-Classicism (Art Council Exhibition, London, 1973)

ANDERSON, ROBERT & IBRAHIM FAWZY, *Egypt in 1800* (London, 1987)

ARNASON, H.H., *The sculptures of Houdon* (London, 1975)

BAILLIO, JOSEPH, *Elisabeth Vigée-Lebrun* (Kimball Museum, Fort Worth, 1982)

ed. BAKER, K.M., *The French Revolution and Modern Political Culture*, vol.1 (Oxford, 1987)

BARNETT, CORELLI, *Bonaparte* (New York, 1978)

BENOIT, F., *L'art français sous la Revolution et l'Empire* (Paris, 1867)

BERGERON, LOUIS, *France under Napoleon* (Princeton, 1981)

BIVER, M.L., *Le Paris de Napoléon* (Paris, 1963)

BIVER, M.L., *Pierre Fontaine* (Paris, 1964)

BIZOT, CH., *Mobilier, Directoire, Empire* (Paris, n/d)

BLACKBURN, JULIA, *The Emperor's last island: a journey to St Helena* (London, 1991)

ed. BLAIR, CLAUDE, *The History of Silver* (London and Sydney, 1987)

BOIME, ALBERT, *Art in an age of revolution 1750–1800* (Chicago, 1987)

BOIME, ALBERT, *Art in an age of Bonapartism 1800–1815* (Chicago, 1990)

trans. ANNE BENNETT, *Roses for an Empress: Joséphine Bonaparte and Pierre-Joseph Redouté* (London, 1983)

BOUILHET, HENRI, *L'Orfèvrerie Française aux XVIIIe et XIX siècles* (Paris, 1910)

BOUILHET, T., *150 Ans d'Orfèvrerie* (Paris, 1981)

BOURGEOIS, EMILE, *Le style empire* (Paris, 1930)

BRÉGEON, JEAN-JOËL, *L'Egypte française au jour le jour, 1798–1801* (Paris, 1991)

BROOKNER, ANITA, *David* (London, 1980)

BRUNET, MARCELLE and PRÉAUD, TAMARA, *Sèvres, des origines à nos jours* (Paris, 1978)

BRUNHAMMER, YVONNE and DE FAYET, MONIQUE, *Meubles et ensembles époques Directoire et Empire* (Paris, 1965)

CLAYTON, PETER A., *The rediscovery of Egypt* (London, 1982)

CONNOLLY, OWEN, *Napoleon's satellite kingdoms* (New York, 1965)

CRONIN, VINCENT, *Napoleon* (London, 1971)

CROUZET, F., *L'Economie britannique et le blocus continental, 1806–1813*, 2 vols. (Paris, 1958)

CROW, THOMAS, *Painters and public life in Eighteenth-Century Paris* (New Haven, 1986)

CROW, THOMAS, *Emulation: making artists for revolutionary France* (New Haven, 1994)

CURL, JAMES STEVENS, *The Egyptian Revival, an Introductory Study of a Recurring Theme in the History of Taste* (London, 1982)

DAUTERMAN, C.C., *Sèvres* (London and New York, 1969)

DESCHAMPS, MADELEINE, *Empire* (New York, 1994)

DELÉCLUZE, ÉTIENNE, *Louis David, son école et son temps* (Paris, 1857)

DELACROIX, EUGÈNE, *Oeuvres litteraires,* 2 vols. (Paris, 1923)

DENON, DOMINIQUE VIVANT, *Voyage dans la Basse et la haute Egypte* (Paris, 1802)

Description de l'Egypte, plates, 11 vols. (Paris, 1809–28)

DOYLE, WILLIAM, *The Oxford History of the French Revolution* (Oxford, 1989)

DRAPER, J.J., *The Arts under Napoleon* (New York, 1969)

Entretiens de Napoléon et Canova en 1810 (London, 1825)

ELTING, JOHN R., *Swords around a throne, Napoleon's Grand Army,* (New York, 1988)

FELICE, R. DE, *French furniture under Louis XVI and the Empire* (London, 1920)

FONTAINE, P.F.L., *Journal,* 2 vols. (Paris 1987)

FURET, FRANÇOIS, *Interpreting the French Revolution* (Cambridge, 1981)

FURET, FRANÇOIS, *Revolutionary France 1770–1880* (Oxford, 1992)

GABORIT, JEAN-RENÉ, *The Louvre: European Sculpture* (London, 1994)

GHALI, IBRAHIM AMIN, *Vivant Denon ou la conquête du bonheur* (Cairo, 1986)

GONZALEZ-PALACIOS, ALVAR, *The French Empire style* (London, 1970)

GOULD, CECIL, *Trophy of Conquest* (London, 1965)

GRANDJEAN, SERGE, *L'Orfèvrerie du XIXe siècle en Europe* (Paris, 1962)

GRANDJEAN, SERGE, *Empire furniture 1800–1825* (London, 1966)

GUERRINI, MAURICE, *Napoleon and Paris* (London, 1970)

HAUTECOEUR, L., *Histoire de l'architecture classique en France,* t.5 (Paris, 1943–57)

HERBERT, ROBERT, *David, Voltaire, Brutus and the French Revolution* (New York, 1972)

HERNMARCK, C., *The Art of the European Silversmith, 1430–1830.* 2 vols (London and New York, 1977)

HOLTMAN, R. B., *Napoleonic propaganda* (Baton Rouge, 1950)

HUBERT, GÉRARD and HUBERT, NICOLE, *Musée National des châteaux de Malmaison et Bois-Préau,* Paris, 1986

HUMBERT, JEAN-MARCEL, PANTAZZI, MICHAEL and ZIEGLER, CHRISTIANE, *Egyptomania. Egypt in Western Art, 1730–1930* (Paris and Ottawa, 1994)

HUNT, LYNNE, *Politics, Culture and class* (Berkeley and Los Angeles, 1984)

INGAMALLS, J., *Wallace collection, Catalogue of Paintings, III* (London, 1989)

JARRY, M, *The carpets of Aubusson* (Leigh-on-Sea, 1969)

JARRY, M, *The carpets of the Manufacture de la Savonnerie* (Leigh-on-Sea, 1966)

JOHNSON, DOUGLAS, *French society and the Revolution* (New York and Cambridge, 1976)

KNAPTON, ERNEST JOHN, *Empress Josephine* (Cambridge, Mass and Oxford, 1964)

KJELLBERG, PIERRE, *Le mobilier français,* t.2 (Paris, 1978)

LE BOURHIS, ed. KATELL, *Costume in the age of Napoleon* (New York, 1990)

LEDOUX-LEBARD, DENISE, *Les ébénistes parisiens, 1795–1830* (Paris, 1951)

LEFÈBVRE, GEORGES, *Napoléon* (Paris, 1965)

LELIÈVRE, PIERRE, *Vivant Denon* (Paris, 1993)

LEMONNIER H., *Gros* (Paris, 1904)

LYONS, MARTYN, *Napoleon Bonaparte and the legacy of the French Revolution* (New York, 1994)

ed. LUCAS, COLIN, *The French Revolution and Modern Political Culture*, vol.II (Oxford, 1987)

MAILLARD, ELISA, *Old French Furniture and its surroundings, 1610–1815* (London, 1925)

MANSEL, PHILIP, *The Eagle in Splendour; Napoleon I and his court* (1987)

MANSEL, PHILIP, *The court of France, 1789–1830* (Cambridge, 1989)

MARKHAM, FELIX, *Napoleon* (London, 1963)

MOSSIKER, FRANCES, *Napoleon and Josephine* (London, 1965)

MOULIN, J-M, *Musée National du château de Compiègne* (Paris, n/d)

PARISET, G., *Histoire de France contemporaine: t.3: le Consulat et l'Empire* (Paris, 1921)

PERCIER, CHARLES and FONTAINE, P.L.F., *Recueil de décorations intérieures* (Paris, 1812)

REYNOLDS, GRAHAM, *Wallace Collection: Catalogue of Miniatures* (London, 1980)

RIBEIRO, AILEEN, *Fashion in the French Revolution* (London, 1988)

RIBEIRO, AILEEN, *The Art of Dress: fashion in England and France, 1750–1820* (London, 1995)

ROBERTS, WARREN, *David and the Revolution* (Chapel Hill, N.C., 1989)

ROSENBLUM, R., *Transformations in Late Eighteenth Century Art* (Princeton, 1967)

RUDÉ, GEORGE, *The Crowd in the French Revolution* (Oxford, 1959)

SAMOYAULT-VERLET, COLOMBE, *Les arts à l'époque napoléonienne* (Paris, 1969)

SAMOYAULT-VERLET, COLOMBE and SAMOYAULT-VERLET, JEAN-PIERRE, *Le château de Fontainebleau, Musée Napoléon 1er: Napoleon et la famille impériale 1804–1815* (Paris, 1986)

SAMOYAULT-VERLET, JEAN-PIERRE, etc., *Arts décoratifs, 1799–1814* (Paris, 1992)

SCHAMA, SIMON, *Patriots and Liberators: Revolution in the Netherlands (1780–1813)* (London 1977)

SCHAMA, SIMON, *Citizens: a chronicle of the French Revolution* (London, 1989)

SCHLENOFF, NORMAN, *Baron Gros and Napoleon's Egyptian Campaigns*, in *Essays in honour of Walter Friedlander* (New York, 1965)

SCHNAPPER, ANTOINE and SÉRULLAZ, ARLETTE, *Jacques-Louis David*, (Paris 1989)

STENDHAL, *Napoleon* (Paris, n.d.)

SUTHERLAND, D.M.G., *France 1789–1815 Revolution and Counter-Revolution* (London, 1985)

THOMPSON, J.M., *Napoleon Bonaparte, his rise and fall* (Oxford, 1963)

TULARD, JEAN, *Napoleon: the myth of the Saviour* (London, 1985)

VIENNET, *Napoléon et l'industrie française* (Paris, 1947)

VIGÉE-LEBRUN, ÉLISABETH, *Souvenirs,* édition féministe, (Paris, 1986)

ZIESENISS, CHARLES OTTO, *Napoléon et la Cour Impériale* (Paris, 1980)

Index